D0436569

# IN THE COMPANY
# OF OWNERS

# IN THE COMPANY
# OF OWNERS

## The Truth about Stock Options (and Why Every Employee Should Have Them)

JOSEPH BLASI, DOUGLAS KRUSE,
AND AARON BERNSTEIN

BASIC
BOOKS

A Member of the Perseus Books Group

*Designed by Lisa Kreinbrink*
Set in 11.5-point Berkeley Book by the Perseus Books Group

Library of Congress Cataloging-in-Publication Data
Blasi, Joseph.
  In the company of owners: the truth about stock options (and why every
employee should have them) / Joseph Blasi, Douglas Kruse, and Aaron
Bernstein.
    p. cm.
  Includes bibliographical references and index.
  ISBN 0-465-00700-7 (alk. paper)
  1. Employee ownership—United States.   2. Employee stock options—
United States.   3. Employee Motivation—United States.   4. Chief
Executive Officers—Salaries, etc.—United States.   I. Bernstein, Aaron,
1955–   .
  IV. Title.

HD5660.U5 B5 2002
338.6–DC21                                                    2002013468

03 04 05 / 10 9 8 7 6 5 4 3 2 1

*To Dr. J. Robert Beyster*

# Contents

# Preface

Stock options have come in for a torrent of richly deserved criticism in the past year or so. It has become all too clear that the runup in the stock market during the 1990s proved to be too great a temptation for many of America's leading corporate executives. At least some of them pursued unethical and maybe even illegal strategies designed not to advance the company's long-range goals, but to pump up their stock and cash in on the profits their options brought them. At a parade of once high-flying companies—icons of the boom such as Enron, WorldCom, and Quest Communications—option-induced avarice spurred corporate chieftains to cut corners, cook the books, and dupe investors into buying shares at inflated prices. Some accountants, analysts, and investment bankers played along, wreaking serious damage to our financial system. The resulting crisis of confidence made options synonymous with greed and excess that distorted the entire U. S. economy.

But the problem with stock options is much larger than a handful of people who flouted the rules to line their pockets. The real issue involves the rules themselves. Most American corporations—including the vast majority who haven't broken any laws—have been on a stock option binge for more than a decade. An overwhelming majority of the country's CEOs used their company's ever-rising share prices as an excuse to stuff their wallets with vast profits from options that they essentially awarded themselves. We calculate that just the top five executives at the 1,500 largest U.S.

companies reaped a total of $18 billion in option profits in 2001, up more than fivefold from the beginning of the 1990s. Over the entire decade, they made a collective total of about $58 billion.

That doesn't count the vastly larger mountain of riches they're still sitting on. Overall, CEOs and a thin layer of other executives and managers in corporate America own a collective total of some 12 billion options today. This gives them control over about 10 percent of all outstanding public shares in the United States, up from next to nothing two decades ago. Even at the end of 2000, after the stock-market had tumbled far from its peak, the top five officers in the largest U. S. companies would have pocketed a total of some $80 billion in profits if they could have exercised all those options at once.

Executives have justified this incredible transfer of wealth by arguing that the incentive it provided would spur them to create more value for their company's stockholders. Unfortunately, economists have found scant evidence to back this theory up, much less to show just how large executives' option grants should be to bring about an improvement in a firm's stock price. Investors bear some of the blame here, since most were all too willing to brush aside questions about executive wealth-grabbing when the market was soaring by 30 percent a year. However, the more fundamental issue with stock options is who gets them, how much they get, and why.

We believe that the corporate malfeasance brought to light by the stock market's collapse stems from the abuse of stock options, not from the concept of an option itself. Most large corporations today are still run on the same top-down pyramid of power that has characterized U.S. business for generations. The CEOs who perch at the pinnacle enjoy virtually unchecked control over most of the major decisions, including their own compensation. Not surprisingly, they have grabbed the largest chunk of stock options for themselves and a small group that usually comprises less than 5 percent of a company's workforce. In the process, corporate leaders have excluded the vast ranks of employees whose dedication and motivation are central to a company's success.

Executive greed has victimized many employees, too. Some have been tossed out of work at the fallen icons such as Enron, which were brought down by the excesses and possible criminality of their leaders. But the greatest losses have come from practices that are much more ubiquitous—and perfectly legal. Many U.S. workers have suffered from their employers' practice of stuffing 401(k) and other retirement plans with company stock. Overall, we calculate that employees have lost more than $260 billion this way since the stock market tanked in 2000.

At the same time, most companies have restricted stock options, a much safer form of employee ownership, largely to the corporate elite. Millions of employees own options in U.S. public companies. However, most of them got a token amount on a one-time or occasional basis. We estimate that at most 3 million workers get options every year, the way CEOs do.

Essentially, corporate America has extended the least risky ownership stake—stock options—to those who can afford to take on the most risk, that is, the highest-income people at the top of the pyramid. Yet it has given the riskiest stake—direct stock ownership locked up in long-term retirement plans—to average workers, who can least afford to gamble their savings on one stock.

The argument of this book is that investors and employees alike would gain if companies turned employees into corporate partners by granting stock options to most of the workforce. Most U.S. corporations would be better run, and in the long run more profitable, if America pursued this approach. We say this because unlike the case with executive options, there's compelling evidence that broad-based employee ownership does in fact produce more value for shareholders. Although many CEOs have twisted the concept of employee ownership for their own narrow self-interest, the underlying idea of using ownership to motivate employees is in fact a good one that has been proven to work. As you'll hear in our book, a number of executives, mostly in high tech, realize this. We will explain how corporations can operate more efficiently when employee ownership is used in a reasonable and appropriate fashion.

The reason is that granting options to an entire company has a very different effect than doling them out to a favored few at the top. The underlying rationale is much the same: to create an incentive to accept a job the executive or the worker might not have taken at the pay offered, and then to work harder or more creatively once they're in it. As Federal Reserve Board chairman Alan Greenspan noted in mid-2002, many high-tech startups might not have survived without employee options.

The basic notion is that options can help to form a partnership of interests between companies and employees. The idea began to emerge as early as the 1950s in companies such as Intel and Hewlett-Packard. As you'll see in the first two chapters, it was developed further over the following decades by Microsoft and other high-tech firms that blossomed in Silicon Valley and elsewhere, finally reaching full form in the Internet companies that sprang up in the 1990s. Even a handful of non-high-tech companies have begun moving in this direction. A few, like Pepsi and Wells Fargo, routinely give options to all workers, while others, including Aetna and Conoco, have made small or one-time option grants to most employees.

The concept has been pushed the furthest, however, at the Internet companies that survived the dot-com shakeout. Although the dot-com heyday has long since come and gone, a viable Internet industry remains today that's no more likely to vanish than the Internet itself. It consists of firms such as Cisco, Yahoo, and eBay, that invented and applied the core technology that made possible the whole phenomenon of individual computers linked up into a global network.

We created an index of the 100 largest high-tech firms that focus on the Internet, which we call the High Tech 100. It shows that employees and executives at these firms hold fully a third of their company's stock. Break that down, and the top five officers hold only 14 percentage points. The other 19 points belong to average employees, 17 of them through options. By contrast, executives in the rest of corporate America own 8 percent of their company's stock, while employees hold just 2 percent—mostly through 401(k)s and employee stock ownership plans (ESOPs).

Instead of an autocratic hierarchy of executive decisionmaking, these companies invented a new version of the employee-owned company. They shaped an enterprise that tries to bring people together as collaborators in a joint undertaking, rather than as workers being told what to do by a boss.

We've dubbed the idea partnership capitalism because it involves thinking of a corporation as a partnership among the people who work there, as well as one between them and the investors who own its stock. You might also call it stock option capitalism, since options for most or all employees are the key economic idea that drives the concept. By offering them to most of their employees, these companies have blurred the notion of private property, spreading ownership among everyone who's using the corporation's assets to generate value. They are engaging in a new form of risk sharing between economic partners. Employees assume some of the risk of ownership in return for a claim on part of the wealth they help to create. Investors, for their part, risk parting with some of their ownership in the hope that doing so will create even greater wealth than they had before.

The new work environment cultivated by companies that extend options to everyone is as important as the options themselves. While they certainly haven't invented a workplace nirvana, many of these firms strive to transform the traditional boss-employee management mentality into something richer and more diverse. Their aim is to spur employees to think of their jobs as activities they do for themselves, not just for their superiors.

The goal of partnership capitalism, then, is to get employees to think of themselves as owners. Doing so motivates employees to work smarter or harder, bringing about a more productive company and, ultimately, rewarding employees and outside shareholders alike. Society at large gains as well, since more productive companies create faster overall economic growth that usually benefits everyone.

The proof that this in fact occurs can be found in America's lengthy history of sharing profits and ownership with employees. For decades, in fact for nearly 200 years, many of the country's leading capitalists have experimented with the notion in one fashion or another. In fact, the broad concept of sharing the risks and rewards of property ownership with workers dates back to the country's earliest days. Usually, property holders have surrendered a portion of their ownership rights in the hope that the prospect of capital income would spur people to come to work for them or apply themselves more vigorously, thus creating more wealth than the original owner could do alone. At various points, many of the most illustrious names in American business have used profit sharing, ESOPs, or other plans that grant employees shares in the company for which they work.

Many traditional companies also have attempted to create workplace cultures that allow employees to take on more responsibility than they do in a conventional corporate hierarchy. Very few have managed to achieve a complete partnership model that couples the financial aspects of employee ownership to cultural changes in the working environment. But each part of the model has been tried by traditional companies for many years, and economists and labor experts have studied the pieces in much detail.

These studies offer powerful evidence that partnership capitalism, unlike executive options, really is a smart investment for companies and their public shareholders. If you sum up all the studies done just in the past two decades or so, they show that even corporate America's limited experiments with the partnership approach produce a one-time, but permanent, boost to a company's productivity of about 4 percentage points, compared to what it would have been without employee ownership. Total annual shareholder returns go up by an average of about 2 points. On average, the companies studied devoted roughly 8 percent of their stock to employee ownership. The higher returns they got came on top of this 8 percent, and thus reflect the net gain corporate stockholders reap from partnership capitalism. This track record strongly suggests that if corporate America used options to share ownership with all employees, and not just top executives, investors would gain more than they give up.

The partnership approach is the closest thing to a free lunch you can find in economics. The higher productivity it brings allows both workers and shareholders to earn more than they otherwise would. Just as employees get option wealth on top of their regular market wage, so do companies and their shareholders stand to earn higher profits and share appreciation than they would if the company didn't engage in partnership capitalism. Of course, nothing in life is really free, and a partnership entails some risks for all involved. For the idea to work, employees must work harder and smarter, and get along in a more demanding and entrepreneurial corporate culture, which is a real cost to them. What's more, they run the risk that their extra effort may not pay off for reasons over which they have no control, whether it's a corrupt or inept management or a larger industry or market collapse.

Shareholders also may extend the promise of ownership to the company's workforce, only to see their stock climb no more than it would have anyway. In some cases, employees might earn extra wealth even though they produced no extra value for shareholders. Still, these risks can be circumscribed for both sides and distributed fairly equally between them. Given the rich evidence that most partnership approaches indeed have paid off for both sides over the long term, the reward seems well worth the risk for everyone, despite today's troubled markets.

That's not to say that the partnership approach could have prevented any deliberate wrong-doing at an Enron or a WorldCom, much less forestalled the collapse of confidence and stock prices that hit corporate America in 2002. Nor will it stop recessions, a slump in a particular industry, or lousy business decisions by a company's CEO. However, forming a wider partnership with employees helps a company to perform better than it otherwise would in most circumstances.

A less autocratic corporation is also far less likely to be a breeding ground for executive malfeasance. If everyone in a company owns a piece of it, they have the same interest in boosting the stock price as the CEOs who let their greed get the better of them in so many firms. Unlike executives, however, average employees usually aren't going to make tens of millions of dollars from their options. Some Internet workers did rake in windfall profits during the 1990s market boom. But most employees in more typical firms and more typical markets stand to make substantial, though not tremendous, sums, on the order of 15 to 30 percent of their annual pay.

As a result, employees in a partnership company are likely to remain concerned primarily about the long-term stability of the company and their jobs. If top executives are cutting corners, workers will have a strong motivation to speak out or resist, as one or two did even at Enron and WorldCom. This is even more likely to be true after the examples these companies set, where thousands of average employees lost both their jobs and their savings while a handful of corporate kingpins walked off with hundreds of millions of dollars. While a nonhierarchical atmosphere can't ward off an executive determined to fiddle with the books, employees are more likely to be attuned to unethical leadership in a culture that isn't the usual "the boss gets everything and the boss is always right."

Just as important is the corporate governance structure a company adopts. U.S. CEOs have been able to award themselves millions in option grants because they essentially set their own pay. Many still handpick the boards of directors that are supposed to oversee management and safeguard shareholder interests. Directors are often former executives of the company, others who have dealings with it in some way, or people the CEO considers unlikely to challenge management. They also almost always run on a single slate proposed by management, so shareholders have no effective choice of candidates. Most boards don't meet separately from the CEO whom they're supposed to be monitoring, nor do they have a separate chairman or lead director who could call such meetings. Until a company runs into problems, many CEOs exercise the full powers of an autocrat. Very few behave like stewards of shareholders' money who must report to a truly independent board of overseers.

Directors have allowed CEOs to ratchet up their compensation to excessive levels with no proof that shareholders gain—or that anyone else who works at the company gets any credit for its success. Cozy boards allowed executives to take most options for themselves, turning away from the pursuit of broadly based employee ownership that some large corporations embarked on in the 1980s through ESOPs.

A partnership approach won't necessarily cure all these ills. In fact, many high-tech firms that grant options to most workers have an even greater proportion of captive directors than more established companies. For the idea to work well over the long run, they, too, will have to change. All companies need better protections for lower-level whistleblowers, and truly independent boards that can hire CEOs who will put a priority on creating entrepreneurial corporate cultures that give all employees a stake.

Investors may rightly feel burned by options today, given how many executives have abused them. But as this book makes clear, using broad-based options to create a partnership model of the corporation will, over the long run, help to make most companies more competitive and create more wealth for shareholders.

Similarly, many employees may not be too interested in the prospect of options in light of the woes of the stock market in recent years. But options remain a good deal for average workers, even today. For one thing, most companies grant them over and above the market wage they pay. They do so because options represent a share of the firm's future wealth; they're a form of profit sharing, which means they're capital income, not labor income. So employees won't lose anything even if their employer gives them options that turn out to be worthless down the road.

In addition, most companies issuing options to all employees do so every year, which means the options carry the lower price if the stock plunges. As the company's fortunes improve, employees will still make money on the new options, even if those granted at the market peak remain worthless. Since most options have a ten-year life span, it's reasonable to assume that stocks will resume their historical upward trend, eventually putting most options in the money.

By massively misusing stock options to enrich themselves, the leaders of corporate America have hijacked what could be one of the most important business innovations in many decades. It would be wrong if the calls for reform lead to the curtailment or elimination of options for a broader group of employees. Adopting a partnership approach in itself wouldn't bring about all the reforms critics have suggested. But it would make U.S. corporations more competitive and profitable, as well as better places to work.

# Acknowledgments

This book is dedicated to J. Robert Beyster, who has been one of the most insightful executives in the area of employee ownership over the past three decades. Beyster is the founder, CEO, and chairman of the board of Science Applications International Corporation (SAIC), a privately held Fortune 500 research and development firm that's owned by its employees. Since founding SAIC in 1969, Beyster has been committed to building the company on entrepreneurial employee ownership and technical excellence. In 1986, he started the nonprofit Foundation for Enterprise Development, which today works to encourage the growth of small- and medium-sized enterprises and the development of entrepreneurs through international contracts and education programs. In 2002, the foundation launched the Beyster Institute for Entrepreneurial Employee Ownership. The institute educates the public through the Internet (www.beysterinstitute.org), national conferences, publishing, consulting, and training programs. We would like to thank the institute for grants to Rutgers to support this study. The ideas presented in the book are those of the authors and do not necessarily represent those of the institute or Dr. Beyster. Blasi is an unpaid member of the institute's board of directors.

We are especially grateful to the managers and employees of many companies who hosted our visits and allowed us to interview them, camp out at their offices, and challenge them in focus groups over many lunches and dinners. All of the nonexecutive employees we interviewed were promised confidentiality and their names appear as pseudonyms. This book could not have been written without the help of dozens of executives and employees and the cooperation of the support staffs of each company. We particularly extend our thanks to several employees of Amazon.com; the management and employees of: Bea Systems, Cisco Systems, Covad Communications, Excite@Home, Infospace.com, Internap, Interwoven, Juniper Networks, Kana Communications, Microsoft, Network Solutions, and Portal Software; several employees of RCN Corporation; and the management and employees of: Redback Networks, RealNetworks, Tibco Software, VeriSign, and Vitria Technology. Nicole Miller of Waggener Edstrom was a helpful host at Microsoft. We also wish to thank Arthur Rock who gave generously of his time on the early history and values of high-technology companies.

A number of experts were kind enough to read drafts of the book during its development and engage in long discussions on our study. Adam Blumenthal has given us special assistance on finance issues. We would also like to acknowledge the continuous assistance and encouragement of Corey Rosen, Ronald Bernstein, David Binns, and a number of occasional readers, including: Al Fortunato, Michael Higgins, Dean Jeff Garten of the Yale School of Management, Stanley Lundine, Bill Scott, Raymond Smilor, Matt Tobriner, Stan Vinson, Joseph Walkush, and Peggy Walkush. Others who have made themselves generously available to help are: Ralph Callaway, Ed Carberry, Michael Keeling, Scott Rodrick, and David Wray. Rutgers historian David Bensman and University of Nebraska historian Bruce. E. Johansen gave comments on the history sections. We would like to thank Richard Freeman of Harvard University for his encouragement and support. Several companies helped us understand their broad stock option programs, especially Louise Blackwell of Charles Schwab & Company, Michael S. Barker of Guidant Corporation, and Nicolas de Porcel of Wells Fargo. Paul Cyr of the New Bedford (Massachusetts) Free Public Library Whaling Archive helped with research on risk sharing among whalers. Jerry of Hello Limousine drove us around Silicon Valley.

Joseph Blasi and Douglas Kruse would like to thank several colleagues at the School of Management and Labor Relations at

Rutgers University: Dean Barbara Lee and Dean John Burton and our department chairs, Steven Director and Paula Voos, who helped us with funding and sabbaticals during the time the book was under preparation, and our graduate program directors, Charles Fay and David Bensman, who were understanding about course scheduling. D. J. Gafgen and Bettylou Heffernan of Rutgers managed our accounts and solved every problem that came up. Joanne Mangels provided computer support. We are especially grateful to Professor James Sesil of Rutgers University School of Management and Labor Relations and Professor Maya Kroumova of the New York Institute of Technology for their important work on stock option research that was key to our argument. Our colleague at Rutgers, Mark Huselid, was helpful in answering questions about his important research. The staffs of the Rutgers University Libraries and the Princeton University Firestone Libraries helped us enormously. The company research would not have been possible without the U.S. Securities and Exchange Commission. We especially want to thank Ms. Seretha R. Pearsall, assistant branch chief of Public Reference at the SEC and Joe Rogers for their assistance to us in tracking down documents. Steve Hekker and Rachel Stern of Factset also provided certain data and assistance. Aaron Bernstein would like to thank his editors at *Business Week* for allowing him to pursue this project.

Our agent, Susan Rabiner, has gone above and beyond the call of duty by serving as a traditional agent, as well as a critic, cothinker, editor, and all-around strategic advisor. She was irreplaceable. Our editor at Basic Books, William Frucht, has believed in this book from the first moment we met him. He has been a patient taskmaster through the many stages of its development. We are very thankful for his staying power. We would not have found either of them without the help of Eric Johnson.

Any errors are the responsibility of the authors. We undertook considerable research that we were unable to include in the print version of the book. Some of this added material can be found on the web site we set up, www.inthecompanyofowners.com.

Most of all, we cannot find the words to express our thankfulness to our families for their unending patience and warm support. For us, their assistance was decisive. Joseph Blasi would like to thank his wife, Nancy, and his family for their steadfastness. Doug Kruse would like to thank his wife, Lisa. Aaron Bernstein would like to thank Margaret, Amanda, and Adam Monahan, who took time out of their lives to support him on this project.

This book is written for general education and interest and should not be used as the basis of investment decisions. More extensive footnotes and additional material are available on our web site: www.inthecompanyofowners.com.

J.R.B., D.L.K., and A.B.

# The History of Partnership Capitalism

# 1

# It All Began with Shockley

Nearly half a century ago, way back in 1957, eight cocky young semiconductor whizzes decided that they could no longer stand working for a brilliant but autocratic inventor named William Shockley. Although his many real faults would later come to be widely perceived as well, Shockley was viewed as a genius by the scientific community of his day. In the 1940s, while employed at what was then AT&T Corporation's Bell Laboratories in New Jersey, Shockley had helped invent the transistor, a feat for which he shared a Nobel Prize in 1956. But Shockley's contribution to his time went even beyond his scientific achievements. To commercialize his world-altering invention, which made possible everything from the portable radio to the personal computer, Shockley left AT&T the year he got his prize and announced the founding of Shockley Semiconductor Laboratories.

In a move whose far-reaching consequences neither Shockley nor anyone else could have predicted, he located his new firm not in some established manufacturing area along the northeast corridor, but in faraway Mountain View, California, next door to his native Palo Alto. The decision turned out to be an unparalleled stroke of good fortune for the area.

Although Shockley chose the location in part to be near his mother, cementing the deal was the fact that nearby Stanford University was offering space in an industrial park it had created to lure electronics companies to the area. Shockley Semiconductor, and the dozens of high-tech spinoffs later started by former employees in this same stretch of northern California, formed the nucleus of what was to become the world's single most important high-tech region, a myriad of computer and software firms now known as Silicon Valley.

Shockley's decision to walk out of AT&T had been precipitated by what he felt was a lack of respect paid to his genius. Management, he thought, behaved as if his contributions were no different from those of any other Bell Lab scientist, or even of the army of technicians and workers who punched in and out for hourly wages. Shockley thought he deserved to be treated as the sui generis article he saw himself to be and asked Bell Labs to give him a share of the royalties it earned from patents based on his ideas.

His request went nowhere. Bell Labs, you must understand, was more than just the research and development arm of AT&T. It was, by any standard, a world-famous laboratory, chock full of brilliant scientists and even other Nobel Prize winners. The lab's philosophy was to give virtually free rein to its researchers, who were in turn allowed to pursue their scientific interests as university academics would, with little thought for any immediate commercial application. The hope was that the few major breakthroughs achieved would generate enough revenue to justify the cost of the entire research program. However, all ideas a lab scientist produced belonged not to the individual, but to the company, which would turn them, if possible, into marketable products. Not surprisingly, AT&T refused as a matter of course to accede to Shockley's demand that he, or any other scientist, be given a share of the royalties derived from patents developed on its dime (a practice still common at most large companies today).

Shockley decided to pack up and start his own company. He turned for help to a fellow graduate of the California Institute of Technology, Arnold Beckman, who owned a Southern California medical instruments firm, Beckman Instruments Incorporated.

Beckman agreed not only to fund Shockley, but to give him what Bell Labs had refused him—the prestige and the financial rewards due a man of his talent and accomplishments. During their initial discussions over money, Beckman wrote Shockley reassuring him that under the terms he proposed, Shockley would find everything he was looking for. Historians Michael Riordan and Lillian Hoddeson discovered the letter in Shockley's papers. It said, in part:

> Your objective in this undertaking is to employ your skills and experience in a manner which will give you maximum personal satisfaction. Important factors are suitable physical facilities, capable and congenial associates, a position of prestige and authority, with adequate voice in policy determination, and financial reward commensurate with performance, which embodies, in addition to salary, some means for obtaining capital gains benefits.

So the deal was closed, and Shockley Semiconductor Laboratory opened for business. It soon became apparent that in addition to all his other skills, Shockley had something of a genius for spotting talent. He quickly recruited a dozen of the country's sharpest young Ph.D. engineers and physicists. Just how good were these people? Several would later go on to found major computer companies, including Robert Noyce and Gordon Moore, who cofounded Intel Corporation. (Moore also authored Moore's Law, which predicted meteoric progress in this new field, holding that the power of a computer chip would double every eighteen months, even as its price fell.)

By rights, Shockley should have known exactly how to keep his troops happy and productive. All he had to do was to give them the same respect he had demanded for himself at Bell Labs. But his overweening ego got in the way. Shockley quickly became a boss with an arrogant management style, treating his band of hotshots even worse than AT&T had treated him. For example, Moore described how several Shockley Labs researchers had once suggested that they would like to publish more of their ideas in academic journals. Shockley went home that night, worked out a theoretical point of his own about semiconductors, and returned the next day to tell them: "Here, flesh this out and publish it."

Soon enough, Shockley's troops rebelled. In 1957, after just a year at the new company, Moore and a few other fed-up researchers appealed to Beckman to bring in a professional manager and make

Shockley a technical consultant. Beckman refused, leaving most of the group feeling that they had no choice but to quit the company. Depart they did, just as Shockley himself had walked away from AT&T's prestigious Bell Labs. But instead of launching out on their own, eight employees—including Noyce, whom they tapped as their leader—decided to offer up their services as a group. They wanted to develop a commercially viable silicon transistor—which Shockley had lost interest in—and thought the project stood the best chance of success if they pooled their knowledge. Their actions became one of the first examples of a high-tech talent rebellion, in which knowledge workers recognized the commercial value of the collective brainpower represented by their team and sought to offer it up as a commodity.

The Traitorous Eight, as Shockley called them, didn't set out to change the world, not even the business world. Originally, they just wanted to find employment in a workplace environment in which they would be treated as the intellectual equals of top management they felt themselves to be. But within a scant few years it became clear that changing the traditional relationship between management and employees was precisely what the burgeoning high-tech business sector needed to allow it to take off as it later did, and that they had taken a giant first step in doing just that.

Just as Shockley had found Beckman to help him, so did the Traitorous Eight hook up with a young New York City investment banker named Arthur Rock, who suggested an unusual move: Instead of trying to find someone to hire them as a team, the group should found their own company.

Back then there was no venture capital industry, and the idea wasn't a conventional business plan that might command funding from a bank or large corporation. In fact, it took Rock thirty-five tries to find a company willing to give the men both the capital they needed and the freedom to use it as they saw fit.

When that funding finally arrived, Rock came up with an unusual business plan. "Each of the eight scientists were given 10 percent, Hayden Stone (Rock's banking firm) got 20 percent, and Fairchild Camera and Instrument lent the group money for an option that they eventually exercised in 1959," Rock recounted in a later interview. Jay Last, one of the eight scientists, said he and his colleagues saw this as a way of "being their own boss." The eight put up $500 each, about a month's salary, and opened their company just down the road from Shockley's shop.

From the beginning, they also insisted with their backers on a culture that would give them the respect Shockley had demanded for himself, but had been too egomaniacal to extend to his own creative team. Largely at Noyce's insistence, they dispensed with titles, dress codes, and reserved parking lots. Instead of a pecking order of different-sized offices, all the scientists sat in an open room. The egalitarianism and lack of hierarchy were designed to create an intellectual atmosphere in which creativity would flourish, producing an unfettered exchange of information and ideas. "Treat workers well and they work harder; treat them harshly and they get even," Rock explained to us in 2002. The formula flowed easily from the men's background as top scientists and seemed more natural in laid-back, sunny California than it would have been in the formal East Coast settings from which many had come.

All this was made possible because Rock had found as the investor for the company a man of unusual foresight, Sherman Fairchild, the inventor of the aerial camera. (His father had financed Thomas Watson, the founder of IBM Corporation, and was IBM's largest stockholder at the time.) Fairchild Camera & Instrument, of Syosset, New York, ponied up $1.5 million. In return, it got what amounted to an option on the new company, which they agreed to call Fairchild Semiconductor. If the startup succeeded, Fairchild Camera had the right to buy it for $3 million.

Sure enough, the company was a success. After two years the startup had done so well that Fairchild did in fact buy out the founders, who came to be referred to as the "Fairchildren," in honor of their angel investor. The purchase left each of the eight Fairchildren holding stock worth $250,000 (equivalent to $1.4 million in 2002 dollars). This was a princely sum. To offer a sense of perspective, Noyce, then thirty-one, had started at Fairchild two years earlier on a salary of $12,000 a year.

"Suddenly it became apparent to people like myself, who had always assumed they would be working for a salary for the rest of their lives, that they could get some equity in a startup company," Noyce remembered in a 1980 interview. "That was a great revelation—and a great motivation." Indeed it was, and not just to the eight original founders. In the early 1960s, inspired by the riches showered on the founders, Fairchild Semiconductor employees began getting ideas of their own about starting up new companies, hoping that they too would be able to negotiate juicy equity clauses when they did.

Noyce, a man of business acumen as well as technical talent, saw that his employees had begun to recognize what he had learned from his own experience—the high value knowledge workers increasingly could command in the market. If he wanted to keep their services, Noyce reasoned, it would no longer be enough to create a nonhierarchical, egalitarian work environment. He had to do for them what he had done for himself and the other founders— give them an opportunity at equity, a share of ownership of the company.

Publicly held companies had long used various kinds of incentive plans to motivate workers, including profit sharing and monthly or year-end bonuses based on productivity, of the individual, team, division, or entire company. But plans that awarded equity, usually in the form of some sort of stock option, had almost always been reserved for top management. The stock option was a favored form of indirect compensation because it conveyed a right to purchase a fixed number of company shares at a fixed price, and thus tied the value of reward to the fate of the company. If the company failed to prosper, and its stock did not rise in price, the option was worth little. But if the price of the stock rose, the value of the option rose with it.

Fairchild, in fact, was already giving options to the most senior engineers and researchers, who tended to have managerial as well as creative responsibilities. But Noyce wanted to extend options to those who had no managerial responsibilities; in other words, to grant knowledge workers, solely on the basis of their unique contributions, perks formerly reserved for management only. Ideally, he may even have wanted to extend these options to non-knowledge workers as well, so that every member of the firm would know that its success meant money in his or her pocket, above and beyond what came from their salary.

But Fairchild Semiconductor was no longer his company. It was now wholly owned by Fairchild Camera back in Syosset. So Noyce, who has been called the father of the Silicon Valley culture, needed the permission of Fairchild Camera to do what he knew needed to be done to keep his company at the head of the pack.

Unfortunately, by this time Sherman Fairchild had died, and his successors balked at Noyce's radical requests. They were plagued by an "East Coast mentality," Arthur Rock said later. "The new management of the parent company were kind of autocratic people located in Long Island and didn't really understand how things worked out here. For instance, they didn't appreciate the concept of giving employees stock options, even though in the year before Intel was formed, the semiconductor division of Fairchild represented 110 percent of the company's profits."

The new bosses in Syosset, including John Carter, Fairchild Camera's recently appointed CEO, instead began to exert more control, squelching Fairchild Semiconductor's independence and demanding that everyone in California report to the East Coast headquarters. This only made matters worse, since the Californians still thought of themselves as owners, even though they had been bought out and technically were now just employees. The clash of perspectives between the Syosset overseers and the California contingent crystallized in a visit Carter paid them one day. In an *Esquire* magazine article some years later, writer Tom Wolfe described the competing worldviews, neatly capturing the distinction between the rigid hierarchy of corporate America and the new style of an employee-owned, California company.

> One day John Carter came to Mountain View for a close look at Noyce's semiconductor operation. Carter's office in Syosset arranged for a limousine and chauffeur to be at his disposal while he was in California . . . . Nobody had ever seen a limousine and a chauffeur out there before. But that wasn't what fixed the day in everybody's memory. It was the fact that the driver stayed out there for almost eight hours, doing nothing.

While John Carter was inside playing CEO, Wolfe went on, "the driver sat out there all day engaged in the task of supporting a visored cap with his head." As word of the sight spread, people started collecting at the front windows just to take a look for themselves. "Here was a serf who did nothing all day," Wolfe reported, "but wait outside a door in order to be at the service of the haunches of his master instantly, whenever those haunches and the paunch and the jowls might decide to reappear. It wasn't merely that this little peek at the New York style corporate high life was unusual out here in the brown hills of the Santa Clara Valley. It was that it seemed terribly wrong."

The visit may have helped Noyce firm up his ideas about how far from the eastern norm the Valley firms were. Wolfe reports Noyce's new understanding:

> Corporations in the East adopted a feudal approach to organization, without even being aware of it. There were kings and lords, and there were vassals, soldiers, yeomen, and serfs, with layers of protocol and perquisites, such as the car and driver, to symbolize superiority and establish the boundary lines . . . .
>
> Noyce realized how much he detested the Eastern corporate system of class and status with its endless gradations, topped off by the CEOs and vice presidents who conducted their daily lives as if they were a corporate court and aristocracy. He rejected the idea of a social hierarchy at Fairchild.

Carter's unwillingness to go along with the budding new culture turned out to be a mistake of historic proportions. By 1968, his California semiconductor division had lost many of its top engineers and executives to smaller rivals. Noyce and Moore finally quit that year as well, along with a hard-charging Hungarian immigrant named Andy Grove, Moore's deputy in research and development. With Rock's backing, Noyce and Moore formed a new company, which they called Intel Corporation, and brought in Grove as one of the first employees.

That the old ways were under strong challenge in this new business environment is glaringly apparent when you look at the fate of these three companies—Shockley Semiconductor, Fairchild Semiconductor, and Intel. By 1963, Shockley's firm, just six years old, had been sold to ITT Corporation and moved back east to Waltham, Massachusetts. Shockley didn't go east with the firm but instead took a Stanford professorship, where he soon earned a reputation of a different kind—one of widespread opprobrium for his energetically expressed racist view that blacks were genetically less intelligent than whites. When he died in 1989 at the age of seventy-nine, he considered his widely rejected racial theories to be more important than all his truly brilliant breakthroughs in the semiconductor industry.

Meanwhile, Fairchild Semiconductor was stripped of much of its talent and gradually lost its standing as the powerhouse of Silicon Valley. Parent Fairchild Camera puttered along, was bought and sold several times, and finally managed to go public in 1999. By 2002, it had a market value of nearly $3 billion—respectable but far from a smashing success.

Intel, of course, went on to become one of America's most successful tech companies, with a capitalization of more than $130 billion—one of the most valuable companies of all time.

And yet, Shockley Semiconductor and Fairchild may ultimately have left a much greater legacy than their economic profiles suggest. For it was the demand for recognition first articulated by Shockley, then by Noyce and the other dissatisfied Fairchildren, that spawned a new corporate model, one that gave intellectual and financial credit not just to management but to workers whose creative talent contributed to the wealth of a company.

This new model, which would evolve into the standard for much of what came to be called the high-tech sector, gained its first foothold in the fertile soil of Silicon Valley. As one history of the area put it, Fairchild "exploded like a seed pod and scattered the germs of new firms throughout the valley." By 1970, forty-two new semiconductor companies had been founded by former Fairchild employees or by the firms they had started, according to one estimate. At the end of the 1980s, more than one hundred firms had lineage that extended back to Fairchild in one way or another. A 1994 book on Silicon Valley described the fact that "many of the region's entrepreneurs and managers still speak of Fairchild as an important managerial training ground and applaud the education they got at 'Fairchild University.' To this day, a poster of the Fairchild family tree, showing the corporate genealogy of scores of Fairchild spinoffs, hangs on the walls of many Silicon Valley firms."

Not surprisingly, as Fairchild workers left for other jobs, they didn't take just the technical skills they had acquired at Fairchild with them. They also shared and extended at least parts of the new Fairchild culture.

In 1967, for example, the Valley firm National Semiconductor Corporation hired a Fairchild manager named Charlie Sporck to be its CEO. Sporck had been one of those most fiercely complaining to his bosses back east about how hard it was to attract new people given Fairchild's restricted options package. Similarly, Advanced Micro Devices was founded by the flamboyant Jerry Saunders, fired from Fairchild in 1969 by new management that tried to rein in the company after Noyce and Grove left. Both companies adopted the open culture of Fairchild and instituted wide profit sharing in the years after their founding, and eventually extended stock options to many employees.

Fairchild also played a key role in the development of high-tech venture capital firms, many of which also propagated the message that an egalitarian culture and a share-the-wealth philosophy facilitate the recruitment and retention of knowledge workers. Eugene Kleiner, one of the Traitorous Eight, joined with Hewlett-Packard electrical engineer Thomas J. Perkins to form Kleiner, Perkins, Caufield & Byers, which found capital for a long string of Valley firms, including Tandem Computers, Amdahl Corporation, a mainframe maker, and Genentech, a leading biotechnology firm, all of which embraced the Fairchild model to one degree or another. Indeed, many of these funding agreements presumed a nonhierarchical culture, and some even required sharing the wealth with a broad range of knowledge workers.

Arthur Rock, too, went on to raise startup funds for many successful Valley companies that later practiced various degrees of partnership capitalism, including Scientific Data Systems and Teledyne. Decades later, when we spoke to him in 2002, he remained as committed to the Fairchild model as ever. "Since Intel, almost every company I've been associated with has given options to all its employees," he said. "People like to know that they are wanted and that management understands they are working hard. Management is diluting their own equity by giving options to employees."

There were two basic strands to the new corporate culture being pioneered in the Valley. One involved trying to give employees more of a say-so about how their jobs should be done, opening up the corporate decisionmaking process, pushing authority down the ranks, and giving more power to ordinary workers. Some gathered workers into teams to encourage this new model to flourish. Others flattened their corporate hierarchies, creating new labor/management systems that put workers on a more equal footing with bosses and allowed employees or unions to participate in the running of the company.

The second approach was financial. As far back as the late 1800s, some of the giants of American business had tried all kinds of schemes to share profits with workers or get them to own company stock. The theory was that if workers, even factory hands, had a financial incentive to think like owners, they would be motivated to do a better job.

But for many reasons, none of these experiments had ever really taken hold as a dominant practice in corporate America. In the decades after Shockley's little rebellion, large corporations would continue to pursue new ways of improving production, such as teams, employee involvement in decisionmaking, profit sharing, and employee stock ownership plans (ESOPs). However, it was the high-tech firms of Silicon Valley (plus other companies scattered around the country, mostly those with ESOPs) that hit upon just the right combination of cultural and financial incentives—especially stock options—to make the concept succeed. They did so not necessarily out of any great insight on the part of their owners and managers. Instead, high-tech firms were led down this path by the particular business environment that developed in the Valley in the 1960s and 1970s—conditions that subsequently came to affect much of corporate America in the 1990s.

For one thing, the computer industry that took shape around the Stanford area after Shockley arrived was highly dependent on intellectual labor. Sure, workers in factories bent and shaped metal to fabricate room-size computers. But most of what transformed those boxy hunks of metal into computers came from the scientists and engineers who dreamed up ever-better ways to make the machines compute faster and perform a greater variety of tasks. The growing importance of software, which is almost pure thought, added further to the incentive for high-tech firms to tap the brains of their employees.

So it was that as the Valley's high-tech industry grew, executives increasingly came to recognize the value of worker knowledge. The trend hit there first, and subsequently spread to other industries as American companies in virtually every industry developed a growing need for more educated workers. The rise of the so-called knowledge worker, a term that only came into widespread use in the mid-1980s, was accelerated further as the U.S. economy shifted away from manufacturing toward a service-oriented economy.

Another factor that motivated high-tech firms to form a new relationship with their knowledge workers was the scarcity of people qualified to fill such jobs. While Stanford and many other universities began to churn out engineers, physicists, and other highly educated graduates in the 1950s, there were never enough to keep up with the rapid growth of the computer industry in Silicon Valley. The shift to services brought mounting shortfalls of more educated workers in many other industries in the 1980s and 1990s. As a result, Valley companies, in industries with steep growth curves, were especially pressed to find new ways to keep their valued employees happy. Many did so by giving them the respect and ownership stake that Shockley had sought for himself. "Sharing the wealth was a natural evolution of the egalitarian culture," said Regis McKenna, a public relations consultant in the Valley who worked with many of its seminal companies, in one interview.

Indeed, the culture of employee ownership that grew in Shockley's wake flourished in the informal, nonhierarchical atmosphere that long had differentiated California from the encrusted traditions of the East Coast business establishment. Treating knowledge workers like partners rather than underlings was a much smaller conceptual and social leap on the laid-back West Coast, where the physical setting itself, notably the temperate climate, encouraged casual dress and looser social codes.

Still, in the years following the Fairchild diaspora in the late 1960s, the road to stock options for knowledge workers remained largely in the dirt-path stage. Almost all of the Fairchildren left with the belief that the rigid management style of corporate America inhibited the freewheeling exchange of ideas and hobbled American industry in an age of rapid technological change. However, they were never all of one opinion when it came to the even more radical issue of sharing company ownership.

In some instances, options were not offered for reasons unrelated to management's belief about their incentive value. For example, some Fairchildren founded firms that never went public and were sold or eventually went out of business. Others were quickly swallowed up by traditional companies such as General Electric, Philco, Motorola, and Raytheon, before they had enough of a chance to develop the distinctive corporate culture that Fairchild pioneered.

Many other firms took years to fully embrace the idea of including everyone in their stock option plan. Even companies such as Intel, whose founders deliberately set out to build off the concept they had encountered at Fairchild, took years to complete the project. While many founders said that all their employees were partners, in reality, the term "all" usually meant all those who counted, that is, researchers and engineers for the most part. It took nearly two decades, often filled with tension and griping, before technical assistants and factory workers were brought into the circle.

For example, in the beginning Noyce and Moore gave stock options to all Intel's engineers and office staff, as they had been blocked from doing at Fairchild. But that came to only about a third of the workforce. All other employees, including the factory workers hired to make chips, only were entitled to buy Intel stock at a discount. The company also had a profit-sharing plan that covered everyone. However, Intel's ownership remained very lopsided. When it finally went public in 1972, Noyce and Moore together owned 37 percent of the stock. Intel only extended stock options to the full workforce in 1997.

You might even draw an analogy between the slow extension of partnership capitalism to all employees and the gradual evolution of democratic rights to all citizens in Western civilization. The ancient Greeks first practiced the concept of democracy in fifth-century B.C. Athens. But in the days of Socrates and Plato, rule by the people excluded most women, slaves, and others who weren't considered citizens. The United States started off in a similar fashion, taking some 150 years to allow women and blacks to vote.

Silicon Valley high-tech firms traversed a parallel arc, although they did so in decades rather than centuries. Shockley's disciples wanted to form companies that treated everyone as equals, but their conception of everyone really meant the scientists and engineers they considered their peers. Slowly, they were prodded by their own rhetoric and the pressure of tight labor markets to expand their definition of who counted to a more inclusive group. But the process took years to play out.

Still, the partnership approach spread steadily across the Valley and by the late 1960s and early 1970s, firms with no direct links to either Shockley's crew or Fairchild had begun to accept that treating knowledge employees like equals and perhaps like part owners could spur creativity and productivity.

As early as 1969, just a year after the Traitorous Eight fled Fairchild, a physicist named Bob Beyster left the General Atomic Corporation to found Science Applications International Corporation (SAIC). The privately held La Jolla, California–based research and engineering company coupled employee teamwork with ownership for everyone through stock options and other forms of employee ownership. The company, which later bought and then sold the Internet company Network Solutions, kept its nonhierarchical culture even as it swelled to a 41,000-employee giant with sales of $6 billion.

Three years later, in 1972, a brilliant computer scientist named Seymour Cray founded Cray Research to make what were then termed "supercomputers," huge metal boxes with the tremendous computing power required by nuclear physicists, aircraft designers, and advanced weapons researchers.

The company soon developed an operating philosophy, based on high value instead of low price, which came to be known as "The Cray Style." A Cray computer could run up to $20 million, five times what a typical mainframe cost back then. The buyer could make up the difference with lower per-unit computing costs. But to remain competitive with mainframe manufacturers like IBM, Cray researchers had to stay several jumps ahead in the race for new ways to multiply computing power. Although Cray stumbled and was sold before becoming independent again, the Cray Style helped the company compete with rivals throughout the 1970s and 1980s.

That style stressed those corporate values that promised to spur creativity. Because Cray believed that scientific breakthroughs stemmed from small groups working in teams, informality was one key element of the style. To encourage experimentation and an entrepreneurial atmosphere, there were no corporate policy or procedure manuals spelling out how work was to be done. Even as the company swelled to several thousand employees, Cray insisted that everyone be treated as a professional, which meant no time clocks, even for secretaries and assemblers. Cray himself set the example, often arriving in the afternoon and leaving late at night by some accounts. While the company didn't employ stock options, it had a generous profit-sharing program that became vested in the employee as quickly as the law allowed. "The reason: Cray Research wants to keep its best talent because they want to stay, not because they are waiting for a vesting date," reported one account in the mid-1980s.

More and more entrepreneurs were coming to accept that when it came to their employees, bread cast upon the waters did truly return. Few of the new high-tech startups organized themselves on the old model that called for a clear demarcation between compensation for owners and employees.

An interesting case is that of Apple Computer, which pioneered a new kind of user- and graphics-friendly personal computer. Founded in 1977, Apple had its roots in the Shockley era. Arthur

Rock was an early investor who helped find venture capital for the company Steve Jobs and Steve Wozniak wanted to start. The two Steves in turn recruited a National Semiconductor executive named Mike Scott to serve as Apple's president.

Apple's early philosophy held that everyone should be encouraged to think like an entrepreneur. But, not surprisingly, at least when it came to stock options, "everyone" meant mostly managers and certain knowledge workers—engineers. The technicians working at the engineers' elbows were excluded, as were factory workers. In part, the company was run in a fairly chaotic fashion initially, with Jobs and Wozniak improvising in many areas as they went along. So they sometimes gave out options rather randomly, even among the managers and engineers, with the awards often determined by who clamored loudest.

The other side of the coin, however, according to several accounts, had Jobs repeatedly refusing to extend options to people he didn't like or care about, even people who had been there from the very beginning. As Apple headed toward its initial public offering (IPO) in 1980, resentment among the staff that had been left out burned hotter. Even within the new Silicon Valley model, there had to be a sense in the workforce that whatever was being offered gave all similarly situated employees a fair chance to participate. The inequities became so glaring that Wozniak took it on himself to help some employees who he felt had been treated especially unfairly. In 1980, he set up what he called the Wozplan, selling 80,000 shares from his personal holdings to thirty-six employees for $7.50 each, three dollars below the value at the time. (His generosity turned out to be vastly larger than that. As one stock watcher noted, anyone who owned 1,420 shares of Apple at the IPO was worth $1 million the next year.)

Sadly, Jobs acted as if his partner were a sucker. "Woz just couldn't say no" when employees asked to buy his stock, Jobs was quoted as saying some years later. "A lot of people took advantage of him." Jobs' attitude, coupled with his refusal to sell his own stock, helped to fuel anger about the ownership differences. "All along Steve Jobs had been talking about such high ideals for Apple," said Trip Hawkins, one of Apple's earliest employees, in a later interview. "He talked about being generous and fair to employees and creating an atmosphere where they could share in the company's success. But in the end it was Woz not Jobs who put that into practice. It really elevated Woz in my estimation and made Steve look pretty bad."

Apple flip-flopped back and forth several times throughout the 1980s on the issue of just who should be considered an employee-owner. Eventually, the company did give options to mostly everyone after Jobs returned to the company as CEO in 1997, and he came to preach the idea fervently. "Of course you want to have your people share in the wealth you create," Jobs explained in a 1998 interview. "At Apple we gave all our employees stock options very early on. We were among the first in Silicon Valley to do that. It's a very egalitarian way to run a company."

A succession of other computer firms followed a similar arc by broadening their wealth sharing. Larry Ellison, who founded Oracle Corporation in 1977 and built it into the $10 billion software giant it is today, insisted early on that everyone should have options, although that changed as the company grew. (In 2000, only about a quarter of Oracle employees got stock options.) So did Alan F. Shugart, who started disc-drive maker Seagate Technology two years later. In 1980, Tandem Computers Incorporated attributed much of its 100 percent annual growth in the early years to a people-oriented management style that included options for every employee, sabbaticals every four years, and an open-door policy that invited employees to drop in for a talk with their managers anytime.

The ideas initially unleashed by Shockley and the Fairchildren also were nurtured by an antibureaucratic, wealth-sharing tradition that had bubbled up in the Santa Clara Valley long before the silicon chip he invented came along to transform its name. Several far-sighted visionaries in the area had long before suggested that corporations should extend the rewards of property ownership to workers. One of the most prominent was the very man who founded the university that first rented space to those early high-tech entrepreneurs—Leland Stanford.

As far back as 1886, U. S. Senator Stanford, who the year before had founded Stanford University, introduced a bill to encourage employee ownership. A railroad magnate who had made a fortune retailing mining supplies to miners during the California gold rush, Stanford had observed up close the desire for personal profits that motivated individual entrepreneurship, and thought extending a share of corporate earnings to employees was the way to harness such power within a business setting. Stanford's bill called on Congress "to encourage cooperation and to provide for the formation of associations in the District of Columbia for the purpose of conducting any lawful business and dividing the profits among the members thereof." He instructed the trustees of his new university "to have taught in the University the rights and advantages of association and cooperation."

In 1938, nearly half a century after Stanford articulated this philosophy, William Hewlett and David Packard, who had met at Stanford as freshmen, started an electronics company in their Palo Alto garage that soon developed many of the attributes we would later associate with the high-tech firms of Silicon Valley.

Like Shockley's successors, Hewlett and Packard recognized that in a business whose growth was dependent upon the inventiveness of knowledge workers, it was critical to provide a comfortable working environment to spur openness and creativity. A casual dress code, informal rules, and free coffee and soft drinks all sprang from Hewlett-Packard's desire to avoid hierarchical management structures that might inhibit the sharing of innovative ideas.

"If a company has the attitude that it needs to control (employees) and that 'we don't trust you,' that will be self-fulfilling," HP's vice president for human resources, Pete Peterson, said in 1990. "We don't try to surround our people with a big, long set of rules and regulations. We prefer to operate on guidelines, describe jobs in broad terms, and give workers the maximum amount of freedom to get the job done." In 1985, Packard said: "If people have some part in making decisions that they're going to be involved with, they're going to be much more effective in implementing those decisions."

HP depended on profit sharing rather than options to share the wealth, in part because for many years it remained a privately held company with no publicly traded stock. However, another pioneering Silicon Valley firm, Varian Associates, gave employees stock options from the day it was founded in 1948. The company, started by Pan American World Airways pilot Siguard Varian and his physicist brother, Russell, developed microwave technology that served as the backbone for the development of radar applications, satellite communications, airplane and missile guidance systems, and television transmission.

The brothers got a helping hand through a professor who had been Russell's roommate at Stanford. The university gave them free use of a lab plus $100 worth of materials per year, in exchange for a 50 percent interest in their patents. In 1953 they became the first tenant of the Stanford Research Park where Shockley, Fairchild, and dozens of other high-tech companies later set up shop. Varian, too, cultivated a freewheeling exchange of ideas among employees, backed up by a financial stake in the firm, which grew to 7,000 employees and $1.5 billion in sales before splitting into three independent public companies in 1999. In a 1996 memoir, Ed Ginzton, who cofounded Varian with the two brothers and became its CEO, wrote: "We appended the word 'associates' (to the brothers' name) to convey the idea that the new company was to become a cooperative owned by the employees."

While these early experiments didn't contribute directly to the widespread propagation of partnership capitalism the way Fairchild did, they did help to create a receptive climate for the new casual corporate culture that would soon come to be associated with the Valley. For example, in 1967 Hewlett took a phone call from a twelve-year-old Steve Jobs, who wanted electronic parts for a project. Jobs got the parts and a summer job at HP's factory, where he got a firsthand look at the HP Way. "What I learned that summer at Bill and Dave's company was the blueprint we used for Apple," Jobs remembered later. Wozniak, his cofounder, also worked as an engineer at HP until he quit to build personal computers with Jobs.

Still, it wasn't until the early 1980s that a critical mass of high-tech companies began to adopt the distinctive culture that came to be associated first with Silicon Valley startups and then with the Internet industry. One factor was the mounting importance of software. Most of the early computer companies in the Valley, such as HP, Intel, and National Semiconductor, focused mostly on producing hardware, electronic equipment, and computers of various sorts. Scientists and engineers were critical to company competitiveness in design and innovation, but these firms still relied heavily on blue-collar workers to manufacture the end product, usually in a factory. But as software became more of a separate function, an end product around which entire divisions or companies could be organized, knowledge workers began to take on even greater importance.

Indeed, a new breed of high-tech firm that grew rapidly in the 1980s often had no physical product to speak of at all. At companies such as Adobe Systems, Microsoft, and Oracle, the creativity of the human mind was what rolled out the door to customers. As a result, it became even more important to nurture employees who had the very special talents required to navigate these uncharted waters. With a distinctively nonphysical product to sell, the creative musings of employees are the means of production.

An intense competition in the Valley for employees with these new talents added to the pressure on high-tech firms to find new ways to recruit and retain valuable employees. Although computer scientists, software designers, and code writers flocked to the area from around the country, almost like a gold-rush migration, the new companies sprang up and grew, keeping available job opportunities always ahead of the expanding labor pool. As early as 1983, startups such as 3Com Corporation, which made networking systems, felt that it was next to impossible to find qualified staff without handing out options to all fifty employees it had back then. (Today, the company has more than 8,000 employees and sales of some $3 billion.) The only way to compete for talent with the larger and wealthier tech firms, which could offer more in salary and better security, was "to make it absolutely clear that there are rewards for coming, for staying, and for working hard," said 3Com founder and CEO Bob Metcalfe in an interview that year. "Without equity, there's suspicion. With it, there's more inherent, intuitive trust."

The shortage of people skilled in the exploding world of electronics took on a particular intensity in the hotbed of Silicon Valley.

As Michael Malone wrote in a book on the region, the two dozen cities that comprise Santa Clara Valley stretch down the San Francisco Bay south from the city, with a low mountain range hemming them in on the other side. They all run together in a more or less indistinguishable mass, creating a dense area of social interaction among the hundreds of high-tech firms that already populated the cities in the early 1980s. Many techies knew each other as students at Stanford and regularly ran into each other in restaurants, bars, parties, and local industry associations. The openness of their companies further helped foster an atmosphere in which ideas were shared not just within firms, but among them as well.

The result, according to a 1994 book, was

> unusually high levels of job-hopping. During the 1970s average annual employee turnover exceeded 35 percent in local electronics firms and was as high as 59 percent in small firms. An anthropologist studying the career paths of the region's computer professionals concluded that job tenures in Silicon Valley averaged two years. These high rates of mobility forced technology companies to compete intensely for experienced engineering talent. Headhunters became common during the 1970s, and firms began to offer incentives such as generous signing bonuses, stock options, high salaries, and interesting projects to attract top people.

Venture capitalists, too, played a key role in bringing about the change. If sharing the wealth and a participative culture was the seed, venture capital was the wind that spread it. People like Rock and Kleiner and Perkins attracted new capital based on their track record of having helped give birth to many successful companies that gave ownership to employees. So they naturally tried to push the idea whenever it seemed appropriate. Many corporate fundraisers who followed in their footsteps felt the same way. "Unless there is broad distribution of major equity portions to the primary key individuals, we're not an investor," said Don Valentine, then president of Capital Management Services Inc., a Valley venture capital firm, in a 1983 interview. "We don't believe you can build a major company with one man owning all the equity and the others being employees with no ownership in the enterprise." Valentine was an early Fairchild employee who later founded Sequoia Capital, which focused on high-tech companies in the Valley and became one of the country's most successful venture capital firms.

Similar views were expressed in the same magazine article by William Hambrecht, who then headed up the San Francisco investment banking firm of Hambrecht & Quist Incorporated. He was particularly aware of the chronic shortfall of skilled labor that every Valley firm faced: "Single ownership doesn't work anymore," he said. "I'm hard-pressed to think how you could go out and acquire good people without giving them a share of the ownership. Most entrepreneurs now understand that. I would have trouble imagining that someone with 80 percent of the stock could keep a key team together and happy." This radical assessment by a respected investment banker illustrates how much had changed over so little time.

The most striking example of the new corporate structure, and one that would inspire both other high-tech companies and the Internet industry, was Microsoft. In Albuquerque, New Mexico, well removed from Silicon Valley, Chairman William Gates Jr. founded what would become the world's largest and most successful software company in 1975. The company, which soon moved to the Seattle suburb of Redmond where it has been ever since, was a small private partnership in the early years and money was tight. Gates balked at paying high wages in those days and even refused to compensate secretaries and other employees for overtime. Eventually, he began giving annual bonuses instead.

In 1981, Microsoft incorporated, creating stock initially held by just a handful of key officers. Gates held 53 percent; cofounder Paul Allen had 31 percent; Steve Ballmer, whom Gates brought aboard in 1980 to be the executive manager, received 8 percent; and the remainder was split among a few other managers. But this didn't sit well with the firm's other fifty-odd employees, who felt left out. In a first attempt to address the problem, Microsoft started a stock option program, but limited it to select employees. The complaints continued as the company grew and prospered, prompting Gates to install a plan in 1986, when Microsoft finally went public, that allowed every employee to purchase company stock at a discount. He also expanded the option program to cover all full-time employees.

"We never thought that offering stock options to all our employees—instead of just to executives, like other companies did—was really that innovative," Gates said in an interview years later. "It seemed totally natural to us . . . . Even back then I felt that great programmers were just as important as great management. If we gave all the options to management, we couldn't hire the best developers." On another occasion, Gates said, "We're using ownership as one of the things that ties us all together."

Microsoft CEO Steve Ballmer, one of the company's cofounders, expressed similar views to us in 2001. "Early on, Bill and I recognized the importance of employee ownership. Microsoft was one of the first companies to grant stock options to all its regular, full-time employees. We believed that people should have a stake in the future success of the company. And by linking employees' long-term interests with the company's, employees naturally have a greater stake in seeing the company succeed. We also knew early on that hiring the most passionate and intelligent people was crucial to Microsoft's success."

Once Microsoft workers are hired, they're eligible for additional options every year, based on their performance, said John Molloy, the company's senior director of Compensation and Benefits. The company also periodically rewards employees with special grants to all full timers. For example, at the end of April 2000, after Microsoft's stock had fallen to almost half its value, the company gave everyone an extra round of options equal to what they had received during their annual performance review the prior July. In February 2001, Microsoft accelerated that year's grants, giving employees the options they had been due to receive the following August. This gave employees an extra six months of upside potential.

In business, as in most areas of life, success inevitably breeds imitation, and Microsoft's wild success contributed greatly to the spread of options and of partnership capitalism. One flash point came in 1992, when a frenzy of publicity arose after a Wall Street analyst estimated that 2,200 of the 11,000 workers on Microsoft's regular payroll that year held options worth at least $1 million. "Not even the height of the Wall Street takeover frenzy of the mid-1980s made as many instant millionaires as did simple employment at Microsoft for the last five years," wrote a *New York Times* reporter.

Gates and Ballmer take no options for themselves, although they hardly need them. Gates still owned 12 percent of the company outright in 2001, worth $40 billion as of the end of the year, while Ballmer's 4 percent stake was worth $14 billion. Still, all the other employees owned 20 percent of Microsoft's shares according to one company estimate, worth some $65 billion in the spring of 2002. While the direct stock-ownership stakes vary dramatically among the company's 48,000 employees depending on their rank and tenure, they held stock options comprising 21 percent of the company's total equity at the end of that year. If all of these options were exercised in the spring of 2002, each employee would have a profit of about $335,000. In stark contrast to the way stock options had been reserved for top management in the pre–Silicon Valley days, the company's top six executives received only 1.6 percent of all options given out in 2001. This represented a broader distribution than had ever been known in the American corporate world.

In addition to the example it set, Microsoft employees went off to start hundreds of companies, spreading widely the new attitudes about worker compensation. One estimate pegs the number of Baby Bills at more than 500, most of them in software and related fields, usually in the Seattle area. Like the Fairchildren, these former Microsoft employees have often taken the options-for-everyone approach with them.

While many American companies offered stock options to executives in the 1980s, the heirs to Gates and Shockley took the further step of expanding them to a wide group of nonmanagement employees. As they did, average workers reaped the rewards of the bull market that followed in the 1990s, right along with other shareholders.

Quite a few of these companies managed to fuse the cultural and economic aspects of the new corporate model. Many pursued the team concept and other attempts at employee involvement, and many pursued ESOPs, managing to put the two strands together into a cohesive whole. Since the 1980s, many leaders of smaller, less noticeable firms around the country have gone down this road. One, for example, was John Cullinane, who in 1968 founded Cullinet Software Incorporated in Westwood, Massachusetts, and soon created a company culture based on employee ownership and a lack of centralized control. As early as 1983, the company had included all 800 employees in its stock option plan and strove for "a lack of bureaucracy that gives employees a chance to impact the success of their project and the company," Cullinane said that year.

A few companies even managed the extraordinary feat of combining East Coast formality with an egalitarian atmosphere that fostered teamwork and communication. At Houston-based Compaq Computer Corporation, founded in 1982, pinstripes and dark shoes were the norm, the Friday beer bashes Valley firms used to lighten the atmosphere were out of the question, and alcohol was forbidden on its premises altogether. Yet somehow, the company meshed such trappings with options for everyone and a consensus management style that eschewed assigned parking places and made decisions in informal team meetings.

But most old-line tech companies have never shaken the autocratic East Coast mentality, whose top-down management style inhibited the open, fluid relationships that mark most Valley companies. Even today, companies such as IBM are still largely run as hierarchies. In fact, the company has a lengthy history of squelching shifts toward a more open culture. Just look at what happened after IBM purchased Rolm Corporation in 1984. Rolm was located in Santa Clara, California, even though it was founded in 1969 by four electrical engineers from Texas's Rice University. The company enjoyed tremendous success making telephone switching gear in the mid-1970s and developed all the trappings of a quintessential Valley tech firm. Rolm had no dress code or set working hours, according to one newspaper account, and employees who stayed with the company six years got a twelve-week paid sabbatical. The paper described the company's headquarters as being in a campus setting with landscaped streams, wooden walkways, a gym, and a swimming pool open to all employees. Rolm also made liberal use of profit sharing and stock options.

IBM took over with vows that it wouldn't disturb Rolm's flexible culture, which IBM officials recognized as a key to Rolm's success. But IBM's almost cultlike uniformity led inexorably toward the same creeping control that Fairchild had faced from its autocratic East Coast bosses. IBM did keep the stock options, but only for select managers. As IBM tightened its grip, more Rolm workers bailed out, including founder Kenneth Oshman, who departed in early 1986 saying he was "no longer needed." In 1987, IBM ended Rolm's status as a separate subsidiary and transformed it into just another IBM division. The unit soon stagnated, and by the end of the following year IBM was forced to pull out and sell its telephone equipment production facilities—and their 2,800 workers—to Siemens, the West German electronics company.

Doubts about the soundness of this approach have plagued some IBM executives for decades. One striking example came in a 1987 interview with former IBM CEO Thomas J. Watson Jr., who at the age of seventy-three expressed remarkably candid views on the subject a full sixteen years after he retired from the company he had inherited from his father. He said:

> My father strove to blur the distinction between white-collar and blue-collar workers. Not only did he pay well, but he eliminated piecework in the factories. In 1958 Jack Bricker, our manager of personnel, suggested that we shift all of our employees [from hourly wages] to salaries, eliminating the last difference between factory and office work. (Later) I considered taking even more radical steps to increase our employees' commitment to IBM. When I talked to my wife at night, I would speak of various ways of sharing our success more broadly. Those at the top were doing fantastically well on stock options. While IBM's workers were making high salaries, they weren't making the kind of capital gains that employees with options were. I even asked myself whether our present system of corporate ownership is the system that will support the free American way long term. Though I never found a practical way to achieve it on a meaningful scale, I looked for ways to increase employee ownership of the business. I disliked applying a double standard to managers and employees.

It may be that Watson would have seen options as the answer he was looking for had they existed in their current form when he was in charge in the 1960s and 1970s. (IBM extended stock options broadly only at the end of the 1990s.) Even if they had, however, it's far from clear that IBM would have ventured into that total revamping of the old ways pioneered by the Fairchildren. Employee ownership is the financial key to risk and reward sharing, but flat hierarchies and shared decisionmaking are just as central to the Silicon Valley concept. Watson and his successors have never given much indication that they had doubts about their company's command-and-control management style.

The ranks of high-tech firms that followed the partnership approach to a greater or lesser degree swelled steadily throughout the 1980s and early 1990s. Individual companies embraced or shied away from employee decisionmaking and ownership in a fairly idiosyncratic fashion, the precise structure adopted in each often related to the beliefs and talents of the founder or CEO. But as labor shortages mounted, more firms moved in the new direction. According to a 1994 survey by Venture One, a San Francisco research firm, only 47 percent of fast-growing small companies in the San Francisco Bay area offered stock options to a majority of employees. However, 78 percent of those founded after 1990 did so, the survey found.

By the time the next wave of high-tech companies sprang to life around the Internet in the mid-1990s, virtually everyone involved in it had brushed aside the reservations of Watson and other high-tech CEOs with barely a thought. At that point, enough Valley firms had opted for the alternative approach that newcomers felt they had little choice but to offer prospective employees similar packages or lose out in what would soon come to be called the talent wars. This was particularly true for companies whose products consisted almost entirely of knowledge.

To understand the revolution brought about by these changes, we must examine the extent to which these new high-tech companies, a brand new subset of the high-tech sector, adopted the new corporate model spread by Shockley's heirs. The next chapter will do that.

# 2

# The Soul of a New Corporation

## How High-tech Companies
## Institutionalized Partnership Capitalism

A t a broad level, the Web is similar to other networks that have
spurred technological innovation as Western economies industrialized over the centuries. Shipping networks, railroads, inter-
state highways, telegraph and telephone networks, and air traffic
control systems have all used the idea of routing among intercon-
nected nodal points to move goods, people, or information.

The network that blossomed into the World Wide Web was started
by the U. S. Defense Department largely in response to the Soviet
Union's 1957 launch of the Sputnik satellite. The following year,
President Eisenhower set up a military agency called the Advanced
Research Projects Agency to compete in the race to space. ARPA soon
developed something called the Semi-Automatic Ground
Environment, or SAGE, which consisted of computers that could receive and interpret a continuous stream of data, piped in over phone
lines, from radar systems that tracked aircraft and satellites.

In the mid-1960s, government and university researchers came
up with the idea of having computers sending and receiving information from different locations, all hooked up together over the
phone. In 1969, the first so-called ARPANET sites were set up at

Stanford, the University of Utah, and the University of California at Los Angeles and at Santa Barbara. The system crashed when Charley Kline, a UCLA undergrad, typed the letter G of LOGIN on the first message.

Universities and military researchers constantly expanded the network over the next decade and set up new ones around the United States. The @ sign was accepted as a standard in 1972, and the next year the first international connections were made, to England through Norway. Email came along a few years later, and discussion groups were added in 1979. In the 1980s, the military split off into its own network (which was killed altogether in 1990), leaving universities as the main users. Their different networks gradually linked up into what began to be called the Internet, shorthand for the inter-networking of networks. By 1987, the number of host computers broke the 10,000 mark.

The Internet opened up to the wider public in the mid-1990s, with the advent of the World Wide Web and browser programs that allow individuals to jump from one host site to another and access clickable documents, pictures, streaming video, and sound. As the number of personal computers multiplied, the ranks of Internet users shot up by orders of magnitude. There were already 727,000 computers with unique Internet addresses when the Web was set up in 1991. But a decade later their ranks had swelled to 175 million. The number of email messages sent in North America jumped from 40 billion in 1995 to 1.4 trillion in 2001. By then, 115 million Americans spent an average of nineteen hours a month online and the Internet had become part of everyday life.

The advent of this new network of communication brought with it the birth of a new industry devoted to developing the equipment and software that make the Internet possible. While some of these companies began life in the Internet's early days, it wasn't until the Web created a widespread public phenomenon in the mid-1990s that they coalesced into a distinct industry.

Many of the companies settled in Silicon Valley, where they formed two distinct subgroups. Some—mostly those that went up in smoke in the tech crash of 2000—focused on selling goods to consumers over the Web. The rest, which form the core of the remaining Internet industry, churned out the Internet's routers, search engines, software programs, and content. Because of their products, everyone from companies and governments to universities and non-profits can display their wares to the public via computer.

It was this branch of the high-tech industry that came, almost by accident, to fully embrace the concept that the prosperity of a company depends on how everyone there performs together. In a way, this isn't all that surprising. After all, these are the very firms serving one of society's most nonhierarchical and communitarian mediums. However, the original impetus came not from some abstract set of principles, but from the brutal market conditions that existed when the industry came into existence.

When the original Internet firms burst onto the scene in the mid-1990s, the high-tech job market was already extremely difficult terrain for employers. For more than a decade, corporate America had been sinking billions a year into new computers and other high-tech equipment. So companies everywhere were scrambling for workers with the special skills and training to adapt the hardware and software to their own particular needs, and then to run and maintain these systems. As well, the hardware and software makers themselves also needed programmers and computer engineers by the thousands, to create new products for this burgeoning market.

As a result, even before many of the new high-tech companies were established, thousands of firms of all sizes were scrambling for computer talent. They dangled all kinds of rewards in front of skilled employees, from bonuses to Porsches, or offered up the right to purchase the company's stock at a discount. Some imported inexpensive programmers from India and other countries and pestered Congress to expand the number of so-called H1B visas, which allow employers to import workers with skills that are in short supply in the United States. But nothing could keep pace with all the new jobs that needed filling. So began what came to be called the talent wars, as companies outbid each other to hire the best, or even the second or third best, in an attempt to find skilled employees.

In this highly competitive environment, startup high-tech companies were at a double disadvantage. First, prospective hires swimming in job choices were being asked to take a chance on unproven firms that often had no revenue to speak of and poor near-future prospects for profits. In fact, the entire Internet concept as a viable business opportunity was unproven. Sure, the pundits back then gushed about the Internet's change-the-world potential. But in the past, many other new industries had streaked across the industrial sky like bright comets and then flamed out. Job hunters were well aware that when recruiters described a company as having "potential," it was another way of saying that the firm had no track record of success. In addition, many Internet startups lacked the cash to shell out above-market salaries that would offset the extra risk employees would run if they jumped aboard.

Stock options gave the budding new industry a way to compete for talent. Although they were already a familiar feature in Silicon Valley, no one really knew how effective a recruiting tool options would become. Would workers leave established companies like IBM for the right to share in the ownership of a place that might become the next IBM, knowing full well that the likelihood of any one company doing so was extremely small? As it turned out, the idea was extraordinarily powerful during those heady days.

"I didn't choose to go to IBM, I didn't choose to stay at another smaller computer company where I was before, which was a company where I would not have had stock options and nine-to-five would have been perfectly fine with them," said Rachel, a forty-something manager at Portal Software Incorporated, a Silicon Valley company that provides billing software for telecommunications companies and stock options for its employees. "I chose to come here, where you have a chance that it might add up to something."

In offering stock options, mind you, founders of high-tech firms didn't envision anything so grandiose as a new model of the corporation or of Western capitalism. To the contrary, their culture started with the same casual hierarchies and stock options prevalent in the Valley milieu of the early 1990s.

But there was a crucial difference. Instead of narrowly defining who would be in the corporate partnership and gradually widening out the group over the years, high-tech firms from the very beginning extended both aspects of partnership capitalism to virtually everyone at the company. Many empowered employees to get involved in decisionmaking about how they did their jobs every day. They also gave options to everyone, so they would have a stake in the company's wealth-generating capacity.

The logic was spelled out clearly in early 2000 by Timothy Byland, a sales executive at Akamai, a Cambridge, Massachusetts, firm that manages corporations' e-commerce infrastructures. He told a congressional committee:

> Employees at all levels can and do play a role in all parts of their company's success, from management to product development to marketing. The concept of sharing the wealth at all levels reflects this culture of contributions. With stock options, I am part of the shared success. I am rewarded for the contributions I make and I am motivated to make them.

Although other Valley companies had begun to move in this direction before, the partnership approach had never snowballed into a broad-based standard until the Internet industry came along. By 1999, when the Internet frenzy reached its height, no high-tech firm in Silicon Valley could remain competitive without offering options to most or all employees and a flattened hierarchy that left lots of room for employees to manage their own time and resources. It didn't matter if the CEO believed in partnership capitalism or not. The concept became the industry norm, and every company had to embrace it.

This remained true even after the high-tech bubble burst in 2000 and pundits began declaring stock options worthless. The following year, Chris Wheeler, cofounder of Internap, which provides Internet routing services, observed: "We would be crucified if it (stock options) didn't exist (in our company), because everybody else does it. In this industry, you absolutely wouldn't be able to survive for one second." Indeed, every single firm in the High Tech 100 index we created offers options to most or all of their employees. Many also operate without the old management hierarchies in place.

Almost by happenstance, the high-tech companies launched a widely watched experiment in partnership capitalism. But why did the idea take off so suddenly and spread so completely across the industry, right from its very beginning?

To some extent, the answer is timing. The industry's decision to move to company-wide partnership capitalism was the culmination of a broader shift underway in America toward a knowledge economy. Throughout the 1970s and 1980s, many traditional manufacturers began to adopt Japanese and Scandinavian concepts, introducing production teams and employee involvement in decisionmaking. They did so because they too began to see that the quality and productivity of their factories depended increasingly on brainpower over muscle power, on new production techniques rather than on heavy equipment.

The early high-tech companies accelerated the journey down this road for similar reasons. They saw that their industry required ever-faster cycles of product innovations, which in turn spurred them to maximize the intellectual output of their staff. Innovation more than capital investment generated corporate wealth. High-tech 100 firms completed the move toward a company in which employees, not machinery, are the fountain of value and wealth. To a large degree, they are little more than a collection of employees and the offices they work in. (Only sixteen manufacture any hardware at all, and most of those consider the software they produce to be as important or even more so.)

The industry's zeitgeist was spelled out nicely in a 1999 book called *Netscape Time*, by James Clark, a cofounder of Netscape Incorporated, which created the first widely used Internet browser. "High technology isn't about software or hardware, but about brains and people," he wrote. Clark understood that even the most dramatic advance could not sustain a company over the long haul. As competitors caught up, the successful company had to keep producing leading-edge innovations to stay ahead of the pack. "Any advantage based on any one breakthrough is short-lived," he wrote. "But good, creative brains will keep producing new and better things. To own something is almost meaningless in the long-run. It's the ability to recruit, inspire, and hold onto smart people that offers the key to ongoing success . . . . That's the one big thing that I know."

Or, as John T. Chambers, CEO of Cisco Systems Incorporated, one of the largest and most successful of Internet firms, once similarly observed in a speech:

> Not long ago . . . the output of machines was the fundamental driver of competitive advantage. We taught our managers to focus on physical assets, the cost of capital, and the value chain. Successful companies built more, for less. In the Internet economy, the dynamics are radically different. Intangible ideas—the output of people, in an economic sense—are the drivers of competitive advantage.

Cisco still produces physical products, like routers, which channel the bits of information around among all the dispersed computers that comprise the Internet. But as software, which is really nothing but thoughts, began to take precedence over hardware, other high-tech companies became even more extreme examples of pure knowledge companies. Today, many Internet companies have no actual physical product to speak of.

The prevalence of stock options says a great deal about the willingness of venture capitalists and other outside shareholders to accept the idea of a company as a partnership. After all, giving options to employees diluted the ownership of the company's founders and investors. Shareholders' willingness to swallow this consequence illustrates that partnership capitalism was accepted as a sound business practice.

The most important relationship to change, however, was not between investors and employees, but between management and worker. High-tech firms still have a hierarchy and the CEO still thinks about the company's overall direction, while a programmer, for example, focuses on a particular piece of software that may earn the company a few more dollars of revenue. But executives don't just give orders that workers faithfully carry out. Instead, the idea is that everyone collaborates to find the best way to achieve the company's goals.

This corporate behavior parallels the leveling values of the Internet itself. On the Web, everyone is linked together in a horizontal network of interactions that lack a central authority. Everyone has an opportunity to speak and to listen, and communication is fast moving, with few formal niceties. Ad hoc groups of individuals come together and break up at will, as in chat rooms. The value of any piece of information is based on its intrinsic utility, not on the authority or credentials of the person who provided it. The idea that every worker's individual prosperity depends on how they all perform together did not have to be sold to people who thrived on the Internet culture. It came naturally to them.

Stock options play a crucial role by giving everyone an ownership stake in the outcome. Once, not long after Amazon did its Initial Public Offering in 1997, CEO Jeff Bezos told a story at a retreat for managers. One who attended remembered it like this: A family Bezos knew owned a beach house that they would rent out for the off season. One summer they came back and found that their tenant had nailed a Christmas tree to the wooden floor of the house. Bezos told his staff: "If [the tenant] were the owner of the house, [he] never would have made that decision. . . . What we need to do in this company is to think like owners. You are an actual owner of the company, and we need to remind people of that, so they will make the right decisions."

Many high-tech firms found that a company of partners who all think and behave like owners enriches both the firm and its employees. This happens in a number of ways. When employees are motivated and given more leeway to make decisions on their own, it spurs innovation and performance from the bottom up. An ownership stake fuels the process by blurring the line between management and workers. Similarly, employees who know they're in a partnership are more likely to work together as teammates, rather than rivals competing with each other to climb the corporate ladder. They're also more likely to remain at the company over the long haul, reducing expensive turnover and helping the company to retain needed skills. In addition, the prospect of economic gain from the company's stock helps them to focus on the company's broadest objectives, with an eye to what's most likely to turn a corporate profit.

"First and foremost, [stock options are] something that apply to all employees, which indicates that every job is important," said Frank Marshall, the vice chairman of Covad Communications, which provides high-speed access to the Internet. "If you have this caste system where there are the hourly workers that don't participate in the equity upside, then you have management that has private dining rooms and stuff like that, and it sets up an attitude that some employees are not important. Stock options send a message to all employees that they have an impact on the growth of the company and they will be rewarded for that impact."

Of course, no amount of innovation or extra effort can overcome larger external forces. The benefits that flow from the partnership approach can't offset illegal actions by rivals, or economic recessions that swamp entire industries. In 2001 and 2002, for example, the economic downturn badly battered America Online, causing AOL Time Warner to rack up billions in losses. Things got so bad that the company was forced to write down a record-breaking $54 billion in losses in the first quarter of 2002, and some observers began proclaiming that AOL's merger with Time Warner had been a big mistake. By August 2002, the company's stock had plunged by more than 75 percent, to a record low of $12.52. Soon thereafter, the company fired Chief Operating Officer Robert Pittman, the person next to AOL founder Steve Case who had been the most responsible for AOL's growth strategy.

That's something else that partnership capitalism can't do a whole lot about: poor strategic decisions by the company's CEO, which can overwhelm any gains from motivated employees. It's not clear whether AOL management did indeed commit major errors, either in the merger or in its core Internet strategy. If anything, the merged company simply couldn't morph itself quickly into the team-oriented partnership capitalism culture of the old AOL. The company gave a one-time grant of stock options to everyone, but there was no serious attempt to meld the cultures. Still, in general, while the partnership method can help a company do better than it otherwise would, it's not likely to be the only factor influencing a firm's fate.

Nevertheless, during 2001 and 2002 we interviewed employees, management, venture capitalists, and founders at high-tech companies about their experiences with partnership capitalism. Time and again, we found that they described changes that fell into one of the following categories.

## Bottom-up Decisionmaking and Innovation

Ironically, there is no better example than AOL (at least before its merger) of how partnership capitalism can improve corporate performance once a company hits upon a winning concept. America Online began life in 1985, first as Control Video Corporation and then as Quantum Computers. It wanted to help people play games over the Internet. In its early years, the company struggled just to stay alive, competing with deep-pocket rivals such as Microsoft and Prodigy. AOL pulled back from the brink of ruin so often that it picked up the nickname "cyber-cockroach" before emerging as the first online media leader when the Internet became accessible to the general public.

Today, of course, AOL dominates the public face of the Web. From its headquarters in Vienna, Virginia, the firm reaches 34 million homes in more than a dozen countries, in seven languages, and delivers more messages each day than the U.S. Postal Service delivers mail. In 2001, it merged with media giant Time Warner.

Almost from the beginning, James V. Kimsey, the founding CEO, gave almost every employee generous option grants. In fact, until the merger, an average of more than 90 percent of all options AOL granted each year went to employees below the top five corporate officers—everyone from customer service representatives to security guards and even consultants. Even after the merger, the practice continued within America Online itself. AOL's culture also has pushed Time Warner to make a symbolic grant of options to all its employees and to begin to emphasize options over other types of compensation. In 1999, Kimsey, who now heads the AOL Foundation as well as his own philanthropic foundation, called the idea of giving ownership to all workers "one of the smartest decisions I ever made."

Before the merger, partnership capitalism helped the company to thrive once it hit upon its proper role in the marketplace. The outcome shows up all the way down to the company's 5,600 call center employees. These are the people on the other end of the phone when you call for technical help or a question about your bill. Like customer service reps anywhere, they are hourly workers strapped to a headset all day, earning about $32,000 a year according to one industry study. But they also get stock options, and have more skill and responsibility than the person you reach at most other customer help lines.

As a result, the reps come up with scads of new ideas, mostly by knowing what customers are looking for. They use a sophisticated database system to help them answer questions and deal with callers. It also helps them to identify problems or features missing in AOL's software. Executives estimate that the constant feedback call reps provide from customers accounts for some 40 percent of the new features in each new version of its software. "These consultants are the only people any of our members will ever talk to," Ken Nemcovich, the head of AOL's Jacksonville, Florida, call center, told an interviewer in the fall of 2000. "It's our secret weapon."

## Teamwork

While employee teams had become a common feature of American corporate life by the late 1990s, high-tech firms built the idea into the fabric of their working relationships from day one. John Chambers, for example, tried to turn Cisco into a federation of entrepreneurial teams by making managers invisible. "I learned a long time ago that in team sports or in business a group working together can always defeat a team of individuals," he said in 1996. "In our organization, if I've got a leader who can't be a team player, they're gone. That doesn't mean we don't want healthy disagreement, but regardless of how well they're performing, if they can't learn over time to be part of the team and to challenge when appropriate, they really aren't going to fit into our long-term culture." To bring this about, Chambers set up a pay system for leaders pegged to the quality of the teams they built.

Some high-tech employees who came from more traditional companies, especially midcareer or older ones, told us that they had to learn to adapt to the new culture. Francine, an engineering vice president at Portal Software who had worked at several non-high-tech places before, described how she had crossed paths with a colleague in another division who wasn't really pulling his fair share of a job the two had to do. In a traditional corporate setting, "I would have been nasty with him," Francine, who was in her mid-forties, told us. But she knew that such behavior wouldn't play at a place like Portal, so she tried to curb her judgmental instincts. Her new strategy: "Instead, I would take him out to lunch and coach him on how to be a manager. I was always looking at what Portal was trying to do and how can we get there."

## Tying Employees to the Company

In addition to spurring innovation and teamwork, stock options also act like financial magnets, binding employees to their companies for the long term. One of the most common refrains you hear from high-tech workers is how the economic incentive that options offer ties them to their company.

This sentiment came through clearly in an informal discussion we had over lunch one day in early 2001 with a half-dozen employees at Portal. Virtually everyone there, from lower-level staffers to a vice president, said they felt much the same way. "I'm willing to stick it out longer and put up with more crap, because there's a financial stake," said Jack, an administrator in the company's finance unit. "There was a time in which I was sorely tested by my manager, and the only reason I stuck around is that we were on the track to that IPO. I knew that if I hung around long enough, it meant millions of dollars to me. That's why I'm with the company now, because it was untenable by every other measure except for that. It is obvious to me that longevity, retention, is really the thing [companies] are buying with stock options."

Added Geoff, a Portal engineer: "Your salary is your reward for doing a good job, and options are an incentive to stay at your job, that's really what it boils down to."

Other high-tech employees felt the same way. For example, in 1992, Rasipuram ("Russ") V. Arun left Sun Microsystems for Microsoft largely for the options the latter offered, which Sun reserved for the most senior executives. He even took a 55 percent pay cut to make the move. "I had no problem leaving Sun because I had no options," Arun told us. "Microsoft was the opposite. It's very difficult for you to walk away." He finally did, joining a Seattle Internet firm called Infospace in 2000 as its chief technology officer. "When I left Microsoft the amount [of options] I left on the table was very large. So I turned down joining Infospace three or four times. Anybody can match your salary and you can just walk away. If you have options, it is very difficult to walk away. It is in the self-interest of the company to reward people like that."

## The Profit Priority

Many high-tech employees we interviewed spoke about how their options encourage a new view of company needs that in turn prompts them to reorder their priorities. Software engineers, for example, are renowned in the tech world for putting their energies into what's hot in their field, the flagship technology of the moment that's both interesting and makes their resumes look good. But their focus changes when they know that their pocket books will grow fatter if they work on something less glamorous, but lucrative for the company.

For example, at a Palo Alto, California, company named Tibco Software Incorporated, a thirty-something events planner named Jennifer told us: "When you have ownership in the company, you . . . watch costs. We're going to Hawaii next week for a sales trip. Well, one person didn't get their travel [arranged] . . . so I called him and said: 'What are you doing, book your travel, if you wait your ticket is going to be so much higher.' You're constantly watching that stuff when you're an owner."

Or take a Portal quality controller named Mitch, who talked about how he is more willing to go to Francine, the engineering VP, and tell her that a product isn't ready yet, or that the company's reputation for quality will suffer if a program is released without doing these three things to it. Mitch attributed his behavior to the ownership stake his options give him. "I'm more willing to raise the issue and take responsibility when I have that much vested interest, as opposed to thinking, 'Oh well, it's not going to affect me, I'll get my salary regardless,'" he said.

Of course managers at traditional companies often use the language of a shared fate to spur employees to consider the larger interests of the company. But motivating people to do so doesn't exactly ring true if you don't give them a direct financial stake in the outcome. Robert, a Tibco employee, described how he had worked at a traditional employer for ten years before joining Tibco. Every year, he got leadership training courses, and the trainers would urge the class "to take ownership in this place." "We used to laugh," said Robert. "Why take ownership in it, you don't get anything out of it? Whereas here, you literally have an impact on the benefit that you're going to get fiscally from Tibco. So when I'm working on a project and I think it can impact how the company can sell our product, it motivates me, without question."

High-tech CEOs say that when employees own a piece of the company, they're more willing to apply their creative abilities to the company's broader interests. "When the company's profits are shared—not the cash profits, but the profits on the growth of the stock price—people in Redback, and people I know in other companies, are more motivated to get deadlines met, to get innovation done faster, and to apply themselves better to achieving company objectives," said Vivek Ragavan, the former CEO of Redback Networks Incorporated, a San Jose, California–based firm that produces software and hardware for broadband and optical networks.

"We have a saying, 'Juniper is my company,'" said Marcel Gani, the chief financial officer of Juniper Networks Incorporated, a Silicon Valley firm that is one of Cisco's largest competitors in the hardware business. "Often in large companies you have these slogans, and people hear the slogan but they don't believe in it. In

Juniper, there is an actual belief . . . that I have a lot of wealth tied into the company, so it is important for me if I see something that's not working properly in my area, I'll fix it. Or if I see something in somebody else's area, I'll go talk to them and say, 'Can't you do this more productively?' So you have this sense of ownership that's really critical to making things work well. And I think it happens at all levels of the organization, across all functions."

## Blurring the Lines Between Worker and Management

To make partnership capitalism work, everyone tells us, executives must take on very different roles. But so too must workers. "We tell workers when they come into this company, 'You're not going to be told how to do your job. You're going to be asked to use your expertise to drive a certain goal, and make sure it's the right goal and then figure out how we should be doing it,'" says Sandy Gould, the director of Recruiting at RealNetworks, which sells software that lets you get audio and video on the Internet.

In this setting, employees come to see taking important issues right to the door of management as appropriate, even to the door of the top executive. In fact, some companies already have a term for walking problems and issues up to management. They call it escalation, as in "She felt she had to escalate the issue, to bring it to the attention of the decisionmaker who could sort the problem out."

Sometimes, if an issue is important enough and involves the broadest interests of the company, an employee may even take it directly to the CEO. Jack, the Portal employee, told us how that very morning he had talked to John Little, the company's founder and CEO. His advice: Portal desperately needed a chief operating officer, someone to take over the day-to-day job of running the company. Jack felt that the task had become too much for Little now that the company had grown to 1,500 employees.

"My exercise price [on my options] is way lower than some of the other people at this table. So I can make a lot of money even at $8.81 a share [the price Portal's stock was trading at that day]. But a fifty- or sixty- or seventy-dollar stock price to me means a hell of a lot. So I'm willing to talk to the CEO and tell him things that might in any other job limit my career. I wasn't afraid of doing it, escalating it, because of my strong financial stake." In early 2002, Portal did indeed create the position of President and Chief Operating Officer.

Executives at many traditional companies would see their authority as challenged if an underling came to them in such a fashion. But in high-tech firms, most of which have functioned like this from the start, executives not only expect such behavior, but perceive it as symbolic of a healthy work ethic. Jay Wood was the CEO of Kana Communications until he gave up the post and became the chairman in 2001. The company sells software to help companies stay connected to customers and suppliers through email and the Web. (He also was the founder of Silknet, a company that Kana acquired.) When Wood worked in a more traditional corporation, a London-based software firm, people were fearful of talking to the manager above their direct boss. But at Kana, Wood said, anybody will come up to him if they have an idea or a suggestion. Or they'll shoot off an email.

Wood put down this blurring of management and worker roles to the freewheeling high-tech tradition but also to the employee's sense of ownership. Employees "tend to feel that it's their right to be able to talk to anyone in executive management," said Wood. "They feel impacted by decisions and want their voice heard. That is tremendously valuable in a company, because some of the most brilliant ideas have come from people who had a suggestion for another department and spoke up."

EBay CEO Meg Whitman expressed similar views in a 1999 Harvard Business School case study. "I've worked in a few companies where senior managers are so afraid of appearing weak that they stand by a point of view even in the face of better, more informed data," she said. "At eBay, we have a no-penalty culture, meaning that there is no penalty for being on the wrong side of an issue or changing your mind in the face of better information."

In fact, the culture at some high-tech firms is so open, so flat and nonhierarchical, that some executives say they feel as accountable to employees as the employees do to them. A lot of this stemmed from the extraordinarily tight labor market that most of these firms experienced throughout the 1990s. Most employees, certainly the programmers and engineers and other skilled workers, knew they could get a job across the street virtually whenever they wanted.

Another factor was the fantastic runup in stock prices. Many high-tech employees were sitting on options worth big bucks (or at least they were for a few years there). Unlike employees in many other industries, who often see themselves as no more than a few paychecks from financial disaster, employees with stock holdings do not live in constant fear of offending their managers. Many employees actually did cash in some of their wealth, and others thought they could whenever they wished. So they didn't see themselves as bound to the company simply because they needed a job and feared losing the one they had. In the absence of such fear, it is human nature to respond well to an opportunity to be innovative, to create something of value in their daily work lives.

"The challenges for executive management are primarily to foster that environment," said Ragavan, the former Redback CEO. "Employees hold us accountable for that . . . . We all have our roles to play. Management still has to make key decisions, and set guidelines . . . . But CEOs who build monuments to themselves in this environment will ultimately fail."

All of these themes could be seen clearly in the birth of Netscape, whose browser made it possible for ordinary people to experience the Internet. Netscape came about for much the same reason that Noyce and Moore walked out of Fairchild: Knowledge workers felt that they weren't being treated with respect and weren't sharing adequately in the wealth their ideas created.

In this case, the workers included Clark, a former Stanford University professor who founded Silicon Graphics Incorporated in 1982. The company blossomed into a billion-dollar enterprise based on Clark's invention of an integrated circuit chip that could transform boring bundles of data into three-dimensional computer images. (It later would become famous for such feats as conjuring up the dinosaurs for the movie Jurassic Park.)

But Clark butted heads with managers; in the Fairchildren tradition, he resented how little control and little equity he had in a venture whose success was based on his knowledge. He also became disenchanted with his inability to persuade Silicon Graphic's professional management to make cheaper computers, which he saw as key to commercial success in a market where personal computers were proliferating. So in early 1994, he walked away, abandoning $10 million worth of SGI stock options in the process. Clark soon met up with Marc Andreessen, a University of Illinois student who had worked on the first Internet browser, called Mosaic, for the university's National Center for Supercomputer Applications. Andreessen got little credit for his breakthrough work, and he too felt that he had not profited financially from it. When the two met, Clark saw Andreessen as another "disenfranchised entrepreneur" frustrated by the university bureaucracy's refusal to recognize his talent.

In April 1994, the two formed Netscape, based in Mountain View, California, not far from the site where Shockley had opened his company nearly thirty years earlier. The two men used the Mosaic software to cook up the first easy-to-use graphical browser for the Internet. It was a stroke of genius. The software program, built of a mere 9,000 lines of code—compared to much more in Microsoft's Windows 95—allowed nontechies to travel from web site to web site by pointing and clicking their way through interlinked text and pictures. Within months, Netscape's software was being used in 75 percent of web applications.

Clark and Andreessen didn't become another arrogant Shockley once they founded their own company. To the contrary, they not only ran their company by the values they espoused but began to articulate publicly the philosophy that stood as the foundation of the Netscape model. Clark wrote in his book:

> Somewhere in this process of equity sharing and technology IPOs is the basis for a new economy that distributes wealth far more diversely than at any other time in the history of business. Contrast the distribution of wealth in the Information Age with that of the Industrial Revolution. The Carnegies and Rockefellers were downright stingy compared to the founders of modern companies. Bill

Gates has enabled thousands of millionaires by causing Microsoft to award generous stock options.

Netscape started by paying its seven original programmers a competitive salary of $65,000 a year plus 100,000 shares of stock, which gave each programmer about 7 percent of the company. "They were partners from the first day . . . . I was intent on giving these young men and the future employees of Netscape a fair shake precisely because I had become so bitter about my early experiences at SGI," Clark wrote in his book. Each year from 1995 until the company was sold in 1998 to what was then AOL, Netscape gave employees stock options representing a tenth to a fifth of all outstanding stock. Clark, Andreessen, and CEO James Barksdale shared in the annual option grant, splitting 9 percent of all the options handed out over the three years.

Netscape built an egalitarian corporate culture that paralleled the wealth sharing. Even in the fall of 2001, after the company had sailed through several ups and downs, and the technology bubble had fully burst, its web site described the firm as follows: "Netscape's dress code is, you have to dress. People are at their best when they're comfortable, and can be themselves. . . . People work hard here and they expect to be treated like grown-ups. Grown-ups don't need dress codes or supervisors breathing down their necks, and they don't need to have their tasks spelled out for them." Even as part of AOL Time Warner, Netscape kept its California location and was proud of its share-the-wealth culture, although the effect of the company's troubled merger with Time Warner remains unclear.

Early on, Netscape grappled with a challenge that many other high-tech companies quickly came to face: how to maintain this casual, partnership-style culture as the firm ballooned from a startup into a billion-dollar enterprise. Cofounder Barksdale's response was to continuously decentralize, by breaking up expanding work groups into smaller teams. The idea was to operate like a large company by building central control systems, but use teams to maintain flexibility and encourage creativity. Every engineering team was pushed to take on as much responsibility as it could.

"Each of the teams working on the different products is pretty much self-contained, and has the ability to make decisions for its product," said Andreessen in a 1996 speech. "They actually set their own schedules, and we have a review process where they tell us their schedules."

Stock options were key to making this strategy work. One of the best examples involved Barksdale's decision in January 1997 to target the groupware market, which is software that allows everyone in a group to communicate with each other over the Internet.

Two journalists recounted what happened in a 1998 book called *Speeding the Net: The Inside Story of Netscape.* They told how Barksdale's goal was to land big-ticket sales to the largest companies or government agencies, entities that needed to connect hundreds of desktop computers. Toward the end of 1996, his staff had come up with a way to license Netscape's software so that buyers would pay fees that rise with the number of users. Early the next year, he told his top executives that he had an idea for how to fire up employees and get them to focus on the new corporate objective. Barksdale said:

> 'We've got to get our people behind us on this. And love and religion ain't gonna be enough to convince them . . . . I think we should put some options behind this . . . . We'll set a goal for sales—and if we meet it, everybody in the whole company will get more options.'
>
> Offering options would be a greater incentive than offering, say, a $500 bonus to everyone on the staff. If the company did well, there was no limit to how much the stock price might increase and no limit to how much the options could be worth someday. About 75 percent of [Todd] Rulon-Miller's [700-person sales] staff worked from field offices around the world, in places like Oslo, Norway, and Stockholm, Sweden, and Melbourne, Australia. If his deployed field operations were to make the design-wins goal [i.e. convincing large companies to use their software designs], they would desperately need the full support of the rest of the company.
>
> With an incentive program to motivate the company's

whole staff, Rulon-Miller decided it would be feasible to aim for a total of two hundred design wins by the end of the first half of 1997. Soon afterward, Barksdale announced an all-hands meeting, to be attended by everyone who worked for the company . . . . Netscape rented space at a nearby college . . . [and] Barksdale climbed up onto the huge stage and said, 'I want to tell you about a new program that I'm calling the two-for-two program' . . . . If Netscape managed to get two hundred design wins by June 30, 1997, every single employee of the company would get options to purchase 200 shares of Netscape stock. The plan was beautifully simple—and guaranteed to motivate everyone from the overseas sales reps to the secretaries, the janitors, and the shipping clerks to do whatever it took to help make these sales.

Feb. 27, 1997. On the wall in the company cafeteria a five foot sign thermometer with the mercury showing Netscape had 20 design wins and 25 or so pending . . . . 'The point is,' Barksdale had told his staff, 'I want everybody to feel like they're a part of this. When the sales force is out in Paris, and they call back to headquarters and say they need help to make a sale, I want the receptionist who answers the call to know how important it is to hook the sales person up immediately to the engineer who's got the little piece of code that will make the difference.'

Soon after the all-hands meeting, Barksdale E-mailed a little reminder to his staff: 'The web site for the 2-for-2 program is up, here's the URL, take a look at it.'

May 5, 1997. 75 design wins on thermometer. May 22, 1997. 100 wins including Bay Networks, Chrysler, Cypress Semiconductor, KinderCare, Eastman Kodak, Prudential Healthcare, Chubb Insurance.

June 30, 1997. Two hundred wins. Barksdale 2-for-2 program had been successful. In the second quarter of 1997, the company sold $135 million in software—an 80 percent increase over the same period of the previous year when sales had totaled a mere $75 million. And every Netscape employee was richer by two hundred shares.

The lure of stock options "motivates people to do great things," Andreessen said in a separate interview in 1995.

Bardsdale said: "This is a great reward for people who have worked so hard to build this company."

Although the big push by employees helped Netscape carve out a new market in groupware, it wasn't enough to offset the devastating loss the company experienced in its core Internet browser market. The cause, of course, was an overwhelming onslaught from Microsoft. In mid-1996, Netscape had 80 percent of the market and Microsoft had 7 percent. By the fall of the following year, by bundling its own browser into the Windows platform preinstalled on most PCs, Microsoft had grabbed 25 percent and Netscape's losses were mounting daily. Netscape's weakened position became untenable and in September 1998 it announced a merger with AOL.

Eventually, in April of 2000, a federal court found that Microsoft had abused its software monopoly on a number of fronts, including the way it snatched away Netscape's browser business. The court then ordered Microsoft's breakup. The ruling was appealed, and the following year a federal appeals court reversed key parts of the ruling. AOL, Netscape's new parent, filed a new lawsuit against Microsoft, but by then Microsoft had snared 91 percent of the market, leaving Netscape less than 9 percent.

The lesson of Netscape's experience, which highlights the promise as well as the limits of partnership capitalism, can be found in the story of Cisco as well, although the company's reversal of fortune wasn't nearly so drastic. Although Cisco's products include hardware as well as software, the collective brainpower of employees has been central to its competitive strategy. Cisco used stock options and a bottoms-up culture of employee ownership to propel phenomenal growth in the late 1990s, much of it stemming from the acquisition of other small startups.

It did so in a fashion that was almost diametrically opposed to the traditional slash-and-burn takeover tactics that were pervasive in corporate America throughout the 1980s and 1990s. Many companies buy assets—technology, brand-name recognition, or market share—and see the employees who had created these assets as secondary or even superfluous. Cisco, however, saw itself as buying people capable of creating future assets, and carefully planned its acquisitions to integrate newcomers into the employee partnership approach.

The company was founded in 1984 by Leonard Bosack, who managed a computer science facility at Stanford, and his wife, Sandy Lerner, who held a similar post at the university's business school. The couple also worked to expand Stanford's own internal computers, and in the course of doing so had applied a technology to link up several separate computer systems around the university. They started Cisco on a shoestring, later securing venture funding from Don Valentine at Sequoia Capital, but the company grew slowly at first. Then as computer networking grew, sales soared from $69 million in 1990 to more than $1 billion in 1995.

By then the couple had left the company after disagreements with a CEO Valentine had brought in to help them manage, and John Chambers took over. Chambers had signed on four years earlier after stints at computer maker Wang Labs, where he had been senior vice president of U.S. operations, and at IBM. His experiences at those two companies taught Chambers everything that was wrong with the traditional top-down cultures of corporate America.

When he took charge, he found a company that shared those characteristics that had come to define so many high-tech companies in Silicon Valley. Senior management worked in cubicles in the center of the fluorescent-lit space while employees got the windows. All offices were the same twelve feet by twelve feet. Employees in sales offices didn't even get their own desks; they all shared "nonterritorial" office space. Chambers and other top executives set an example of frugality and equality by flying coach wherever they went and eschewing the trappings of CEO power favored by most East Coast executives.

Cisco backed up the employee-centered strategy with generous stock programs that covered virtually everyone. Each year, employees have the right to purchase $25,000 worth of company stock at 15 percent off the opening or closing price of the previous six months, whichever is lower. They also all participate in a stock option plan that typically gives nonexecutives more than 90 percent of all options handed out.

Especially striking was how Chambers managed to keep this approach even as Cisco embarked on its wild acquisition binge. From the day he took over to the time the high-tech stock market nosedived in early 2000, the company bought sixty-nine companies. Chambers used corporate purchases as a way to grab every market opportunity in a business where the average product tends to have a life cycle of six to eighteen months. Since Cisco didn't have the internal resources to develop every new product quickly enough to meet the demands of this fastest growing sector of the economy, it tried to buy its way into market share on a broad front.

But Cisco's method of buying market share focused as much on the employees as on the product to be acquired. Typically it would identify a small, technology-driven firm with sixty to one hundred employees whose product had not yet hit the market. The ideal candidates frequently resembled the early-stage Cisco and were referred to within the company as "Cisco kids."

"When you combine companies, for a period of time, no matter how smoothly they operate, you lose business momentum," Chambers said in 2000. "Our industry is not like the banking industry, where you are acquiring branch banks and customers. In our industry, you are acquiring people. And if you don't keep those people, you have made a terrible, terrible investment. . . . So we focus first on the people and how we incorporate them into our company, and then we focus on how to drive the business."

When Cisco thought it had identified a potential acquisition, the initial step began with informal conversations between senior Cisco managers and the CEO and senior team of the target firm, according to a study by two Stanford professors. This would be followed by an exchange of documents on technology and human resources. Part of the assessment process evaluated what information the target was prepared to share. Early on, the study said, Cisco decided that excessive secrecy may signal a lack of the openness and honesty that Cisco insisted upon with its own managers. It also used these preliminary conversations to get a handle on how flexible the target firm's managers were and how widely they shared their equity within the company. "An unwillingness to share the equity may signal a misfit for Cisco's values," the professors wrote.

"This is an empowerment culture, a customer-focused culture, a culture of equals," Chambers explained in a mid-2000 interview. "If someone has an office four times the size of mine, if all the stock options are at the top of the organization . . . we don't touch that company."

Once the purchase was made, Cisco moved immediately to fold the newcomers into the family. Management, the Stanford study said, would assign an integration team to hold orientation sessions and explain company values to the newcomers. The sessions would involve employees from previously acquired companies who offered their insights. Cisco also assigned "buddies" to the new group to facilitate the bonding process. "The buddy system involves pairing each new employee with a seasoned Cisco veteran of equal stature and similar job responsibility," the Stanford professors wrote. "The buddy offers personalized attention better suited to conveying the Cisco values and culture." Of course, new employees also were plugged into Cisco's discount stock purchase plan and its stock option program.

The outcome of all this effort to retain intellectual assets can be measured by looking at how many acquired employees left the company. In the late 1990s, Cisco had an overall voluntary attrition rate of about 8 percent, which itself was unusually low at a time when at any given moment virtually every techie in Silicon Valley had several alternative job options and job-hopping was common. Even more extraordinary, Cisco lost only 6 percent of the employees who joined it through acquisition. It was Chambers's position that so many acquisitions did not work out because "Most people forget that in a high-tech acquisition, you are really acquiring only people."

Cisco's laserlike focus on employees was a central component of its phenomenal growth after Chambers took over. From 1995 through the tech market crash in 2000, Cisco zoomed from $1 billion in sales to $22 billion, with 37,000 employees in 54 countries.

Still, employee ownership couldn't insulate Cisco against the slump any more than it could protect Netscape from Microsoft.

Like so many other high-tech companies, Cisco was blindsided by the abrupt collapse of hardware sales that came with the crash. By mid-2001, its revenues had sunk an astonishing 30 percent, leaving the company stuck with $2.5 billion in inventory. As the industry went on developing new products, this enormous inventory became obsolete before Cisco could move very much of it. The company announced up to 5,000 layoffs, 17 percent of its total workforce—a move Chambers had vowed never to make. The meltdown ravaged Cisco's stock value, slashing it by some 70 percent, or a stunning $282 billion. The company also halted a building binge and left empty structures half constructed in San Jose.

The disaster, occurring as it did to the company that was almost an icon for high-tech super growth, may also have stemmed from so many rapid-fire acquisitions. For example, in August 1999, Cisco paid $6.9 billion for Cerent Corporation, a two-year-old startup that had run at a loss throughout its short life span. Cerent, which was supposed to jump-start Cisco in the optical network components market, had just 287 employees when it was purchased. Using Chambers's own analysis that in any acquisition the most important asset acquired is people, Cisco had forked out an incredible $24 million per employee. But by mid-2001, Cerent still had not gained a foothold in the optical network business.

A much smaller 1999 purchase turned out even worse. Cisco that year paid $500 million for Monterey Networks, another optical company. But Monterey's $1-million-plus optical router flopped, and Cisco was forced to kill the product in the spring of 2001.

Nonetheless, by the middle of 2002 there was no sign that Cisco's employee ownership culture was unraveling. The company issued new options to employees at prices that matched the much lower stock level, giving them new upside potential that helped offset some of the options rendered worthless by the market downdraft. Chambers also continued to stress equality and openness in the workplace. "I'd like to be the world's most successful company and yet be known as the world's most generous, giving-back, highest integrity, fair company," he said about six months after tech stocks began their descent. "No, I don't think those are opposite goals. I think you can be the most influential company in history and yet be known as the most fair and the most trusting."

The story of how Cisco's partnership survived the test of a major setback can be found in many other High Tech 100 firms. While a handful did go bankrupt in the tech crash that brought down the dot-coms, most hung on and began to grow again. More important to our story, employees didn't abandon ship in large numbers. They hung on too, as did the culture of employee ownership. Most continued to work hard and still thought of themselves as having a stake in the company that was worth fighting for just like any other owner.

The reason lay with management's continued commitment to the egalitarian culture they had started with, and with the ongoing financial motivation provided by employee stock options. Unlike other forms of worker ownership that American companies have tried over the decades, options withstood the test of the tech stock slump.

They did so in several ways. First, employees don't need to use their own money to buy options, as they must do with employee share purchase plans and company stock in 401(k) plans. Instead, they pay for options by working harder, or smarter. So the loss in a down market, while painful, doesn't undercut employees' current living standards or their retirement security.

Second, options were especially lucrative for many high-tech workers, leaving many with gains despite all the potential wealth they lost when the market crashed. Even before the slump, High Tech 100 workers as a whole averaged an astonishing $300,000 per person from selling stock they had obtained through options. We'll look at this figure in much more detail later on, but suffice it to say that such good fortune bought tremendous goodwill and loyalty.

In addition, while High Tech 100 workers suffered huge paper losses from their options due to the tech stock collapse, some options they had received before the crash were still in the money afterward. The reason: The options had been granted at such low prices that they remained higher than the value of the company's stock despite the 96 percent falloff in the value of the High Tech

100 between the tech market high point in March 2000 and August 2002. Again, we'll discuss this more fully in a later chapter.

Third, after the slump most high-tech companies continued to do what they and other firms that issue employee options had done before: give employees a new round of options every year. Since options are set at the market price on the day they're granted, High Tech 100 employees received options at the much lower levels. This gave them a whole new ownership stake, with the potential to reap new rewards if the stock rose again.

Indeed, the culture of sharing the wealth remained firmly entrenched in the High Tech 100 companies. We did most of our reporting for this book in 2001 and 2002, after the industry's setback. Virtually everyone we spoke with, employees, executives, and company founders, reaffirmed their commitment to the partnership approach.

We found one example at Tibco, whose software helps financial institutions and others provide real-time data on the web. Tibco's stock followed the same steep arc as most other high-tech firms: It went public in 1999 at $5 a share, peaked at $138 in early 2000, and was trading all the way back down at $9.50 in March 2001.

In the spring of 2001, when Tibco's stock price was trading at that $9.50 level, a fifty-year-old software engineer named James described how his unit had a major product presentation coming up with Accenture, a multibillion-dollar management consulting firm that recently had been spun off from Andersen Consulting Worldwide. This was a major opportunity for Tibco, one that would open up an entire new line of business crucial to its plans for rapid growth. James and a colleague, Bill, flew to Dallas, where they were going to run through a detailed description of Tibco's software. The audience: a top-level Accenture team that had the power to say yea or nay to the whole Tibco account. The duo was supposed to give a live, three-hour demo of the software, which required endless preparation—and perfection.

James and Bill slaved all night to get everything just right. Then, at 8 o'clock the next morning, Bill got a call that a family emergency had come up. He agonized about what to do. "It was one of those bottom-of-the-ninth, tie score, bases loaded kind of things," remembered James. Ultimately, James convinced his friend to go home and leave him to pinch hit. But that meant James had to redo the entire presentation to fit his own style of presentation. "It ended up that instead of going to bed at 8 A.M. and napping for a couple of hours, I had to work straight through," said James.

By the time he finished the demo that afternoon and attended the cocktail party with the Accenture folks that evening, where he had key conversations with their managing partners, James had been going for forty-two hours straight. The fact that the stock market depression had left his options so far underwater, rather than making him wonder if he should kill himself, actually drove him to put in the extra effort. If Tibco hadn't snared the deal—which it did—"we wouldn't have been able to achieve the growth rates that are a prerequisite for our success," said James.

Numerous other high-tech employees expressed similar sentiments when we spoke to them in 2001, when the industry was still struggling to emerge from the high-tech slowdown. "In a way the stock bust, while it's not nice for me, it is nice for Portal, because it keeps me working," said Francine, the Portal vice president. "I continue to think that the [stock price] is going to go up again."

Robert, the employee who used to laugh when his previous company had urged him to take ownership of the place, described how, the week we spoke to him, Tibco had allowed employees to exchange the expensive options they had received when the stock was trading much higher for lower-priced ones that would be worth something even at the stock's current market price. The action, he said, communicated the company's ongoing commitment to its employee-owners even after the bust. Said Rick Tavan, a Tibco executive vice president: "A company that is owned in part by its employees is going to be more effective than a company that is owned by an insurance company in Hartford."

The new culture is as important as the financial aspect. If you visit one of the High Tech 100 today, even after the crash has taken the wind out of the industry's sails, in many cases you'll encounter very different relationships than you find at even many lauded stalwarts of corporate America. Said Vivek Ranadive, an entrepreneur who founded Tibco in 1985 and later developed it into a pure Internet software firm:

> The Internet Age is a back-to-the-future kind of a thing. In the ten thousand years of human civilization, corporations have only existed for two hundred years. Before that, everybody was an individual entrepreneur, a shopkeeper, craftsman, farmer, and that was how people made a living. Then corporations came along and tried to organize, for economies of scale and efficiencies and so on.
>
> What the Internet economy does is, everybody becomes an individual entrepreneur again. Basically, companies are collections of entrepreneurs that are organized to bring creators of value and consumers of value together. It's with this basic understanding that reward systems and compensation systems are structured. I think of it as jazz, where I've got all these different people and they each do their own thing. My job is to let them do their own thing and hopefully make music at the end of it. It is not a Souza marching band, which was the corporation of old where everybody had a little thing they did and they marched to the tune of the same drummer.

This is more than just some self-serving rhetoric you hear from the people in power. Rank-and-file high-tech employees articulate similar feelings. "A good part of this is trusting your employees and giving them the authority to make the right decisions," said Joe, a Tibco software engineer. "The point of upper management should be to set the overall company's strategic direction and allocate (resources) across departments. Then let those smaller groups run on their own. That's one of the bigger changes between the new Internet companies and old companies. People feel so much more a sense of ownership, and not just because of the stock options but because of the culture in the companies."

Ranadive's jazz metaphor doesn't hold true in every high-tech company all the time. They're run by humans just like any other company, and some of them are greedy, arrogant, or poor leaders.

But it does capture the feel of what many are striving for and how they go about it.

This view stands in stark contrast to the approach found in most of corporate America, where most executive power rests with the almighty CEO, and it becomes the role of each tier of managers to support the decisions and carry out the policies of the managers above them. To a large degree, most traditional CEOs have been unwilling to let go of this hierarchical management structure, which has characterized most American corporations from their earliest history.

Thus it's not surprising that when it comes to employee compensation, corporate America has become more, rather than less, top-heavy. It is commonplace for corporate leaders to talk about how highly their enterprises value their employees and depend upon them for success. But in a culture in which money is the arbiter of status and worth, the true expression of a company's views can be found in the way it pays its employees. While stock options have been a democratizing force in the high-tech industry, they have played exactly the opposite role in much of the rest of corporate America. Because they have been justified as necessary to lure and retain only top management, options in most traditional companies have been handed out mostly to CEOs and a handful of the highest-ranking officers.

To see how this odd turn of events came about, let's take a closer look at what an option is and how it evolved from a way to manage the uncertainty of future risk into a vehicle for fantastic riches for an elite few. In doing so we will tell the story of how employee stock options have been used in the non-high-tech side of corporate America, the subject of the next chapter.

# 3

# The Soul of an Old Corporation

## From Thales to Executive Stock Options

The concept underlying an option has a pedigree stretching back thousands of years. In his book on politics, Aristotle tells the story of Thales, one of the legendary Seven Wise Men of antiquity who lived in the sixth century B.C. Thales spotted an economic opportunity in the olive oil business. While the olive crop fluctuated year to year, the number of presses available to make olive oil remained virtually constant. As a result, a bumper crop would leave farmers stuck with extra olives they couldn't press into oil. A skimpy harvest, on the other hand, left press owners with underused presses and a lower income.

In exchange for a right to some of the potential reward, Thales took on some of the risk himself. As economist Marilu Hurt McCarty told the story in a 2001 book, Thales offered press owners a small fee in advance of the harvest, before anyone knew how it would come in. The fee gave him the right, though not the obligation, to rent the presses at harvest time. If the crop was bountiful, Thales exercised his option, rented out the presses to make olive oil, and made a handsome profit.

If, however, the crop was poor, Thales simply let his right lapse without exercising it. If that happened, he had lost only his upfront fee. The press owners earned less income than they did in bountiful years, but at least they had Thales's fee as a partial offset. The first year Thales tried his scheme, the autumn olive harvest produced a bumper crop. Aristotle wrote: "When the harvest-time came, and many [presses] were wanted all at once and of a sudden, he let them out at any rate he pleased, and made a quantity of money."

Thales's little scheme stands as the earliest recorded use of an option. His insight was that you can manage the risk of ownership by buying and selling the right to use a property in the future. Because none of us can ever predict what's going to happen with complete accuracy, an option allows both a property owner and an investor to protect themselves against extreme outcomes. Property owners surrender a portion of the potential profit they might earn in exchange for getting someone else to share part of the uncertainties of ownership. In doing so they give up the chance to exploit a huge windfall to its maximum, but they also guard against the danger of being wiped out by a catastrophic loss.

On the other side of the transaction, the option buyer gets the rights of a partial owner for a much smaller investment than would be required to actually buy part of the property outright. Even more comforting, because the buyer has no obligation to exercise the option, the size of his or her loss is limited to the price of the option.

Options granted to employees to purchase their company's stock aren't all that different in concept from what Thales cooked up 2,500 years ago. Basically, they give employees the right to buy a set number of their employer's shares at a certain fixed price, specified at the time the option is granted to the employee. The price at which the stock can be purchased by the person holding the option is often called the "exercise price" or "strike price." Usually, the employer sets the strike price at fair market value, meaning the price the shares are trading at in the open market at the time the options are issued.

The company also must specify a time period the employee must wait before the option can be exercised (usually called the vesting period). Most companies choose three to five years. Some companies stagger the vesting, so that, say, a third of the options vest in the first year, another third in the second, and the remaining in the third year. Options help tie the employee's economic interests to the firm's long-term outlook. Most employers require workers to make up their minds whether to exercise their options within ten years. So they usually have a window of five to seven years to decide whether and when to exercise them and buy the stock.

While options have lots of complicated rules, the practical consequences for employees are straightforward enough. If the company's stock price rises above the strike price, the employee can exercise the option and buy the shares at a discount off the price at which the stock is currently trading. The employee then has two choices. He or she can hold onto the stock, which can be risky. Or employees can sell the stock immediately and take the cash profit, as nearly all do.

However, if during the exercise period the stock price remains flat or falls, the option is worthless and is usually referred to as being underwater. In that case, the employee doesn't exercise the options. He or she gets no benefit. But unlike a regular public shareholder who purchased the stock on the open market, neither does he or she stand to lose anything. So options provide the holder an opportunity for wealth sharing with a limited downside risk of a loss.

Still, options present workers with a complex set of choices that are much trickier than just getting a raise or a bonus. The first is when to exercise it. If the employee had a strike price of, say, $80, and the stock rose to $100 by the end of year three, should he or she jump at the $20 profit? Or would it be wiser to wait for a few years, perhaps even to year ten, to make sure the stock is not about to take a tumble soon after the stock is purchased? Employees must grapple with all these decisions and make up their own minds, based on their tolerance for risk and on what they think will happen to their company's stock.

To further complicate matters, employees also must decide what to do with the stock they get if they do exercise their options. Once the employee purchases the stock, it's just like any other share he or she might have bought. But employees get no profit from their low option price until they actually sell. Sure, they were able to buy a $100 share for $80. But until they sell the stock, all that has happened is they spent $80 on something which at that point in time is valued in the marketplace at $100. If they sell right away, they pocket the $20 profit. However, if the employee waits, the stock could rise in price, increasing his profit. Of course, the price also could fall, wiping out some or all of the profit, or even leaving the employee with a loss.

To avoid having to deal with such complex decisions, most employees simply sell the stock when they exercise their option. In fact, research on the stock option behavior of 50,000 employees in eight companies (which were unnamed in the study) suggests that 90 percent sell their stock immediately after exercise. Many exercise and sell simultaneously in a cashless transaction that doesn't require them to put up any money to pay for the stock.

A close cousin of the option is the futures contract, an idea employed for hundreds of years to trade mineral and agricultural products. While futures perform a function similar to options, giving people a way to manage risk, there is a key difference between the two. The former usually obligates its buyer to buy the corn, pork belly, or whatever, at the price agreed upon, no matter which way market prices go in the interim. The purchase is not optional. An employee stock option, by contrast, gives buyers the choice—that is, the option—to purchase the stock. An option allows buyers to simply do nothing if they would lose money by exercising it.

In the modern era, futures contracts became a way for buyers of commodities to protect themselves against the risk of extreme price fluctuations. They also allow commodity sellers, including farmers, to hedge against the chance that prices may fall before the harvest is complete. The U.S. futures market began to take shape in 1848, with the founding of the Chicago Board of Trade, where most commodities are still bought and sold. At first, traders mostly dealt in futures for grain and other farm crops. Later they extended the idea to livestock, then to metals such as iron and steel, and to lumber. Since the 1970s, futures trading has been adapted to a bewildering variety of economic transactions, including mortgages, bonds, electricity, and most recently to stock market indexes such as the Dow Jones Industrial Average.

Options, too, have been adapted to many situations over the millennia. Both the Romans and the Phoenicians optioned cargo on their trading vessels. Before a ship set sail, an investor could buy an option on the shipment for a fraction of what it would cost after it arrived. This removed the risk of holding an interest in the cargo if the product went bad or the ship sank. After the ship landed, the investor could exercise the option, purchase a portion of the cargo, and pocket a profit. On the other hand, if the voyage turned out badly, there was no obligation to go through with the purchase. The investor lost the upfront fee, but nothing more. Option sellers reduced their risk, too, since the fee they got functioned like insurance to cover the cost of any failed trips.

Still, investors looked askance at options for many years. In his classic 1973 study of investing, *A Random Walk Down Wall Street*, Burton Malkiel wrote that options got a bad name when they were widely used in the Dutch tulip-bulb craze in seventeenth-century Europe. When sky-high tulip prices collapsed in 1636, speculators in options were wiped out. Still, options and similar instruments continued to dominate the Amsterdam stock exchange in the 1600s, when the city functioned as Europe's financial center. Finally, options were declared illegal on the London Stock Market by the Barnard's Act of 1733.

Trading in options and futures has a longstanding—though also controversial—tradition in the United States as well. Commodity options were used in colonial times—they were first traded on the New York Stock Exchange in the 1790s—and flourished until the Civil War. Thereafter, they came to be regarded as mere gambling contracts by the Progressive political movement. In the latter part of the 1800s, there was an active informal market in options on railroad stocks.

It's not clear exactly when U.S. corporations issued the first stock options for employees. One of the earliest recorded examples involved the New England Norton Company, a leader in grinding wheels, machines, and abrasives, which began awarding options to its top sales, financial, and management people in the late 1890s. However, it was the rise of the publicly traded corporation that really gave the idea a lift. During the Robber Baron era of the late 1800s, many big corporations were owned largely by the entrepreneurs who founded them, people like Andrew

Carnegie, John D. Rockefeller, and the Dupont family. In the first decades of the new century, ownership widened as major companies sold stock to millions of individual members of the public. One consequence of this shift was that control began to pass to a new class of professional managers.

The separation of ownership and control that accompanied the advent of publicly held corporations posed a major dilemma for American business in the 1920s and 1930s. There was much concern at the time about the potential pitfalls of so-called managerial capitalism, where hired executives rather than founders ran companies. One key issue was whether the new class of CEOs would rip off all those anonymous public shareholders, whose vast ranks precluded a close involvement in the day-to-day operations of the company. Shareholder suspicions were fueled by many exposés of insider dealing and stock speculation by executives, who weren't required to publicly disclose their salaries until the federal Securities and Exchange Commission (SEC) was created in 1934 to regulate public companies.

Options seemed like a good solution to this so-called "agent" problem. They very publicly tied the fortunes of executives to those of shareholders. If one prospered, so would the other, leaving a diminished incentive, it was hoped, for CEOs to bilk the company with secret deals. Shareholders also took comfort from the fact that while the new hired guns didn't own a huge chunk of their company's stock the way the founder had done, stock ownership by managers ensured that they had the interests of the corporation at heart. At the same time, options were a recruiting tool. Talented managers who asked to add their intellectual capital to the company were more likely to sign on if they got a chance to share in the wealth they helped to create.

Stock options for executives spread steadily throughout the 1920s and 1930s. The stock market crash of 1929 undercut some of the interest, since many once-burned executives were now more inclined to want hard cash. However, others soon began demanding options from Depression-struck companies that couldn't afford to pay big salaries. In fact, they became a favored way for troubled companies to attract expertise. For example, James O. McKinsey, who founded the consulting firm of McKinsey & Company, received an extremely generous option package in 1934 when he became chairman of troubled Marshall Field and Company, the department store chain. Walter Chrysler was given options when he turned around the feeble Maxwell Motors, which later became the Chrysler Corporation. Similar arrangements took place at Gillette and National Cash Register in 1931 and 1932. By that year, fully a third of the firms traded on the New York Stock Exchange used options to pay their executives, according to Harvard University business professor John Calhoun Baker, who performed the first exhaustive study of options in 1937.

Still, options remained controversial even as their use increased. Many shareholders felt that directors who approved them were simply handing out corporate assets that rightfully belonged to the stockowners, Baker wrote. He was also critical of the practice of setting strike prices too low, "to a figure where . . . the executives can make an easy profit." (The government didn't require the price to be set at the market level in those days.) The practice, Baker thought, "dispels much of the incentive romance . . . and raises embarrassing questions." Moreover, he did not find clear evidence that stock options improved corporate performance. Critics, he concluded, felt that "executive options furnish a heads-I-win, tails-you-lose proposition."

Plenty of others felt the same way, and the intellectual battle seesawed back and forth for decades. Shareholders filed lawsuit after lawsuit, attacking the very idea of options as a giveaway of private property. The courts and the IRS fought to collect personal income taxes on options, which they saw as a substitute for salary, and in 1945 the IRS won a significant ruling on the issue from the U.S. Supreme Court.

On the other side, companies increasingly came to see options as a way to align the interests of executives and public shareholders. They won a victory in 1934, when the New York Supreme Court directly tackled the notion that only shareholders were entitled to share in the capital gains from property ownership. It wrote: "We have long since passed the stage in which stockholders, who merely invest capital and leave it wholly to management to make it fruitful, can make absolutely exclusive claim to all profits against those whose labor, skill, ability, judgment and effort have made profits available."

In 1950, Congress overruled the U.S. Supreme Court. It passed a law that allowed executives—or any employee, for that matter—to pay the capital gains tax rate, which is lower than the tax rate on regular income, on the profits they make from selling shares purchased with options. The reasoning from Washington was very much like that of the New York Supreme Court. Congress said it wanted to make sure that professional managers were owners and partners in corporations. It also believed that options could help firms retain good people and improve their operations.

The 1950 law gave executives an even greater incentive to demand options than they have now, since the capital gains rate was just 25 percent at the time. By contrast, the top personal income tax rate back then was 91 percent. Of course, virtually no one ever paid the top rate, because they took other adjustments to income and deductions. Still, it was very difficult to whittle the effective rate all the way down to 25 percent, so options remained for executives an attractive alternative to salary increases. By 1952, a third of the 1,084 companies on the New York Stock Exchange were using executive stock options.

But the law did little to quash the complaints. Throughout the 1950s and 1960s, the business press ran articles such as: "Are Stock Options Legal?"; "The Booby Trap in Stock Options"; "Under Fire: Stock Options"; and "Tightening Tax Laws on Stock Options." The 1953–59 bull market helped executives make a lot from options by lifting stocks nearly threefold. A common criticism at the time was that these bonanzas came from the general market and not extra or unusual efforts by management. In fact, many politicians saw the favored tax treatment of options as little more than a giveaway to the rich, because the recipients were typically a very tiny corporate elite. In the 1960s, Senator Albert Gore Sr. of Tennessee (the father of the former vice president) and others tried repeatedly to get rid of the favored tax treatment provided by federal law for profits earned through the exercise of options. In 1964, Congress enacted a variety of strict rules for stock options, which made them virtually useless.

Then in 1976, Congress essentially legislated stock options out of existence by making employees go back to paying the regular personal income tax rate on option profits. By then, Washington had slashed the top tax rate to 70 percent, but the move still put a chill on executives' desire for options in lieu of direct compensation. At the same time, the stock market performed poorly in these years, so options didn't seem like such a hot idea anyway.

Two developments in the 1970s laid the groundwork for the explosion of options that came in the following decade. In 1970, three economists—Fischer Black and Robert Merton of the Massachusetts Institute of Technology and Myron Scholes of the University of Chicago—came up with a way to put a price on the value of an option (any option, not just ones granted to employees). Despite the long history of options, it always had been difficult for buyers and sellers to tell how much they were worth. After all, an option is really little more than a bet on what's going to happen in the future, whether it's the value of that year's olive harvest or the price of a company's stock three to five years out. The uncertainty didn't stop people from issuing and buying options, but until 1970 it often was something very close to gambling.

The new pricing system was a breakthrough that lifted confidence in options. The method, which came to be called Black-Scholes, involves a complex formula that correlates the current price of a stock, its price volatility, the risk-free interest rate, the strike price of the option, and its time to expiration. Throughout the 1970s, Black-Scholes gradually became a conventional tool by which investors—and employees—could put a price on options. (In 1997, Merton and Scholes won the Nobel Prize in Economics for their work. Black was excluded by his death two years earlier.)

Options got a further boost in 1973, when the Chicago Board of Trade opened the first public market for stockholders to trade options on the shares of public companies. Before that, options had been traded over the counter (meaning not through an organized market). By providing an open market, the Chicago Board Options Exchange (CBOE) further increased the general comfort level with options and helped to turn them into a mainstream investment. Today, the CBOE lists options on about 1,500 individual companies, and these kinds of options are traded on five U.S. exchanges. Options even trade on broad stock market indexes, such as the S&P 500.

By the early 1980s, the stage was set for executive options to go mainstream, too. The economy went through a wrenching recession in 1981 and 1982 that threw many workers out of a job. When it emerged, companies spent much of the decade engaging in very visible, often controversial, mergers, takeovers, and leveraged buyouts. Usually these changes brought massive layoffs. At the same time, the public was beginning to realize that these and other trends were holding down the wages of average workers, while the pay of CEOs and other top executives kept hitting record levels every year.

Options for senior executives offered a way to blunt some of the criticism of these huge CEO salaries in the face of shrinking worker paychecks. They made it more difficult to compare executive pay to worker pay, since options vest over several years and don't have to be exercised for many more. CEOs also renewed the argument that options gave them a bigger incentive to boost the company's stock price, thus aligning the CEO's personal motivation more closely with the interests of shareholders. The long bull market that began in 1982 added to the allure of options, as executives saw just how valuable they really could be.

Congress helped out, too. In 1981, under President Ronald Reagan, Congress set aside worries about inequities and created what's called an incentive, or qualified, stock option, which provides a tax break for capital gains. In addition, the capital gains tax rate itself was cut from 28 to 20 percent. Then Congress slashed the personal income tax rates, first to 50 percent and then to 28 percent. Since then, companies have had a choice. They can issue incentive options, which are taxed at the low capital gains rate. Or they can use what are called nonqualified ones, meaning options that don't qualify for the special tax break and are subject to regular income taxes.

All these strands came together in 1987, when the top executives at Toys "R" Us Corporation raked in one of the first great option jackpots. The company's founder, Charles Lazarus, had sold the toy store chain in 1967, but it foundered in subsequent years, finally sinking into bankruptcy. When it emerged in 1978, Lazarus returned to the helm and set aside 15 percent of the company's shares for executives and store managers in the form of options. The chain's fortunes soared in the following years and Toys "R" Us became the country's top toy retailer. By 1987, the company Lazarus had sold for $7.5 million twenty years earlier was worth $5 billion.

That year, Lazarus earned a bonus of $3.3 million, which itself was large by the standards of CEO pay at the time. But it paled in comparison to his option payoff, which came to an eye-popping $56 million. Toys "R" Us president Norman Ricken pulled down $11 million, and even store managers found themselves with sizable windfalls.

All of a sudden, other CEOs woke up to the stock option bonanza. Instead of earning a million or two a year from a traditional salary and bonus, they saw that options could deliver them true wealth, tens of millions of dollars or even more. Corporate America's leaders quickly came to see options as "The Next Best Thing to Free Money," as a 1997 *Fortune* magazine piece explained in its title.

Soon, eager executives were ladling out options to themselves by the bucketful. In 1992, the top five executives at the 1,500 largest U.S. corporations cashed in about $2.4 billion worth of options. By 2000, they were exercising more than $18 billion worth. President Clinton fueled the option trend in 1993, when he pushed a law through Congress that limited companies from getting a tax deduction for salaries greater than $1 million. This gave companies an incentive to shift CEO pay to options, which retain their tax break. The bulk of the options, of course, go to top corporate executives. Indeed, you'd be hard-pressed to find a CEO of a major company who doesn't get an option package today.

One lesson CEOs didn't learn was the next step taken by Toys "R" Us. If options were so great, why not dole them out to everyone, or at least to managers or knowledge workers, as Intel, Apple, and other high-tech companies already had begun to do in the

1970s? "We thought, This will be a great motivational tool," Michael Goldstein, who joined Toys "R" Us in 1983 and became its CEO in 1989, told *Fortune.*

Relatively few major companies have followed the example set by Toys "R" Us. For the most part, the idea of giving a lot of stock options to ordinary employees has remained confined to the high-tech industry, and particularly those that focus on the Internet. Traditional CEOs have used options to bring their own financial interests into line with those of their company's stockholders. But they often have excluded most other employees from this relationship, keeping all the risk—and all the reward—for themselves.

One reason lies with the predominant view about who in a corporation is responsible for creating the wealth it produces. Think back to that 1934 New York Supreme Court ruling for a minute. Essentially, it agreed with critics that options confer the benefits of property ownership on employees (whether they're top executives or lowly janitors made no difference to the tax question before the court). But the court concluded that it's proper for those benefits to go to those employees "whose labor, skill, ability, judgment and effort have made profits available."

By and large, corporate America has felt that only top executives fall under this definition. For example, in 1953, William J. Casey, the New York corporate lawyer who later would head the CIA under President Ronald Reagan, wrote a monograph on employee stock options. His conclusion: "The best opinion seems to be that stock options should be restricted to key executives who can contribute significantly to profits and stock values."

A decade later, a writer at the *Harvard Business Review* published a book that reviewed the whole question of pay incentives for top executives. It quoted Thomas Ware, the president of International Mining, who defended the practice of restricting options to a few people at the top of the corporate pyramid. "I agree that the stock option is discriminating. However, I feel this is fitting since it is intended only as an incentive for those who bear the burden of decisions and take consequent risks. This is in keeping with the management philosophy that rewards should be comparable to risks."

The Conference Board agreed in a 1993 study, writing: "Many employees contribute to the overall success of the company. However, stock options are awarded to those who have the greatest opportunity for long-term effect upon the value and success of the business."

That fairly well sums up the attitude of many large companies today. Throughout the 1990s, much of corporate America gradually spread options to lower-ranking senior executives and to middle managers. But as we'll see later in the book, only about 6 percent of large corporations come close to the high-tech practice of giving them to most or all employees. Many companies talk about their workers being their most important asset. But they don't back that up by sharing the risks and rewards of ownership with them. Instead, most companies use options to allow higher-paid executives to become owners without using their own cash, while lower-level employees usually must use their savings to buy their employer's stock.

High-tech firms, by contrast, have gone to extraordinary lengths to bring most or all of their employees into the circle of corporate ownership. The next chapter demonstrates just how far they have gone.

# PART TWO

# Sharing the Company with Employees

# 4
# How High-tech Firms
# Share the Wealth

When we examine who owns the great corporations of the United States, we see that very few of them remain in the hands of their founders or heirs of the founders. Instead, most are owned by the public at large, either directly as individual stockholders or indirectly through financial institutions, such as pension funds, banks, insurance companies, and mutual funds. We've seen how in recent years it became common for publicly held corporations to extend options to the highest-level executives, both to motivate and to reward them. In prior decades, many mainstream corporations had experimented with a host of ways to extend ownership of one form or another to a broader range of employees, through ESOPs, 401(k)s, and other plans that allow employees to buy discounted company stock. However, the extent to which high-tech firms that are focused on the Internet have granted ownership to their employees has no precedent in modern American history. No other industry has ever attempted, much less achieved, the depth, breadth, and extent of wealth sharing found among these firms.

To determine just how broadly the industry has embraced partnership capitalism, we decided to focus on the newer high-tech companies that emerged in the 1990s with the growth of the Internet. We did so because we found that virtually all of them have gone the options route, something that not as many older high-tech companies have done. So we drew up the High Tech 100, which consists of the hundred largest public companies that generally derive more than half of their sales from the Internet. The index was constructed very much like the Standard and Poor's 500, which is comprised of the largest companies in the major U.S. industries. To identify the hundred largest, we measured size by each firm's market value as of October 2000, the date we began the project. (A more detailed explanation of how we constructed the index can be found in the notes. If you want to look at the entire list of companies, see Appendix A.)

Our High Tech 100 allowed us to separate the viable Internet industry from all those ephemeral dot-coms that jumped on the online fad—by trying to sell anything from pet food to wine over the Web—but which didn't survive the market crash of 2000. The High Tech one hundred companies certainly suffered then, too. In fact, when we look at the damage investors sustained as a consequence of the wildly unrealistic stock market runup of the late 1990s and the subsequent bursting of the high-tech bubble, these companies bear much more responsibility than the failed dot-coms.

Just look at the dizzying ride on which they took investors. At the March 2000 peak, the High Tech 100 index stood at $10,563. By July 2002, the index had collapsed to just $430, a stunning 96 percent decline. The total value of all public shares of these hundred companies was worth about $1.3 trillion at the beginning of 2000. By the end of July 2002, their value had sunk to just $162 billion. That's nearly a trillion dollars in real wealth that vanished in two years.

Put another way, these one hundred high-tech firms were responsible for almost a quarter of the entire decline in the NASDAQ. Over that same period, the total value of all 4,100 NASDAQ stocks plummeted by $4.8 trillion, to about $1.9 trillion. Since all but one of the High Tech 100 trade on the NASDAQ (AOL trades on the New York Stock Exchange), it's clear that the trillion-dollar loss they generated was one of the largest contributors to the rise and fall of high-tech stocks.

Nonetheless, the High Tech 100 are no market-bubble mirage like most of the dot-coms that enjoyed a brief moment of glory during a market runup. As of July 2002, eight of the hundred had declared bankruptcy. More surprisingly, from the end of 1999 to the end of 2001, the total employment of the hundred firms actually had climbed by 26 percent, to 177,000. These companies have real customers and real sales, which continued to grow after the high-tech bust and the demise of the dot-coms. Indeed, the combined sales of the High Tech 100 climbed by 78 percent between 1999 and the end of 2001, to $59 billion. Only three of them experienced falling revenue (excluding the bankrupt ones).

Federal Reserve Board chairman Alan Greenspan made much the same point in mid-2002, although he didn't distinguish between dot-com and Internet infrastructure companies the way we have done. He said: "The dot-coms that went under went under because they did not [add] value, but a lot of them are still around, [and] they've produced major advances in technology and improved our standards of living."

In addition to tracking stock market swings, our High Tech index let us measure the extent of employee ownership among these leading firms in the industry. This ownership consisted of the future stock to which employees had a claim through stock options, plus the much smaller amount of stock they owned directly. There's no widely accepted term for the combination of stock employees currently own and the options they hold to purchase stock in the future, so we decided to call it "employee equity." Thus the term refers to both the actual and the potential ownership held by employees below the top five officers of each firm.

We found that these high-tech firms really had embraced partnership capitalism to an extraordinary degree. On average, employee equity in these hundred companies totaled 19 percent as of December 31, 2000. This was greater than the 14 percent held by the top five officers in each company, which represents an unprecedented development. As far as we can determine, never before in the history of the modern corporation has an entire industry handed over so much potential ownership to a broad cross section of employees.

The High Tech 100 index led us to other findings as well. One of the most startling was the inaccuracy of the popular perception that high-tech employees had been left with little or nothing when high-tech stocks collapsed. After the crash, virtually the entire high-tech industry suddenly looked like a dead end, and all the options they had handed out so freely soon were being ridiculed as worth little more than deeds to Arizona oceanfront property. The twenty-something millionaire next door was no longer planning a retirement in the South Seas by age forty. Huge losses suffered by former high-fliers made a natural news story, and the media milked it for all it was worth. It quickly became the norm for business-school grads and other new hires to deride the promise of equity and ask for hard greenbacks, the good old currency of the suddenly solid-looking Old Economy. Keep those options, the new view went, they're just worthless pieces of paper now.

But this new conventional wisdom missed what really had gone on in the high-tech industry. True, hundreds of dot-coms closed their doors, shutting out the dreams of option wealth for their employees. In addition, workers at High Tech 100 firms lost a stupendous amount of paper wealth. We calculated that at the peak of the market, their options would have been worth $175 billion, or an average of about $1 million per employee. (The top five executives at all one hundred companies held options with a paper worth of another $43 billion, collectively—an amazing average of $86 million each.) As of July 2002, 83 percent of employee options were below their company's stock prices at the time and therefore worth nothing. So we estimate that they lost a total of $171 billion. Or at least, they lost that much on paper, since options don't require employees to shell out a dime of their own money.

Still, if you stand back and look at the broader picture, you'll see that partnership capitalism showered most High Tech 100 workers with magnificent—though to some degree undeserved—profits, despite all the potential wealth they lost in the crash. Even at the bottom of the market, the remaining 17 percent of employees' options were worth some $4.4 billion, or an average of about $25,000 per worker. Of course, this included some options that hadn't vested. But even if you look just at their vested ones, they still owned options worth another $3 billion that they could have cashed in at the time.

In addition, we found that High Tech 100 workers actually have taken home a total of some $78 billion in profits from all the options they have cashed in since their companies went public. We calculated that between 1994 and 1999, they collectively had exercised options that gave them profits of some $53 billion. (The top five executive officers of each company took out a combined total worth of an additional $10 billion.) This was actual cash profits employees and executives made from their stock options. It wasn't paper wealth; they really got the money.

Many investors may be surprised, and perhaps angered, to hear that High Tech 100 employees made billions more even as the market dropped in 2000 and 2001. Because many started at their companies early on, they still held options granted at IPO and pre-IPO prices. Even in July 2002, the stocks of forty-three of these firms remained above the IPO levels. Eight of them were actually more than 1,000 percent higher. AOL Time Warner, for instance, was trading at $10.90, an amazing 12,000 percent above the 9 cents that AOL went public at in 1992. As a result, all High Tech 100 employees were able to collect profits of $25 billion in 2000 and 2001 on options they had received in those early days. That's an average of some $125,000 each. (For more detail on the stock performance of the High Tech 100, see Appendix B.)

Employees probably deserved only part of all these gains. A fair amount of the $53 billion they took home prior to 1999 came because the stock market ballooned to unrealistic heights. Many investors foolishly sunk money into high-tech companies during the irrational exuberance that gripped much of the stock market. They left at least a portion of their dollars in the pockets of those employees lucky enough to have cashed in their options in those heady years.

Rank-and-file workers probably don't bear that much responsibility for the market's runup. But those who cashed in their options at the top received a huge windfall on top of what they would have earned if high-tech stocks had climbed at a more reasonable rate. This is money that came at the expense of dot-conned investors. Still, most of the rest of what employees made represents true wealth sharing between investors and workers.

Much of the $4.5 billion would seem to fall into this category, since that was their ownership stake after the air had been let out of the stock bubble. The same holds true for a lot of the $25 billion they earned in 2000 and 2001.

For the most part, all this option wealth came on top of high-tech employees' regular salaries, which averaged a very respectable $70,000 a year in 2000. Since the $78 billion works out to a rough average of $425,000 per worker, partnership capitalism paid these workers an additional six times their annual pay on average. (We'll see later that some firms treat options as a substitute for part of their workers' pay, rather than as something extra. However, even the companies that did this usually abandoned the practice after a few years.)

| TABLE 4.1 | **The Options Sweepstakes**<br>Value of Stock Options Held or Exercised by High Tech<br>100 Employees |
|---|---|
| **As of the market's top in March 2000** | |
| Paper profits[*] | $175 billion ($1 million per employee) |
| Actual profits[**] | $53 billion ($300,000 per employee) |
| **As of July 2002** | |
| Paper losses[***] | $130 billion ($970,000 per employee) |
| Remaining paper profits | $4.5 billion ($25,000 per employee) |
| From vested options | $3 billion ($17,000 per employee) |
| From unvested options | $1.5 billion ($8,000 per employee) |
| Actual profits[****] | $25 billion ($125,000 per employee) |

NOTES: [*]Value of outstanding options whose exercise price was above the company's stock price at the time.
[**]Profits on options exercised prior to 2000.
[***]Loss since March 2000 on options whose exercise price was below the company's stock price in July 2002.
[****]Profits on options exercised in 2000 or 2001.
SOURCE: Authors' analysis of SEC filings.

Having said all this, you also should keep in mind that few workers match precisely the experience of the average worker. Individual High Tech 100 employees experienced a wide range of outcomes with their options. Virtually every firm had people who, mostly due to luck and timing, fell into a variety of camps. A few really did walk away with those million-dollar windfalls you read about. Many more got thousands or tens of thousands of dollars. Others made the big bucks on paper, but didn't exercise enough options in time, or didn't sell the stock they bought when they exercised before the market slumped. Of these, the fortunate ones were left with nice sums, but not spectacular ones. Others held tight to their options or shares while the market was rising. They bought in to all the gushing rhetoric about new rules for the New Economy, and thought high-tech stocks would rise forever. They "drank the Kool-Aid," as the saying goes (a somewhat macabre allusion to the follow-the-leader suicides in Rev. Jim Jones's commune in Guyana), and wound up with zip.

To appreciate the magnitude of the wealth sharing inside high-tech firms, it's helpful to begin with an overview of their financial architecture. The data we gathered for the High Tech 100 came mostly from the SEC, the federal agency that oversees publicly traded companies. The SEC requires every company whose shares trade on a public stock market to file a report each year describing exactly how many of its shares are owned by corporate insiders.

The SEC divides insiders into two camps. First are the company's top five executive officers, which the agency defines as the CEO plus the four other most highly compensated officers. Then there are the members of the board of directors, who typically are venture capitalists, wealthy individual investors, executives of other companies, as well as former executives, public figures, scientists, professors, or experts. The directors may also include very large outside shareholders who have special status as insiders by virtue of the amount of stock they control. They usually are privy to confidential information that's unavailable to the public and other outside shareholders.

The SEC reports told us how much stock each group held outright, as well as how many options they had. The commission also requires companies to report the total number of options held by all employees. By subtracting the total held by the top five officers, we found out how many options were held by all other employees, from vice presidents to receptionists. The SEC doesn't require companies to specify just how many employees actually participate in any stock option programs. Many volunteer the information anyway. We contacted those who don't, and their responses gave us complete data on all High Tech 100 firms.

Now let's look at how much of the High Tech 100 these different groups own. There are two ways to think about corporate ownership. The standard approach is to look at the percent someone holds of all outstanding shares. If you have a million shares and the company has issued 10 million, you own 10 percent of the company.

But in companies with scads of options, you have to take into account what would happen if they were exercised. Options are really potential, rather than actual, ownership. After all, they may expire before the holder exercises them (which occurs when the share price falls below the strike price and stays there). When that happens, the ownership stake represented by the option evaporates.

If the options are exercised, though, more outstanding shares are added to the pile the company already had issued. The previously issued shares then become a smaller portion of the larger total. So if the company with 10 million shares outstanding had granted 10 million options and they were all exercised, there would be 20 million shares outstanding at that point. The million shares you had before would shrink to a 5 percent ownership stake. This is called dilution.

Because the high-tech industry relies primarily on options to share the wealth with employees, it's important to include them when we look at how ownership has been divvied up. We think the best way to do so is to treat all options as if they could be cashed in immediately for stock, that is, after dilution. This runs the risk of overstating employees' true ownership stake, which can decline if falling stock prices wipe out some of their outstanding options. But it's the only way to tally up both stock and option ownership on a consistent basis. Looking at the value of stocks and of options on a postdilution basis provides the best way to measure who owns how much of the High Tech 100. The following table breaks down the industry's ownership after the dilution by options, as of the end of 2000.

**TABLE 4.2  Who Owns the High Tech 100**
Average Potential Ownership Stake as of December 31, 2000, by Type of Owner

|  | Stock (%) | Option (%) | Total Equity (%) |
|---|---|---|---|
| Employees[*] | 2 | 17 | 19 |
| Top Five Officers | 10 | 4 | 14 |
| CEO | 7 | 2 | 9 |
| Other Four | 3 | 2 | 5 |
| Total Equity of Employees and Officers | 12 | 21 | 33 |
| Directors[**] | 8 | 1 | 9 |
| Total Insider Equity[***] | 20 | 22 | 42 |
| Public Shareholders | 58 | 0 | 58 |
| Total |  |  | 100 |

NOTES: [*]Excluding top five officers. Stock holdings include estimated purchases through employee share purchase plans.

[**]Includes stock owned by companies, such as venture capital firms, with which directors are affiliated.

[***]Employees, top five officers, and directors.

All three columns are calculated as if all options, both vested and unvested, had been exercised, i.e., on a post-dilution basis.

The first column shows the percent of the High Tech 100's stock each group would own under this post-diluton scenario.

The second shows the percent of stock each group's options would represent.

The last column combines the first two to show each group's total potential ownership stake, including their diluted stock plus the stock they would have received if they had exercised all their options.

SOURCE: Authors' analysis of SEC filings.

The first point to appreciate is just how much of the industry was owned by all insiders, including employees, officers, and directors. At 42 percent, the insider share was several times greater than the average in most traditional companies. Of course, some of this has little to do with a philosophy of employee ownership. Instead, it reflected the startup status of most High Tech 100 firms. By and large, they only began selling shares to the public very recently, in the 1990s. Before that, many were private, which meant that by definition, insiders owned all their equity. Typically, most startups go public in stages, because the original owners want to hold onto as much of their ownership as possible. So insiders usually own a lot more than the norm during the first years after a company has sold stock on the open market.

More relevant is how the 42 percent was split up among the different inside groups. The 9 percent share held by High Tech 100 CEOs was quite large, especially their 7 percent direct stock ownership. The 5 percent share of the other top four officers was high, too. In part, this reflects the fact that most of these companies were started as entrepreneurial firms. The founders and the first executive team were given or purchased a lot of the initial stock at very cheap prices, often as part of the original incorporation process, before the company went public. By getting in on the ground floor, top High Tech 100 officers ended up with a lot of direct stock ownership. However, it's also true that they take a lot of their companies' options for themselves. They're much more generous with their workers than the rest of corporate America, but High Tech 100 executives still don't take much less for themselves than most of their counterparts in more traditional industries.

The truly astonishing figure, though, the one that would have been virtually impossible a generation ago, is the 19 percent of total equity held by High Tech 100 employees (excluding the top officers). Just 2 percent of this was direct stock ownership, with the rest coming from options. Most employees own few shares outright, because they weren't at the company in its earliest days and didn't have access to restricted stock or to founder's shares. After the IPOs, most of these companies offered employees the opportunity to buy stock through employee share purchase plans, which typically offer a 15 percent discount off the market price. Most employees accumulated their 2 percent direct stock ownership through such plans.

(A related point of interest here is that virtually none of the 2 percent represented stock held in 401(k) retirement plans. The meltdown of Enron Corporation in early 2002 brought close public scrutiny to the way many large corporations fund their 401(k)s with their own stock, and then encourage employees to buy company stock with their savings. This is a form of employee ownership, but a vastly different, far more risky one than what's provided by stock options.

Most companies who match 401(k) contributions with stock are using employee ownership as a partial substitute for the regular compensation they provide their workers. In other words, they recognize that the labor market requires them to offer a retirement plan, but they fund it partly or even wholly with stock instead of cash. They do so for several reasons: because it's cheaper or keeps cash within the company; because management believes it can avoid hostile takeovers more easily if their stock is in the hands of employees; and because at least some of them want the economic and cultural benefits that flow from employee ownership.

High Tech 100 firms, by contrast, fund their 401(k)s with cash. Almost all have such plans, but only a handful use company stock in them. Those that do have less than 1 percent of the plan's total assets in their own shares, versus nearly 30 percent in other public companies that have company stock in their 401(k) plans. The reason: Most high-tech firms see options as sharing the risks and rewards of property ownership with workers, not as a substitute for compensation. Nor do they want to expose their workers to even more risk by using their savings and retirement plans to buy more employee ownership. We'll examine this point in greater depth later on, but for now suffice it to say that in high-tech firms, option wealth usually comes on top of regular pay and benefits.)

The 19 percent ownership stake held by High Tech 100 employees is huge. In just a few short years, they had accumulated more of their companies than their bosses or the directors. True, their ownership was contingent in ways that much of that held by the top officers or directors was not. For instance, employees' options may not vest if they leave the company too early. Options also may sink underwater and stay there until they expire. Even so, as far as we can determine no other industry in the United States has ever even offered to share so much wealth with employees. This didn't change with the stock market crash, either. That 19 percent stayed in the same range in 2001, at 20 percent.

Nor does extensive employee ownership seem to be a function of the startup, entrepreneurial nature of High Tech 100 firms. This conclusion may be somewhat premature, since the entire industry is less than a decade old. But so far, there's no evidence that High Tech 100 firms have dialed back on sharing the wealth as the companies expand and become more established. For example, we found that employee equity didn't shrink as companies grew. Nor did employees in larger High Tech 100 firms have less equity than those in the smaller ones; option ownership averaged 21 percent in those with market capitalizations of greater than $1 billion as well as in those with less than $1 billion. In fact, some of those with the highest market value had even higher employee equity, such as Amazon, BEA Software, Broadcom, Cisco, eBay, Siebel Systems, and VeriSign.

Microsoft illustrates the point as well, even though it's not in the High Tech 100. Bill Gates cofounded the company in 1975 and took it public in 1986. In 2002, Microsoft's employee option program put workers' equity at 22 percent, while Gates owned 10 percent.

The High Tech 100's large employee equity stake is tangible evidence of the industry's commitment to partnership capitalism. Most of these companies were founded by entrepreneurs who dreamed up the business idea and bore the initial risk of putting it into practice. Many put in their own life savings. They got outsized rewards for doing so, which is the traditional way U.S. capitalism is supposed to work. It's also standard practice for company founders to surrender large chunks of ownership to venture capitalists and other large shareholders who step in with funds in the firm's crucial initial stages.

The break from tradition came when high-tech founders used options to promise their employees more of the company's future

**TABLE 4.3    How Founders Share the Wealth**

While a Few High Tech 100 Founders Still Hold the Bigger Stake

| Company | Founder | Founder's Total Equity* (%) | Employees' Total Equity* (%) |
|---------|---------|---------|---------|
| Microstrategy | Michael J. Saylor | 43 | 18 |
| Infospace | Naveen Jain | 24 | 15 |
| eBay | Pierre Omidyar | 23 | 11 |
| CMGI | David S. Wetherell | 10 | 7 |

**...Many have given more to employees**

| Company | Founder | Founder's Total Equity | Employees' Total Equity |
|---------|---------|---------|---------|
| RealNetworks | Robert Glaser | 25 | 26 |
| Amazon | Jeffrey P. Bezos | 21 | 24 |
| Siebel Systems | Thomas M. Seibel | 11 | 26 |
|  | Patricia P. House | 1 |  |
| Freemarkets | Glen T. Meakem | 10 | 18 |
| Doubleclick | Kevin J. O'Connor | 7 | 13 |
|  | Dwight Merriman | 3 |  |
| Akamai | F. Thomson Leighton | 6 | 12 |
| Yahoo | David Filo | 6 | 19 |
|  | Jerry Yang | 4 |  |
| Juniper Networks | Pradeep Sindhu | 4 | 17 |
| WebMD | Jeffrey T. Arnold | 2 | 24 |
| E Trade | William A. Porter | 2 | 9 |
| AOL** | Stephen M. Case | 2 | 17 |
| Lycos*** | Robert Davis | 2 | 14 |

NOTES: *All outstanding shares and all options on December 31, 2000, after dilution, i.e., assuming that all the options had been exercised.

**Before merger with Time Warner Incorporated.

***Before merger with Terra Lycos.

SOURCE: Authors' analysis of SEC filings.

wealth than they had reserved for themselves. These entrepreneurs made a fundamental decision about property sharing in the firms they founded. They embraced substantial dilution of their own ownership stakes because they believed in the incentive effect of stock option capitalism.

Another significant finding that emerged from our research was that property sharing by the High Tech 100 includes virtually all employees. In recent years, a growing number of mainstream companies have begun to grant options to employees below top management. But they usually include only lower-level executives. Some extend the privilege to managers as well. However, it's much less common for corporate America to give options to every employee, or even to 80 percent or 90 percent of them, as do nearly all of the High Tech 100.

Other than general speculation in the press that high-tech companies seem to give stock options to a lot of employees, there has been little hard information on this question. To answer it, we scoured SEC filings, the High Tech 100's corporate web sites, magazine and newspaper clippings, plus some of the help wanted ads on Internet employment sites. Finally, where good information was not available, we called or emailed seventy of the companies directly.

We found that ninety-eight of the High Tech 100 provided options to most or all of their employees. Among the two outliers, MRV Communications Incorporated gave options to nearly half its workforce and was expanding the program further in 2001. The other, Checkfree Corporation, said that 40 percent of its employees received options, and a majority were enrolled either in the option program or the employee share purchase plan.

The extraordinary wealth high-tech workers received from options came largely from the decision of the companies' founders to share ownership with so many employees from the firms' earliest days. Most of the $78 billion employees cashed out was made by those lucky enough to get hired on before their companies went public. These employees got options with incredibly cheap strike prices, usually under $5 and sometimes just pennies. Then when the company did its IPO, the stock prices shot up into the $100 or

$200 range and employees who cashed in their options pocketed the difference.

Between 1994 and 2000, eighty-eight of the High Tech 100 did IPOs. All told, the workers employed at these companies when they did their IPOs raked in about $21 billion, or nearly one-half of the total option earnings through the end of 1999. This IPO wealth works out to an average of $540,000 per worker for those employed at the time of the offering.

The explanation for such enormous wealth isn't difficult to find: Most of these companies were still small when they went public. If you add up all the people working at each company when its IPO was done, it came to just under 39,000 employees, versus 177,000 employed by the High Tech 100 as of December 2001. So the $21 billion was divided among the 39,000. Of course, it wasn't parceled out equally. Those hired earlier usually got options at cheaper strike prices, so they made more. Higher-paid employees also often received a larger number of options than lower-paid ones, so they too made more. Still, because almost all workers got options, most shared in the IPO profits.

These founder employees got true insider prices on their options. If you average all their exercise prices together, treating all eighty-eight IPOs as if they were one giant offering, each worker paid just $1.27 a share for his or her stock.

Compare that to the investors who, by their connections, good fortune, or astute market sense, were able to buy a share of this IPO when it first hit the market. Average their purchase prices and you get $8.61. That may not sound like so much until you put it in percent terms. The founder employees already had a whopping 700 percent gain the minute their company's stock became publicly available. It was before much of the runup on many of the stocks started.

A rapid, and we now know irrational, runup is precisely what did occur with most High Tech 100 stocks. At the end of the very first day of public trading, the average High Tech 100 had shot up by a mind-boggling 29,083 percent, or 290 times the exercise price of the cheapest employee stock option that the company had granted to employees in the years before the IPO. Since the stock market was in the middle of a general runup when these IPOs occurred, these first-day gains were just the beginning. Three months after each IPO, their average stock price had jumped by an even more unbelievable 42,600 percent, or 426 times the exercise price of the cheapest employee stock option.

To see how this shower of gold came pouring down on those lucky first employees, look at what happened to our friends at Portal. The company was founded in 1985 as an Internet service provider, then shifted to developing software for other service providers and communications companies. When the Internet began to expand exponentially after 1994, Portal went along for the ride. Its sales doubled in each of the succeeding years, hitting $103 million in 1999. Yet it had just 754 employees.

Portal had been granting options to all employees since its founding. Every employee got options when they were hired. Most got them annually, based on their performance, as well as for promotions and special achievements. Portal's goal was, and still is, to give options to at least two-thirds of its employees every year. In 2000, for example, the company provided options to 80 percent of its employees.

Portal went public in May of 1999, the height of the Internet boom. Its stock soared 167 percent, to nearly $12 that day. By the time the employee cash-out date arrived six months later, the stock had hit $30. Over the ensuing year, Portal's share price fluctuated between $84 and $27. We assumed that employees sold at the average of the two, or $56, and that nearly all immediately sold the shares they received. Of course, not all these people remained millionaires. Some exercised their options but didn't immediately sell, so they lost money when the stock later fell. Some who did sell may have invested in other stocks that also nosedived when the market crashed. Still, the outcome was an estimated $1.3 billion windfall, for an average of $1.4 million each. Not every employee got this much, since some owned more options than others. But Portal said later that its IPO created 350 millionaires, according to a study by the National Center for Employee Ownership.

One of those millionaires was Francine, the Portal vice president who learned to curb her judgmental instincts. She lost out on the chance to rake in several million dollars that her options could have brought if she had cashed them all in before the company's stock sank. In part, she was blocked by Portal's rules about when managers could exercise their options. She also didn't sell all the shares she did get from the options she had been able to exercise, because she believed that the market would eventually lift them up again. "I still kick myself that I didn't sell all of them," she said. Still, because she joined Portal in 1997, about two years before its IPO, she came away with plenty enough for most people: $6 million.

Francine's colleague, Jack, the finance administrator, raked it in, too. He hired on in April 1997, got a wad of options, and cashed in enough to take home $3.5 million after selling the stock. True, he held onto thousands more options, which were worth about $1 million at one point. But he still made about thirty times his annual salary, in less than four years on the job. "My expectation coming in here was that if I did one to two times my salary over the three or four or five years, $200,000 to $500,000, I thought I'd be fat, dumb, and happy," he said. "So I've got no complaints."

Or take Jennifer, the Tibco events planner. She started at the company in 1995, four years before it went public, and cashed in enough options to leave her with nearly $5 million. But it was an emotional ride, deciding when to sell, and how much. All told, Jennifer said, she could have made about $18 million if she had been able to time the stock market perfectly. Sometimes, she even felt not like she made $5 million, but that she lost $13 million.

"It was a very emotional internal battle, and extremely stressful for me," she said. "It is very hard to sell stock when it is going up all the time, extremely hard. And it's double hard to sell when it's on the way down. But it was too uncomfortable for me to hang on to too much."

Then when she did sell a lot, in 1999, "suddenly I was faced with tons of wealth. I came from an upper-middle-class family with a culture of, you never discuss money with people. I paid a million dollars in taxes in 1999 and I remember writing the check to the government. I literally had to write it three different times, because I never had spelled out that word on a check. I literally wrote it wrong and I had to start over. My hand was trembling as I wrote the check."

Plenty of others went through the emotional wringer, too, although it's tough to feel sorry for someone who made millions but lost out on millions more. Owen, an Amazon manager we interviewed, pulled out some $5 million from his options, but missed the chance for $2 million to $3 million more. "I remember I said to my wife, 'We just lost one of the nicest homes in Seattle,' which is what I could have bought," he said.

"I'm not a real sob story, but I had nightmares about it. One of the most painful parts was the regret, which was the exact thing I had been most worried about. I never wanted to have regrets about any of this. But at that exact moment, I realized I had been drinking the Kool-Aid. Even on the day when our stock was at $30, I had a spreadsheet showing what it would be worth at $80. Finally, after a week or so, I just said, move on."

Another way to get a feel for the $78 billion windfall High Tech 100 workers lucked into is to look at the total they got at an individual company. At Tibco, for example, all employees including the top five officers exercised options worth an estimated $1.35 billion after its 1999 IPO. Of that, those below the top five took out $777 million. That averaged out to $1.6 million per worker (although of course all those options weren't distributed equally among the 490 workers on Tibco's payroll that year). They made more in the following years, about $400 million in 2000 and another $137 million in 2001, even though the stock price collapsed from $140 to about $5.

Employees of VeriSign, a 2,000-employee company that registers Internet addresses, got some $721 million since its IPO. Of that, $578 million went to non-top officers, or an average of $1.5 million for each of the company's 394 workers in 1999. The next year, after the firm had acquired Network Solutions, employees cashed in another $695 million, although the profits were split among many more people since the workforce had expanded to 2,200.

Even employees of the At Home Corporation, a High Tech 100 firm that went bankrupt in 2001, made a bundle on pre-IPO options. As of the end of 1999, employees of Excite@Home, as the company was commonly known, had cashed in some $660 million worth of options since the firm's 1997 IPO. That worked out to an average of $283,000 for each of the 2,319 workers the company had at the time.

Despite all the cheap options high-tech employees had received at pre-IPO prices, many still suffered the psychological blow of losing out on so much more. Just ask Mitch, the quality controller at Portal who spoke to us about how his ownership stake made him more willing to tell his boss if the company would suffer from releasing a product before it was ready. He had come aboard in 1997, before Portal's IPO. He got 5,000 options, which climbed to 30,000 with later stock splits. Mitch exercised all of them early on, at a nickel a share.

But then he held onto the stock, on the assumption that it would build wealth over the long term. At the time we spoke to him, in April 2001, Portal was trading at $7 a share. So his stake was worth $210,000 at that point. But he would have cleared $2.5 million if he had sold at the top, when the stock hit $84. "I have not sold a share," he said. "My philosophy is, hold it and wait to see what's going to happen."

That hurt, just as it hurt Rachel, the manager who had left a company with no options for the chance to hit it rich at Portal. She didn't even want to talk about how much she lost. Her strike price was a dollar or so. She had a standing order to sell if Portal's stock fell to $80. "But you know what, I drank the Kool-Aid, too," she said. "I thought we were going up to $140, so I cancelled my order. Now we're trading at $7. I didn't sell, because I viewed this as a long-term proposition."

Of course, having the right to pay a dollar for shares you can sell for seven is a nice return under any circumstance. Rachel also said that she did sell some, enough to give her savings of about as much as she earned from her salary in a year. So she could afford to put her kids in private school, and the mortgage didn't worry her anymore. "But I felt stupid," she said. "For a long time I kept saying, 'I know it's going to go up, I know it's going to go up.' Until fairly recently I could grit my teeth and say, 'It's a long-term play.' It is much harder for me to believe now."

While High Tech 100 employees had a potential equity stake of 19 percent as of the end of 2000, a skeptic might retort: "Yeah, but I bet most of their options are underwater today. So their ownership probably doesn't amount to much anymore, not after the crash."

There's at least some truth to this. As we mentioned above, we estimate that 83 percent of the options held by High Tech 100 employees were indeed underwater as of July 2002. Some hadn't cashed in these options because they hadn't vested. Others chose to ride the market and came to regret it. No question, though, some high-tech employees emerged from the boom and the bust with little to show but the salaries they had earned.

Just ask Peter, who joined Tibco in 1999, right before its stock split two for one. He got 16,000 options with a strike price of $70. Within two months, Tibco's stock doubled, to $139, making him worth $2.2 million on paper. But he hadn't vested, so he couldn't exercise them. In 2000, he watched as the stock slipped lower and lower. By early 2001, it was down to just $10 and his millions seemed like a dream.

"I knew I didn't vest for a year, but it was already money in the bank for me," said Peter, who was about thirty at the time. "At certain times, I had these little visions of dollar signs dancing in my head. It doesn't really affect me, because all along I've thought of it as a lottery ticket."

Jay Wood, the former CEO of Kana who's now the chairman, said that the employees who felt the worst were those who counted their paper profits and thought they had won the lottery, only to find their dreams crushed. "They missed the opportunity, which is a hard thing psychologically to overcome," he said.

The people who felt just as bad were those who came in near the top of the market. Some had a chance to make a little from their options, but mostly they watched as the lucky ones spent their winnings. Many came down with severe cases of option envy. Wendy, a Tibco marketing official, started at the company in November of

1999, just five months before the stock peaked. She got a total of 10,000 options, but they didn't vest until her one-year anniversary came up. She cashed out some of her options while the price was already headed down, so she made a few thousand dollars. But that was it. By the spring of 2001, all options she still held were underwater.

The hardest part, she said, was watching everyone else in her department spend all their loot. "I saw other people buying new clothes, getting new cars, buying houses. I was the last of the group to vest, and when I vested the price wasn't as high. I definitely experienced the envy."

Although most high-tech employees either made money from options or just didn't exercise them if they wouldn't have made a profit, a few unlucky people actually lost their own money, sometimes buckets of it, because of the strange tax rules that apply to most options.

Federal law recognizes two types of options, which get taxed in very different ways. One is called a qualified, or incentive, stock option, which means employees can pay lower capital gains taxes on any profit, if they hold the stock for a certain period. The second is a nonqualified option, meaning it doesn't allow employees to qualify for capital gains. They must pay the ordinary income tax on the profit. Most of the stock options in the High Tech 100 are of this type.

A problem arises when employees with nonqualified options exercise them but don't immediately sell the shares—and the share price falls dramatically. That happened to some unlucky employees during the market downdraft of 2000. The IRS reasoning goes as follows. Say you exercise an option with a strike price of $5 and your company's stock is trading at $100 that day. The IRS says you just received compensation from your employer of $95, so you must pay tax on it immediately. That's not difficult if you actually sell the share and collect the profit. But if you chose to gamble by not selling your shares and actually collecting your profit, well, that's your problem, you still owe the tax. The same thing would happen if a relative gave you a gift of stock that you claimed as income, and then the stock price declined.

This is what happened to Jerry, an Excite engineer who spoke to us with a group of his colleagues in early 2001. He had been worth $15 million for one magical moment in 1999, when his company's stock was worth about $200 a share. He exercised his options at a much lower price and immediately owed Uncle Sam ordinary income taxes on the paper profits. But he didn't sell the shares he received and take his cash profits. His mistake in not selling, he said, stemmed from the arrogance that came when the stock price just kept climbing.

"I just kind of had this invincible thing, like if all my stock vests in another year, I'll be worth $4 million, so big deal, who cares (about the tax), I'll just sell some more stock. Once, I went out and bought a $3,600 gold watch just on a whim. The money just disappeared like you would not believe. I thought I knew what I was doing and knew all the tax laws. So I thought, I'll just hold on, it keeps going up. I had no reason to sell and minimize the taxes, because you never never could foresee that the stock would fly from $100 to $4." When he finally sold his stock, he got far fewer profits and had to struggle to pay his taxes.

Another problem had to do with the Alternative Minimum Tax (AMT), a federal tax designed to make sure rich people don't take so many deductions that they pay no federal income tax at all. Some employees with incentive stock options exercised their options, had terrific paper wealth, and once again held onto their shares rather than sell. However, they did so in order to get that special lower capital gains treatment.

This happened to John, another Excite@Home engineer. When he joined the company in the late 1990s, John had received several thousand options that quickly became worth hundreds of thousands of dollars, at least on paper. In April 1999, he was house-hunting and quickly locked himself into escrow on a $600,000 house. Excite's stock was soaring skyward, jumping from $120 a share to $175 in the space of a month. John's first tranche of options vested on May 1, and if he had exercised and sold, he would have had more than enough for a $25,000 down payment, as well as the $60,000 BMW he wanted, and still had enough left over to pay the tax bill.

That spring, he exercised his options just below Excite's $200 high and had enormous paper wealth. But he held tight, selling nothing. His plan was to hold the shares for a year so that he could qualify to pay the lower capital gains tax. Then the stock began to nosedive. At $135, John sold enough to make the down payment. However, he continued to hold the rest of his shares, still thinking Excite's stock price would rebound as it had in the past. In April 2000, he got hit with a $130,000 tax bill from the IRS because the Alternative Minimum tax on his paper profits now applied. He had no cash to pay it. Fortunately, he didn't have to sell his home to pay off the feds, because he could take out a home equity loan instead. But he has lamented his greed ever since. He had taken a risk to pay lower capital gains taxes and lost the gamble.

"What's stupid is that I could have sold at $175, but I waited because there was this whole jackpot mentality," said John. Now, "the problem is that my mortgage payments are $4,200 a month between the two loans, so I am literally teetering on the edge. I think I have like $400 left in the bank right now. It's ridiculous. I'm making a six figure salary and I'm living paycheck to paycheck." By the end of the year, he had even worse problems, since he lost his job when Excite went down the tubes. Of course, his stock became worthless, too.

On tax day, 2001, some employees got hit with AMT tax bills that occasionally ran into five figures. News reports said that many were unable to pay even after they dumped their stock, sold their homes, and cashed out 401(k)s and other savings. "What are they going to do if we don't fix this—spend the next five years paying the IRS taxes on something they never had?" U.S. Rep. Zoe Lofgren, a San Jose, California, Democrat, complained to the *San Jose Mercury News* that April. "That's not fair."

Lofgren and lawmakers from Silicon Valley and other tech hotspots pushed for federal legislation that would provide retroactive relief for thousands of workers caught in this dilemma in 2001. If the bill ever passes, workers who exercise stock options no longer would face the AMT on their paper profits. Instead, they would be taxed on any actual gains they made from selling stock. "There's something fundamentally troublesome with the concept of taxing income that never existed," said Lofgren.

Plenty of high-tech employees caught in this dilemma said they didn't understand the tax consequences of the various courses of action they might take with their options, nor how to avoid all the potentially calamitous pitfalls. According to a 2001 national survey by Oppenheimer Funds, more than half of employees who receive options know little or nothing about their tax implications, yet 50 percent seek no advice before exercising them. But some also concede that they got caught up in the Gold Rush fever. They thought the stock price would keep doubling every year, which would render the tax consequences inconsequential. So they exercised their options and held onto the shares in the hope of really making a killing. Then when the market suddenly crashed, they were the ones that got killed.

Some employees compounded their financial misery by borrowing on their stock, often at the urging of stock brokers. This happened to dozens of Microsoft employees in the 2001 tax season. One midlevel employee of the firm told the *New York Times* that the Microsoft stock he acquired from his options was worth $1.5 million when the company's share price peaked in 2000. He owed taxes on the paper profit, but instead of selling the stock to pay it, he held on, assuming the market would keep lifting Microsoft's share price. So he borrowed money from his broker, using the stock as collateral, a practice known as a margin loan.

But when the market fell and Microsoft's stock collapsed by 50 percent, disaster hit. The employee, who declined to give his name, found that his brokerage firm had the right to begin selling his collateral shares at the lower price to pay off his margin loan. By tax day, most of his stock was gone and he still owed $100,000 in taxes, more than his annual salary. More than two dozen Microsoft employees in similar situations wound up filing for bankruptcy.

A big part of the problem is that even the financial experts can't agree on what employees should do with options. Generally speaking, their advice falls into three camps, says Corey Rosen, Executive Director of the National Center for Employee Ownership, a nonprofit organization in Oakland, California. One group says you should hold options as long as possible if you believe that the stock will go up over the long term. Corporate executives, the employees most likely to get options, are often faulted for selling too early.

Another school of thought says that you should not be trying to guess the market or react emotionally to your company's stock price. This group wants you to sell on an orderly, phased schedule once the options vest.

A third group talks of critical capital, by which they mean the amount of risk that is prudent given your own financial situation. Part of the consideration should be just how many retirement nest eggs you have in any one basket of stock. If a lot of your savings are sunk into the company where you work, through a 401(k) match, for example, you might want to regularly diversify into other investments—even if doing so sacrifices some upside potential. Rosen puts it this way: "If you are making $50,000 a year, are middle-aged, and have a daughter going to college next year on option wealth, then you may have a reason to take your profits now. But if you are making $50,000 and have money saved for your retirement and no immediate needs, you may not want to rush into exercising options."

Unfortunately, none of the pundits worried much about the peculiar tax complications of a catastrophic crash in market values. So some employees who used options to buy stock and hold it got caught. Still, most employees who get stock options don't end up in such a state, because most simply sell the stock and take their profit at the same time they exercise an option.

Options can be tricky, and sometimes financially dangerous. But it remains the exception for employees actually to lose money on them. If a company's stock price keeps rising above the exercise price, then by definition employees gain. If the market value falls, however, most employees usually have enough time to realize what's happening and just don't exercise the option. In that case, they incur no paper profit and the IRS doesn't come knocking at their door. Those who got hit in 2001 were unfortunate enough to exercise just before an abrupt, and very large, slump.

While on average many high-tech workers made significant amounts of money from their options throughout the industry's boom and bust, that still left the question of what would happen to them from then on. True, the new conventional wisdom didn't accurately assess just how much wealth their options gave them. But when the glory days ended and the Internet's prospects started to resemble those of more traditional industries, were the new B-school grads right to think that a stock option isn't worth the paper it's written on?

There are two issues to consider. First, some high-tech firms used stock options to bargain down what they had to pay talented new hires, a practice that was especially prevalent in the industry's early days. Since it's highly unlikely that the High Tech 100 will repeat the crazy stock gains they enjoyed in the late 1990s, it's possible that some employees could earn less from their ownership than they give up in the form of below-market salaries.

On the other hand, there's another largely unnoticed feature of stock option capitalism that cuts the other way. The High Tech 100 don't just issue options as a one-shot deal to lure workers in the door. The vast majority also grant them on an ongoing basis, usually annually. This isn't apparent in the total employee equity figures we presented in this chapter. These numbers add up all the options employees ever had received in their company's entire history that remained outstanding in December 2000.

The question is, what's the value of the options that high-tech workers get every year? If it's high enough, they could offset the lower pay some receive. For the majority who do earn market-level salaries, the issue is whether the new options are sufficient to compensate for the extra risk of working in an industry whose long-term outlook no longer seems quite so shiny and bright.

# 5

# Why Companies Hand Out
# New Options Every Year

It's clear by now that many High Tech 100 employees showed a net profit from the stock options they received, including many who exercised their holdings after the bust. Yet this bottom-line way of looking at stock options doesn't reveal the whole story. It considerably understates just how much these employees already have benefited from partnership capitalism, and stand to gain again when the stock market eventually improves.

The reason lies with what experts call the run rate, which simply means how much equity a company hands out in the form of employee options in a given year. You might think the amount is fairly obvious. After all, in Chapter 4 we learned that the top five officers of the typical High Tech 100 firm owned 14 percent of their company's total equity as of 2000. All other employees at the firm owned another 19 percent. So you might reasonably conclude that on average, each group probably got roughly the same amount of stock and options every year. Otherwise, they wouldn't have ended up with more or less the same total equity stakes after years of option grants.

However, what actually happened was more complicated. In a typical year, High Tech 100 firms hand out many more options to average employees than they do to the top officers. This generosity allowed workers to catch up to the equity stakes held by the firm's founders, who are also often CEOs or other top officers.

Usually, the person or small group of people who founded the company owned most or all of it to begin with. In order to bring in the financial resources necessary to expand their firm, high-tech founders gave up a lot of their ownership, just as most corporate founders do. Employees got some, mostly through stock options. Then venture capitalists were allowed to buy shares at insider prices. When the firm did its IPO, the public at large got to buy the company's stock, too, although they usually paid the highest price for their ownership stake. Despite all this stock being issued to so many groups, a high run rate that goes mostly to employees allows employees to gain ground on the founders and other shareholders.

By looking at the SEC filings, we determined that the average run rate among the High Tech 100 was about 8 percent a year between 1997 and 2001. In other words, they granted 8 percent of their total equity to employees and top officers in the form of options every year. The bulk of this combination of actual and potential ownership—typically 7 of the 8 percentage points—went to average employees. The top five officers received only the remaining point. As a result, employees quickly caught up with and then surpassed the top five, despite the huge ownership stakes with which most top officers started. Nor was there any sign that the bust caused these companies to change the pattern: High Tech 100 firms gave employees about 90 percent of all outstanding stock options in the years before and after the stock market sell-off.

The run rate gives a more comprehensive picture of the industry's extensive commitment to sharing risk and reward than the 19 percent snapshot of employee equity we saw in the last chapter. It's one thing to find that many workers lucked out by getting into the industry before its stock soared to unbelievable heights, and that many were left with quite a bit more than worthless dreams when the market sank. But to get an idea about whether options are likely to make much of a financial difference to employees in a more normal economic environment, we need to look at what happened on an ongoing basis.

Examining how high-tech firms hand out options every year also sheds light on the ability of stock option capitalism to withstand wild market gyrations. We've already seen how the popular perception that high-tech workers got stuck with worthless paper after the 2000 crash was at least partly inaccurate because of all the cheap pre-IPO options they had received early on. However, an equally important reason lies in the run rate, which shows that high-tech firms continue to grant options every year. Since each new grant comes with an exercise price pegged to the current stock price, the stock option model automatically readjusts employee risk sharing for even the most severe market swings, by renewing the upside potential every year. While employees still had plenty of underwater options after the crash, the run rate has been steadily building up a new stock of in-the-money ones.

"At times, the market may get ahead of itself; at times, behind," Cisco CEO John Chambers told an interviewer in May 2000, shortly after the high-tech stock collapse had begun. "We pass out stock options every year so that [employees' holdings] don't go up and down based upon what their initial [exercise price] was. So I don't worry about the short-term fluctuations" of the stock market.

A widespread lack of knowledge about the run rate has contributed to the inaccurate notion that the high-tech bust proved what a lousy deal options turned out to be for average workers. Even many experts don't take into account how annual option grants re-equilibrate employees' ownership stakes and keep intact the partnership among capital, management, and labor. In mid-1999, for example, a leading national expert on employee relations gave a newspaper interview that illustrated the misapprehension. "The great Achilles' heel of all these [stock option] programs is that if the stock market turns, . . . you've built an enormous castle of sand," said Edward Lawler III, director of the University of Southern California's Center for Effective Organizations. "All of a sudden, you've got a lot of people with underwater options [that are worthless] and nothing to hold them to the company."

While Lawler is correct in pointing out that many employees suddenly found themselves with worthless options, he didn't stress the fact that many employees are given new options at in-the-money prices every year, no matter how many underwater options they're stuck with from prior years.

The run rate helps to make sense of something else, too. For all the grand talk about sharing the wealth and having employees think like owners, some high-tech companies—like Amazon, for instance—consistently underpaid their employees in the early years. Economists have their own name for this phenomenon as well. They call it "wage substitution," meaning that the company is substituting options for a part of the normal market wage.

While not every high-tech firm lowballed salaries in this way, the run rate became particularly crucial for those that did: The new options they granted every year were necessary to continue to offset the artificially depressed wages. From the perspective of the employees, the more options they received, the more likely they were to come out ahead from the wage substitution. Either way, there was no guarantee, since the stock market can be so fickle. But to learn whether employees lost money from wage substitution, we need to determine the value of the options they received every year through their company's run rate.

To get a better handle on the run rate, think of the difference between a snapshot and a motion picture. The total equity table in Chapter 4 took a snapshot of the High Tech 100 as of December 31, 2000. It told us that employees had accumulated 19 percent of their firms' total equity over the years. But because that table measures employees' potential ownership stake as of a certain point in time, it says nothing about how many options they received on an ongoing basis every year. All we discovered was that employees held 19 percent as of the time the camera flashed at the end of the year.

The run rate, on the other hand, measures the flow of options to employees every year. It's like training a financial video on the industry, to follow the trail of options as companies grant them. To get a better feel for the average High Tech 100 run rate, look at Table 5.1. It shows the share of the firm's total equity granted as options each year, and how the pie was divvied up between employees and the top five officers.

These are extraordinary numbers. They tell us that the average High Tech 100 firm granted about 8 percent of its future ownership to employees every year. True, this is potential, not actual, owner-

**TABLE 5.1    The Annual Option Spigot: High Tech Workers Get More Than Their Bosses** (Share of the High Tech 100's total equity granted as options each year)

|         | Employees' Share % | Top Officers' Share % | Total % |
|---------|--------------------|-----------------------|---------|
| 1997    | 8                  | 1                     | 9       |
| 1998    | 8                  | 1                     | 9       |
| 1999    | 7                  | 1                     | 8       |
| 2000    | 6                  | 1                     | 7       |
| 2001    | 4                  | 1                     | 5       |
| Average | 7                  | 1                     | 8       |

NOTES: All outstanding shares and all options after dilution, i.e., assuming that all the options had been exercised.

Employees refers to everyone but the top officers, who are the five highest-paid executives at each company

SOURCE: Authors' analysis of SEC filings.

ship, because options can't immediately be cashed in for stock. Still, it's clear that most options go to rank-and-file employees and lower-level managers, not CEOs or upper-level managers, as is the case in most of the rest of corporate America. The founders and executives of these companies seem committed, by an ethos that hardened into a competitive standard, to spreading the wealth to generate more wealth.

Take a look at 2000, for example. The High Tech 100 handed out 7 percent of their total equity to employees and the top five officers that year. Nearly all of this run rate—about 6 percentage points—went to average employees. The top five executives in each firm received just 1 point. To put it another way, the High Tech 100 granted 1.5 billion options in 2000. The top five officers got 164 million of these, while everyone else split the remaining 1.36 billion. In a fifth of the companies, the top five received 5 percent or less of all the options granted that year. Not one High Tech 100 firm gave the top five officers more than employees.

If you run the video for all years since the High Tech 100 were founded, you find that they had granted 11.5 billion options as of the end of 2000 (including the ones that had been exercised). Of that total, some 9 billion, or nearly 80 percent, had gone to employees. The top five officers got the remaining 20 percent.

These figures drive home the extent of high-tech firms' commitment to stock option capitalism. Sure, executives took plenty of options for themselves, especially when you consider that there were only 500 top five officers and 177,000 employees as of 2001. But there's no question that executives back up their shared-ownership rhetoric to a vastly greater degree than their counterparts in any other industry in America.

The moving picture view of options also makes clear why employees so quickly caught up with the ownership stakes of their company's founders. The original owners may have started with most or all of the company's stock. But in every subsequent year they gave their employees nine options for every one they gave themselves. At that rate, it didn't take long for employees to pass them by. As a result, the employee share of the High Tech 100 total equity pie expanded steadily, from 17 percent in 1999 to 19 percent in 2000 to 20 percent in 2001.

To illustrate the point with a typical company, take Yahoo. When Jerry Yang and David Filo started the Internet search engine in 1994, they owned 100 percent of the stock. Soon after, they sold shares to Sequoia Capital, a venture capital firm, for $1 million. They diluted their holdings again when they got more funding from Softbank, another Internet firm. They also granted a slew of options to most employees. Then Yahoo sold shares to the public in 1996. At that point, Yang and Filo each owned only about 11 percent of the company (after accounting for the potential dilution from stock options). Other officers and directors held 7 percent, including Tim Koogle, Yahoo's first CEO. Sequoia held 13 percent and Softbank had 27 percent. Employees' options came to another 17 percent, leaving public shareholders with the remaining 14 percent.

Yahoo continued to grant options to employees in subsequent years that represented about 9 percent of the company annually. Overall, Yahoo handed out almost a quarter of a billion options between 1994 and the end of 2000. Of that total, it gave 12 percent to the top executives and 88 percent to employees. By 2000, Jerry Yang's and David Filo's ownership stakes had shrunk to 6 percent each. Employees had accumulated a total potential ownership of about 20 percent, almost entirely through options. This is the amount they hadn't exercised, either vested or unvested. They also had exercised many options along the way. That's more than Softbank and more than Jerry Yang and David Filo combined.

The run rate shows that high-tech firms didn't just share the wealth once, in a burst of generosity during their heady startup days. Instead, they did it every year. This renewed commitment became very important after the market crash. The bursting of the stock bubble drove more than 80 percent of the options held by employees underwater. If options had been one-time deals, many would never see any value from those they still held at the time.

Of course, High Tech 100 companies didn't continue to issue options just to keep employees in the money. Their primary motive was the same as it had been during the boom days: a need to be competitive in attracting, retaining, and motivating talented employees. The setback in the market, which undermined confidence in the Internet as the market of the future, tested this human resources strategy. Some high-tech companies really hadn't had enough time to get out of the startup mode, though over time the strongest of them had begun to resemble solid operations likely to survive and thrive over the long haul. But after the bubble burst, even the most promising high-tech companies that focused on the Internet were once again viewed as risky job situations. Traditional companies looked more secure as a place to build a career.

In mid-2001, Vivek Ragavan, then CEO of Redback Networks, a Cisco rival that builds Internet equipment, explained why he continued to grant options even though the labor market for high-tech workers had cooled. "We don't have billions of dollars of cash sitting on the balance sheet, and we don't have a stable base of revenue yet," he said. "The early guys who joined took more risk, and now they are taking a little less, but it's still risky. And because we are still a startup, people feel that if they take a risk they should get the reward, and they are willing to work for it."

Other high-tech companies believe that employees' stake in the firm must be constantly refreshed so the ownership culture will thrive. We've seen how the special culture that options helped to form is as important as the options themselves, for employees as well as the company. But the financial stake for employees is the glue that helps hold it all together. If that stake isn't renewed, especially after a big stock slump, employees may lose their motivation and the culture might well begin to atrophy or even dissipate altogether. "If you took Juniper and said, We're going to do the same things, but we won't have stock options, I don't think you would get the same results," said Marcel Gani, Juniper's CFO.

The run rate helps to keep alive the sense of employee ownership and the productivity gains it brings. The high-tech companies that issued new options after the market collapse did so at the sharply lower stock prices that prevailed at the time. As a result, workers continued to earn a fresh stake every year in any future gains their labor might help produce. In addition, new hires were brought into the ownership fold. One testimony to the retention value of options is the fact that High Tech 100 employees didn't desert in droves for traditional companies after the stock market meltdown.

"We have had a policy since day one of sharing the equity with employees, and we continually refresh [their] option positions," Siebel Systems CEO Thomas Siebel said in a television interview in April 2001, after the company had announced a doubling of its first-quarter profits. "We've been doing that now over the last seven years to make sure that we have a company where all the employees are owners. I think they find their stock options are very motivating. This has been a major, major reason why Siebel Systems has been as successful as it has."

Pegging the strike price of newly issued options to current stock levels automatically injects new hope for financial gain. Old options that had a paper worth of $100 at the height of the bubble were undercut when the stock price fell to $40 or $20 or even $1. But the new ones carry the lower exercise price, so employees stand to make a profit if there's any upward movement at all.

Lower-priced options can even make a company look more attractive to new hires. This may seem counterintuitive. After all, few people want to sign on to a company whose stock had just lost 90 percent of its value, since there's a big risk that it might go out of business altogether. But when the market had been at its peak, some potential hires had begun to wonder just how much higher it could go. Getting options in a company whose stock already had shot up 1,000 percent didn't always seem likely to lead to a new windfall, since it would be increasingly difficult to keep growing as such an incredible pace.

But if the underlying business remained sound, options in a company whose stock had fallen back to a few dollars left plenty of room for another payoff. "It becomes increasingly difficult to hire people when your stock is so high," said David Callisch, director of market communications at Alteon Websystems in a 2000 interview. "The fact that the stock is lower now, that's the one good thing now about this whole stock market collapse." Alteon, an Internet software firm later acquired by Nortel, was trying to hire about 100 people at the time and offers stock options to all its employees.

Still, the crash was an acid test for the High Tech 100's stock option culture. Some employees became disheartened as they watched the value of their potential ownership shrivel or even vanish altogether. Many had felt a sense of entitlement during the boom times. So it was a heavy psychological blow to wake up one day and find out that a lot of their unexercised options were worthless, despite the 17 percent that were still in the money and the profits they already had made from those they had cashed in.

"This is an incredible challenge now in the Valley," said Jay Wood, the chairman of Kana, in early 2001. "People were so motivated in that frothy market we saw in the beginning of last year. Now the market is depressed, and there are people that have $100 options but their stock is sitting at $1. They are not going to realize anything from that and probably never will. So what companies have been challenged with is, 'How do you reset the bar and give these people value?'"

Added VeriSign CEO Stratton D. Sclavos: "Over the last twelve months, you see a dramatic number of companies whose stock price has gone down by 70 percent to 99 percent. You have a high degree of your workforce who believed options were a wonderful thing, but now they're not necessarily convinced that those options will ever achieve an above-water situation. This is a time that tests the stock option recruitment and retention theory."

To preserve employee loyalty and motivation, many high-tech firms took extra steps to offset the psychological impact of the crash. Although the options employees get from the run rate each year give them a new reason to remain at the company, they do little to compensate for the great sense of loss they suffered when their old options became worthless. High-tech firms used a variety of stratagems to deal with this problem.

One approach was to hand out a pay raise, as Microsoft did to its lower-ranking workers. In a seven-page memo sent to employees in December 2000, Microsoft CEO Steve Ballmer explained why it did so:

> It's critical that we continue hiring great new people and investing in our existing employees. Our ongoing goal is that our base salaries are higher than two-thirds of the companies in the industry. We have drifted behind that target and the stock market drop makes employees, new and old, more sensitive to cash compensation. Stock options remain a great long-term opportunity for employees to share in the success of the company. That remains important, but reality has set in— here and industry-wide. The world is not full of get rich quick opportunities, but everyone here has an opportunity to do very well long term.
>
> In the next month we will review all employees at level 67 and below (roughly the bottom half of Microsoft's workforce) for consideration of a base salary increase, or, for sales people, an increase in bonus opportunity. These increases are not automatic; they will target strongest performers, and good performers who are lower in their salary ranges. None of this is in lieu of the normal August reviews. While we will have many fewer open positions, we must ensure we continue to find and hire the right new people and fully use our salary ranges as an aid.

That year, Microsoft had moved to solve another personnel problem brought on by one of its employee ownership programs. The firm's full-time employees get an option grant when they're hired, plus continuing grants, and they get to buy stock at a discount in the employee stock purchase plan. However, one long-running sore spot at the company had been management's strategy of excluding employees it designated as temporary workers from the purchase plan. They sued in a case that eventually covered 10,000 current and former temp employees, or a quarter of the company's total workforce. In 1999, Microsoft lost a lengthy court battle in which temps had argued that they should be considered regular employees. After losing the case, Microsoft sharply reduced its temp workforce, bringing a larger share of its workers into the stock purchase plan.

Not many high-tech companies had the financial wherewithal to follow mighty Microsoft's move and raise pay to offset employees' option losses, especially in a sinking stock market. Instead, the majority used their option programs in various ways to compensate employees for their underwater ownership stakes.

The most straightforward tactic was to simply raise the run rate and hand out more options. If, for example, a company had planned to issue options worth 8 percent of the company in 2000, it could lift the grant to 9 percent or 10 percent. Microsoft had done this in April of that year, even before the pay raise and just days after the tech sell-off began. The company made an extra award of 70 million options at $67 a share, a much lower price than the $90 ones employees had received the previous July.

Overall, 47 percent of the High Tech 100 lifted their run rates in 2000. Most did so without stinting: The average increase came to 4.4 percentage points, lifting the run rates of this group to more than 12 percent. "We will go and look at the entire base of employees, determine how much of their vested and unvested shares are underwater, and then do an incremental grant [of new options] between zero and 30 percent [of the number employees already had], to create some adjustment," said VeriSign CEO Sclavos, who issued new options that year.

While the other 53 percent reduced the number of options they granted in 2000, many nonetheless used options in other ways to help workers who had lost out in the market slump. In fact, nearly half of this group—roughly a quarter of the entire High Tech 100—pursued a controversial approach that exchanged old options for new options after six months. This essentially repriced employees' options. Repricing means that your employer changes the strike price of an option you already own, reducing it to the current market price or even lower. Say your options came with a strike price of $10. Then the stock price shot up to $100, but sank back down to $5. The company would reset your strike price to $5 or less.

Repricing kicked up quite a fuss, for understandable reasons. Outside investors saw it as cheating. After all, being a part owner means sharing in the risk as well as the reward of ownership. Other shareholders lose just as much as employees when the stock price tumbles. In fact, they're usually worse off, since most had to shell out hard cash to buy their stock. Employees, on the other hand, got their options just by working. So why should they get protected from a market slump if no one else does? "Shareholders out there say, Well, no one is repricing my shares," said Jay Wood, Kana's CEO. "I bought them at $100 and now they are $1. Why should you get any more?"

Still, Amazon repriced in early 2001. Owen, the manager who told the story about Amazon CEO Bezos and the beach rental, explained why. The company's stock price had plummeted in the prior year, from a high of $107 all the way down to $30. As it fell, it drove an increasing number of employee options underwater. "It just grew and grew and grew until we got to a point where, because I joined before the company went public, I was one of 3 percent or 4 percent of the company that actually had options worth anything," Owen said. "This was a huge problem, because now everybody is left with options that are worthless, and retention becomes an issue."

A combination of disappointment, resentment, and a diminished confidence in the company's future was soon reflected in changed work habits. People stopped working as hard, Owen explained, and began going home at 5 P.M. or 6 P.M.—something that never used to happen when the stock was soaring. "I felt that I really couldn't push on people," Owen said. "It's hard to do anyway, because we really don't have that kind of culture. But I can't really ask people to feel like they are in some kind of jihad anymore. I was always walking on thin ice with folks, wanting to motivate them but not wanting to push too hard, because they might walk out the door."

Amazon employees expressed similar views. "Morale in the group was directly tied to the share price," said James, a thirty-six-year-old software engineer who had come to the company as a contractor and become a permanent employee in mid-1999. "The group I was in had about thirty people in it," he told us in the spring of 2001, not long after he had left Amazon again for another job. "You could see as the share price started slipping, people still did the work but the morale wasn't there, and the fervor was not as high as it was back in 1999. The morale was pretty low after that. It's like, why are we bothering implementing new features, it's not going to change anything."

In fact, you could track morale levels by the comments employees wrote on the white boards Amazon had in its elevators. Some, said James, would write "'We hope that'. . . and then they drew a little *boing* like we were going to bounce. Then other people drew a slow vertical drop straight down off of that and said: 'No way, we're going down, this is it.' When the share price started sliding comments show up about Amazon.bomb and Amazon.gone. Then when it went back up, you'd start seeing more positive things in the elevator."

By August of 2000, Bezos decided to take action. In an email to Amazon employees, he explained that the company was giving them a special new grant of options. But by the following February, it had become clear that the supplemental grant wasn't enough. Nearly 70 percent of the 70 million options held by Amazon employees had strike prices ranging up to $83, yet the stock was trading at $16. This time, instead of another round of new options, Bezos repriced. Technically, what he did was allow workers to trade in older options with higher exercise prices for fewer options that carried strike prices that were at least 15 percent lower.

This was a bold move. Although Amazon had been the poster child of the e-commerce boom, some investors had begun to sour on it by 2000. Stock analysts complained that Amazon kept pushing back the year when the company would turn its first profit. In 2000, Amazon posted a $545 million loss. Bezos "was making a pretty big statement," said Owen, "which is that I still believe in ownership of the company as the way to go. He has not abandoned that as a guiding philosophy for the company. We responded by trying to get it so that ownership once again can become the driver for us." Indeed, Bezos was so aggressive about swapping out his workers' high-priced options that by July of 2002, only 13 percent of them were underwater even though Amazon's stock was still trading in the $16 range.

The repricing strategy was a risky one for many companies, because they had to reduce their earnings when they did it. The need to do so was spelled out in 2000 by the Financial Accounting Standards Board (FASB), an industry oversight body that sets the accounting rules for corporations. That year, FASB issued guidelines saying that employers who reprice must subtract the gain employees get from the company's own earnings statement. In other words, their profits are cut by the amount they reprice.

Few high-tech companies took the official repricing road, largely because they didn't want to take an earnings hit. All told, we found only three High Tech 100 firms that used this approach in 2000. "The FASB rules really have tied the hands of management in trying to incent people," said Wood. "I think it is a bit of a shame really, because what we want out of our economy is better productivity out of our employees. By instituting these accounting standards, it makes it virtually impossible to re-incent employees with stock. Some companies have done repricings and their shareholders have punished them mercilessly for it."

To get around FASB, many high-tech firms employed a loophole that first seems to have been uncovered by Sprint, the long-distance telephone company. In the fall of 2000, Sprint realized that the newly issued FASB rules didn't bar it from simply canceling underwater options. All a company had to do was wait six months, then issue new ones at the market price of the day. The move, called a slow-motion swap or a 6-&-1 repricing (six months and one day), didn't trigger the rule requiring an earnings charge, even though it clearly is intended to achieve the same result as a repricing. The time period is the key factor. FASB considers it repricing if a company cancels old options and issues new ones within a six-month period. One that does exactly the same thing after the six months and a day is just exchanging or swapping options, and isn't required to take the earnings hit. After Sprint spotted the strategy, many high-tech firms jumped to exploit it, including a third of those High Tech 100 firms that had decreased their run rates.

In reality, a swap is still a form of repricing, even if it does skirt FASB's fine print and avoids the official label. High-tech companies also faced other limitations in how far they could take it. Companies must ask shareholders' permission to grant options. They do so by specifying how many options they want to give out, and then allowing shareholders to vote on it. If stockholders say yes, as they almost always do, the company can't exceed the specified amount without going back for another shareholder vote.

"Some of us have tried other creative ways that are acceptable by the accounting standards, but it's not easy," said Kana's Wood. "If you're going to increase it beyond what has been preset, you have to go to your shareholders and get approval. And shareholders are not very happy when the price is down. So you get yourself caught. Some companies have such large pools that it doesn't matter. But it still looks messy."

When shareholders ask why repricing or regranting is fair, said Wood, he responds by telling them, "'Because you're asking the employee to work their tail off to give you more value. You're not sitting here working sixteen hours a day. Let these people have an opportunity to be successful again and you'll get more out of the company by getting these people to work hard.' If I were a shareholder, I'd say, 'Reprice the damn things, I don't care.' But it's not the way it works."

Other high-tech CEOs disagree. "I never reprice options," said Bill Coleman, the chairman and cofounder of BEA Systems, an Internet software company based in San Jose, California. "Right now, there's a bunch of software companies out there that do because they found a new loophole. My view is, if you're repricing, you're admitting to the world that you are never going to build enough value to get back to that price again. The second thing is, you are taking the responsibility for failure away from the people who maybe made that happen."

Still, nearly half of the High Tech 100 did some version of an exchange or repricing in 2000. When you throw in those who jacked up their run rates (some of whom also repriced), fully two-thirds helped employees to offset the market crash in one way or another. Overall, the number of cancelled options jumped to 29 percent in 2000, from 11 percent the year before, as companies wiped out old high-priced options and replaced them with ones carrying strike prices at lower market levels. The practice accelerated dramatically in 2001 as the stock market continued its swoon. In fact, cancellations soared to a stunning 62 percent that year as employers struggled to cope with the morale impact of so many worthless options. All these cancelled options had the odd effect of driving down the run rate, which sank to 7 percent in 2000 and to just 5 percent in 2001. In reality, companies were handing out more options in those years, not less. But because they cancelled so many old ones, the net number fell.

Investors who just looked at the falling run rates might conclude that high-tech firms were scaling back their option grants. While new grants were in fact smaller, the extra options they handed out to offset the cancelled ones meant that the scaling back was much less than it appeared. Indeed, the drop in the run rate had nothing to do with de-emphasizing partnership capitalism. Just the opposite was true. Companies were canceling options with $100 exercise prices and replacing them with fewer options that carried $10 exercise prices. Public shareholders, of course, are bearing more of the risk of dilution when this happens.

Shareholders gain risk either way, but most of the companies felt they had little choice but to try to help employees. "Every employee has the power to reprice their options package. . . . It's called, 'I quit,'" said Amazon spokesman Bill Curry in a 2001 news interview. In other words, they can simply walk out the door and get options at a new company that carries the current market price.

Another reason why some high-tech companies were so anxious to make sure employees didn't wind up with worthless options involves the implicit promise they extended to employees. This has to do with the wage substitution issue we mentioned earlier. While most paid salaries equal to those at any other company, some undercut the market wage and used options to make up the difference.

For the most part, this happened in the company's startup period. Some high-tech CEOs offered a fairly sophisticated explanation—or perhaps it was really a justification—for why they did it. Naveen Jain, the CEO of Infospace, argued that in the early days of his company, employees were in effect subsidizing its startup phase by working for below-market wages. He could have gone to venture capitalists to raise enough money to pay them more. But then they would take a piece of the ownership pie, along with the potential rewards it would bring. Why not instead let employees play the role of venture capitalist?

"When I started Infospace, I went to each employee and told them, 'Look, if you were going to the open market, you can make $100,000 a year,'" he said. "'I will pay you a $100,000 a year, too, but that means I have to go raise that money. If I do, I have to give part of the equity to somebody else. Do you want to take a $30,000 salary and become the venture capitalist yourself? That way, the only person who will make the money from your blood and sweat will be you, not somebody else. How would you feel when somebody is sitting at the beach, and you're working hard twenty hours a day but he's the one making the money? Probably you'll not feel very good.' So I think turning the employees into the venture capitalist is probably the best thing you can do."

Here, too, Amazon was perhaps the most prominent example of a high-tech company that paid below-market wages. During its first few years, Amazon did surveys of labor markets to determine how much it should pay employees. The surveys, which usually are done by private consulting firms, tell companies what the average salary is in a given city for any type of worker, whether it's a midlevel manager or a low-skilled warehouse worker who packs the books Amazon ships to its customers. Most large companies use these surveys to set pay levels. However, Amazon deliberately pegged its salaries in the bottom quarter of the levels found in the surveys.

Amazon and a few other high-tech companies skimped on wages for a simple reason: They couldn't always afford to pay competitive wages. While they wanted the most talented workers, so did the likes of IBM and Intel, which had a lot more money to throw around. "When you are starting a company, a high-tech company in particular, most of the alternatives these people have in terms of other jobs come from more established companies, whose salary scales are probably higher than yours," said VeriSign CEO Sclavos. "So [an option program] gives you an offset to that."

Many employees were willing to go along, especially after high-tech stocks started to soar. They watched other high-tech workers getting rich from options and thought a lower wage would be a good tradeoff for a chance at the jackpot. A broad range of workers felt this way, from managers who could earn six figures to the customer service representatives who handle calls from the public.

Owen, for example, started at Amazon with a salary of $60,000 a year, plus thousands of options. "I had also gotten an offer from a consulting firm that I had worked for over the summer," he remembered. "Their offer was $120,000, including a salary of $95,000 or $100,000, with bonus on top on that. If I had gone to a consumer products company, it probably would have paid me $80,000 or $90,000. So I knew I was not only below market but probably at the bottom of my entire [business school] class." Bezos, he said, was open about the tradeoff, and told employees that Amazon was giving them ownership in the company instead of a full salary.

Zach Works thought options were worth a lower wage, too. A senior customer service representative in Amazon's Seattle office, Works had earned $10 an hour when he started with the company in 1998. While this was $2 less than what he had made at his prior job, Works also received 1,500 options. In December 1999, when Amazon's stock hit its peak, they had been worth $169,000, far outweighing the $4,000 or so a year he was giving up by earning $2 an hour less.

But by the fall of the following year, Amazon's stock was at $29. Since Works's strike price was $21, the bonanza he was counting on had shriveled to just $12,000 and was getting closer to zero every day. "And I'm the exception, since most of my colleagues started later and are underwater," he said that fall. Toward the end of 2000, Amazon's stock sank to almost $15 and Works's golden pile was worthless.

As this happened to more high-tech employees, wage substitution all of a sudden became a major morale problem for companies like Amazon. Instead of feeling like they had lucked into an opportunity, many felt ripped off, and perhaps a little foolish for having uncritically accepted their company's grand vision. Some may have been angry with themselves for having bought into what seemed increasingly like a bad deal.

So it wasn't surprising that Amazon led the way on repricing. "We ask people to take lower salaries when they come to Amazon.com in exchange for ownership in the company," Bezos said when making the case to shareholders at Amazon's 2001 annual meeting in May of that year. "Since the stock price went down, employees were granted an opportunity to exchange their options for ones at a lower price."

Amazon's repricing proved to have tactical value as well. Disappointed workers in several cities actually tried to form labor unions in the fall of 2000—a shocking break from the hip, individualistic culture of high tech. That November, the Washington Alliance of Technology Workers (WashTech), which had been formed to help permatemp programmers at Microsoft, began a union recognition petition among Amazon's 400 or so Seattle-based customer service representatives. Works joined, along with dozens of others.

The wage versus options issue exposed other grievances as well. The service reps called their group "Day2@Amazon.com," because "Bezos is always telling us, 'It's Day One, we can't stop or rest,' and we think five years of Day One is generating lots of problems for us," said Works.

He and other reps complained that management no longer listened to their problems. They routinely worked fifty-hour weeks, going up to seventy in the holidays, said Jennifer McDaeth, another rep in Amazon's Seattle office. The company also changed their shifts, sometimes on as little as a day's notice, making the job even more stressful, she said. Reps complained repeatedly, she said, but management did nothing to solve any of the problems. The group's mission statement called on Amazon to make "a true commitment" to reps on compensation, job security, and respect, among other values.

The morale problems cast a light on the distinctly Old Economy underbelly among the workforce at Amazon and some other high-tech companies, one that almost no one ever talked about. As one of the largest Internet firms serving the public directly, Amazon had built up an extensive national operation to ship books and other products to customers' homes. It included seven warehouses, staffed by some 5,000 workers who were even lower paid than the service reps.

Two labor groups tried to form a union among the warehouse workers that fall. One was the United Food and Commercial Workers (UFCW), a large union that represents supermarket and other retail workers, including warehouse staff much like those at Amazon. The second group was called the Prewitt Organizing Fund, an unusual freelance union recruitment outfit based in Washington, D.C.

Although Amazon's warehouse workers comprised more than half of the company's workforce, they were largely excluded from the stock option culture Bezos worked so hard to cultivate. They earned $7.50 to $9.25 an hour, with skimpy benefits. This was considerably less than what similar workers made who belonged to the UFCW or other unions. Warehouse workers, too, often had to put in fifty- and sixty-hour weeks, especially during the holiday rush. But unlike the reps and other high-tech workers, they got only 100 options, vested over five years. These, too, had been rendered largely worthless by Amazon's falling stock price.

Amazon successfully defeated the union drives. In February 2001, it cut back operations when the peak Christmas season didn't bring as much business as management had planned for. In the process, it shuttered the Seattle office, laying off all 400 sales reps—effectively squelching the union drive.

On a second front, Bezos moved to phase out the wage substitution. Amazon began trying to peg salaries to the 50 percent mark in market surveys, up from the 25 percent it had previously targeted. In other words, the company began adjusting wages so they would be closer to the market average. "You bet the wage substitution has diminished," said Owen in the spring of 2001. Between this change and the repricings, employee morale gradually began to improve.

Other high-tech firms had to reverse course, too. "When the market starts going down, you find that you can't compete (for good employees) when your stock isn't growing at the rate that it used to, so suddenly we had to start getting our wages into the market arena," said Chris Wheeler, the chief technical officer and co-founder of InterNAP Network Services Corporation in Seattle. His company, which had 770 employees at the end of 2000, provides companies with Internet routing services. Wheeler estimates that InterNAP paid engineers 20 to 30 percent under the market wage from its founding in 1995 to the market crash in early 2000.

Some companies began to phase out wage substitution for newer employees who had missed the wealth that options brought during the boom days. "Our executive salaries are particularly low for a company that has 2,000 employees," said VeriSign's Sclavos. "But most of my executive management has been with me for four years and has seen the positives of the stock. New executives, on the other hand, end up having not quite the same upside potential. Therefore, executive comp on the salary and bonus is going up. You have to start balancing it back the other way."

It's difficult to say just how many High Tech 100 companies used options as a substitute for below-market wages. Most of the employees and executives we interviewed said that companies primarily did this in the startup phase, and usually abandoned the practice in later years. Two surveys back up this notion, although neither measure the High Tech 100 directly. One, by a high-tech compensation consulting firm called iQuantic Incorporated, surveyed 200 high-tech firms in 2000, some of which were likely in the High Tech 100. It found that 86 percent of the 200 companies said that they paid between the fiftieth and seventy-fifth percentiles of the market wage. The other 14 percent paid more. The other survey, also taken in 2000, looked at twenty pre-IPO dot-coms in Silicon Valley and the San Francisco Bay Area. It found that the companies had begun paying competitive salaries.

While wage substitution was a way for companies to make employees shoulder a larger share of the risks of ownership, options sometimes can have the opposite effect. For a few heady years during the late 1990s, some high-tech employees made so much money that they could just up and leave whenever they wished. At some companies, some workers, even a few lucky low-level ones, enjoyed windfall gains far beyond what they ever imagined possible. When that happened, some workers decided to drop out or retire and enjoy their newfound wealth.

During our discussion with the Portal employees, for example, Francine, the vice president, mentioned how she had cashed in $6 million worth of options before the stock price fell. Most of the others, who hadn't profited as handsomely, thought they might not still be working there if that had happened to them. "I mean, frankly, I'd be out of here," said Tom, a technical staffer. "Six and a half million, I'd have gone, too," agreed Jack, the finance administrator. Even Geoff, the engineer, said: "Yeah, I have to say, I'd be gone."

High-tech employees also talked about the mixed or even negative effect on morale that can occur when their vesting period approaches. Some employees start to focus on the riches they stand to make and tend not to care as much about their job. Vest in Peace, the joke went.

High-tech companies may have inadvertently contributed to the problem by being too generous with options at various times. During the market runup, companies as well as employees were caught up in the let's-all-get-rich-quick frenzy, so much so that even some employees thought their companies were passing out too many options. "A lot of the equity problems in the Valley and elsewhere come from kind of a 'They're doing it, so I have to,' thing," said Jerry, the Excite@Home engineer who at one point had options worth $15 million. "That's how it has gotten out of hand. A lot of us played other companies off of each other to get our current jobs. We said, 'Well they're giving me 10,000 options, so give me

20,000.' Then that offsets the scale internally to what other people have been brought in at. So it's just been this huge mess."

His colleague, Joe, felt likewise. "When I vested, I had my initial 10,000 options. Three months later, I got another 8,000 options, and a month later I got another 7,000. So I had 15,000 more options in my first four or five months of working there, and I don't even know why. I thought that I was doing a good job, but the person who was the senior VP of our work at the time just really liked me. The senior VP must have been given large pools of options every month to give out and I think he just picked out his favorites."

Whether it was the excessive generosity of employers or the excesses of investors madly driving up high-tech stock prices, CEOs had to cope with the inflated expectations many employees came to hold. Some executives dealt with the issue by trying to get employees not to obsess about the stock price. There's a story at Tibco about how Vivek Ranadive, the CEO, once tried to drive the point home. It was 1999 and the company had just gone public. The stock was shooting up and up every day and employees were buzzing in the halls, talking about the new kitchen they would put in or the new car or house they wanted to buy. One employee in particular—call him Paul—just couldn't contain himself. He was a New Yorker, an Italian, very loud, very funny, and his enthusiasm for the topic infected everyone.

One day, Ranadive happened to walk by when Paul, gabbing in the hall with friends, said: "If the stock hits a hundred in another week, I'm going to wear a dress to work." Ranadive heard him, and sure enough, the next day Tibco's stock not only hit a hundred but went to a hundred and twelve. So Ranadive put on a fashion show for Mr. Stock Obsessed. He brought in a catwalk, put on lights and music, and corralled some employees to act as judges. To outfit Paul, a large man, Ranadive got an aide to buy half dozen size 13 pumps and six long gowns, size 18.

Paul was a good sport about it. He agreed to put on makeup and wear hats and gloves, plus a sash and a crown. Employees voted on the dress they liked the best and crowned him Miss Tibco. Everyone laughed and had a good time, including Paul. At the end, Ranadive got up and grabbed the mike and thanked him for playing along. But, he said, the point he wanted to make was a serious one: Don't focus on the stock price. Instead, everyone should focus on the customer. "I don't want to hear anyone else talking about it," he warned, "or you never know what will happen to you."

Sclavos, the VeriSign CEO, had a similar view. He pointed out that it can be risky for management to hype potential option winnings as the motivation for working so hard, since the stock market can be so volatile. Workers quickly realize that the up and down movement of the stock price doesn't correlate to their own dedication to the job day by day. Those whose options hadn't vested by the time the market peaked saw their paper wealth go up in smoke, no matter how much time they had put in.

Still, the wild stock market ride has proven the durability of the stock option model. A lot of employees significantly expanded their incomes with option wealth. A few super-lucky ones made millions and quit with their loot. Plenty of others thought they made millions while the market was flying high, then watched in frustration and dismay as their paper wealth slipped away when share prices sank. Latecomers could only stand by helplessly as sagging stock values made their high-priced options worthless.

Throughout it all, the good relationships have survived. Options lifted up the hopes of many employees to crazy and unreasonable levels, and dashed them right down again, but most high-tech employees didn't turn against their employers. "The underlying motivational results that we see options create for people is real," said Excite chairman Bell. "I don't know why that would go away."

Bill, the young Tibco techie who helped out Jennifer, the events planner, had similar feelings, even after his company's stock sank in early 2001. "In these last couple months, when we've lost 80 percent of our value, or 92 percent, I have buddies calling me to say, 'What happened to your stock? Is everybody grumbling and talking about leaving?' I don't hear any of this. Because there is so much meat to the company, and everybody believes and is motivated. It's a good place to work."

We've described options as a form of risk sharing between employees and corporate owners. Originally, high-tech firms offered options to

lure workers to a new industry. Workers took on a greater risk of losing their livelihood than they would have had if they had taken a job
in a better-established corporation. In exchange, the company's
founders and outside shareholders gave them a chance to share in
any wealth the company would create if it was successful.

The run rate adds to the complexity of the equation. If options
were offered solely to induce an employee to join a company with
uncertain prospects, why should management keep issuing more
every year? The answer from executives was retention; they needed
options to make sure they didn't lose the talent they had worked so
hard to get.

However, repricing or exchanging options seem to undercut
some of the risk-sharing aspects of partnership capitalism. After all,
high-tech workers knew when they signed on that options would
only pay off if the company prospered and its stock value increased.
Making sure they get paid even if it doesn't seems like changing the
rules of the game after it has been played. It seems to turn options
into something of a free lunch.

Wage substitution, on the other hand, seems to cut the other
way. Although the practice diminished in most companies after
their early years, it nonetheless implies that at least some high-tech
firms wanted employees to foot part of the bill for options, on top
of the job-security risk they took on by joining a new and untested
industry. Alternatively, you might argue that the company founders
were really trying to freeload not so much off of employees, but off
outside investors. A skeptic might say that entrepreneurs like Bezos
and Sclavos used investors to pay part of their wage bill.
Companies too unprofitable to support the market wage for qualified workers used investors' equity to help them out.

To make sense of all these puzzling issues we need to answer another question: How exactly do options create wealth for the companies that grant them? If high-tech companies only handed them
out because they were startups desperate to attract and retain workers in a tight labor market, they would have stopped doing so as the
industry matured or when the national unemployment rate shot up
in 2001. If that had occurred, it would suggest that stock options
are a short-lived phenomenon that probably don't have much to of-

fer to the rest of corporate America, at least over the long term. A large corporation might consider options for all its workers if it was caught in a particularly frenzied labor market, as indeed many were in the late 1990s. But a prudent CEO might not want to start passing out ownership stakes that stretch out over a decade or more just to deal with a labor crunch that would very likely ease after a few years. Certainly after the 2001 recession that reason didn't seem so compelling anymore.

However, stock options, and the employee ownership culture that goes with them, are part of a larger shift in corporations towards sharing equity with knowledge workers. This is happening because a partnership approach generates value for corporations that goes beyond recruitment and retention. To understand this new reality, let's look at the economics of options for the companies that issue them.

# 6

# What Shareholders Gain
# by Giving Up Some of
# Their Ownership

Despite the staggering wealth high-tech employees lost when the stock market sank, by and large options have been a good deal for many of them, certainly for those who joined the company early on. But what about their employers? Do companies and their public shareholders come out ahead when they grant options to workers? Many High Tech 100 stockholders rightly believe that most of these companies' founders and many of their employees got a lot more from options than shareholders got from their stock. After all, employees cashed out a total of $78 billion from an industry that wiped out more than $1 trillion of investors' money.

So are options a zero-sum game? If that were the case, every grant would represent a potential gain to employees and a corresponding potential loss of equal value to the shareholders. Our view is that options can be a net plus for both sides, at least in a normal economic environment. High-tech workers did indeed come into a windfall that was at least partially undeserved during the market bubble. But in a market that rises and falls with less extremes, as is mostly the case in modern economies, options will bring benefits to shareholders and employees alike if they're used as part of a broader commitment to a culture of employee participation.

No question, though, public shareholders initially surrender something of value every time a company whose stock they own grants an option to an employee. The reason: Options water down their ownership, at least if they're exercised. Whenever an employee cashes in an option for a share of stock, the company then has more shares outstanding, diluting the percentage each stockholder owns. Of course, if the stock price doesn't increase, outside shareholders face no dilution from options. In effect, options have a built-in self-moderating mechanism. When the pie is growing, stockholders face a diminution of their percentage of ownership, but when it's not, they give up nothing.

Shareholders may feel generously inclined toward the workforce when the company's stock price is rising. But options represent much more than a good-times expression of gratitude. We believe they can help to create extra value that offsets the dilution. How? First, by attracting and retaining employees with experience, talent, and drive, options help management to build a workforce that can create innovations and grow the company. Second, in a participative corporate culture, options encourage employees to think and act like owners, thus spurring them to work more diligently and more efficiently. In addition, because options are a handoff of value from outside shareholders to employees, they put pressure on management and employees alike to make the company more successful than it otherwise would have been. The company must create enough extra wealth to offset the potential shift of ownership to employees.

Let's look at the mechanics of dilution to see how this works. Take a company that we'll call America Incorporated. It's founded with three shares of stock and is trading at $1 a share, so it has a market capitalization of $3. The founder owns one share, or a third of the outstanding stock. Two outside investors, maybe venture capitalists, each own one as well. All three owners thus have a third of ownership, entitling them to a third of the voting rights.

One day America Inc. decides to grant a stock option to an employee. The option entitles her to buy one share for $1 any time within the ten-year window that's typically found at most companies. America Inc. doesn't actually issue the share until the employee exercises the option. But the company has made a commitment to issue a new share, at least if the stipulations are met, such as a requirement that the employee remain with the company throughout a set vesting period. Finance experts often refer to the share promised through an option as the stock option overhang. In this case, America Inc.'s overhang is 33 percent.

If the stock price rises and the employee goes ahead and purchases her share when she's allowed to do so, the company then will have four shareholders, and four shares of stock outstanding. As a result, the 33 percent overhang will transform into a 25 percent real ownership stake. When that happens, the three original shareholders have their ownership diluted, from 33 to 25 percent each. Before the option was issued, the original shareholders could count on getting one-third of the future wealth America Inc. produced. Or if the company had been sold, each stockholder would have been entitled to a third of the sale price. Now, each person has only a 25 percent share of any transaction. Their voting rights in the corporation are likewise slashed to 25 percent.

Of course, employees have to pay money to buy the stock that an option entitled them to purchase. This goes to the corporate treasury. However, employees only exercise an option if the strike price, that is, the amount they must pay to the company, is below the market price. So if the option is exercised, the company won't gain enough income to completely offset the dilution of the original stockholders' ownership stake.

In large public corporations with millions of shares, the company often tries to offset the dilution by repurchasing shares on the open market. In other words, if our employee sold her $1 share on the open market, as most employees do when they exercise options, America Inc. could simply buy it back. However, it would have to pay the current market price. So if, for example, America Inc.'s stock had jumped to $2, the employee would sell it for a $1 profit. America Inc. would get the $1 strike price from the employee, and it would have to pay $1 to buy the stock in the marketplace. The original three shareholders would now each own a third of the company again, but America Inc. would be out $1 that could have gone toward expenses, profits, or new capital investments. So the cash cost of options to a company is the difference between the strike price and the market price at the time the option is exercised.

Most financial experts use the overhang as a measure of a company's potential dilution. Companies that offer options typically publish the information needed to compute this figure in their annual SEC filings. Wall Street looks at this and says: "America Inc. has a 33 percent overhang, so it has promised to dilute its ownership by a third."

We decided to use another approach to calculate a company's potential dilution. Instead of overhang, we looked at the amount of stock ownership employees and investors would have if all options were exercised. We use the term "total equity" to describe this combination of stock and option ownership, the same phrase we used in previous chapters to measure ownership in a company that issues options. We think this is a useful way to measure the potential dilution a company faces from options.

To see how much dilution occurred among the High Tech 100, let's look again at who owns these companies. We have already discussed the numbers in a different context, in Table 4.2 in Chapter 4. There, we showed how much potential and actual ownership High Tech 100 employees had accumulated through 2000. (The potential part was the total number of unexercised options they held as of that year. The actual part was the amount of stock they had.)

Table 6.1 shows employee options again, but this time with the dilutive effect they would have if they were cashed in.

Look how much public shareholders stood to have their ownership diluted by employee options. If no options were exercised in subsequent years, their ownership would represent 74 percent of the High Tech 100. If employees cashed in all their all options, the outside shareholders' stake would get knocked down to 58 percent. The only way they wouldn't lose these 16 percentage points is if the stock had remained flat or had fallen, dragging the options underwater. But of course, in that case the options would have no effect on outside stockholders.

Stock option capitalism involves risk sharing by all three partners in a corporation: shareholders, management, and employees. For example, the same dilution effect suffered by outside share-

**TABLE 6.1   The Dilution Public Shareholders Face from Employee Options**
(Average ownership shares of the High Tech 100 as of December 31, 2000)

|  | Stock before Dilution (%) | Options after Dilution (%) | Total Equity after Dilution (%) |
|---|---|---|---|
| Public shareholders | 74 | 0 | 58 |
| All insiders* | 26 | 22 | 42 |
| Employees** | 3 | 17 | 19 |
| Top five officers | 13 | 4 | 14 |
| CEO | 9 | 2 | 9 |
| Other four | 4 | 2 | 5 |
| Directors*** | 10 | 1 | 9 |

NOTES: *Total holdings of employees, top five officers, and directors.

**Excluding top five officers. Stock holdings include estimated purchases through employee share purchase plans.

***Includes stock owned by companies, such as venture capital firms, with which directors are affiliated.

The first column shows the percent of the High Tech 100's stock each group owned, before any outstanding options are exercised.

The second shows the percent of stock each group's options—both vested and unvested—would represent if they all had been exercised.

The third shows the percent of the stock, both from direct purchases and from options, that each would have owned if all outstanding options had been exercised.

SOURCE: Authors' analysis of SEC filings.

holders applies to the CEOs, other executives, and to the directors and the shareholders with whom they are affiliated. In trying to make the case that options are perks that management awards to the employee at the expense of the company's public shareholders, the press and many shareholder groups often lose sight of the fact that management's equity is diluted just as much as that of public stockholders. This is why a company's leaders must truly believe that options improve a company's performance; they're putting their own equity on the line with every option they issue to the workforce.

Another point to keep in mind: Even employees get diluted. While High Tech 100 workers don't hold that much direct stock ownership, even their 3 percent stands to be reduced when new options are granted. In fact, every new option issued also stands to dilute any existing options employees still own. So while the run rate replenishes an employee's ownership stake, it simultaneously waters it down as well. This adds further incentive for employees to strive to create extra value and increase the size of the pie for all stakeholders.

It's also clear that dilution isn't the same as the cumulative run rate. In the last chapter, we saw that the High Tech 100's run rate averaged 8 percent a year between 1997 and 2001. Yet shareholders in 2000 faced only a 16 percentage point dilution, not the 40 points you might expect if they gave away 8 percent a year for five years. You can't measure dilution simply by adding up how many options a company hands out every year. If that were the case, a company with a 10 percent run rate would transfer its entire ownership to employees after ten years. This doesn't happen because employees typically sell the stock they get from exercising their options. Since these shares are sold in the public market, they revert to outside shareholders again. As a result, annual option grants continually dilute outside shareholders, but the total dilution—and employees' collective ownership of the company—is kept largely in check.

The 16-point loss is thus a snapshot of the potential dilution outside shareholders faced as of 2000. It doesn't tell you how much their ownership already had been diluted in prior years. Nor does it tell you how much value they gained as an indirect result of that dilution. In addition, the number doesn't completely predict how much dilution shareholders actually will experience in the future. The 16 points may be lifted up or down by exchanges, regrantings, and repricings. It also may be altered by a lousy stock market, which could render some options worthless by the time their expiration date arrives. Still, this is about the best way possible to get a ballpark idea of how much ownership high-tech firms have promised to transfer from outside stockholders to their employees.

Now that we know at least roughly how much potential dilution high-tech shareholders accepted, we can begin to think more clearly about what they stood to get in return—and whether it was worth it. The first point to keep in mind is that options cost shareholders nothing if the company's stock price falls below the option's exercise price. Other stockholders are worse off due to the falling value of their shares, but the unused options don't alter their plight one way or another. This is just what happened to many high-tech and Internet firms after the market crash. Most employees lost much of the value of their options, so shareholders weren't diluted and won't be unless their company's stock price recovers.

If stock prices do rise, however, companies get numerous benefits that help to offset the dilution their shareholders face. One is a break on federal taxes. Typically, when an employee exercises an option, the tax code allows the company to deduct the "spread," which is the difference between the exercise price at which workers bought the stock and the market price at which they sold it. This can be a whopping number. For example, Microsoft racked up a $2.1 billion tax benefit from options in 2000, according to one estimate, while Cisco took $1.4 billion and Dell and Intel got roughly $900 million apiece.

The company gets the tax deduction even though it didn't actually spend any money to provide the option. The reasoning goes something like this: If the company wanted to replace those shares, it would have to go into the market and pay the going price. So it has given that much value to employees, a value the government treats as compensation. (We don't believe that it's accurate to think of options as compensation for labor performed; instead, it represents capital income that workers receive for sharing the risk of property ownership. But we'll leave that discussion for later on.)

Employers get to deduct the wages they pay their workers from the corporate tax bill, and they receive a similar deduction for the money employees get from their options. The result is that the company gets a nice tax subsidy from the feds for options. The tax break is no greater than the amount the employer would get if it had paid employees the same sum in wages. But of course, by using options the company didn't have to part with actual cash to get the tax savings.

The same thinking, however, doesn't carry over to the way a company reports its earnings to the public. Some critics of options see this inconsistency as allowing executives to dress up a company's image. Even though employers get a tax break for the cost of an option, they don't have to treat that very same option as an expense when it comes to reporting their profits to shareholders. Say Cisco gives its employees options worth 10 percent of its total outstanding stock this year. Now it's the end of the year and Cisco issues its annual report, telling stockholders how much money the company earned. Instead of calculating its profits by subtracting an estimate of the value of the 10 percent that employees stand to earn if they exercise their options down the road, Cisco can simply state the total profit figure as if the options never existed.

The critics say this allows companies to hide the true cost of employee options from their outside shareholders. While Cisco doesn't spend any actual cash to issue the option, it has given the employee something of value. In addition, many companies do wind up spending their profits after an option is exercised, in order to offset the dilution that occurs. This group holds that options should be treated at a real expense by the company, which should subtract their cost from its profits. Supporters, however, argue that the true impact of options is measured by the share dilution they bring. Companies already are required to report their earnings as diluted by options, they say, which is good enough.

The critics say it's a double standard to treat options as an expense for tax purposes but not for earnings reports. It can also be deceptive to shareholders, they argue. In 1997, Microsoft became one of the first companies to tell shareholders how much options might slice off the company's bottom line, although it did so only in a footnote. The answer was a lot: 17 percent to be exact, at least that year. Microsoft said that calculated the traditional way, it had earned $3.43 a share in the twelve months ending in June 1996. However, its profits fell to $2.85 once its estimate of the cost of employee options was included.

Microsoft acted because a few years earlier, the Financial Accounting Standards Board had tried to force all companies to treat options as an expense when calculating their profits. But the board had run into a flurry of protest and ultimately backed off. As a compromise, FASB required companies to report their option expenses in a footnote, which even today, after options have become so widespread, is all they must do. Microsoft hadn't changed its mind about the FASB effort, which it had opposed. But "we do recognize that options have a cost," Greg Maffei, Microsoft's chief financial officer, said at the time.

In 2001, the collapse of Enron Corporation drew attention to the issue all over again. Critics pointed out that Enron had received a large tax break for the options it gave to executives and other employees, which was part of the reason it paid no federal taxes between 1996 and 2000. The ensuing outcry triggered a great debate in Congress the following year about whether to get FASB to draw up new rules requiring companies to knock option costs off their profits. Critics such as Federal Reserve Board chairman Alan Greenspan began to push the idea. Earnings grew by 12 percent a year among the S&P 500 between 1995 and 2000, a figure that would have been slashed to 9.4 percent if companies had expensed their stock options, he said, citing internal Fed research.

In the summer of 2002, Senator Carl Levin, a Michigan Democrat, tried to get an amendment passed in Congress that would require companies to treat options as an expense. After it was blocked, he vowed to introduce the idea as a stand-alone bill in the fall. He won support from others, including Senate Majority Leader Tom Daschle, a Democrat. Several companies decided to get on board, too. The Coca-Cola Company, the Washington Post Company, Bank One, General Electric, General Motors, and Citigroup all announced that summer that they would begin counting options as an expense against profits. Even Amazon, which relies much more on options than those companies, said it would start expensing them.

Once you set aside the tax issues, however, the primary benefit options bring to companies is a motivated workforce. As we keep saying, giving workers an incentive to think like owners can be valuable to shareholders if it helps to make the firm more productive.

Initially, most high-tech companies threw options at employees not to make them more productive, but just to get them in the door. Very quickly, options became the norm and high-tech firms found that they couldn't hire anyone without an option grant, even if they had wanted to. "Silicon Valley is now twenty years into it, so everybody expects" options, said BEA Systems chairman Bill Coleman. "In a high-growth industry, the options are imperative. You are only high growth if you can hire the great people. You can only hire the best people if you are giving them not only the challenge and the opportunities, but the ability to benefit from the growth."

Still, options work as a long-run strategy only if they cause the company to grow fast enough to support a reasonable run rate. If options are not an ongoing part of the picture, employees may slip into a "What have you done for me lately" mindset.

At a more conceptual level, partnership capitalism is an attempt to address one of the great mysteries of economics: Where do productivity advances come from? To economists, productivity means how much someone can produce by working for some unit of time, usually an hour or a day. Increases in productivity are the key to higher living standards in industrialized countries. The more value each person can produce in an hour, the more wealth there will be in the economy. If productivity grows faster, the economy has more goods and services to offer. If it slows or falls, so, over time, will consumption and living standards.

The same holds true for individual companies. If stock option capitalism helps firms to boost their productivity and profitability and, ultimately, the value of their shares, the options will pay for themselves, even over and above the recruitment and retention value they bring.

Economists have never really been able to pinpoint the precise causes of productivity growth. For decades, they focused mostly on capital investment, which helps companies buy the new equipment that makes it possible for the same number of workers to produce more in an hour or day. Investment also funds the research and development needed to come up with advances in technology that achieve the same purpose. But as the economy began to shift away from manufacturing toward services, economists began to consider the role of human capital as well.

Today, 80 percent of the U. S. workforce is involved in nonmanufacturing activities that depend as much on human knowledge as on the equipment workers use. As a result, economists are no longer so confident that they know the precise causes of productivity growth. "Knowledge is not like a stock of ore waiting to be mined," wrote Zvi Griliches, a leading productivity expert and Harvard University economist, in a 1994 article on the subject. "It is an assortment of information in continuous flux . . . . It takes effort . . . to access, retrieve, and adapt to one's own use."

In fact, in most modern theories of how economies work, a good portion of productivity gains are simply assumed to happen. Economists have been unable to define with absolute clarity the conditions that bring about the breakthrough technologies or work methods that lead to higher productivity. They know some advances come from inventions, such as the light bulb, the personal computer, and so on. Others come from a critical examination of current production methods, leading to innovative changes that promise to wring more goods or services out of an hour's work.

But why such advances happen when they do is less clear. Inventions and innovations are the deus ex machina of economic productivity theory. They're what economists call "exogenous" or outside, factors, meaning they're not something for which they can specify the cause. Although economists do discuss how factors such as market structures can enhance or retard innovation, they can't predict when these things are going to happen. Sometimes they occur more frequently, sometimes less so.

Partnership capitalism is an effort to sidestep the unresolved questions about the sources of productivity improvements. While the partnership approach doesn't exactly answer those questions, either, it does rely on the assumption that changes in employee behavior can be a key cause. High-tech companies certainly haven't come up with a way to guarantee the invention of the steam engine, the assembly line, or the next Internet. But the atmosphere of employee ownership they have cultivated improves the conditions in which inventions and innovations are most likely to occur.

How? By encouraging employees to put their minds to work. Scientists and researchers need to be motivated to strive for the inventions. Similarly, innovations in the workplace, which often come from those directly involved in producing a good or service, require a collection of people sharing common attitudes toward group goals. The financial incentives options bring are designed to spur individual employees to work together, so that the social bonds among them encourage everyone to work harder or smarter on the job every day.

If the options culture works properly, it spurs workers to produce more in a day's work, bringing gains for employees and outside investors alike. "There is a tradeoff between dilution of the shareholders and wealth creation," explained Vivek Ragavan, the former CEO of Redback Networks. "I come up on the side of more dilution, because ultimately it creates more value. The more equitably options are distributed among the company's employees, the better, because it helps to grow the company fast, to create faster cycles of innovation, to create more new compelling products. So the dilution is drowned out by the value created."

Other executives express similar views. Richard Tavan, the then executive vice president for Engineering at Tibco Software, explained to us how he thinks about this issue in a 2001 interview.

> We're creating a company in which human resources are key, in which innovation is our lifeblood. The physical barriers to entry in the software industry are very low. Anybody can put together a team of programmers and write a piece of software. Our advantage is in the experience that our employees build up working with us, their ability to make the thousands of decisions. Programmers make a lot more decisions than assembly line workers. For programmers, every line of code is a decision. You want to make sure that they make every one of those decisions in a way that's going to further the objectives of the company.
>
> There is no way management can control that directly, so you just have to create an environment where people are learning all the time . . . and a culture where everyone feels a sense of ownership. An engineer gets out of a meeting and he walks off in a snit and he sits down in his cubicle to write a piece of code, if he is sitting there fuming at the boss, chances are he is not going to be doing the best programming that he

might otherwise be capable of doing. If that ends up in a bug being delivered to a customer in an obscure situation a year later the customer is going to be upset and it's going to reflect negatively on our company.

Many high-tech founders believe firmly that options pay back more than they cost. "When you start a company, you own 100 percent of this pie, which consists of zero at that point," says Naveen Jain, the Infospace CEO. "If you can somehow have ten other people who believe it is their pie and they want to make their small section of it be bigger, that means you're going to have an even bigger pie. So [granting options] is a very selfish thing to do. If my employees work hard for themselves, they are really working hard for me."

The same logic, Jain argued, applies to outside shareholders as well, who prosper when the company they own goes well. "For the company to be successful, everybody has to think they own that piece of pie, and that they are trying to make a big pie out of it."

Still, it's possible that the option incentive will create extra productivity, but not enough to offset the dilution it entails. One famous statement of this view comes from Warren Buffett, the chairman of Berkshire Hathaway Incorporated and one of America's most successful investors. Buffett once called options a "royalty on the passage of time." In other words, if a company's stock price improves, employees get wealth from their options even if they do nothing to earn it. His notion is that options give employees a free ride, since the stock market has generally gone up (even after you factor in all the down periods like the most recent slump). Employees get wealth not for investing capital as other shareholders do, but simply because they happen to be employed at a company that offers options.

Buffett fired off a related criticism in early 2002. In a letter to Berkshire shareholders, he said that options don't require their holders to take as much responsibility for their decisions as direct stock ownership does. He described a firm Berkshire had acquired the year before in which fifty-five executives and managers had put up $100,000 each to buy part of the company. "As they would not be if they had options, all of these managers are true owners," Buffett wrote. "They face the downside of decisions as well as the upside. They incur a cost of capital. And they can't 'reprice' their stakes: What they paid is what they live with."

While Buffett frequently is quoted as a critic of options, he mostly seems concerned with executive options. It's not entirely clear if he holds the same views about partnership capitalism, which extends options to most or all workers. In 1985, long before the high-tech option culture became widespread, he wrote about employee options in his annual letter to shareholders. He said: "I want to emphasize that some managers whom I admire enormously—and whose operating records are far better than mine— disagree with me regarding . . . options. They have built corporate cultures that work, and . . . options have been a tool that helped them. By their leadership and example, and by the use of options as incentives, these managers have taught their colleagues to think like owners. Such a culture is rare and when it exists should perhaps be left intact—despite inefficiencies and inequities that may infest the option program." Buffett may well have in mind the culture at Microsoft; his respect for Bill Gates, reportedly a personal friend, has been widely noted in the press.

The critique implicit in Buffett's negative view of options is powerful, but we believe ultimately unpersuasive. What Buffett misses is that employees aren't really getting something for free, at least not if options work as they're designed to do and the company builds a strong "think like an owner" culture. While workers don't part with financial capital to get their ownership stake, most do invest their human capital: their skills, their know-how, their teamwork, their willingness to participate in a demanding entrepreneurial work culture, or even just their plain hard work, as so many high-tech employees have done.

The valid aspect of Buffett's criticism is that public stockholders have no guarantees about how much extra productivity employees will bring about if they're granted options. But the problem is narrower than Buffett's statement assumes. To see why, imagine that a company's stock price would rise by 10 percent a year if it didn't issue options to employees. Now take the same company and assume that it does grant options, diluting public shareholders by, say, 8 percent a year (the average run rate of the High Tech 100.) For investors to come out ahead, employees generally must generate enough extra productivity gains to offset the 8 percent dilution, and still leave the company with a return that surpasses the 10 percent investors would have enjoyed if they hadn't gone the option route.

If the company's stock price improves only as much as it would have done anyway, then Buffett's criticism would be accurate. Employees would have gained option wealth without producing enough extra value to offset the dilution shareholders experienced. This is a real issue, and not a trivial one. But it by no means stands as a reason to reject the whole option approach. Instead, the potential gap between shareholder dilution and the extra productivity options can bring represents the portion of the risk investors assume under stock option capitalism.

For companies and their investors, the risk is that employees won't work any harder or smarter even if they get their options. If the stock nonetheless rises above employees' strike price, their options would be in the money and they would get the free ride Buffett worries about. In that case, investors would foot the option bill with diluted ownership. But if the incentive works, productivity rises more than it otherwise would have done, leading to greater profits and a higher stock price, at least in the long run. When that happens, stock option capitalism isn't a zero-sum game, since investors and workers both come out ahead.

Buffett's concern, that options provide investors with no guarantee of a payoff, is certainly valid. But that's true of any corporate investment. A company can overpay for an acquisition, or sink money into a new product that doesn't work or that no one wants to buy. Likewise, it can invest in a worker incentive program and get no return. However, this isn't a good reason to dismiss options as worthless, as long as the chance of the reward is commensurate with the risk involved.

Options are actually even better than many other investments, because they offer a greater measure of downside protection than usually is available. Why? Because unlike most investments, failure costs stockholders nothing since no dilution will occur if the stock price goes nowhere at all. Buffett is right if companies reprice or ex-change their options, as many High Tech 100 companies indeed did. Aside from this, however, shareholders gain if options bring a higher stock price than would have occurred, but they lose nothing if the stock goes nowhere. So their only risk is the relatively narrow possibility that the stock will muddle along somewhere in between, giving workers a free ride. That's the nature of risk sharing. It's pos-sible to shrink the risk to shareholders even more, as some in-vestors want to do, by indexing options to a company's perform-ance. For example, a company could grant options that only can be exercised if the firm's stock price beats the average share perform-ance of the industry it's in, or of a broad market average. Of course, doing so would put more of the risk onto workers and lower the in-centive effect options bring.

One big exception is a stock market bubble like the one high-tech and many other companies experienced in the late 1990s. Employees' creativity and hard work certainly played a major role in the birth and success of the Internet, which contributed greatly to the meteoric stock gains of the era. But even ardent supporters might be hard-pressed to argue that rank-and-file tech workers cre-ated an average of $300,000 each in extra value (the amount High Tech 100 workers got from cashing in options prior to the 2000 crash). In light of that $1 trillion investors lost when the bubble popped, workers' options winnings may seem excessive and at least partially undeserved in terms of how much economic value they likely created.

While we believe that some of this windfall was indeed excessive, it's also true that many investors made windfall profits as well during the stock market bubble. Remember that for every person who bought a share as prices rose, there was someone else on the other side of the transaction who made money by selling. Stock bubbles are like games of musical chairs: Everyone wins except those stuck holding the stock after the peak. The investors who raked in billions didn't deserve that money any more than employees.

One indication of this can be found in the track record of the High Tech 100. We saw in Chapter 4 that on average, their shares collapsed by 96 percent from the peak of the market in early 2000 to the end of July 2002. Fully 57 percent of these companies were trading below their IPO price as of that date, leaving most of their public shareholders with substantial losses. However, the other 43 percent were still ahead, even after all the air had gone out of the high-tech bubble. Eight of the companies, including Cisco and AOL, still boasted astounding returns of more than 1,000 percent since their IPOs. Many of the others still above their IPO prices posted returns of 100 to 500 percent over their lives as public companies. Despite the downturn, some investors clearly came out ahead, just as some workers did—assuming, of course, that they had the foresight to invest in the companies that would form the High Tech 100. (See Appendix B for their stock performance.)

Risk sharing in extreme situations like stock market bubbles is much messier than in a normal stock market environment. But it remains risk sharing nonetheless, with investors and workers both subject to gains and losses from the property they share.

Bubble aside, if we return to Buffett's passage-of-time statement, it's clear that it misses another aspect of how options distribute risk to both employees and investors in a normal stock market. If options function like they're supposed to, employees work smarter or harder. Yet just as investors can spend their ownership and suffer more in dilution than they win back in higher productivity, so can employees expend their human capital and get back nothing in return.

This can happen if their company's stock price doesn't rise above their strike price despite all their extra effort, as is bound to occur in some companies at least some of the time. After all, markets aren't perfect. Even when a company does well, its stocks can fall as part of an industry or market retreat. Employees also may find themselves working at a company with a lousy management. If the top officers make major strategic mistakes and the stock suffers, workers with options will lose out right along with other shareholders. In such cases, no amount of additional diligence on their part will make up for management's errors.

Workers take on risk individually as well. They may be highly motivated and work harder than they have ever done before. But their effort may be wasted if, for example, they have the misfortune to be thrown in with fellow employees who don't become motivated by their ownership, or simply aren't very talented.

The conclusion we reach is that partnership capitalism spreads both risks and rewards fairly evenly between shareholders and employees alike (particularly if companies don't reprice). For both groups, it's a little like the old saying, "You have to spend money to make money." Employees face relatively little risk if they just do their job the normal way and earn a standard wage. But if they work harder, and invest extra human capital in their firm, options may return them a measure of the extra wealth they helped to create. Stockholders face a complementary equation. Options entail a risk that a stockholder will surrender equity and receive little or even nothing in return. But they bring a promise of greater reward as well.

SAIC CEO Bob Beyster says he granted workers majority ownership of his company because he thought it was fair, but was surprised at what happened. "The crazy thing about it was, the more I gave the company away, the more money I made," said Beyster. "At one time, I had 20 percent of the company. Now I have 1.5 percent." (SAIC had a market value of about $6.7 billion in 2002.) "I don't know what would have happened if I had kept it all. But I do know that the more I parceled the stock out to people in the company, the more my own stock was worth. When I founded SAIC, I could have chosen to not make available as much equity to the employees. Had I done that, I am convinced that today I would own a much larger percentage of a far less valuable company." Today, SAIC's 41,000 employees own 79 percent of its stock.

Plenty of other high-tech founders feel the same way. For example, Chris Wheeler, the InterNAP Chief Technology Officer, owned 25 percent of the company when he cofounded it with colleagues in 1995. By the end of 2000, he owned just 3 percent and employees owned 16 percent. Why did he go along with such dilution? "Here in Seattle it all centers around Microsoft," he told us in mid-2001. "Microsoft was a great example for us. They got great people and those people worked like crazy, twenty-four hours a day. We thought that this sharing-the-ownership issue was a gigantic piece of why people did that. People we knew who worked there felt like they were part of the company, like they were making a difference, and the company actually rewarded you for making that difference. So we looked at ourselves and said, 'We want the employee ownership of this company to be as large as it possibly can be."

Still, if options make sense for investors when employees produce more than they otherwise would, that leaves the question of whether this in fact actually happened with the High Tech 100. Put it another way, would investors have fared any differently if the companies had not diluted shareholders by handing out so many employee stock options? There's no way to answer with ironclad certainty, since no one can repeat history to see what would have happened absent options. However, there are several clues that suggest that the answer is yes for many of the companies and their investors.

One very broad answer is that many of the High Tech 100, or maybe even most, might not even have existed without such financial incentives. We already discussed how the Internet industry was born amid intense competition for the kind of talent these firms needed. Many of the firms very well may not have been able to hire or retain competent people in such a labor market. Many of the breakthrough ideas might not even have happened if these mostly startup firms hadn't been able to use options to lure some of the most innovative employees away from more established companies.

Another perspective comes from the dozen or so high-tech CEOs and top officers we spoke with about the issue. Most of them remain convinced that options more than paid for themselves. Since most were major stockholders, and usually the founders to boot, they personally would bear much of the financial loss if they were wrong. Also, high-tech CEOs continued to pass out options after the market crash, suggesting that even such an extreme test didn't shake their faith in the partnership approach.

There's also some evidence that Wall Street went along with the theory of options. After all, few high-tech firms encountered a wave of investor complaints about the practice, even after their stocks plunged by 90 percent.

Some critics argued that the entire industry gave away far too much equity to workers, and that the excessive dilution ultimately led to the 2000 crash, or at least exacerbated it. To test this hypothesis, we did numerous statistical analyses of the relationship between the size of option grants and the stock performance of the High Tech 100.

We found no correlations to support the hypothesis. The stock prices of those firms that had been the most generous with options didn't do any worse in the crash than their stingier rivals. Their fall was no greater from the top of the market in March of 2000 to its first bottom in September of 2001. What's more, the shares of the firms that handed out more options actually rebounded more quickly in the initial recovery that had taken place by the end of January 2002. We found that for every 1 percent increase in option ownership by employees, there was about a 3-percentage-point higher rebound in the stock price from that September to January of 2002. Similarly, the High Tech 100 firms with the most total employee equity, from both stock options and direct stock ownership, also had a better rebound.

The implication: Excessive options played no role in the bursting of the high-tech bubble, at least not among the top hundred companies in the sector of the industry focused on the Internet. The findings also suggest that it made sense for High Tech 100 companies to keep partnership capitalism going through the bust, and that it would have been self-defeating to abandon the idea when trouble came along.

These data suggest that stock options may have helped—and certainly didn't hurt—the performance and survival of the High Tech 100. Nonetheless, these companies can't tell us definitively whether options are a net plus for shareholders or not. Most of them simply haven't been around long enough to compile a track record that would satisfy a rigorous economist. In addition, there's no control group: They all use options, so there's no way to get an objective comparison with similar firms that chose more traditional ways of recruiting and compensating workers.

Instead, the most compelling evidence that shareholders gain over the long term from employee ownership through options comes from corporate America itself. High-tech and other traditional firms have used options for several decades, most just for top executives, but some of them for all or almost all of their employees. Other companies have embraced employee ownership through ESOPs, as well as profit sharing and similar financial incentives.

In addition, since at least the late 1970s, U.S. companies have experimented with just about every workplace innovation used by the high-tech firms, as well as many others, including teamwork systems; the Japanese notion of *kaizen*, or continuous improvement; "horizontal" (that is, more equal) management; employee participation in decisionmaking; and quality circles.

As we'll see in the next chapter, economists and academics have raked over every one of these efforts, and come to the conclusion that in general, they all pay off if done properly. Not for every firm that has ever tried one, and not in every year. But on average, over the years, numerous studies have shown that every form of shared ownership has added to the corporate bottom line in a multitude of ways.

# 7

# The Evidence that
# Shareholders Come Out Ahead

The High Tech 100 didn't come up with the idea that sharing ownership with employees might be a good way to stimulate greater productivity. For more than a century, major corporations have been experimenting with a variety of such plans, including stock options, profit sharing, and direct employee ownership of stock through ESOPs, 401(k)s, and stock purchase plans. Many employers also have embraced nonhierarchical workplace themes designed to encourage employees to think and act like owners, such as bottom-up decisionmaking, teamwork, and fewer levels of management. These are often summed up by terms such as employee participation, employee involvement, or high-performance work systems.

The High Tech 100's signature contribution has been to fuse all of these elements together and attempt to make them the norm across an entire industry. We came up with the phrase partnership, or stock option, capitalism to get across the idea that there is more at work here than options alone. A new form of capitalism, and of the corporation, has been created by the combination of financial ownership for a broad group of workers and far-reaching changes in workplace culture.

But does this new corporate form really make sense for corporate America? In the last chapter, we explained how partnership capitalism can pay off for companies and investors over the long term if they gain enough added productivity to offset the dilution of shareholders' ownership that stock options entail. But is there any tangible evidence that companies do in fact enjoy such gains?

Our answer is that such evidence exists in abundance, even though we can't prove it with companies as new as the High Tech 100. Instead, the proof lies in the rich history of sharing the risks and rewards of ownership at traditional companies, which has existed in various forms in the United States for more than 200 years. Stock options are one of the newest forms, but as we'll see in more detail in the next chapter, most companies have reserved them for the corporate elite.

Even setting aside stock options, though, employers today share ownership with workers at nearly 12,000 U.S. companies that offer their employees shares through one or more of these plans. All told, they covered about 24 million workers in 2002, or 23 percent of the workforce. Employees owned a majority of their company in nearly a fifth of these firms, and 31 to 50 percent in another third of them. Nearly 70 percent of the 24 million employee owners work in large public companies, where they typically own less than 5 percent of the stock. However, those with stakes above 5 percent owned an average of 12 percent of the stock. The other 7 million or so work at some 9,000 private companies, mostly smaller ones. (See Appendix C for a more detailed picture of employee ownership in America.)

In the past twenty-five years, researchers have done more than seventy empirical studies of these forms of risk sharing. Taken together, the studies provide compelling evidence for the net gain that the partnership approach can produce for a company's public shareholders.

This is a pivotal point of the book. We believe that the high-tech approach of bundling together a range of different risk-sharing ideas, with stock options at the core, is a worthwhile investment for many traditional companies and their shareholders, no matter what industry they're in. We will show that on average, over many years, each one of the ideas the High Tech 100 pulled together clearly has boosted corporate performance in traditional companies—even after dilution is taken into account.

The three of us have been studying and writing about various forms of employee ownership and profit sharing for most of our professional careers. The two academics among us have written numerous books and articles on most of the elements of partnership capitalism. For example, in 1988, Blasi surveyed everything he could find on the subject in a book called *Employee Ownership: Revolution or Ripoff?* In 1991, he and Kruse wrote *The New Owners,* which documented the emergence of widespread employee ownership through ESOPs, 401(k)s, and profit-sharing plans. In a 1993 book called *Profit Sharing, Does It Make a Difference?,* Kruse analyzed all the studies others had done on profit sharing up until then, and added new evidence. In 1995, we surveyed the literature on ESOPs for the National Bureau of Economic Research, which we then did again in 2001.

For this book, we did a similar survey of all the major studies we could find on the four key aspects of partnership capitalism: direct employee stock ownership, profit sharing, broad-based stock options, and employee participation. The studies look at how each one affects measures of corporate performance such as productivity, profit margins, return on assets, and return on equity. In addition, we looked at studies that tried to analyze the combination of financial ownership and cultural changes.

The results surprised even us, not because they were positive, but because they were so extensive and so uniform. We had read most of the studies when they came out, and of course we had done a fair number of them ourselves. But no one, including the three of us, ever has taken the time to stand back and synthesize all the findings gathered over the years. When we did so for this book, it became clear that more than enough evidence now has accumulated to draw firm judgments about the economic effects of employee ownership.

The most striking conclusion: Every major study found that investors come out ahead if their company adopted key elements of partnership capitalism. Not one found a negative result in terms of the total returns shareholders experienced. In fact, when you look at the major studies of stockholder returns, none even found that investors simply break even by investing in a basket of companies that adopted these approaches to employee ownership. All showed that public shareholders came out ahead. Of course, not every single company profits when it pursues one or more of these ideas. Studies look at averages, and by definition some companies are above the average and some below it. Still, it's clear that on average, the various approaches to employee ownership produced strongly positive results for shareholders.

So how big are the gains to investors? While each study found somewhat different results, they all came within more or less the same broad range. We added up all the conclusions and averaged them into a single finding for each of the four elements. Roughly speaking, we found that the partnership approach improves a company's productivity level by about 4 percentage points, compared to firms that don't adopt such practices. Total shareholder returns increase by some 2 percentage points relative to other firms. Profit levels—as measured by return on assets, return on equity, and profit margins—jump by about 14 percent.

It's important to be clear about the difference between higher levels and higher rates of growth. The studies we looked at found that productivity, profits, and shareholder returns get a one-time bump up to a higher level. In other words, if a company's productivity is one hundred units of goods or services an hour, partnership capitalism would bump that up to a hundred and four. It doesn't mean that the company's productivity growth rate would improve from say, 3 percent a year to 7 percent a year and remain at the higher level, which would be unrealistic.

Similarly, if a company's total shareholder return averaged 10 percent a year without employee ownership, it came in 2 points higher, at 12 percent a year, with it. The higher levels, not a higher annual rate of increase, are sustained indefinitely. So a company that creates a successful culture of risk sharing will lift its productivity and profits, and keep it at the higher level. It's a one-time gain, but a permanent one as long as the risk-sharing system remains in place.

There's another important point to keep in mind here as well. The gains in profits and returns came after the dilution borne by outside shareholders has been factored in. On average, we estimate that the companies in all these studies granted roughly 8 percent of their shares to employees. These shares are counted in each company's total, along with all the shares held by outside investors. So when a study examines how the company's stock price fared, for example, it's looking at the performance after this 8 percent dilution has occurred. In other words, the studies show that on average, companies and their investors made a profit on partnership approaches, including stock options, over and above any ownership they dished out to employees. They gave workers an 8 percent ownership stake, and in return enjoyed an average of a 2-percentage-point higher return on the diluted shares they still held.

**TABLE 7.1  How Risk Sharing Pays Off for Companies and Their Shareholders**

| Performance Measure | Gain from Partnership Capitalism |
| --- | --- |
| Total shareholder returns | 2 percentage points |
| Productivity | 4 percentage points |
| Return on equity | 14% |
| Return on assets | 12% |
| Profit margins | 11% |
| Average employee ownership | 8%* |

NOTES: *After dilution

Total shareholder returns include stock price appreciation and reinvested dividends.

Productivity is defined as output per employee in some studies and as value-added per employee in others.

Return on equity is defined as after-tax profits divided by the outstanding shares.

Return on assets is defined as pretax profits divided by a firm's assets.

Profit margins are income before extraordinary items, taxes, and depreciation, divided by total sales.

SOURCE: Authors' analysis of more than seventy empirical studes.

These numbers are based on evidence gathered over the last several decades. However, similar experiments have gone on for much longer. To fully appreciate the context in which such ideas arose and just how solid the findings about them are, you need to understand the extensive history of partnership capitalism in the United States. The idea, broadly conceived, has a lengthy pedigree that actually predates modern capitalism, stretching back to seventeenth- and eighteenth-century America. Indeed, the underlying concept—sharing property ownership to produce greater economic wealth—has popped up in the most unexpected places in American history. For example, before the European settlers showed up, the Iroquois allocated land to clans who used it to jointly farm and hunt (although their notion of property as communal rather than individual provided a much different context).

Not long after, European settlers employed indentured servitude as a way to share economic uncertainty within the Western concept of individual private property. Indentured servitude today is usually seen as something akin to virtual slavery, which indeed the practice often degenerated into. Still, it also sometimes helped property owners in the New World to attract and motivate workers from Europe. Similarly, it allowed some workers a chance to escape feudal Europe and work toward a financial independence they could never achieve at home. American landowners shared some of the cost of the voyage across the Atlantic, as well as the value of their property, with people willing to come from Europe and work for a set period of time. Rather than today's wage and salary system, servants worked for food and lodging, plus in many cases capital assets such as tools, a share of the crop, or even plots of land they could get after being released from their contract. Like modern-day companies that share stock ownership with employees, property owners sometimes extended rough forms of profit sharing or a promise of partial ownership rights to workers in the hopes that the land would generate more value than it otherwise would.

Probably the purest form of risk sharing between capital and labor in America came on nineteenth-century whaling ships. Early in the 1800s, most whalers were small vessels that took short voyages. Each trip was organized as if both the ship's owner and all the crew were investors. No one got a wage, and all profits were split amongst owner and crew according to a set formula that gave each person a share called a "lay." The lay certainly isn't something that most Americans today would perceive as an equitable division of risk and reward. But the practice, at least in abstraction, represented a clear notion of owners and employees as partners. As such, it was a marked departure from the standard view of property owners as capitalists who hire workers for a fixed wage, even though the system often degenerated into the exploitation of sailors.

Another manifestation of the partnership approach came in the Homestead Act of 1862, which was an ambitious effort to use the power of government to stimulate widespread property ownership. The law, signed by President Abraham Lincoln, allowed men over twenty-one and women who headed a household to take legal ownership of any public land, up to 160 acres, after they had farmed it for five years. (However, native Americans largely were excluded.) While homesteading involved farming, a job far afield for most Americans today, the basic concept shared many similarities with modern-day stock options. Homesteaders could get property from sweat equity, that is, from the work they performed, rather than from any cash they paid. The right—or option—to obtain the property could only be exercised after a specified period of work. In other words, it vested over a certain number of years. Individuals could buy and sell both their option to the property, and the property itself, once they gained possession. The option was made available to a broad number of people, and individuals could accumulate several options over their lifetime.

The intent of homesteading (though not always the reality) was to extend property ownership to those who couldn't accumulate enough capital to purchase it on their own. The idea illustrates just how deeply the notion of widespread property ownership is embedded in the American psyche—and how the federal government time and again has acted to advance it. Homesteading represented a remarkable attempt at social engineering, and gave a wide range of Americans access to property ownership in an economy where farmland was a key source of capital wealth. By doing so, the government blurred the line between owners of capital and common workers, allowing the latter to share in some of the wealth that comes from owning a productive asset.

About the same time that (usually white) settlers were homesteading in the West, newly freed slaves adopted a very different form of property sharing during the Reconstruction era of the post–Civil War South. Sharecropping emerged after promises to extend land ownership to free blacks were abandoned by the government. The term "sharecropping" leaves a bad taste in the mouth today, conjuring up images of dirt-poor black farmers in thrall to abusive white owners. These connotations have much validity, since there was considerable racism and exploitation in many sharecropping relationships, which grew directly out of the slave system that preceded it. Still, the practice, at least in theory, had elements of broad-based risk sharing that are not widely recognized today.

Sharecropping evolved as a way for white landowners to cope with the uncertainties of farming amid the ruined economy of the defeated South. Landlords provided the land and all supplies, including food, a horse, a mule, and use of a house. In return, the worker supplied the labor, and agreed to hand over a quarter to a half of the crop to the landlord at the end of the season. The worker also promised to live up to the landlord's expectations and be open to advice. Every plantation owner had to worry about whether there would be a crop each year, as well as whether it would get harvested and what price the market would pay for it. Sharing crops split these risks between the owner and the workers even though these risks weren't fairly shared and sharecropping did little to lift up American blacks.

While we certainly don't endorse sharecropping or indentured servitude, they illustrate the repeated efforts America has made to create alternatives to the standard wage system. Neither represented true partnerships between capital and labor, and in practice both caused extensive suffering. But to the degree that the idea can be separated from the practice, they and homesteading can be seen as attempts to spread the fruits of property ownership among many people as a way of coping with economic uncertainty. One goal was to entice employees to work harder and share in the risk of ownership so that the property could be used more efficiently, thus creating more wealth than the original owner could do alone.

By giving up partial rights to their property or profits, asset holders hoped to persuade workers to act like owners and take part in new labor markets, despite the tremendous uncertainty and risk involved for them. Owners also wanted to get the labor they were having trouble obtaining by just paying a wage, as well as more motivated workers. For their part, workers at least sometimes became stakeholders in a profit-making venture. They often gained access to capital that they couldn't afford simply by saving money from their wages. Some also got the right to a portion of the financial reward typically reserved for property owners.

In the end, whaling, indentured servitude, and sharecropping all failed as alternatives to the system of paying conventional wages. They did so in part because workers in those days largely lacked the power to defend their interests, and no authority did it for them. As a result, property owners took advantage of them, which ultimately caused each idea to collapse when workers found alternative ways to earn a living. Still, imperfect as they were, all of these experiments demonstrate the powerful incentive property owners have had to share ownership and risk with workers. They also show that Americans have tried numerous times to create alternatives to the standard practice of paying a wage for a day's work. All of these approaches involved an easing of the rigid definition of private property that has dominated Western political thought since the days of the philosopher John Locke.

Similar efforts have been tried time and again within modern capitalism. Throughout American history, some of capitalism's most illustrious stalwarts have preached, and practiced, the virtues of making employees part owners of the companies that employ them. Some of the earliest efforts involved sharing profits with employees. While not every profit-sharing plan gives workers actual stock ownership, they all divvy up its risks and rewards with them. Albert Gallatin, who was secretary of the Treasury when Thomas Jefferson was president, set up a profit-sharing plan in 1795 at a company he owned called the Pennsylvania Glass Works. Other businesses tried similar approaches throughout the 1800s, often involving a significant degree of ownership by workers. For example, starting in the late 1790s, small groups of skilled craft workers such as ironmongers and glassblowers set up firms they owned themselves. They did so to resist mounting efforts by entrepreneurs to organize skilled workers into factories and pay them low wages.

By the late 1800s, profit sharing and employee ownership were widespread in a variety of industries, including shoe making, furniture production, gas companies, and printing and publishing, including the *Boston Herald.* In 1886, John Bates Clark, a founder of the American Economics Association, wrote a book calling for widespread profit sharing and employee stock ownership because he believed such incentive plans improved business performance.

In 1882, Charles Pillsbury, founder of the baking company, began splitting profits with a quarter of his mill workers, an idea he later extended to half the workforce. Rand McNally, the mapmakers, shared profits with all of its workers starting in 1886. The following year, Robert Brookings, after whom the Brookings Institution is named, espoused widespread employee ownership as a way to increase efficiency. Colonel William Procter, a founder of Procter & Gamble Corporation, set up a profit-sharing plan at the soap maker the same year. In 1890, it gave workers stock in the company as their share of the profit. Even today, both ideas continue to play critical roles at the company.

In 1903, Lincoln Filene and his brother, Edward Albert Filene, who helped found the U.S. Chamber of Commerce, combined profit sharing and an employee council at Filene's Department Store in Boston to create a model that received a lot of attention in the press and led to much public discussion. Kodak started profit sharing in 1912 that gave workers corporate earnings in the form of stock, as did Sears in 1916. Both plans became famous for the wealth they brought to average workers.

About the same time, a few influential business leaders took the next step and began systematically to turn their employees into shareholders. In 1893, the 61,000 officers and employees of the Illinois Central Railroad were allowed to buy the company's stock on favorable terms. One traveling salesman, a man named King Gillette, was so taken by the general idea of cooperative wealth sharing that he wrote a book about it in the 1890s. When his views got no notice, he invented the safety razor to make money to promote the idea, or so he later claimed.

In 1900, the Pittsburgh Coal Company began selling stock to its employees, as did the National Biscuit Company and the First National Bank of Chicago the next year. Alfred DuPont, an heir of the chemicals company that still bears the family name, began a profit-sharing plan in 1909 that paid out stock to his workers. DuPont was also one of the first companies to use stock ownership to hold onto workers. In 1927, the company began giving employee shareholders a special bonus in stock if they were employed on February 25 of each year. DuPont believed that turning workers into owners would "gradually result in the elimination of the line between capital and labor."

In 1919, George Eastman became one of the first "high technology" moguls of his day to embrace employee ownership. That year, he offered more than 8 percent of Eastman Kodak's stock—from his personal holdings—to employees at a steeply discounted price. The reason he gave: to reward employees for developing the company and to encourage them to remain as employees. All those who had worked at the company for two years were eligible to buy in. By 1927, 15,000 workers—58 percent of Eastman Kodak's workforce—owned stock in the company.

Most of these early advocates pushed employee ownership as much for ideological reasons as for economic ones. Gallatin thought it would help to develop democracy in the United States. He introduced his profit-sharing plan by saying: "The democratic principle on which this nation was founded should not be restricted to the political process, but should be applied to the industrial operation as well."

Other proponents saw sharing the wealth as a way to tamp down worker unrest and head off unions, or even to inoculate America against socialism and communism. The United States experienced extensive labor unrest in the early 1900s, when labor unions doubled their share of the workforce. In response, hundreds of corporations cooked up all kinds of labor-friendly practices. They tried everything from employee stock ownership and profit sharing to private unemployment insurance, pensions, athletic facilities, worker councils, paid vacations, health insurance, mortgage assistance, and employee training. By 1914, the National Civic Federation, a reform group comprised of prominent business and community leaders, counted 2,500 firms pursuing one or another of these policies. In 1917, Charles W. Eliot, who had been Harvard University's president for forty years until 1909, wrote a forceful article advocating profit sharing as well as the sale of company stock to workers at reduced rates to make them owners. "Cooperative management," wrote Eliot, was needed to tie it all together.

Many of the country's largest companies set up employee ownership plans of one type or another in the hopes of buying industrial peace. In 1919, John D. Rockefeller Jr. formed a group called the Special Conference Committee, composed of executives from two of his former companies, Standard Oil of Indiana and Standard Oil of New Jersey, as well as from many of the industrial giants of the day: AT&T, Bethlehem Steel, DuPont, General Electric, General Motors, Goodyear, International Harvester, Irving National Bank, U.S. Rubber, and Westinghouse Electric. The goal was to come up with an approach to industrial relations that would unite labor and capital. "The only solidarity natural in industry is the solidarity which unites all those in the same business establishment," Rockefeller said.

The committee was chaired for many years by Clarence Hicks, Rockefeller's personnel manager from Standard Oil of New Jersey. Rockefeller adopted the committee's ideas, such as selling discounted stock to workers. Within ten years, employees owned about 4 percent each of Standard Oil Company of New Jersey, Standard Oil Company of California, and Standard Oil Company of Indiana, making workers the second largest shareholder block in each company.

Other companies on the committee also sold stock to the rank and file, who by the late 1920s owned about 6 percent of AT&T and 7 percent of Bethlehem Steel and of International Harvester. Employees owned 12 percent of Proctor & Gamble, a majority of the Philadelphia Rapid Transit Company, all of the Belmont Iron Works, and nearly all of the Fuller Brush Company. The General

Electric Company even organized a separate corporation, the General Electric Employees' Securities Corporation, which sold GE bonds to employees that paid 6 percent interest, plus an additional 2 percent if the employee held the bonds and stayed on the payroll. The company, an investment trust, was an early precursor to today's ESOP. GE's president, Gerard Swope, wrote articles endorsing widespread employee stock ownership.

Many business chiefs espoused employee ownership in other forums as well. Owen D. Young, GE's CEO in 1927, gave a speech at Harvard University that year in which he suggested that workers should buy into the American business system through stock purchases and create a peoples' capitalism. His views were one reason why the *New York Times* suggested him as a Democratic presidential nominee that year.

Still, despite all the big names, employee ownership never really spread beyond a thin layer of the leading companies in the early 1900s. In 1928, the Conference Board, a business group founded twelve years earlier, estimated that about 800,000 employees owned a billion dollars worth of stock in more than 300 companies. At the time, that represented about 1 percent of the stock market's total market value.

These efforts came to a crashing halt with the Great Depression. The stock market debacle of 1929 wiped out the value of many worker investments, underscoring the excessive risk workers bore when employee ownership was based almost entirely on the use of their savings to buy company stock.

Risk-sharing ideas resurfaced as the Depression wound down, only now the motivation of corporate leaders shifted from politics to economics. In 1939, Republican Senator Arthur Vandenberg sparked congressional interest by holding hearings on the subject. He concluded that profit sharing was associated with business success and "was essential to the ultimate maintenance of the capitalistic system." The evidence, he said, was too significant "to be ignored or deprecated."

World War II gave profit sharing a major, though unintentional, shot in the arm. To boost production during the war, the U. S. government slapped controls on prices and wages. But the caps didn't apply to benefits. The new rules also allowed companies with profits that exceeded certain limits to get a tax break if they shared some of their earnings with workers.

This kicked off an explosion in benefits of all kinds as companies and workers, patriotic though they might have been, looked for ways to skirt wage controls. Many companies set up profit-sharing plans in order to keep and attract workers at a time when the war made labor scarce. The tax breaks also prompted companies to expand stock bonus programs as well as stock ownership plans, mainly for salaried employees.

After the war ended, the prosperity of the 1950s and 1960s brought a boom in corporate profits, which further fueled the profit-sharing binge. Thousands of companies, large and small, set up such plans. Many of them functioned like savings or pension plans, by deferring the payout until retirement. Many also covered all employees, such as those at Sears, Procter & Gamble, and Harris Bank. Fisher Price provided up to 22 percent of its profits to employees, capped at 15 percent of their salary. Through profit sharing that often was distributed in company shares, employees became major shareholders at Safeway Stores, Standard Oil of California, and J.C. Penney.

Profit sharing reached its peak in the early 1980s, when a sixth of the 500 largest companies had such a program. Some plans gave workers significant economic rewards. However, others faltered because of insignificant amounts of profit sharing that were more symbolic than real, or because there was little or no attention paid to supporting cultural changes designed to create mutual interest between employers and workers.

At that point, federal policy and the economy intervened once more, effectively stalling a trend of nearly forty years. A few years earlier, in 1978, Congress had created the 401(k) plan as part of an overall move to use tax incentives for individuals to encourage more retirement saving. Little happened at first. The 401(k) allows workers to put pretax income into a retirement plan, with the company kicking in if it wishes. While many profit-sharing plans functioned like retirement plans, too, there was no significant tax penalty to a company if it did both. Many companies integrated their profit-sharing plans with 401(k) plans and made them dependent on worker savings.

However, in 1986 Congress enacted major tax reform to lift taxes and slow down the burgeoning federal deficit. The new rules set overall limits on how much a company could sock away for an employee in all types of retirement plans. As employees signed up for 401(k) plans and increased their pretax contributions, companies with existing profit-sharing plans began to bump up against the limits. Ever since, 401(k)s have been squeezing out most serious attempts at profit sharing. Many workers choose or are steered to buy their employers' stock as part of their 401(k), and companies often add even more by paying part or all of their match in the form of stock. As a result, employee ownership has expanded steadily. But it has become even more like a retirement plan than it was in most profit-sharing plans.

Meanwhile, in a parallel development after World War II, employee ownership also got a big boost from the advent of the ESOP. An investment banker named Louis Kelso set up the first one in 1953 at Peninsula Newspapers Incorporated, a California company. Kelso and the philosopher Mortimer Adler wrote *The Capitalist Manifesto*, a book about broad-based employee ownership. For years afterward, Kelso proselytized tirelessly for the idea, as did Russell Long, a powerful U. S. senator from Louisiana who played a key role in shaping retirement tax law from his lengthy perch as head of the Senate Finance Committee. The two of them were primarily responsible for convincing Congress about the merits of ESOPs. Congress passed the first laws to encourage them in 1974, and has passed more than a dozen changes since then.

While ESOPs can be structured in several ways, the basic concept involves workers obtaining their company's stock through a trust that management sets up. The company puts some of its shares in the trust, which sets up stock accounts for each employee. Employees usually build up stock ownership over a number of years, only taking possession of it when they retire or leave the firm. Some companies borrow the funds to buy the stock, so they can give it to employees immediately. The employer gets a tax break on the contributions it makes to the ESOP or on the payments it makes on the loan, if there is one. The idea, Kelso pointed out, was to let companies use debt as leverage to buy ownership for workers, just as they use loans to purchase machinery or assets that they repay from the profits produced.

Kelso and Long argued that ESOPs produce many economic benefits, as well as social and political ones. Ownership makes workers more committed to their jobs and their companies, they said, lifting productivity and profits. Such plans also lead to more equality in the workplace and eases tensions between workers and managers. (Union strife was once again a major national concern in the late 1960s and early 1970s, when Kelso and Long campaigned to get ESOP laws enacted.)

The number of ESOPs in the United States climbed steadily through the 1970s, then soared dramatically in the 1980s. During that decade, thousands of companies rushed to put stock in workers' hands to gain the tax breaks or to ward off takeovers by putting a big chunk of their ownership into the friendly hands of employees. Many also acted out of a conviction that employee-owners would give a boost to the bottom line.

The growth of ESOPs stalled out in the 1990s, in part because some companies had set up modest ESOPs without making any real commitment to creating a culture of ownership. As a result, they found the idea difficult to sustain. Employees also lost interest at companies that didn't set up ESOPs large enough to give them a meaningful financial stake.

At the same time, the threat of takeovers diminished among public companies, leaving CEOs less worried about creating a block of friendly stock. In 1992, the accounting profession also changed the rules for how public companies book ESOP purchases on their income statements. Because the new method made corporate income look smaller, it put downward pressure on an ESOP company's stock. So CEOs began to shy away from the idea. Some firms continued to use ESOPs to stave off bankruptcy, funding them with wage and benefit concessions. However, they represent a small percentage of all ESOPs.

ESOPs still flourish at privately held companies today. One big reason is the federal tax incentives they provide their founders and family owners, who can be excused from capital gains taxes if they sell more than 30 percent of the business to employees. The memberships of the country's two major ESOP groups, the ESOP Association and the National Center for Employee Ownership, increasingly are made up of such companies, which now often have a majority of their stock in the hands of employees.

Employee participation in managerial decisions doesn't have quite the pedigree that financial incentives do, but the idea still dates back nearly a century. In the 1920s and 1930s, some British companies looked for ways to boost productivity and quality by making work more meaningful and less repetitive. Several high-profile factory experiments attracted great interest.

The idea of involving employees in decisionmaking spread rapidly after World War II, in both Europe and the United States. The Germans took a top-down approach, setting up formal factory councils, or groups of elected worker representatives with which companies must consult by law. Companies there also must have employee representatives on their boards of directors. So-called works councils remain a key facet of German labor relations today and are found across much of Western Europe. In 2002, the European Union decided to establish similar councils at most of the companies of its member states in the coming years.

Teamwork, too, took off in the 1940s, initially in Britain, Sweden, and the United States. The idea has gone by many names and has taken various forms. Quality circles, for example, are usually groups of workers that meet to solve problems that crop up on the job. Cross-trained teams, often also called self-directed teams, typically means five or ten employees trained to do each other's jobs who often rotate through several jobs during the day. All the variations involve the basic concept of giving workers a greater say-so over the day-to-day tasks they perform on the job.

In the United States, labor relations experts extolled the virtues of worker participation starting in the 1950s. Within a decade, it was taught widely in business schools. Teams and other ways to empower workers got a further boost in the 1970s, when many U.S. factories fretted about job alienation among blue-collar workers. While many labor unions were skeptical at first, the competitive threat from Japan, which set up teamwork-run factories in the United States in the 1980s, spurred widespread imitation in the United .States.

Over the past two decades, much of corporate America has adopted some kind of teamwork or worker participation system. A majority of workers are involved in a group similar to a quality circle in roughly half of workplaces, while about a third of all workplaces have at least one self-directed work team somewhere in the organization, according to an analysis of Census Bureau data Blasi and Kruse published in 2000.

Although teams seem like an integral part of the corporate landscape in America today, they're actually not all that common. For instance, while a lot of workplaces have teams, only 12 percent of companies actually have a majority of their employees on one. Despite all the hype in the business community about high-performance work systems in recent years, most companies involve only a fraction of their workforces in most of these practices. In fact, only 1 to 2 percent make widespread use of multiple innovative work methods.

Because employee participation, as well as all the financial risk-sharing ideas, has been around for so long, economists and labor experts have had plenty of time to scrutinize them closely. Many of the studies they've done have focused on one specific form or another, largely because few companies have melded all these ideas together the way the High Tech 100 have done. Below we summarize the most important studies of each element separately, starting with options. We focus on those done in the past two decades, which tend to be more rigorous than ones done earlier in the 1900s.

## Stock Options

There are only three significant studies of stock option plans that include most or all employees, largely because the idea only took hold in the past decade or so. Blasi and Kruse, along with Rutgers colleague James Sesil and Maya Kroumova of the New York Institute of Technology, published one in 2000 that examined 490 companies, in a variety of industries, that offered options to most or all of their employees. (No High Tech 100 firms were included.) They were sizeable companies, averaging $3 billion in sales with 14,000 workers. Nearly 90 percent had set up their plans after 1987. The study compared the firms to all public companies, except those few that also had broad-based option plans. It also compared each company to the next largest and the next smallest firm in its industry.

The result: The broad-based option companies performed better on a range of corporate measures. Between 1985 and 1987, and 1995 and 1997, their average productivity grew 6 percentage points faster than the companies with no employee option plans. It also climbed 7 percentage points faster than the productivity of the matching firms. Their return on assets increased more over the period, too: 16 percent more than all public companies, and 10 percent greater than the larger and smaller firms with which each had been matched.

The stock market returns of the companies with options for everyone were higher as well. Between 1992 and 1997, the years for which complete data existed, the broad-based option guys saw their average annual stock returns jump by 23 percent, versus 18 percent for all nonoption companies in the public stock market and 22 percent for the 500 largest public companies.

A follow-up study in 2002 by the same authors homed in on 229 "knowledge industry" companies out of the first sample, most of them in communications, high-tech manufacturing, pharmaceuticals, and computer software. It found that between 1985 and 1987, and 1995 and 1997, these companies' average productivity grew 20 percentage points more over the decade than the firms that had no broad-based option plans. They also posted higher stock market returns: The option firms gained an average of 26 percent a year between 1992 and 1997 (the period for which complete data exist), versus 23 percent for nonoption companies in the public stock market and about 17 percent for comparable "knowledge companies" among the 500 largest public companies.

Another study found that options pay off the most when they go to mid- and lower-level employees. It was done in 2001 by three professors at University of Pennsylvania's Wharton School of Business who are widely respected experts on compensation issues. They looked at 217 high-tech firms, 70 percent of which had gone public in the previous ten years and had median market capitalizations in 1999 of about $1.6 billion. (Although they didn't name the companies, some almost certainly are in our High Tech 100.)

Between 1998 and 1999, the companies that gave more options to employees posted higher-than-average returns to shareholders. By comparison, those that granted more options to top officers, including the CEO, vice presidents, and directors, did no better for their shareholders than the rest of the group. "The benefits to providing additional grants to mid-level employees can be greater than grants to executives," the study concluded. In other words, options create added value, but only if they go to many levels of employees.

## Employee Stock Ownership

Because ESOPs have been embraced by so many mainstream corporations, they've been studied more closely than any other form of risk sharing. Many experts believe that employee ownership spurs workers to do a better job when combined with a participative culture. As a result, the most common question researchers have asked is whether ESOPs or similar plans have any effect on a company's productivity. Four times since 1995, two of us have reviewed the major ESOP studies (including several by us) done in prior decades that had focused specifically on the productivity question. The studies ranged in size from one that examined forty-five ESOPs to another that covered almost 2,000 in a wide variety of industries.

Our last effort was in 2001, at which point eleven such studies had been done. They all compared companies with ESOPs to similar non-ESOP firms, using common statistical methods to rule out as many distorting factors as possible, such as the size of the company, the industry it was in, or how capital intensive it was. They also looked at each company over time, to see what had happened to productivity before and after the ESOP was adopted. If you average the findings of the eleven, companies saw a 4.4 percent increase in productivity after they put in an ESOP.

Another study Blasi and Kruse coauthored in 1996 looked at how all forms of employee ownership, not just ESOPS, affected productivity between 1980 and 1990. We used data we had collected in our 1991 book on the subject, *The New Owners*, which documented the existence of a thousand employee ownership plans in public companies. The study compared all public companies in which employees owned more than 5 percent of the stock (there was data for the whole decade available for 562), to all other public firms with that much data (a total of 4,716). On average, employees held 13 percent of their company's stock. The result: The companies with 5 percent employee ownership enjoyed productivity growth that was 7 percentage points higher over the decade than that of all public companies (although the effect diminished as the employee stake grew).

Employee ownership seems to pay off in the stock market, too. After publishing *The New Owners,* we looked at the stock gains of those 562 companies with more than 5 percent employee ownership. Between 1980 and 1990, they had an average total return to their shareholders of 207 percent, compared to a 94 percent average for all other public companies. That translates into a 2-percentage-point annual edge. The effect was stronger in smaller companies.

Other analysts also have found that ESOPs correlate with higher stock prices. In 1999, for example, the consulting firm Hewitt Associates and an economist now at the Federal Reserve Bank of New York looked at data on 382 companies for two years before they set up ESOPs, and for four years afterward. The ESOP companies saw significantly faster growth in their average annual return on assets, compared to similar firms in the same industry. ESOP firms also enjoyed total shareholder returns of 26 percent over the four years, compared to 19 percent for their non-ESOP peers.

Similarly, a study Blasi and Kruse completed in 2000 with economist Margaret Blair of the Brookings Institution looked at the stock performance from 1984 to 1997 of all twenty-seven publicly traded companies that had at least 20 percent employee ownership in 1983. No matter how we sliced it, the employee ownership firms came out ahead of either the S&P 500 or forty-five matching firms comprising the next largest and next smallest companies in each industry.

We grouped the twenty-seven together as if they were holdings in a single mutual fund, weighting each one as an equal investment. They beat the average annual total shareholder return of the S&P 500 by 2.5 percentage points over the thirteen years, and the forty-five matching firms by about 2 percentage points. We got similar findings when we weighted the group according to each firm's market capitalization, and when we adjusted the returns for any greater risk they had compared to the S&P and the forty-five firms.

The employee ownership firms also proved to be more stable than other companies. Some 60 percent survived from 1983 to 1997, compared to 51 percent for the matching firms and only 38 percent of all public companies. None succumbed to bankruptcy, compared to 2 percent of the matched firms and 4 percent of all public companies. Some 37 percent of the employee ownership firms were acquired or merged, compared to 25 percent for the matching companies and 27 percent for all public companies.

We also did an analysis of ESOPs' effect on sales and employment growth. In 2001, two of us completed the most extensive examination yet done on the subject. We looked at all privately held ESOPS set up between 1988 and 1994 for which complete data was available (a total of 343 companies), comparing how the firms performed before and after the ESOPs were established. We also matched up each ESOP firm with a company of similar size in the same industry that had no ESOP.

The outcome: The employment of the firms that adopted an ESOP climbed 2.4 percent a year more rapidly in the subsequent three years, compared to those of the non-ESOP firms. Among those with sales data, per employee grew 2.3 percent a year faster, too, while their overall sales expanded 2.3 percent more rapidly. These might seem small at first glance, but they imply that a company would be about 25 percent larger after ten years with an ESOP than it would have been without one.

This isn't just true for the first few years after companies set up an ESOP. We compared all ESOPs at companies with more than fifty workers in 1988 to non-ESOP companies in the same industries and with similar workforce sizes. We found that both the sales and the sales per worker grew about 1.2 percent a year faster at the ESOP companies between 1983 and 1999.

The same study also suggested that ESOP companies even seem to survive better. It compared 1,200 privately held ESOPs that existed in 1988, most of them small businesses, to 1,200 matched non-ESOP firms of similar size and industries. Some 70 percent of the ESOP companies were still in business as of 1999, versus 55 percent of the non-ESOP companies. Of the companies that did disappear, the ESOP ones were less likely to have gone bankrupt. Only 35 percent of them vanished due to bankruptcy or a cessation of operations, versus 58 percent of the disappearing non-ESOP firms. (Presumably, the rest were acquired by another firm.)

## Profit Sharing

Today, it's accepted wisdom among many prominent economists that profit sharing can lift a company's productivity. In 1984, Harvard University economist Martin Weitzman wrote a book called *The Share Economy,* which suggested that there might be important macroeconomic effects from profit sharing. In 1990, he and Kruse summarized the firm-level evidence on productivity for a book called *Paying for Productivity,* which was edited by Alan Blinder, the former vice chairman of the Federal Reserve Board.

In his 1993 book on the subject, Kruse examined twenty-six studies that had been done over the prior fifteen years. A majority of them concluded that splitting profits with workers did indeed improve a firm's productivity level, by an average of about 4 percentage points. However, cause and effect weren't clear, because most didn't try to look at companies before and after they had adopted profit-sharing plans. Kruse's book tackled the issue with new evidence, finding that the adoption of a profit-sharing scheme lifted a company's productivity level by an average of up to 5 percentage points.

Six years later, Kruse updated the survey, examining 34 studies, including all of the original twenty-six. The findings were similar:

Profit sharing brought productivity gains of about 4.5 percentage points.

A more recent study, in 2000, echoed those results. An economist from Tufts University and another from the Federal Reserve Board of New York looked at 760 randomly selected manufacturing worksites that had been surveyed in 1994 and again in 1997. They, too, found that the adoption of profit sharing heightened productivity, by an average of about 16 percent over that period.

## Employee Participation

While the studies of financial incentives for workers to act like owners show unmistakable benefits to companies, none of them have been able to discern if it's really the incentive alone that does the trick. The reason: Some of the monetary reward schemes adopted by companies in recent decades have gone hand-in-hand with efforts to create a workplace culture of employee participation. So is it the prospect of extra money that motivates employees, or the new workplace culture that comes with employee participation efforts?

The answer, many experts say, is that both are necessary. Money talks, but employees can't think for themselves and make more creative contributions to productivity if companies don't alter the traditional, "I'm-the-boss, do-what-I-say" mentality so often found throughout corporate America.

At the same time, the reverse holds true as well. As Robert, the Tibco Software employee pointed out, telling employees to "take ownership" of their jobs rings hollow if management doesn't offer actual financial ownership or some share in the improved performance for which they are responsible. Without wealth sharing in some form, it feels like the company is just trying to con you into working harder.

Several studies have come to this conclusion. A 1995 book of the history of employee involvement called *Re-inventing the Workplace: How Both Business and Employees Can Win*, argued that sharing financial gains is a key element of participatory corporate cultures. It concluded that it's difficult to sustain effective participation if workers don't feel that they share the benefits of their extra efforts and commitment.

A 2000 study found much the same thing in one of the most thorough analyses ever done on the subject. Two economists randomly chose 193 manufacturing worksites and looked to see if innovations such as problem-solving groups and self-directed work teams had any effect on productivity. Those that used such ideas by themselves, with no financial rewards, showed no significant impact at all.

The following year, two economists looked at 433 worksites over a sixteen-year period and 660 more over nineteen years. They, too, found that high-performance work practices such as self-directed work teams, job rotation, cross-training, and problem-solving groups had no effect on productivity. But self-directed work teams contributed more to productivity when they were combined with profit sharing.

One of the few studies to look at the combined effect of both employee participation efforts and financial incentives came out in a 2001 book called *The HR Scorecard*. It examined 2,800 publicly traded corporations between 1992 and 1999 with sales above $5 million and more than 100 employees. It focused on those that had dramatically altered both their corporate cultures and their approach to pay. These were firms that carefully selected most new hires, trained them extensively, and involved almost half of them in self-directed work teams. The companies also paid above-average wages and tied more than 6 percent of workers' incentive pay to clear improvements in individual performance.

The results were stunning. The companies that did such a big overhaul increased their market value in the subsequent year by 24 percent. Their return on assets climbed by 25 percent, and their sales per employee by about 5 percent. Turnover was cut by about 8 percent. Firms that took a more modest approach show similar, but much less dramatic, results. "We find very powerful support for a relationship between a High-performance Work System and firm financial performance," the authors concluded.

Earlier studies found a similar pattern of synergy between participation and incentives. One of the earliest, done by the National

Center for Employee Ownership in 1986 and published in the Harvard Business Review, was also the first to show a specific causal link between employee participation and company performance. It examined forty-five ESOPs set up in 1981 or earlier, assessing their track records for five years before and after the ESOP was established. It also compared each company to about five similar non-ESOP firms in the same industry and geographic region.

First the study assessed the ESOP itself. It found that the sales of the companies that had set up ESOPs grew 3.5 percent a year faster than they had before it was established, while their employment climbed nearly 4 percent a year faster.

The study then ranked each company's culture of participation, based on an extensive survey the authors had conducted of both managers and workers at these firms. The companies were grouped into three categories. The ones with lots of participation saw their annual employment grow 8 percent faster than before the ESOP. Their annual sales grew 16 percent faster, and their sales per employee climbed 4 percent more rapidly. The midrange companies had 6 percent better employment growth, 5 percent faster sales growth, and 6 percent quicker productivity growth. The bottom group, companies that ignored participation altogether, showed a 4 percent annual decline in employment growth, a 16 percent annual decline in sales growth, and a 6 percent annual decline in productivity.

A year later, in 1987, the General Accounting Office, an arm of the U. S. Congress, shed even more light on the issue. It, too, did a before-and-after study of ESOPs, and also matched each one to similar non-ESOP companies in the same industry. The GAO collected data for six years on 110 firms that had set up ESOPs between 1976 and 1979, using information from corporate tax returns supplied by the IRS.

The agency found that just putting in an ESOP had little effect on profitability or productivity (although it also said that the sample of firms may have been too small to make a reliable judgment). However, when the ESOPs were coupled with various forms of participation, productivity grew by 52 percent in the year after the ESOP was set up, compared to the non-ESOP firms. "We found that the greater the degree of employee participation in corporate deci-sionmaking, the higher the rate of change in our measure of pro-ductivity between the pre-ESOP and the post-ESOP periods," the GAO concluded.

Four years later, in 1991, the National Option Research Center of the University of Chicago surveyed 727 employers. The center found better performance at companies that offered profit shar-ing or stock options and that also had invested in training their employees.

Perhaps the most unusual assessment of the whole subject came from a 2000 Harvard University study. Instead of looking at exter-nal criteria such as productivity or sales growth, the authors asked employees themselves about how the company and their fellow workers performed. The idea grew out of a national random survey of all American workers the authors had commissioned that had questioned 2,400 employees across the country in 1994 and 1995. This was more than enough to adequately sample the 70 million employees who comprised 70 percent of all private-sector workers at the time (excluding the self-employed and those at companies with just a handful of employees). It represented the most extensive analysis of American workers' attitudes toward the workplace in more than two decades.

The purpose of the broader project was to look at what workers wanted from their companies, a subject that was turned into a 1999 book called *What Workers Want*. The survey included an elaborate set of questions about participation, ownership, and pay. In 2000, one of the authors wrote up a separate analysis on this issue.

The survey asked employees about any participation efforts go-ing on at their companies, as well as about employee ownership and any shared compensation plans, such as profit sharing. To get a measure of productivity gains, it also asked them how often they made productivity-related suggestions, and how often these sugges-tions were heeded by the management.

The companies with shared compensation had higher levels of this self-reported productivity than companies that just paid a regu-lar wage or salary. Workers at these companies also said they were more satisfied with their jobs and more loyal to their employers.

However, firms with more employee participation ranked even higher on productivity, job satisfaction, and loyalty. Workers at the shared-compensation companies gave their colleagues higher marks on their concern for the success of the company and their willingness to take on new responsibilities and work hard than did workers at companies without shared compensation schemes.

The highest scores came at companies that combined shared compensation, participation, and employee ownership—in other words, something very much like what we call stock option capitalism (although some of the companies that do this used ESOPs and other ownership stakes instead of options). "The highest outcomes occur when firms combine three shared institutions: pay for company/group performance, ownership stake in the firm, and employee involvement committees," the study concluded. Echoing earlier findings, it also found that "the impact of (shared) compensation practices appears to be contingent on such decision making structures."

We pointed out earlier that employee participation isn't really all that widespread in the United States today. One reason may be that many companies have been unwilling to provide the financial incentives, such as stock options or other forms of employee ownership, that are required to make the idea work properly. Financial ownership for employees is much more limited than participation efforts. Yet ownership provides the motivation that spurs employees to throw themselves into teams or an entrepreneurial culture and actually make them pay off for the company.

This link came through clearly in the analysis of Census Bureau data we did in 2000. It showed a strong tie between higher pay and the more widespread use of various participation methods. In other words, the 1 to 2 percent of companies that involve most of their workers in teams and other participation efforts also pay them more for doing so. Other companies refuse to pay a lot more for the extra effort these ideas require to function correctly.

The conclusion we draw is that employee participation alone isn't enough. The tangible rewards of employee ownership or some form of sharing the fruits of ownership must go hand in hand with work practices that give workers greater decisionmaking. Where the two aren't paired, a company's productivity isn't likely to improve enough to make the effort worthwhile. The same holds true of the culture of the High Tech 100. Stock options give companies a way to compensate workers for accepting more demanding work systems that contribute to higher productivity—and therefore higher profits.

We hope by now we've convinced most readers that partnership capitalism benefits companies and their shareholders, as well as employees. By virtually any measure, companies that use any aspect of the partnership approach are better off. The studies we summarized give a range of outcomes, not a precise set of numbers like those in the table at the beginning of this chapter. Still, if you average all the results together and sum them up, as we did in that table, it gives a fairly good idea of the order-of-magnitude gain that investors stand to make if they pursue stock option capitalism. The conclusion: Shareholders come out ahead, whether you look at productivity, profits, or stock gains.

However, these findings present a challenge of another sort. Why hasn't the new approach swept across corporate America and become the norm at most companies? Sure, tax and accounting rules stymied profit sharing and ESOPs. But stock option plans like those adopted by so many high-tech firms don't face that problem. Nor do employee participation efforts.

If the substantial economic payoff from partnership capitalism is really as great as the studies show, why haven't corporate leaders been pursuing it? Why didn't other industries adopt it wholesale before high-tech? Surely, CEOs in every part of the economy are in the business of maximizing their company's profits. Why has corporate America basically ignored all these voluminous studies—particularly since they were done at many of these same traditional companies, not new-fangled high-tech ones that you might argue have atypical workforces?

We believe there are a number of complex reasons. All these studies were done largely by academics in a piecemeal fashion. Until now, no one really took the time to pull them all together and say: Hey, this stuff really works. As a result, no one has presented corporate America with the evidence. In addition, while many companies have tried both participation and financial incentives, separately or together, such efforts can be difficult to pull off. They involve a cultural transformation of the workplace that requires managers and executives to take a lot of risks.

However, it also seems that some basic human emotions have played a role. All too often, the CEOs and other top executives of corporate America have been unable to let go of the traditional, top-down power structures they have used, in one form or another, since capitalism began. Some of them also may have been driven by self-interest to avoid sharing the wealth with employees, the better to keep it for themselves.

At the same time, public shareholders, and the boards of directors whose putative duty it is to represent them, have let CEOs get away with such self-interest because they were distracted by two factors. As we'll see in the next chapter, one was the bull market of the late 1990s. The other was the superficially compelling justification CEOs have given for grabbing the wealth for themselves.

# PART THREE

## A New Corporate Model

# 8

# Top-down Capitalism

## What Would Have to Change in Corporate America

Most traditional companies are just as concerned as high-tech firms are about motivating employees and improving their efficiency. In a trend that spread quickly in the 1980s and became virtual dogma in the 1990s, corporate America, at least rhetorically, embraced much of the same philosophy expressed by the High Tech 100. Most CEOs today would readily volunteer that owners treat property better than renters. They're fully aware of the payoffs that stem from flattening rigid corporate hierarchies, setting up teams, and getting employees more involved in decisions. Many say that's what they're trying to achieve in their own companies. Employers routinely try to connote shared ownership by referring to their employees as "associates." They exhort their employees with phrases such as "act like an owner," "sense of ownership," "run it as if you own it," and "think like owners, not caretakers."

But for most companies outside the Internet and high-tech industries, the reality belies the rhetoric. As we saw in the last chapter, less than 2 percent of companies actually involve more than half of their employees in joint decisionmaking and back them up with the right approach to recruitment, training, incentives, and culture. They do little better when it comes to sharing ownership with workers. Many companies pay lip service to the idea, and quite a few also have an ESOP, profit sharing, or incentive plan of one sort or another. However, most of these either don't involve meaningful financial rewards or aren't integrated into a culture of employee participation.

What's more, the largest chunk of employee ownership in corporate America doesn't represent extra wealth that employees get on top of their regular wages and benefits, as is the case with most of the options granted by the High Tech 100. Instead, workers buy much of their stake with their own earnings. Consider the 24 million workers in the last chapter who own shares in the companies they work for. If we exclude stock options, the aggregate market value of all these shares came to roughly $400 billion, or about 5 percent of the total value of all publicly traded shares in the country.

However, we estimate that employees paid for about 64 percent of all this stock ownership themselves. This includes shares they bought through employee share purchase plans and company profit-sharing plans. Workers also used savings they diverted from other investments to buy employer shares through 401(k)s. Only the remaining 36 percent of the $400 billion represents true property sharing. Included here are company contributions to profit-sharing plans, ESOPs, and the matching stock that many companies contribute to their employees' 401(k) plans.

By contrast, executives have used the same justification—that ownership in the company spurs them to better performance—to lift their own pay to Olympian heights. Options, of course, have been the primary vehicle. As of 2000, the 1,500 largest public companies in the United States had issued about 12 billion options (both vested and unvested ones). The shares underlying these options had a market value of some $1.2 trillion at the end of that year (which had plunged to roughly $820 billion by August 2002). This comes to about 10 percent of the value of all outstanding shares in these companies, which themselves represent most of the value of all publicly traded shares in the United States.

Almost all of this fantastic wealth is held by the corporate elites. Roughly 30 percent of all options—some $400 billion worth in

2000—are in the hands of the top five executives. If they could have cashed them all in at the end of 2000, America's business leaders would have pocketed profits of some $80 billion. This is additional paper wealth they hold even after taking home profits of about $58 billion on options cashed in between 1992 and the end of 2000. Most of the remaining 70 percent is spread very narrowly among other executives and managers, who typically comprise less than 5 percent of traditional companies.

Except for a minority of firms that have embraced high-tech-style options for everyone, very little goes to average employees, whether they're blue-collar workers or white-collar and professional ones. Millions of workers hold options in public companies in the United States. However, most get a handful on one occasion, or are given a small symbolic grant every few years. We estimate that only about 6 percent of the country's 10,000 public companies offer most of their workers options on a regular annual basis. However, many of them are on the smaller side, so only 2 percent of the U.S. workforce, or 2 to 3 million employees, get options every year.

To put it another way, executives have grabbed 10 percent of the ownership of corporate America for themselves and a small group of top-tier managers, up from 5 percent in 1992 and virtually nothing a decade earlier. Very little of this goes to average workers, who also must buy the majority of their ownership with their own money.

Shareholders, and boards of directors, allowed companies to turn away from the employee ownership path many had set out on in the 1980s because it no longer seemed to matter in the 1990s. In the 1970s, U.S. productivity growth collapsed from around 3 percent a year to about half that. The resulting stagflation prompted CEOs to search for ways to reinvigorate their companies. The onslaught of globalization and other factors in the 1980s ratcheted up the pressure even more. Throughout the decade, many companies, led by large manufacturers, embraced employee involvement and participation as an answer. The crises also led some traditional companies to pursue ESOPs and other employee incentives in the 1980s and early 1990s.

But the booming economy of the late 1990s took the edge off these concerns. As productivity sprang back to near its preslump levels, U.S. factories regained their competitive edge against Japan and other global rivals. As a result, stockholders no longer felt a need to pressure CEOs into bold, creative action to increase company performance. Further, the stocks of traditional companies also shot up much faster than any rational investor could have expected. In a market that was jumping up at 30 percent a year, no one really cared whether the CEO was being greedy or not. After all, the amount he or she took out of the pot seemed very little compared to the total wealth the company generated for shareholders. The idea that there could be a better way, which had seemed so important in the tough times of the 1970s and 1980s, seemed irrelevant. The fact that employees were left out of the bargain got lost in the process as well.

The top-heavy approach that prevails today undermines corporate America's efforts to achieve the motivated workforce many companies claim to desire. Many corporate leaders want the higher productivity gains that an employee ownership mentality can bring. But they want it on the cheap, without having to pay for it with dilution that accompanies a true sharing of property and risk. Companies urge workers to act like owners, but when they refuse to make them actual owners the exhortations ring hollow. Instead of offering to share the pie as an enticement to hard work, too often the message at traditional companies is: "Treat this place like you own it, work like crazy, produce as much as you can—and here's your annual wage, plus maybe a small bonus if you do a bang-up job."

At the same time, most employers have failed to significantly alter the hierarchical pyramid of power that has characterized large companies for so long. Indeed, they've reinforced it by doling out huge amounts of corporate wealth to the upper crust of executives, widening the gap between those at the top and everyone else.

The justification many CEOs used for their wealth accumulation highlights the discrepancy. While many companies today still use the rhetoric about how employees are their most important asset, some CEOs have argued that they deserve the lion's share of employee options because they were responsible for the leaps in shareholder value during the bull market. Of course, few CEOs actually say, "My actions alone lifted the stock price, the employees had nothing to do with it." But that's the implicit rationale when they explain their option millions. They take the reward, leaving little for all the other employees, and then cite the stock gains as justification.

The financial press exacerbated the problem. With fawning stories about the glamorous lives and bold actions of individual CEOs, it fueled a cultlike worship of CEOs as all-powerful Masters of the Universe single-handedly capable of turning around huge corporations. The media wrote about how the management style of one CEO or the strategy of another turned red ink to black in one company and vaulted another to heights never before scaled. This encouraged the impression that the CEO alone makes the difference between a corporation's success and failure.

Many CEOs naturally fell into this flattering role, acting as if they and a relatively small group of other executives and managers are the only ones who matter in a company, or are motivated by corporate ownership. Human capital may provide a growing share of the value the U.S. economy creates every year, but in most companies it seems to be only the intellectual assets of a small number of people who count. The theory of aligning employee interests with those of outside shareholders holds for this group, but not for the broad rank and file.

The irony, of course, is that there's plenty of evidence that companies perform better when employees are owners, as we showed in the last chapter. However, there's very little proof that this holds true for the gargantuan ownership stakes executives have claimed.

To flesh out the stark difference between employee ownership in mainstream corporate America and high tech, we created an index of traditional public companies comparable to the High Tech 100. We call it the Corporate America 100. We constructed the index in much the same way we did the High Tech 100. We took a representative group of corporations listed on the New York Stock Exchange with market values that exceed $1.6 billion (the size of the smallest High Tech 100 firm in October 2000). We chose the hundred at random so they would be representative of corporate America as a whole. (These companies can be found in Appendix D.) Filings

**TABLE 8.1    Corporate America's Top-heavy Wealth Sharing**
(Average Ownership Stake* in the Corporate America
100 as of December 31, 2000, by Type of Owner)

|  | Corporate America 100 % | High Tech 100 % |
|---|---|---|
| Top five officers | | |
| Stock | 5 | 10 |
| Options | 3 | 4 |
| Other executives and managers** | | |
| Stock | — | — |
| Options | 6 | — |
| Total top tier | 14 | 14 |
| Employees*** | | |
| Stock | 2 | 2 |
| Options | *** | 17 |
| Total employees | 2 | 19 |
| Total for both groups | 16 | 33 |

NOTES: *Total potential ownership, i.e., the percent of all stock and options
each group would have owned if all issued options had been exercised.

**Typically less than 5 percent of the company. Many undoubtedly own stock
directly, but the SEC doesn't require companies to report it. Also, the
High Tech 100 offer options to everyone and don't break out the holding of
this group separately. So their assets are lumped in with those of employees.

***All other employees in the company

****Less than 1 percent

SOURCE: Authors' analysis of SEC filings.

from the SEC told us how much stock and options were held by executives and employees as of 2001. The comparison is shown in
Table 8.1.

The broadest conclusion we draw from the table is that risk shar-
ing in corporate America is barely over half what it is among the High
Tech 100—and essentially stops at the upper management level.
Look down at the totals in the bottom row. The average large com-

pany in the United States has granted 16 percent of its actual and potential ownership—that is, stock and options—to officers and employees, roughly half the 33 percent found in High Tech 100 firms.

Of that 16 percent, the top five corporate officers have 8 percent. Another 6 percent goes primarily to the company's lower-level executives, occasionally including some managers and professionals. However, this group typically constitutes less than 5 percent of the workforce, leaving just 2 percent to be split among the other 95 percent of employees.

Now contrast this with the High Tech 100. As we've said, their top-tier officers certainly aren't shy about rewarding themselves. They get the same 14 percent share as their Corporate America 100 counterparts. The figure would be even larger if we had been able to segregate the holding of the other high-tech executives and managers. However, high-tech companies typically don't have special option plans restricted to this group. Instead, their stake is lumped in with all the other workers in the firm.

Many high-tech CEOs may not be quite as open to criticism for their wealth taking as their counterparts in traditional corporations. Remember that a lot of these companies are new, so their executives often are still the founding officers. As a result, they're more likely to hold some of the assets they had when they set up the firm in the first place. So you'd expect them to hold bigger stakes than CEOs in corporate America, who are usually hired managers, not founders.

The big difference, though, is that high-tech executives are even more generous with average employees than they are with themselves. Their employees hold a 19 percent ownership stake. By comparison, Corporate America 100 officers give their workers just 2 percent. The small amount of direct stock ownership derives principally from ESOPs, 401(k)s, and employee share purchase plans. Except for the ESOP stock and employer matches in 401(k)s, employees bought most of this with their savings. Executives' shares, by contrast, come mostly through options, which represents wealth sharing on top of their regular salaries.

What's more, there's little evidence that average employees actually get much option ownership. Instead, much of their options are held by a small fraction of workers. Only 6 percent of the Corporate America 100 regularly give options to a majority of their workers the way the High Tech 100 do: 99 Cent Stores, Charles Schwab, Compaq Computers, Guidant, PepsiCo, and Wells Fargo. Even some of these provide relatively small numbers of options to lower-level employees. Another 5 percent have given options to most employees, but only on a one-time or occasional basis. Aetna, Conoco, Lexmark, and Sunoco fall into this category, as does AOL Time Warner since its merger, which has significantly watered down AOL's original partnership capitalism culture. Overall, corporate America doesn't even grant options worth 1 percent of its shares to regular workers.

The same pattern holds true if you look at the run rate. The Corporate America 100 devote about 2 percent of their shares to options every year, compared to 8 percent annually at High Tech 100 companies. But because CEOs at traditional companies are rarely the founders, they didn't start with a huge ownership stake. Instead, they typically take a large chunk of options for themselves every year, and give most of the rest to a narrow group of other leaders in the company. Of course, since this group can consist of hundreds or thousands of people in a very large company, the top five get hundreds or even thousands of times more options per person than the rest of the managerial ranks. For example, of all the options the Corporate America 100 granted in 2001, 27 percent went to the top five executives alone. Most of the rest went to the next few levels of management.

This is employee ownership for the bosses. Almost everyone else, including most middle managers and professionals, are left out. Of all the Corporate America 100, fully ninety-six offer an employee stock option plan. But only the six firms named above include most of their employees in their option plans.

(There is a widespread misperception that a greater number of large companies offer broad-based option plans. It stems in part from a 2001 survey done by William M. Mercer Company, a benefits consulting firm, that was widely quoted in the media as finding that 54 percent of the 350 largest U.S. corporations made most employees eligible to receive stock options. That's an accurate statement as far as it goes, but putting employees in an eligibility pool doesn't always assure that they will get to enjoy the benefit. The details of the study made clear that a broad group of employees actually only got options in about 5 percent of these companies, and some only get them over a two-year period at that. Moreover, many companies gave just one-time or occasional grants of a small number of shares to each employee, and then forgot about the whole thing. The average paper value of all these grants was insignificant, too, at just $2,000 per employee.)

To put traditional companies' employee ownership figures in perspective, we calculated them in dollar terms. As of August 2002, the 2 percent stock ownership of employees in the Corporate America 100 was worth an average of about $6,727 per worker. However, employees in about half of the companies owned no stock in their employers at all, in any form. So the true holdings of the other half actually was much larger than $6,727, perhaps as much as double.

At first glance, this seems to be a significant amount, since the average annual salary of the 3.5 million employees in these companies was about $40,000 in 1999. However, it's a lot less than you might think. Remember that employees bought a lot of this investment with their own cash, through 401(k)s and stock purchase plans. In addition, this $6,727 was largely accumulated over many years, because ESOPs, 401(k)s, and share purchase plans usually are set up to stretch out over time. So the sum represents long-term savings, most of which is locked up in plans that workers can't get at until they retire or leave the company. It's very different than high-tech-style option wealth that workers usually receive every year and cash out on an ongoing basis.

By contrast, executives in the Corporate America 100 have used employee ownership to enrich themselves to an ever-increasing degree. In 1980, the two highest-paid executives at a sampling of nearly 500 of the largest U.S. corporations earned an average of $1.35 million each, in today's dollars. Most of their pay came from a base salary, plus annual bonuses. Only about a fifth came from stock options. By 2001, their average total pay had multiplied to $11 million each, with 80 percent of the total coming from options. "Twenty years ago, CEOs made fifty times as much as the average worker," venture capitalist Arthur Rock told us in the midst of the corporate scandals of 2002. "Now they make 500-fold more. This is unconscionable."

You can see how this occurred by looking at how executive options paid off over the past decade. We calculated how much the top five executives at the largest 1,500 U.S. firms made from cashing in their options every year. Their collective annual winnings jumped from a total of $2.4 billion in 1992, when the first detailed data became available, to $18 billion in 2000, an increase of nearly 650 percent. Overall, the top five collected some $64 billion through 2001.

They got more, too. Bonuses and long-term incentive plans—which sometimes include stock grants—multiplied from a total of $1.6 billion in 1992 to $4.7 billion in 2000. Grants of restricted stock more than tripled, to $6 billion. In sum, executives granted themselves higher annual increases than workers in every form of compensation.

But these annual compensation figures are dwarfed by the paper wealth executives have accumulated from the stockpile of options they own but haven't yet cashed in. If these options were all exercised at once, they would have brought the top five officers a total net profit of nearly $80 billion at the end of 2000, after they had paid the market value for each share. This is a more than tenfold increase from 1992, when the top five held options with a paper value of $7 billion.

It's no secret why this happened. For all intents and purposes, many CEOs in corporate America set their own salaries. In most large corporations, the board of directors decides, at least on paper, how much to pay top management. But everyone knows that CEOs handpick many of the directors and usually dominate the board.

Indeed, shareholders' advocates have been agitating for some twenty years to reform boards controlled by management. There has been halting progress, and CEOs in many large companies have grudgingly gone along with a move toward more independent directors. Still, the basic system remains largely in place. A recent description of it was given in a 1999 article by Kevin J. Murphy, an economist at the University of Southern California who is a leading expert on executive compensation. He wrote:

> Although all major decisions related to top-level pay are passed through this [compensation] committee, the committee rarely conducts market studies of competitive pay levels or initiates or proposes new incentive plans. Rather initial recommendations for pay levels or new incentive plans typically emanate from the company's human resource department often in conjunction with outside accountants or compensation consultants. These recommendations are usually sent to top managers for approval and revision before being delivered to the compensation committee for consideration. The CEO typically participates in all committee deliberations, except for discussions specifically dealing with the level of the CEO's pay.

The ability of executives to influence their own pay explains many puzzling features of the CEO compensation system in the United States, according to a 2001 study by a Harvard University Law School professor and two others. In early 2002, Federal Reserve Board chairman Alan Greenspan also expressed concerns about the dominant role of the CEO in determining who sits on his or her company's board: "The board of directors appointed by shareholders are in the overwhelming majority of cases chosen from the slate proposed by the CEO. . . . Shareholders usually perfunctorily affirm such choices."

In a system like this, it takes a brave director to tell a CEO that his or her pay is out of line and should be reined in. Certainly, there's scant evidence that anything like that has happened in any systematic way. It's no easier for directors to suggest that there's a wider pool of intellectual capital in the company that should share in the benefits of successful company performance.

Then there's the role of the executive compensation consultants. These are firms such as Buck, Mercer, Pearl Meyer, and Watson Wyatt, which offer a wide range of consulting services to corporate America. One of the more lucrative is running the executive pay schemes.

The consultants take elaborate steps to set up these plans. They diligently perform "market surveys" of CEO pay, which are used to determine how much each client company should pay its own chieftain. This gives the plan a veneer of objectivity, allowing the board of directors to sign off on it without seeming to be favoring the guy who gave them their board seat. It also gives directors legal cover, since angry shareholders would find it more difficult to take directors to court for overpaying executives if an outside professional creates and signs off on the pay plan directors adopt.

The problem is that the consultants, too, get their job designing the plan at the discretion of the CEO. They wouldn't last long if the person who signs their check saw his take-home languishing while his rivals soared up to the golden pinnacle of success. A 2001 article in *Fortune* magazine expressed this in stark terms. The authors interviewed seven directors at major corporations about how CEO pay is set, promising confidentiality in return for candid talk. One of them, himself a CEO who serves as a director of several other companies, put it like this:

> You can have a very sophisticated board—and it'll still be amateurs vs. pros. . . . I'm classing the directors, in most cases, as amateurs, and management, together with the compensation consultants they hire, as pros. . . . I would say that it is unusual to find a consultant who does not end up, at the least, being a prostitute. The consultants are hired by management. They're going to be rehired by management. There's some thought given by conscientious compensation committees to hiring their own consultants. But the consultants don't want to be hired that way, because then they cut themselves off from management.

Many directors feel trapped by the system, too. As *Fortune* put it:

> The directors come from varying spots on the spectrum of opinion, though all believe unequivocally that pay should be related to performance. The trick is in making that happen. The surprise in what many of these directors say—and they are all smart, strong-minded people—is how helpless they sometimes feel in the grip of a system

that inexorably sweeps executive pay toward ever higher levels. Said one director defeatedly: 'You sort of get rolled over by the system even if you try to do well.'

CEO wealth has been fueled further by the Lake Wobegon effect. The market surveys used to justify outsized executive rewards are usually fairly objective in themselves. But every corporate leader seems to think that he or she is above average. So their pay packages are rarely designed to keep pace with average CEO pay, the way most employee pay plans keep pace with average worker pay. Instead, executive compensation plans often target the upper quartiles of the companies surveyed.

The result has been a glorious game of financial leapfrog. Once a few executives struck it rich with options and other long-term stock incentive pay systems in the 1980s, others quickly followed suit by citing the new, higher "market" average for CEO pay. Since they all try to put themselves in the upper brackets, their pay has spiraled ever upward.

This is where Warren Buffett's gimlet-eyed view of options as a free ride applies in spades. The theory behind options for CEOs is similar, at least in broad terms, to the one that explains why they make sense for all employees: Ownership spurs them to do a better job of creating wealth for shareholders. But they should get premiums over and above their regular annual salaries only if they generate extra value. Some experts have found at least superficial evidence that this occurs. The benchmark study of current CEO pay practices was done in 1998 by two Harvard economists, Brian J. Hall and Jeffrey Leibman, who examined the total compensation of CEOs at large public companies between 1980 and 1994.

They found that CEO pay closely tracked a firm's stock price. For example, those whose annual stock price change ranked in the bottom 30 percent of the group over the fifteen years earned $1 million each. But CEOs with returns in the top 30 percent took home $5 million. A CEO whose company's stock performed in the top 10 percent earned $9 million more than one whose stock came in at the bottom 10 percent. The authors' conclusion: There's "a strong link between the fortunes of CEOs and the fortunes of the companies they manage," with virtually all of the link being "attributable to stock and stock options."

But this doesn't tell us whether CEOs create extra value that offsets the dilution triggered by their stock and option compensation, the way employee ownership typically does. To begin with, there's no clear evidence of cause and effect. In 1999, Murphy reviewed decades of evidence on this question. He noted that there's what he calls a mechanical relationship between the value of CEO stock and stock options and total shareholder return. In other words, if a CEO owns 2 percent of his company's stock, either directly or through options, then of course the value of his stake will parallel the company's stock performance. If the stock performs in the top 30 percent of all stocks, so, more or less, will the CEO's pay.

The real issue, though, is whether the CEO whose company performed above average caused the higher growth (or caused the sub par performance of a laggard). On this score, Murphy is clear (if a bit academic). "Unfortunately . . . there is surprisingly little direct evidence that higher pay-performance sensitivities lead to higher stock price performance." It's difficult, he concluded, "to document that the increase in stock-based incentives has led CEOs to work harder, smarter, and more in the interest of shareholders."

Our conclusion is that America's top executives have taken 8 percent of their company's stock for themselves, plus another 6 percent for their chief lieutenants, without any clear evidence that the shareholder dilution this brings has been offset by their extra contribution. A charitable analysis might hold that there's little hard evidence to the contrary. Still, it seems clear that investors have accepted largely on blind faith the substantive dilution brought about by the award of stock to executives.

There are ways to hold CEOs and other executives to the same standard of risk sharing as employees. One method would be to make their option awards pay out only if their company's share price exceeds the overall market average, or at least the average for their particular industry. The conventional view in corporate America is that a CEO's primary job should be to maximize value for shareholders. If CEOs do their jobs adequately, they should be expected to match the market or their peers in similar companies.

But they shouldn't get a windfall just because they did their job adequately and the market happened to soar, as it did in the late 1990s. After all, why should investors agree to give a CEO part of their ownership stake just for returning them as much value as they could get by investing in an index fund that tracks the market?

If, for example, GE's stock goes up 10 percent a year and so does the market, CEO Jeff Immeldt shouldn't get extra compensation from options. However, if he delivers 12 percent when the market rises 10 percent, then investors have earned something in return and his options should reward him. Plenty of other experts on CEO pay have made this argument, including Hall and Liebman. As they put it, "CEOs should be paid relative to some market or industry-wide index."

By this standard, it's clear that many high-tech CEOs, too, have taken too much wealth for themselves. One of the more egregious examples came in 2001, when E*Trade Group Incorporated CEO Christos M. Cotsakos managed to earn a total of $80 million (of which only about $6 million came from options). He did so even though the online brokerage company's stock had plummeted from around $70 in 1999 to barely over $7 in mid-2002, when the company released his compensation figures. So great was the outcry that several days after the news was announced, he agreed to give up about $21 million of his pay.

Across corporate America, even a rough calculation makes it clear that CEO compensation has vastly outpaced the stock market for many years. For example, we said earlier that the top five executives at the largest 1,500 companies enjoyed a 650 percent increase in the value of the options they exercised annually between 1992 and 2000, and a more than 1,000 percent increase in the paper wealth of their unexercised options. Yet these companies' total market value climbed by only 350 percent over this period. Of course, the market crash that followed has made the discrepancies much more glaring. What did executives do to deserve so much more than what they delivered to their shareholders?

Even this approach doesn't tell you whether the dollar amount of options executives receive is the level required to spur better performance on their part. No one has studied how large an award is needed to get them to beat the market, or even to match it, for that matter. CEOs' influence over their own pay has largely governed the size of option grants, which are often justified by market surveys that simply report what CEOs have given themselves at other companies. Do executives really need to get almost $11 million worth of options every year, plus millions more in unexercised options, to stimulate them to do better? Why not half that, or twice as much? Have they really performed better than when they took home just $1 million a year?

One answer, or at least some context, comes from other industrialized countries. For example, in 1997, the CEOs of the largest U.S. public companies earned 190 percent more compensation than their counterparts in England. The Americans received 1.48 percent of the average increase in shareholder value that year, versus 0.25 percent for the English CEO. Why do Americans require, or are allowed to take, so much more? Maybe during the U.S. bull market you could argue they turned in a better performance, but that argument doesn't look so good after the market stopped growing.

Many critics in the business community have been making these arguments for years, but to no avail. Executive pay has continued to climb, and executives maneuver to make sure that no brake will be put on it. One example came in mid-2002, when in the wake of the Enron collapse the New York Stock Exchange (NYSE) mounted an effort to require the companies it lists to put all stock option plans before shareholders for a vote. Even before NYSE officials had announced the plan, executives swung into action to head it off. The Business Roundtable, a prominent group of CEOs of large corporations, initially wrote to the head of the NYSE to denounce the move, with General Mills Corporation CEO Stephen W. Sanger calling it "counterproductive."

Perhaps the most startling finding about American CEOs' share of the option pie relative to employees came from a study we did in the course of writing this book. Using the same data on the 1,500 largest public companies in the United States, we calculated the total amount of options they granted between 1992 and 2001. We then determined what share went to the top five officers in each

company, and tried to correlate their relative share to the performance of the firm's stock three years after the options were granted.
(You need the time lag because of the vesting period that applies to
most options.)

Our finding: There's no correlation. The companies whose executives took more had no better returns in the following three years
than those that took less. Worse, the firms whose corporate chieftains were most likely to take a bigger share had sub par performance to begin with. Since the extra ownership made no difference,
the shareholders with the greediest CEOs were just throwing good
money after bad. The relationship held true regardless of the size of
the corporation, as measured either by its market value or by how
many employees it had.

At a minimum, we conclude that there's little rhyme or reason to
the disparity between the number of options many CEOs receive
and those granted to the employees they govern.

Overall, it seems clear that options have been seriously misused
as a tool for motivating executives. CEOs have taken much more
wealth than they can justify, and they've shared too little with average employees if the goal is to create a more entrepreneurial workplace. Corporate America's CEOs cut themselves and an elite group
of executives and other employees in on an unbelievably lucrative
ride, and left almost everyone else in their companies sitting back
on the roadside.

Investors have lost out, too, since they've surrendered tremendous ownership to executives with no clear evidence that all of
these stock options were judiciously spent. They've also lost out on
the proven gains they could have received if their companies had
shared the wealth with average employees and changed their corporate cultures accordingly. "Management has an obligation to recommend option grants that make the pie bigger for all shareholders," said Adam Blumenthal, New York City's first deputy
comptroller, whose job overseeing city employees' massive pension
fund makes him a leading advocate for institutional shareholders.
"They also have a responsibility to not recommend grants that are
only good for them personally." But in light of the scandals at companies such as Enron, WorldCom, and Global Crossing, "we see

that there's no reason to think those two are the same. Many executives have shown that they have a conflict of interest in deciding who gets options in their own companies."

The ultimate irony is the stated justification many corporations employ for their executive compensation practices. The language comes right out of the rich tradition of employee ownership. Listen to how General Motors describes its executive risk-sharing program. "A significant portion of each executive's total compensation is linked to accomplishing specific measurable results intended to create value for stockholders both in the short-term and the long-term . . . . Options are granted to emphasize the importance of improving stock price performance and increasing shareholder value over the long term and to encourage executives to own GM stock." GM approved its most recent plan in 1997, allotting more than 100 million shares to it. The company said it expected to give options to 4,000 employees a year. While 4,000 may sound like a lot of people, it represents only about 1 percent of the auto giant's 365,000 employees.

Even companies that have extended motivational wealth sharing to a broader group typically still top-load their plans. For example, in its 2001 shareholder letter, GE said:

> Over 30,000 employees below the executive officer level have been awarded one or more stock option grants under a broad-based stock option program initiated in 1989. This program . . . reinforces in the Company the entrepreneurial environment and spirit of a small company by providing real incentives for these employees to sustain and enhance GE's long-term performance. The Committee believes that the superior performance of these individuals will contribute significantly to the Company's future success.

Still, the 30,000 are mostly executives and managers, and they represent less than 10 percent of GE's 317,000 workers. That's a far cry from the solid majorities or entire workforces included in the option programs of the High Tech 100 and some other high-tech firms. Like most other traditional companies, GE acts as if the fate of the company lies with a small minority of its employees. All the rest don't matter.

Lurking beneath these explanations is a view of the world that comes straight out of the American thinker Ayn Rand's paeans to individualism. In novels such as *The Fountainhead* (1943) and *Atlas Shrugged* (1957), Rand waged ideological battle against the evils of socialism by arguing that the entrepreneurs and titans who run corporate America are the true "creators" or "prime movers" of capitalism. Their genius, their ingenuity, their spark of initiative, she proclaimed, is responsible for all the bountiful wealth our economy produces. Her books sold millions, and she developed a cult following

In *Atlas Shrugged*, Rand drove home her point with a tale about what would happen if all the CEOs went on strike. Sure enough, the motor of capitalism is cut dead. Economic activity sputters to a crawl, and the country sinks into a barren existence even gloomier than life in the old Soviet Union.

Corporate America's pay practices embody a similar view. Few people express it this way and maybe most CEOs and shareholders don't even think it consciously. But you sometimes get a glimpse of such a mentality when overpaid CEOs are put on the spot about why they don't share the option wealth more broadly with their fellow employees. For example, at a 1999 corporate meeting of Disney Inc., CEO Michael Eisner said: "You don't think we should give stock to the guys [attendants] in the parking lot, do you?" A Disney spokeswoman later explained that he was referring to the dilution costs of widespread options. But Eisner exemplifies the overpaid CEO whose option payouts far exceed the return to shareholders Disney has delivered under his rule.

The boss-gets-almost-everything stock option philosophy doesn't square with a perspective that sees the corporation as a complex ensemble of people who all must be motivated to play their part in a harmonious whole. Nor does it mesh with the mounting importance of intellectual capital in advanced economies. Instead, most large companies act as if the director of the marching band alone, or maybe the top few percent of those directors, determines its fate. All of his or her band members are just so many interchangeable players, who can be replaced with another just as able to carry a tune if only the director tells them when to play and how.

Corporate America's standard employee option plans dilute public shareholders on the belief that five employees, or at best a small slice at the top, alone determine the company's fate and fortune. Traditional companies have taken all the lessons about employee participation and ownership they learned in the past two decades and applied them only to this thin top layer.

There is a better way to do it, namely, sharing options more broadly. This approach also makes sense in other corporate settings, as some CEOs realize. The general theory behind most employee option programs in corporate America "is that only [senior executives] make a difference," said D. Wayne Calloway, the CEO of PepsiCo, in a 1989 newspaper interview. "We don't think that fits our company." That year, Pepsi put that philosophy into action by rolling out a stock option plan, called SharePower, which now covers 500,000 employees who average at least 1,500 hours a year. On average, they get options worth 10 percent of their annual pay.

To see how other companies can do the same thing, let's look at what it would take to apply the principles of partnership capitalism in a traditional corporate setting.

# 9

# Partnership Capitalism

## How to Put It All Together

We believe that partnership capitalism as practiced by the High Tech 100 provides constructive lessons for corporate America. They're not model companies in many respects, particularly in light of the vast wealth they lost for many investors. Still, the new form of the corporation evolving in the industry offers a role model on which others can draw.

As we've stressed throughout the book, high-tech firms haven't really discovered anything new. Instead, they have synthesized a range of ideas about employee ownership that traditional companies have grappled with for many years. Quite a few early technology firms came to similar conclusions many years ago, especially in Silicon Valley, as did thousands of mostly closely held companies that have used ESOPs as the center around which to build participatory cultures.

The one aspect that is new, however, involves the comprehensive use of stock options to turn their employees into owners. We've come to the conclusion that the addition of options to the employee ownership mix offers both companies and workers a more attractive and versatile approach than ESOPs, 401(k)s, and other methods of employee ownership. The fact that virtually all the leading companies in the industry have articulated, and put into practice, the same vision also shines a powerful light on the concept of stock option capitalism. More established companies now can see for themselves that combining the financial and cultural aspects of employee ownership into a unified approach can, if done right, provide a better alternative to the traditional corporate relationship among shareholders, managers, and employees.

The partnership approach to sharing the risks and rewards of property ownership promises to improve the prospects of the major stakeholders in a public company. For companies and for shareholders, the idea makes sense if the ownership they surrender inspires employees to work harder or smarter. If motivated workers generate sufficient extra growth for the company, public shareholders will own a smaller, but more valuable, share of a bigger pie. Stock options also provide a measure of downside risk not available with most other forms of employee ownership, since investors suffer no dilution if their company's share price falls or fails to rise.

For employees, partnership capitalism can provide a less hierarchical workplace environment, one that gives them greater input into their daily jobs. It offers the satisfaction of owning a piece of the company for which they work. Employees also enjoy the prospect of a significant financial reward beyond their basic salary. One important lesson from the High Tech 100 is that a partnership built around options allows employees to become capitalists without investing their own savings to purchase company stock. Options allow average workers to buy ownership with their sweat equity, a much more affordable prospect.

Such rewards may offer one way to reverse the stagnation of the average American worker's hourly paycheck, which has risen by a grand total of only about 3 percent since 1973, after adjusting for inflation. While wages have outpaced consumer prices since 1996, capital has provided a far greater source of increased income in America in the past three decades. Partnership capitalism can bring average workers into the capitalist ranks, letting them share more fully in the bounty the economy creates.

Stock option capitalism also offers a more prudent division of risk and reward than other kinds of employee ownership. Critics have rightly pointed out that the single largest form of worker ownership today, the company stock held in 401(k)s, ties up savings in the shares of a single company, which violates the time-proven investment caveat against having all your eggs in one basket. Many employee share purchase plans do the same thing. This became all too clear after the stock market slump, which wiped out that $260 billion worth of employee ownership in America—about 90 percent of it from these two kinds of plans. (See Appendix C for more details.)

Employee options minimize these problems or avoid them altogether. Workers can cash out when their options vest, so they're not locked into one stock for many years and won't face the Enron calamity of losing their job and their savings in one stroke. Because employees lose nothing if their options aren't in the money, options also put important circuit breakers on their risk of capital ownership by providing limits on the downside.

Such an economic partnership does involve risks, but they're shared more or less equally by everyone. For shareholders and companies, the risk is that they will surrender future ownership stakes that, at least under some circumstances, may accrue to employees even if they don't lift the company's value to a higher level than it would have achieved without the options. Similarly, employees may throw themselves into their jobs with much more vigor than they would in a conventional corporate setting, only to watch their stake in the firm's future profits evaporate due to a slowing economy, poor luck or lousy management at their particular company, or some external factor like a recession. Some of these problems can be overcome by, for example, indexing employee options to an industry or market average. Either way, the partnership approach to value creation would bring a range of gains to most corporate partners, most of the time.

Having said this, however, any company intrigued by the idea still is left with the question of how to apply it to a more traditional corporate setting. The first task must be to alter the less flexible corporate hierarchy that still grips many large U.S. companies. Clearly, changing a corporation's culture is a much more arduous undertaking than setting up a financial scheme to share wealth with employees. For that reason, it's probably the most important component of partnership capitalism. The top-down approach made more sense when it was devised a hundred years ago, under the name of scientific management, or Taylorism (after Frederick Winslow Taylor, an early proponent). Back then, many large companies were manufacturers that maximized efficiency by telling their workers every move to make. Today, most companies need employees to think on the job, whether they labor in a factory, write software, or work with customers in a retail establishment.

Partnership capitalism works best in an entrepreneurial corporate culture. It requires firms to try to spread power, prestige, and resources broadly among employees, and attempt to equip them with the skills and information they need to achieve the goals of the company. Flat corporate hierarchies require managers and executives to listen to employees and even to accept criticism from them. "If you are not able to allow people to criticize you, you will never be able to make the best decisions," said Infospace CEO Naveen Jain.

"It doesn't mean that you make the decisions by committee. But you do allow people to come and say that is the stupidest thing they ever heard. You allow them to explain why they believe that. You sit down and say, 'Look, for these five reasons I don't think what you are saying is right.' You may still say, 'Look, great, why don't you stick to your coding and let me do my job.' But nonetheless you heard their arguments, and lot of times you come back and say, 'You know what I think, you are right.'"

A true partnership requires meaningful wealth sharing as well. Over the past decade or so, corporate America has used stock options to create a form of partnership with CEOs and other high-level executives and managers. Average workers, for the most part, mostly hold ownership in 401(k)s and employee stock purchase plans. Aside from ESOPs, much of this isn't risk sharing at all, since workers usually must purchase their ownership stake with their own money.

Essentially, corporate America has extended the least risky ownership stake—stock options—to those who can afford to take on the most risk, that is, the highest-income people at the top of the pyramid. It has given the riskiest stake to average workers, who can least afford to gamble their savings on one stock. This is just what happened at Enron: Average workers lost most of their 401(k) company stock, while executives used their more flexible option and other stock incentive plans to bail out before the company collapsed.

Any large company that wants to embrace a true partnership with its employees must decide how much property to share with them. The High Tech 100 may not be a particularly useful guide for much of the rest of corporate America in this regard. Most conventional companies aren't startups in which a few founders have invested small sums of capital that they often perceive as a financial gamble. Instead, a mainstream company has many thousands of shareholders who spent hard cash to buy their stake and want a sound, steady return on their investment. Most corporations also operate in industries that have been around for decades or even longer. It's unrealistic to expect that they can grow at anywhere near the rates achieved by high-tech companies in the late 1990s, no matter how motivated employees become. So it may not make sense to part with the 17 percent option ownership stake the High Tech 100 have extended to their workforces.

In addition, high-tech firms are built mostly on knowledge, or human capital. Their primary asset resides in the minds of their employees, who must think up the new software or design the new hardware. While traditional companies are moving in this direction, most still rely more heavily on physical capital, whether it's an auto factory required to produce cars or the computers and real estate a bank needs to service its customers. You can see the dividing line clearly by looking at how much capital is invested in each.

On average, the High Tech 100 give each of their employees just $65,000 worth of equipment, while the Corporate America 100 back up each one of theirs with $250,000 worth. Companies that use more human capital to produce wealth usually can reap higher returns from employee ownership than ones that rely more heavily on physical capital. After all, partnership capitalism creates extra value by spurring employees to do a better job. If they're responsible for a greater share of the wealth produced in the first place, the amount of extra gain they are capable of producing should be higher as well.

So instead of using our High Tech 100, we can turn again to corporate America's own experience to get some guidance as to what level of worker ownership might make sense in a conventional business setting. There are several relevant examples. The first is the extensive employee ownership history we reviewed in Chapter 7. We saw that companies that used significant employee ownership in the past several decades, such as ESOPS or profit sharing, gave their workers a rough average of 8 percent of their shares (after dilution is taken into account).

This 8 percent is broadly analogous to the 17 percent option ownership stake held by High Tech 100 workers. It suggests that as a very rough guide, the average large corporation could expect to reap higher profits and see its stock price jump if it shared a total of about 8 percent or so of its ownership with its workforce. That's not a hard and fast figure by any means. But it offers a reasonable starting point.

There's also the question of the annual run rate. Here other guideposts illustrate what might make sense for much of corporate America. Most traditional companies might overdilute if they tried to match the high annual option grants found in the High Tech 100, which by coincidence happen to come out at 8 percent, too. (Don't confuse these two figures. The 8 percent in the preceding paragraph refers to the total amount of employee equity a company has outstanding at any given time. The 8 percent run rate measures how much employee equity high-tech firms grant every year.)

Probably the best example can be found in the traditional companies that offer options to most employees. For instance, in Chapter 7 we discussed a study of 490 firms that did so. They exclude Internet and other technology firms and thus provide a good idea of what companies in other kinds of industries might be able to do. The study showed that these companies, which include everything from industrial manufacturers to communications and pharmaceutical firms, outperformed similar companies on several measures. On average, these 490 companies had run rates of about 3 percent.

Another study was done in 2000 for a handbook on broad-based stock options by the National Center for Employee Ownership. It looked at 150 traditional companies with such plans (software and e-commerce firms were excluded). Those had run rates averaging a little over 4 percent.

Further guidelines come from the run rates that fund the executive stock option plans of virtually every large company. The 1,500 largest corporations in the United States gave a little more than 2 percent of their ownership to top-level executives in 2000 in the form of options (a number, by the way, that doubled for the 500 largest firms over the 1990s as executive stock options ballooned). Of course, as we found in Chapter 8, there's scant evidence that shareholders have profited from such large handouts. However, since all the research we've found shows that companies would make money if they shared ownership with the rank and file, it could make sense to use at least part of the existing run rates to make partners out of everyone in the company. The other possibility, of course, is simply to increase run rates to make more options available for the rank and file, which is what many companies with broad-based option plans have done.

All of these figures are very rough averages that summarize what has happened at many companies over a number of years. So they certainly don't constitute a precise answer about the level of total dilution or the run rate that would produce greater returns for the shareholders of a typical company in corporate America. Still, they provide some parameters about where to start constructing the financial side of partnership capitalism in a traditional setting. Indeed, the numbers provide a conservative view, since most of the firms in these examples didn't put together the entire package of cultural and financial changes the way the High Tech 100 have done. Theoretically, companies that are able to shift to full-fledged partnership capitalism might see even greater returns from greater risk sharing with employees.

Our conclusion, then, is that many large corporations in the United States could safely set up a stock option plan that gives employees something like 3 or 4 percent of the company each year, with a maximum employee equity of something on the order of 8 percent. If they did, they could expect to see their stock price climb by at least 2 percentage points more than it would having done otherwise (the average gain from all the employee ownership studies we reviewed in Chapter 7).

This may not sound like much, but in fact it's a lot. To see why, look at how the average company performs. Since 1926, the U.S. stock market has risen by 10 percent a year. This is a long-run average, which includes wide swings such as the Great Depression and the bull market of the 1990s. As a result, it doesn't tell you with any precision what the stock of an individual company is likely to do in a given year, or even in a given decade. But it's the most conservative guideline to use for our purpose, since it tells you what all companies on average can reasonably expect to achieve over the long haul.

Adding 2 percentage points to the 10 percent average means that stock option capitalism can give shareholders 20 percent (2 points out of 10) more value than they would get if their company just sticks to the conventional corporate model. Compounded over time, this quickly adds up to a meaningful advantage. For example, say you invest $10,000 in the S&P 500 or the corporate America 100. Using our 10 percent guideline, your investment would grow to about $16,100 after five years. Now say you invest an equal sum in an index fund comprised of similar large corporations that have chosen to pursue stock option capitalism. On average, you should earn 12 percent, which would leave you with about $17,600. This additional $1,500 means that the stock of the partnership firms returned 25 percent more after five years. In fact, the gain would be even larger, since we haven't accounted for reinvested dividends here. Remember, this is how much you would earn after you've accounted for the extra stock ownership you dole out to employees each year. A return of that magnitude should be enough to cover the potential risk that comes from trying a new corporate model.

Of course, these general guidelines, an 8 percent maximum employee equity and an annual run rate of 3 or 4 percent, only describe the expected tradeoff between dilution and shareholder return in very broad terms. For stock option capitalism to pay off for traditional companies, they must carefully adapt the concept to fit their own financial structure and prospects. They also must do so within the context of an entrepreneurial corporate culture, or the financial returns are likely not to occur.

In some companies, it might make sense to complement options with other forms of employee ownership. For example, as a general rule of thumb, firms with higher stock market values for each employee will have an easier time issuing options. The reason: The 3 or 4 percent they grant to employees annually will come to a larger amount per worker than the same percentage would be at a company with lower market values. As a result, these firms can deliver more wealth sharing to their employees for the same run rate.

Companies or industries with low market values per worker could find it easier financially to pursue partnership capitalism by mixing option grants with ESOPs, employee share purchase plans, or profit-sharing plans. ESOPs, for example, can sometimes bring companies a greater tax advantage than options, which allows them to share more wealth with their employees. Stock purchase plans might sometimes be more affordable, too, since they require less dilution from public shareholders. Profit sharing brings the advantage of only costing public shareholders after the profits are earned, which can put less of a strain on the company's finances than option dilution. Given the tremendous diversity in corporations' financial structure and outlook, the best approach is for a company to begin with a vision of the employee ownership it wants to achieve, and then figure out which mix of methods can work best given its situation.

From the standpoint of employees, partnership capitalism offers the prospect of significant capital gains. There is a widespread notion in the United States today that employee stock options are just another form of compensation, like salaries and benefits. Many experts made this point repeatedly during the national debate on stock options that arose after the failure of Enron in early 2002. Luminaries such as Federal Reserve Board chairman Alan Greenspan and his predecessor Paul Volcker both described options as compensation numerous times (although they were focused almost entirely on CEO options, not the broad-based kind we're talking about in this book). In May of that year, Standard and Poor's Corporation, which rates corporations for investors, introduced a new set of measures for earnings that count options on a company's expense line, just like other compensation.

We believe this view fundamentally misunderstands the nature of employee ownership in general and stock options in particular, at least regarding average employees. Far from being compensation for labor performed, options are instead a form of capital income. They represent risk sharing based on joint property ownership. Options turn employees into economic partners in the enterprise. As such, they stand to share in the stock appreciation that they help to bring about. Essentially, options offer employees a way to become shareholders by spending their human capital instead of their cash. They're still employees and they still get paid their regular wages and benefits. But options provide an additional dimension to their employment relationship, allowing workers to participate in both the risks and the rewards of property ownership.

There's substantial economic evidence that options bring workers capital rather than labor income. Labor economists typically think of compensation as an earnings package whose value is set by the supply and demand for the particular labor the employee can provide. From this standpoint, there's little distinction between hourly wages, an annual salary, and benefits such as health care or pensions. All of it adds up to a compensation package whose level is largely determined by market forces.

However, the earnings workers get from options comes on top of their regular market wage. It's true that some high-tech firms, the ones that engage in wage substitution, do effectively require workers to pony up their own money to become property owners. These firms basically get employees to buy their options with a part of their salary. But this isn't a necessary feature of employee options, or a usual one.

Several studies demonstrate this. For example, the point came through clearly in the study of the 490 non-Internet firms with broad-based option plans. On average, they paid their employees about 8 percent more than all other public companies between 1985 and 1987, when most of them set up their option plans. A decade later, they still paid about 8 percent more, excluding any money workers got from options. In other words, these employees got option income on top of the same pay hikes everyone else in the United States had received over the decade.

The same is true for ESOPs. Several studies show that companies offer them in addition to any other retirement or savings plan they set up to be competitive in the marketplace. For example, a study we mentioned in Chapter 7 that compared 1,200 ESOP firms to 1,200 similar non-ESOP ones showed that the ESOP companies were four times more likely to have a traditional pension and five times more likely to offer a 401(k). The conclusion: ESOPs don't substitute for a retirement benefit that companies give their employees to remain competitive. Instead, it comes on top of market-level benefits.

Two smaller studies buttress the point. One compared ESOP and non-ESOP firms in Massachusetts, while the other did the same in Washington state. Both found that the levels of pay and other benefits were higher at the ESOP companies. Similarly, the wealth of literature on profit sharing indicates that such earnings generally don't substitute for pay or benefits.

Options and other forms of employee ownership deliver extra gains because employees do something more than their regular jobs in the companies that grant them. For partnership capitalism to work, employees must make more use of their abilities and intelligence, or their options or other property sharing could wind up worth nothing. The harder they work, or the smarter, the more their equity will be worth. Working harder or more efficiently is a real cost to employees, but it's often a lot easier way to pay for ownership than the direct wage sacrifice typically required when workers buy company stock in 401(k) or stock purchase plans.

So how much could workers in a traditional corporation expect to get if their employer adopted partnership capitalism? The reward must be large enough to command the attention of employees, otherwise they won't be motivated to put out more effort. We have concluded that workers should get a minimum of 15 percent of their annual paycheck every year to begin to achieve the desired incentive effect.

In the model we've sketched out so far, all the employees of a company would split options worth 3 or 4 percent of its ownership every year (on a diluted basis, as usual). But the monetary worth of this figure to employees will differ widely, depending on the nature of any particular company and how the total option pie is split up among the workforce. Once again, many high-tech firms aren't too helpful in illustrating what workers stand to earn, since very few companies are lucky enough to experience the jackpot stock runups they enjoyed in the late 1990s. However, we can get at least a ballpark idea by looking at more conventional companies that offer options to most of their workers.

One example can be found in the study of 150 such companies we mentioned above by the National Center for Employee Ownership. The study didn't report how much income employees at these companies actually had made from their options. However, it did tell us the average number of options employees received in 1999, according to broad job type, as well as the average strike prices at which they had received them. These two facts allowed us to calculate the initial value of all the options the average employee got that year. This is the amount each employee would have to pay to exercise the options when they vest. They get to keep any additional money that would come if the stock price rises from the exercise price.

Of course, we have no way of knowing how much the shares of all these companies rose after 1999 or will rise in the future. But to get some idea of what employees could expect, we returned to the same 10-percent-a-year scenario we used to estimate the returns shareholders stand to make. Using that assumption, we calculated how much individual employees would earn if the options they received in 1999 vested in five years and they sold the stock as soon as they were able to exercise them. The outcome: Hourly workers would take home option profits of roughly $5,600, or 16 percent of

**TABLE 9.1   What Employees Could Expect to Earn from Partnership Capitalism**
(Average Profit on 1999 Option Grants after Five Years, Assuming 10 Percent Annual Stock Price Increases)

| Job | Salary | 1999 Option Grant | Profit in 2004* | Profit as a Share of 1999 Salary (%) |
|---|---|---|---|---|
| Hourly | $33,000 | $9,200 | $5,600 | 16 |
| Non-technical | $53,000 | $29,300 | $17,800 | 34 |
| Technical | $76,000 | $48,000 | $29,300 | 38 |
| Sales | $92,000 | $76,500 | $47,600 | 51 |
| Middle mgr. | $83,000 | $70,800 | $43,300 | 52 |
| Senior mgr. | $134,000 | $173,800 | $106,100 | 79 |
| Executives | $159,000 | $531,000 | $324,800 | 204 |

NOTES: *Projection based on the assumption that employees exercise all their 1999 options after five years and sell the stock for an immediate cash profit.

SOURCE: Authors' analysis of "Current Practices in Stock Option Plan Design." National Center for Employee Ownership, 2000.

their 1999 pay, after five years. Employees at higher levels get an increasing share of the profits. The breakdown for all the employee groups is shown in Table 9.1.

Obviously, employees wouldn't be guaranteed these sums, just as shareholders aren't assured of getting an extra 2 percent return in exchange for the options the company issues. For example, in the bull market of the late 1990s, when stocks climbed by 20 to 30 percent a year, these figures would have been more than several times larger. In a flat market, employees may go years with little or no profit. But these figures give us at least a rough estimate of what employees might initially earn if corporate America embraced stock option capitalism with annual run rates of 3 or 4 percent a year.

Over time, they would probably get quite a bit more. The reason: Option profits grow with the market value of the company. In the survey described in the table, employees' option grants totaled about 4 percent of their company's ownership on average (after dilution). In our model, they would receive that much every year. As a result, their option profits would increase in tandem with their company's market capitalization, at least within reasonable limits. So, for example, if a company had a market value of $1 billion in 1999, employees' 4 percent stake would have been worth $40 million that year. If the stock rose by 10 percent a year as we assumed in the table, they would earn a collective $24 million profit after five years. (Their stock would have a market value of $64 million and they would have to pay $40 million—their strike price—to buy the stock when the options were exercised.) This is just another way of describing what workers could earn from their 1999 options, only now we're lumping all employees together.

Now look at what would happen if the company prospered and its market value doubled to $2 billion. Say this occurred in seven years, which it would if the firm's stock price rose at 10 percent a year. Every year, employees would get option grants that climb by that much as well. By 2006, they would split 4 percent of the $2 billion, or $80 million. Five years after that, they would earn a collective $49 million profit—nearly double the amount earned five years earlier. (Again assuming 10 percent annual stock price growth, their shares would be worth $129 million and their strike price would be $80 million.)

Of course, any company growing at such a steady pace would undoubtedly be hiring along the way. So that $49 million would be split among more workers. In addition, salaries hopefully would climb over the ten years, so each worker's share of the $49 million wouldn't double as a percent of their annual pay. Still, it's clear that even hourly workers would be earning much more than 16 percent of their annual pay at that point. After all, their capital income would be rising at 10 percent a year, far more than anyone could reasonably expect average wages and salaries to increase.

Indeed, a smoothly functioning partnership company would go a long way toward offsetting a repeat of the wage stagnation that gripped the U.S. economy starting in the early 1970s. For more than twenty years after U.S. productivity growth began to stagnate in 1973, the typical American worker saw pay hikes that gradually left them farther and farther behind inflation. Wages did finally grow fairly quickly in the late 1990s, as the economy boomed and productivity growth soared. But by 2001, average wages for non-supervisory workers were just 3 percent higher than they were at the 1973 peak. If even hourly workers could have earned something like 16 percent more each year, with the amount increasing annually with the stock market, American family incomes would be dramatically higher today.

Options also alleviate a major drawback that exists with most other forms of employee ownership, namely the lack of diversification they entail. It's a staple of financial investing that you shouldn't own too much of one stock, because the risk that it will underperform the market is just too great. Enron, where most workers had a lot of their 401(k)s locked up in the company's shares, is a prime example. ESOPs have a similar problem, although it's much less of an issue since they aren't purchased with worker savings and provide employees with a benefit that comes on top of their regular pay and benefits. Workers would come out ahead if they could sell their ESOP shares and diversify, but since they probably wouldn't get those shares without the ESOP, they're better off getting extra earnings in a single company's stock than not getting the extra earnings at all.

Options, however, allow workers to take their wealth as soon as they vest. If options are granted every year, employees can and usually do cash out on an annual basis as options granted three or four years ago vest and become exercisable. This allows employees to diversify their wealth on an ongoing basis. It doesn't completely eliminate the diversification problem, but it minimizes it.

The greater liquidity options provide mean they offer an extra financial buffer against corporate failures like Enron, Global Crossing, and WorldCom. Most companies don't go bankrupt, of course. But when those collapsed, many employees lost much of their retirement savings, which had been tied up in their company's stock through 401(k) and stock purchase plans. At Enron, for example, 60 percent of the company's 401(k) was invested in Enron stock, a practice management had strongly encouraged. As a result, workers and retirees lost more than $1 billion worth of retirement assets in 2001 as the company's shares collapsed.

This generated tremendous debate about the extremes of employee ownership, prompting the introduction of several bills in Congress to limit the share of company stock employees could have in their 401(k)s, to force companies to allow employees to diversify their 401k company stock holdings, and to limit management's ability to prevent employees from selling their shares in down markets while management safeguards its own interests. Although none had passed by the time this book went to press, the last two proposals had widespread support. The episode gave something of a taint to employee ownership. While the critics have a point, stock options limit such damage, because workers can cash out a portion of their wealth each year instead of being forced to keep it in a 401(k) until retirement.

Sharing the wealth doesn't mean socialist egalitarianism. Partnership capitalism doesn't necessarily undercut the traditional system of pay differences, which, at least theoretically, rewards individuals according to what they contribute to an organization. High-tech firms cultivate flat hierarchies that promote workplace equality, but that doesn't mean the financial rewards need to be distributed equally. Employee ownership is a way for property-holders to motivate the people who can enhance the value of their property. If those with higher skills can bring greater value, they get greater reward.

BEA Systems chairman Bill Coleman said:

> The more senior people get more stock options, because they can influence a lot more of the success of the company. Relative to their income, you need to give them more to actually make a difference in their thinking and their perception. I spent ten years at Sun [Microsystems] and Sun had the same philosophy that we do. We do an annual merit refresh for the top 75 percent [that is, he gives a new round of options every year to employees whose individual performance puts them in the top 75 percent of the workforce]. The top 25 percent get probably twice as much as the third quartile. And the bottom quartile, they don't get any refresh [just their initial option grant]. You really want to retain those top people. You want their handcuffs [from the option wealth they stand to collect when they vest] to get bigger and tighter.

It may be, in fact, that high-tech firms doled out larger option shares to lower-echelon workers in their earlier days simply because they were growing so rapidly. As growth rates come back to earth, option compensation may start to tilt even more toward the top. Rick Tavan, an executive vice president of Tibco, put it like this:

> If you look at a seventy-five-year-old smokestack industry company, you're going to find a very different distribution of equity than you find in a Silicon Valley startup. When that startup is seventy-five years old, [it will have] something closer to what you call the old economy distribution of wealth potential. No, I don't think it's temporary. I think the concept of universal ownership is here to stay. When my company is seventy-five years old, everybody will be a shareholder. But I think maybe we'll see more disparity between the top and the bottom, because it is easier to attract more junior people into an older company than to attract executives.

It's clear that companies don't necessarily have to hand out options equally to everyone for partnership capitalism to be successful. True, executives in corporate America can't easily justify the large equity stakes they already take out for themselves. As a result, it could be psychologically difficult to persuade shareholders to issue even more options. Still, a number of large corporations have begun to move in this direction, including the 6 percent in the Corporate America 100. Doing so makes sense for shareholders, since the same philosophy of ownership executives apply to themselves should hold equally well for their employees. History also shows that most investors will come out ahead if they do.

# 10

# Conclusion

The central argument of this book is that most corporations in America would enjoy more motivated workers and larger profits if they embraced partnership capitalism centered around employee stock options. This model of the corporation stimulates better economic performance through a new division of the risks and rewards of property ownership. Many technology companies came to this conclusion as their industry grew. It seems likely that their approach will survive the tech shakeout and stand as an example for other industries. "Awarding stock options to all of our eligible employees has been a successful practice for our company," Microsoft CEO Steve Ballmer told us in mid-2001. "It's clear that a sense of ownership seems to be strongly linked to corporate success in many industries. I think you'll see a continuing shift towards remuneration packages that incorporate some form of ownership for employees."

These lessons aren't new. Traditional companies have learned at least parts of them several times over the decades. They in turn were tapping into a much longer history in the United States of property holders discovering and rediscovering the benefits of sharing the risks of ownership with employees. Government, too, has played a key role at various stages, supplying new tax incentives and accounting rules that have fostered different types of employee ownership.

But somehow, these ideas never seem to stick. Many corporations pursued employee ownership, but often based it largely on worker savings rather than true property sharing. Many also skimped on the amounts, failing to provide workers an opportunity to earn a meaningful incentive every year relative to their salary. Similarly, many corporate leaders began to alter their companies' cultures to give employees more input, then lost sight of that goal when it no longer seemed so necessary. It's almost as if American companies behave like the proverbial monkeys, who only think of fixing the leaky roof when it's raining outside. When corporations run into problems, like slumping productivity, fears of foreign competition or domestic takeovers, or chronic labor shortages, they turn to their employees for help and relearn the benefits of employee participation and ownership. Then when the picture brightens, executives tend to forget all that and slide back into the old, easier habits of autocracy and top-down management.

Many new tech companies may well turn out to be no different. They reinvented employee ownership largely out of a desperate need for talent, just like some technology companies before them. Now that the industry's growth has slowed and workers aren't in such short supply, the High Tech 100 may start to find that it's easier to tell employees what to do, instead of involving them in decisions. However, there are few signs of that happening so far.

Partnership capitalism may not be suitable for every company or even every industry. Certainly, many high-tech companies are a specialized breed that seem especially well-suited to a jazz-ensemble management style. They tend to be smaller and many have a stronger sense of camaraderie, born of shared technical interests, than many other companies in corporate America. These factors may limit the applicability of the model, or at least make it more difficult to achieve at companies that have more diverse workforces.

To some degree, the model offered by the High Tech 100 also may be limited by their knowledge-intensive nature. Most of these come close to being pure knowledge corporations that rely almost entirely on brainpower instead of physical equipment. Their employees tend to be highly educated, with many holding college degrees. That's not true of the American rank-and-file as a whole, among whom only about a quarter have graduated from college. "We don't have any manufacturing, we don't have any distribution," said Bill Coleman, the BEA Systems Chairman. "Virtually everyone in this company is a college graduate, and we hire almost nobody out of school. They're only here because they are good at what they do. If you're not empowering them, all you are doing is handicapping all this brainpower you've got."

Still, we believe a fundamental shift is under way as the role of intellectual capital looms larger than physical capital throughout much of today's postindustrial economy. As late as the early 1980s, tangible assets such as equipment and goods held in inventory comprised more than 70 percent of all the assets of nonfinancial corporations in the United States. By 2000, that figure had fallen to just above half, with the rest coming from intangible items such as patents, copyrights, software, and research and development—in other words, assets created by thoughts rather than muscle.

In emerging industries that depend as heavily as the Internet on human knowledge—such as biotechnology, for example—employee equity delivered through stock options approaches High Tech 100 levels in many leading firms. As far back as 1979, two senior experts on the corporation, Professor Michael C. Jensen of the Harvard Business School and Professor William H. Meckling, the then dean of the University of Rochester Business School, wrote that "in circumstances in which a disproportionately large fraction of an individual's wealth is represented by his human capital . . . we also expect to see profit-sharing partnerships arise."

There's some initial evidence that the partnership approach is starting to be taken seriously in a broad range of companies, and for workers with almost any level of skill or education. Just look at the 6 percent of the Corporate America 100 that have option plans open to a majority of their employees. These companies aren't practicing all the elements of partnership capitalism. Some, for example, don't give meaningful amounts of options to their employees. The difficulties some have encountered, such as media giant AOL Time Warner, underline the complexity involved in introducing an entrepreneurial culture to an old-line enterprise. Still, their efforts suggest that traditional corporations can at least begin to move in that direction.

Mainstream companies who wish to pursue employee ownership must adapt the concept to their own circumstances. To be successful, they can't simply pluck out one element of partnership capitalism and hope that it will be a magic wand to boost performance. Instead, traditional companies must look at the full range of financial incentives and participation methods, and combine those that make the most sense in their situation. They also must extend the changes across the entire organization, embracing everything from recruiting and training to teams, daily management, and compensation.

Most companies will never expand at the phenomenal rates the Internet firms achieved during their heyday. Rapidly growing companies or industries can support a lot of dilution. Slower-growth ones must proceed more cautiously, because growth can't compensate for as much dilution. As a result, options aren't going to shower most employees with riches of the magnitude many high-tech workers enjoyed in the late 1990s. "The highest value of a stock option is at the small companies that are going to grow explosively," said Covad vice chairman Frank Marshall.

Most investors in non-high-tech parts of the economy aren't going to reap such rewards either, so they shouldn't give away such large amounts of ownership. If they do, they're quite likely to lose more in dilution than they can ever hope to earn back from higher productivity. However, modest incentives can make a huge difference if combined with the right corporate culture.

Stock option capitalism may very well be more difficult to get right at established corporations. It's tough to ask managers and executives to give up power that they already have and treat employees more like partners than underlings. Most high-tech companies have had the benefit of creating their workplace cultures from scratch. A General Motors or an American Express would have to change an existing system that has a rich—or maybe entrenched—history. That's a far tougher proposition.

A partnership approach also is likely to be more of a challenge at big companies. Many companies in corporate America are much larger than high-tech ones and have many more employees. The Corporate America 100 average 35,000 workers each, while the High Tech 100 average a mere 1,760. Size tends to breed bureaucracy, which can be a daunting thing to change. There are some very large companies that so far seem largely to be making it work, such as Cisco, which is a High Tech 100 firm, and Microsoft, which isn't. But of course, they're both high-tech firms, with a similar culture.

A company with a cast of thousands is more likely to be dragged down by free riders, too. Skeptical economists long have argued that the incentive effects of employee ownership can get hopelessly thinned out as the size of an organization grows. In a large company, they say, rewards that flow to the entire group give each individual a powerful reason to shirk. The reason: Any employee's contribution to the firm's overall success will of necessity be very small. After all, if there are just ten workers and all contributed equally, any slacker would cut the company's performance by 10 percent. But if there are 10,000, any individual may correctly think, If I don't put in extra effort, the effect will be minuscule and I'll still collect the benefit of the extra productivity gain everyone else produces. The problem, of course, is that if everyone did this, there wouldn't be any extra gain.

"Even in the New Economy, as the company gets bigger, each person cannot make as much impact," said Naveen Jain, the Infospace CEO. So some employees may become "what you call 'tagalongs,' in other words, they become successful just because they happen to be there" as the company prospers, Jain said. "This is the Microsoft phenomenon. A lot of people made money not because they contributed to the wealth, but because they just happened to be there when the wealth was created. That does happen."

Some high-tech employees feel this way as well. John, the Excite engineer who didn't sell his options before the crash, said that "Equity in a bigger company doesn't seem that important, because it's harder to affect the stock price. Sure, I own a piece of the company and I can definitely make a difference. But how much does that difference matter? It is not like I can move the stock price myself, so it's much harder to make a long-term difference."

In recent years, experts on employee ownership have come to believe that the free rider problem can be overcome by encouraging cooperation among employees. Although significant financial incentives help to sustain workers' interest in collaboration, money alone won't suffice. Instead, companies must adopt teams and other forms of employee participation, which inhibit free riders by making individual employees feel a sense of obligation to their colleagues. Teamwork also motivates everyone to monitor the behavior of those they work with, to make sure they pull their weight. Many high-tech companies back up this approach by awarding larger option grants to team players.

"You can be a real star performer, but unless the entire team does well that doesn't count," said Tom, the head of a Cisco market group, in a 2001 interview with us. "You better operate as a team or none of us survive. We're all measured on our customer satisfaction rating every time we go in front of a client. Our customer client scores are posted and everybody has a right to look at them. So I (might) say, 'John, you're one of my team mates and you're dragging us down.' Or I may have a very very high score for a quarter, but the fact is, if my other teammates aren't meeting a certain minimum, we're all in trouble. I can't pull them out alone."

Still, the challenge this represents for large companies adds to the difficulty of spreading partnership capitalism widely throughout corporate America. The culture of employee ownership may not "translate very well to large traditional corporations," says Marcel Gani, the Juniper CFO. "I don't think you are going to change the behavior if you just add a lot to the ownership pot. You have to change the organization itself and the employee involvement has to feel true. It has to be kind of a cradle-to-grave thing, where people feel proud and you have an open culture where people feel like they can speak their mind. This goes together with having shares in the company. It's all of those things that make people willing to contribute. If the culture of the company changes tomorrow and we became more of a rigid, bureaucratic company, people would have the equity, but I don't think they would put in the extra effort."

Other high-tech CEOs see a culture clash, too. "The biggest thing I notice when we work with Old Economy companies is the slow decisionmaking processes," said Sclavos, the CEO of VeriSign, a 2,000-employee company that registers Internet addresses. "Part of that is the size and the bureaucracy. Part of it is forgetting how to make fast decisions, and not empowering decisionmaking down lower into the organization. There's almost a bull-in-the-China-shop analogy: We go in assuming that everybody at every level feels comfortable making decisions quickly for the corporation and takes risk. But that's not generally true."

Sclavos argues that traditional companies should use options to help change the culture. If he were put in charge of one, he said, that's just what he would try to do. "I believe that's the most important thing. Equity participation would be part of helping to show that management is sensitive to everyone needing to change. And if we do it, everyone will benefit. Options are the reward for the culture changing."

Employee ownership also helps to focus employees on the company's larger goals—the same rationale executives use to explain why they should get options. "There is a psychological buy-in that needs to take place in more traditional industries," said David Allen, the CFO of Interwoven, a High Tech 100 software firm. "You want people to participate because then they'll share in the ultimate objective of the company, which is to create shareholder value."

Jay Wood, the Kana chairman, agrees, although he acknowledges the magnitude of the challenge traditional companies face. The partnership culture "is transferable, but it's the old analogy of turning a big ship in a small river. In those large companies, cultures are so ingrained. People come in through the training process and are told, 'This is how we do things here.' So it's like moving a mountain. It's hard to take a traditional company and change the way it operates. Companies make these changes when they fall on difficult times. Then all of a sudden, there's an attitude shift."

The shift must also take place in the minds of the executives who champion partnership capitalism. SAIC CEO Bob Beyster said he came to see a policy of granting options to everyone as a means of rewarding and motivating employees at all levels of his company. "Employees earned it," he said. "They made something a success, helped solve a problem, all the things that make companies hold together. Those that were willing to do that deserved to own some of it. You have to subjectively say, 'This guy, although he did something different, is equivalent in importance to this guy over here who sold this ten million dollar contract.' A lot of people that do different things are in the same category."

Another key aspect of this attitude shift involves the concept of a career that undergirds the conventional corporate pyramid. The bureaucracy in many traditional companies is fueled and maintained by the calculating maneuvers of those trying to climb the narrow slopes of the pyramid. The flatter hierarchy found in many high-tech firms, coupled with the prospect of financial reward that options bring, can help to mitigate the corporate infighting that plagues many large companies. The partnership approach allows employees to share the wealth at different levels of the corporate hierarchy, which undermines the traditional corporate bureaucracy. "We don't have nearly as much of the politics associated with people worried about checking that box in my career, I should have that job, that's where I need to go," says Interwoven's Allen. "The people who come here say, 'How can I contribute. I want to work for a good company. I want to make some money.' We don't have nearly that type of water-cooler bullshit going on, and in talking to my peers in other Internet companies, I don't think they have as much of that either, because the classic career ladder just doesn't exist."

Partnership capitalism has potential pitfalls. For example, it's possible that a company can get carried away and grant too many options. If so, the dilution would be greater than any return and shareholders would lose out. As we saw in Chapter 5, even some High Tech 100 employees thought that their companies sometimes overdid it.

"They handed out options like they were going out of style, for bonuses, just for no reason," said Randall, a product engineer at Excite who spoke to us before the company's bankruptcy in 2001. At one point, he said, "It was almost every other month or something. It was at price points that are underwater today, but back then it was a big thing. They did it more when the stock had started to slide. I think they tried to use it more as an incentive. In June of 1999, they gave us a ton of options, but a month later all of them were underwater by the time we received the letter in the mail saying we got them. So they reissued even more than they had done before."

A related problem is whether employees who hold options might be tempted to look for ways to artificially pump up their company's stock, even if it means cutting corners. There was much discussion of this issue as it relates to executive stock options in 2002, following the collapse of Enron, which gave options to a majority of its workforce. In hearings on Capitol Hill, luminaries debated whether the lure of option wealth drove the company's top management to cut corners on accounting and break accepted business practices or even federal laws.

"I think there is a legitimate question in some cases as to whether the slogan of aligning the interests of management to the stockholders gets reversed and the interest of the stockholders is being aligned with the interests of the management, which is not the way it's supposed to be," said former Federal Reserve chairman Paul Volcker at one Senate hearing on Enron.

The partnership approach may offer some help in preventing options from distorting management's perspective. Because most rank-and-file workers aren't likely to rake in hundreds of thousands of dollars from their options, much less millions, their long-term financial interests still link primarily with their regular salary and overall health of the company. As a result, they have less incentive to cut corners to hype their company's stock. In fact, most have a good reason to object if top executives try to cook the books the way WorldCom leaders were charged with doing in 2002.

Another safeguard against the perverse incentives options created for corporate chieftains is to have a strong, independent board of directors. The Enron debacle prompted renewed calls for corporate America to embrace directors with more independence from the CEO. Enron directors, like so many of those at other companies, were handpicked by the company's CEO and often had relationships with the company of various kinds that seemed likely to compromise their independence. While there's no sign that many High Tech 100 firms have run into widespread corner-cutting like Enron or the other scandal-ridden companies that were exposed in 2002, their boards are even more insular than those at other large companies.

In part, that may be because many of these companies are still relatively new and relatively small. High-tech firms have an average board size of seven, compared to twelve at the typical large corporation, one study found in 2000. We looked more closely at the boards of the High Tech 100 and found that two of the seven are from top management. Of the remaining five outsiders, one was often from a venture capital firm or someone else closely connected to the company. In addition, even many of the five outside directors often have historic ties to management, lessening their neutrality. High-tech boards tend to have fewer independent directors and make virtually no use of special director committees to monitor corporate governance.

All of this seems inadequate. Both high-tech firms and any others that pursue partnership capitalism need powerful boards that can closely monitor the company's culture and ensure that wealth sharing doesn't warp behavior and mores. A strong board is also necessary to make sure that broad-based option programs are combined with the shift to a less hierarchical culture. Otherwise, public shareholders may not benefit and options can turn into a corporate giveaway.

Partnership capitalism also would seem to call for an employee representative to sit on the board. After all, if workers own a total of 8 percent or so of the company, as our model suggests would be feasible, they should be entitled to as much say-so on its top decisionmaking body as outside shareholders who own such a large stake. In fact, the standard assumption on Wall Street is that a 5 percent ownership stake is the threshold that entitles a shareholder to participate in the company's governance. Nor is an employee director such a strange idea. It happens on occasion in the United States, usually at unionized firms with large amounts of employee ownership. Workers on boards also have long existed in many European countries, where the practice came about as part of their more consensual style of labor-management relations. In the long run, a partnership corporation is only likely to succeed if boards of directors are truly independent from management. Part of that independence includes separate representation for employees—an idea that would serve technology companies well, too.

Another way to mitigate any perverse incentives for executives and employees to pump the stock would be to ensure shareholder approval of all option plans. Currently, management has the discretion to set up such plans and decide how much dilution shareholders should swallow. Some major shareholder groups called for this during the 2002 corporate governance debates following the scandals at Enron and WorldCom.

Partnership capitalism raises plenty of other issues. For instance, what happens in a prolonged bear market? Even if options do motivate employees, how many would stay psyched up if their employer's stock price is dead in the water for five or ten years? The cultures of most High Tech 100 firms seem to have survived the 2000 crash. However, it's not clear how well the model would hold up if employees had to wait many years for their company's stock price to grow again. One solution, which many high-tech firms used, is to set up or add to cash profit-sharing plans during times when the stock market is weak but the company continues to prosper. However, most companies can't and shouldn't continually reprice, regrant, or exchange options to keep employees motivated. Doing so usually would shift too much risk onto outside shareholders.

In fact, it's possible that the employee ownership culture found in the High Tech 100 only really works if the company's stock price is rising, even if it's not shooting up at double-digit rates. Amazon, if you remember, repriced its employees' options in early 2001, after its stock price had plunged from $107 to $30. Not long after, Owen, the Amazon middle manager, talked about employee morale before the repricing.

> I think the ownership culture depended on the stock price. It really did. The 'think like an owner' culture worked when the stock was going up. And it fell on deaf ears when the stock was going down. It ate on people's belief in the company. Not right away. But it just sort of ate on peoples' mood.

I'm a manager of about forty or fifty people, and I'm constantly looking for ways to motivate those folks. To be honest,
I feel that trying to motivate them with a speech about ownership in the company at this stage would be very unwise. It's a
sore subject for people. We now have a year and a half where
the stock has been going down. Everybody who joins the
company over that period gets their options set, and then a
few weeks later they're below water, then deeper below water,
then deeper below water. To feel the ownership, you have to
start to feel that you have something. They never really felt like
they had anything. The options were like window dressing for
them.

Still, using options to support a culture of employee ownership
is likely to achieve better results than methods that rely on direct
stock purchases. This seems to be one lesson to be learned from
United Airlines Incorporated's ESOP, which has been one of the
largest experiments in employee ownership in the United States in
recent times. In 1994, most of the airline's unionized workers
bought 55 percent of the company's stock, which they paid for
through large wage and benefit cuts and work rule concessions.
The effort began to transform employee attitudes and lift productivity in the first few years under the leadership of CEO Gerald
Greenwald. However, his successors increasingly alienated many
workers. A lot of employees also became increasingly disillusioned
with their investment as the company's once-soaring stock sank in
the late 1990s.

By the time the ESOP came up for renewal, labor and management were at each other's throats and the unions decided not to set
up a second one. The bitterness has been so great that much of the
cultural changes have long since dissipated. So has most of the positive views toward employee ownership, which has seemed like a
lousy deal to many as the carrier's continued woes dragged on and
on. Stock options might not have kept the new attitudes alive in the
face of all the missteps. Still, with the company teetering near bankruptcy in the summer of 2002, workers' expensive stock purchases

seemed unlikely to ever pay off. If, by contrast, their ownership stake had come largely through options that hadn't involved pay and benefit cuts, the experiment might have stood a better chance of weathering so many years of financial turmoil.

The most important ingredient in partnership capitalism is the cultural transformation it entails. Vivek Ranadive, the founder of Tibco Software said:

> There are scary elements to it. There are many in Russia who say, 'Maybe we would be better off if we went back to communism. At least things were secure. There was some order and we had to wait in long lines but at least we got food when we waited in those lines.' Now, you're going to have to be responsible for your own career. You're going to have to think about how I am going to have value and there is no such thing as a stable job. I have to do this, too. I'm the CEO, but if I don't add value I'll be tossed out. I should be tossed out.
>
> On one level it can be viewed as being scary, because there is no stability. Now, every person is an entrepreneur, just like the old days. You were a shopkeeper, and if your shop didn't do a good job then you went out of business. And so that's the world. It's back to the future, back to how it was 200 years ago. There were no corporations and every person was a value creator. Every person was an individual entrepreneur. And so the Web makes that possible. It's the craft economy.

Perhaps the biggest transformation must come from top executives. As the cult of the CEO grew in the 1990s, many large U.S. companies have become even more autocratic than they were before. Part of this may stem from the enormous chasms in pay that opened up with the spread of executive stock options and the soaring stock market. With CEOs now taking home an average of $11 million a year, they typically earn several times more than the next layer of management. The inner circle, in turn, takes home much more than the next group, and so on down the line.

Since how much you make frequently denotes power and prestige, wider pay gaps tend to push authority up the corporate pyramid. The effect is magnified because a larger share of white-collar pay comes in the form of options and bonuses related to performance. How someone performs has a large subjective element to it, which means that bosses have even more power over their underlings' immediate financial prospects than they do under a fixed salary system. As a result, everyone has an even larger incentive to please the boss than before. On a psychological level, the glorification of corporate America's top leaders makes it difficult for many executives to become true partners with employees. It's a challenge for most people to give up power. It's also a lot harder to listen to other people's ideas, instead of just telling them what to do.

But when employees are also owners, this approach won't work anymore, even if gradations in pay remain. "You need to be more persuasive than demanding," said Kana's Wood. "Employees feel like they own something here, and they want to understand why. If you're making a salary of $60,000 a year and someone says, 'Paint that blue instead of yellow,' you say, 'Okay, what's it matter to me, I'm getting my $60,000.' But if you think, 'Wow, painting that blue is going to change how successful this company is, and I own some stock in this company and it could affect my value,' well, then you're going to approach it differently. You might come back and say, 'Hey, how about we paint it green, and here's why.' It affects attitudes and it affects the way you have to approach people."

Corporate America has already been pushing for more employee teamwork and worker input into decisionmaking. To make these ideas work, managers have had to become less authoritarian. Partnership capitalism pushes managers in the direction of becoming coaches. Indeed, in the long run, corporate managers may have to become more like pro sport coaches, who must learn to draw out talent rather than command it. Such a redefinition of roles, which requires managers to share prestige with underlings, touches virtually every aspect of management.

This doesn't mean some kind of radical egalitarianism, where everyone has an equal voice. "We try to set up an environment that has participative management, which means that somebody is empowered to do something and they involve all the stakeholders when it's necessary to make a decision," said BEA's Coleman. "But when they make a decision, everybody else gets out of the way, as opposed to the consensus management that ends up happening when everyone can say no, no one can say yes, and everybody is in everybody else's way. So it is a balance."

Jain and other high-tech CEOs believe that sharing information is equally important. There's not much point in making employees shareholders, or partners in an enterprise, if they don't have enough information to identify with the company. "Most shareholders have more information about the company than the employees themselves," said Jain:

> That's very counterproductive. If your most important shareholders, the ones who can make a difference to other shareholders, don't even have the information that can allow them to change something or make it successful, then sharing equity is not going to solve the problem.
>
> The idea is to listen to your shareholders to see how to improve the company and the wealth in the company. Unless you can change the way management communicates with employees, making them shareholders is not going to fundamentally change how things happen in the company. So my advice, if you are the CEO of a large railroad or some other traditional company, is make sure you treat your employees like shareholders first, before you make them real shareholders.

This is a skill that much of corporate America has yet to learn, despite all the rhetoric about pushing decisionmaking down the ladder. To make employee ownership work, executives and managers must figure out how to help workers relate their daily activities to the company's larger goals. "I know as a manager that I have financial targets that I have to deliver to the company, so that we can make all of our numbers," said Owen, the Amazon manager.

I'm an MBA, so it is very easy for me to tie my efforts to the company, and to my stock price and my personal wealth. Especially when companies are bigger, you need managers—it can't just be the CEO—to translate your team's goals into an individual's specific day-to-day responsibility, and to draw out that math from what you do to how it affects the stock price.

That does not happen a lot. It really requires managers who are good teacher types, because it is not clear to the average employee how this connects. You can't feel ownership unless you understand how your actions affect this thing that you own. That doesn't work for a lot of people who haven't had that explained to them or haven't really thought it through. Especially in large organizations. When the company was small, everybody's job had a noticeable impact. Today, it has to be explained.

Although the decision to pursue partnership capitalism must come from a company's executives and employees, the federal government has a motivation to step in and play a role as well. Over the decades, Washington has been key to the spread of employee ownership in the United States. Congress established both ESOPs and 401(k)s, providing some favorable tax treatment as an incentive for companies to pursue these ideas. Doing the same with broad-based stock options would be a continuation of the same effort. ESOP incentives, too, should be expanded, to provide more flexibility for public companies that can't move toward partnership capitalism entirely with options.

There are many approaches under discussion. In 2002, politicians spent much time debating whether and how to rein in stock options for executives, which were widely perceived to be excessive and abused after the Enron disaster. One response might be to use tax breaks to encourage companies to pursue partnership capitalism by tilting the balance of options away from CEOs toward employees. Congress could, for example, reduce or eliminate the current tax deduction for options at firms that don't grant most of their options to most or all employees.

Supporters see plenty of precedent for such an approach. Already, the Feds slap a higher tax on regular executive pay, excluding options and bonuses, that exceeds $1 million a year. In addition, companies with 401(k)s must run financial tests every year to make sure that the highest-paid employees aren't getting too big a share of the firm's contributions. If they are, the company must reduce its contribution as well as the amount high-end employees can contribute.

Another possibility would be to give preferential tax treatment to companies that offer options to most workers. Some political and business leaders have suggested this at various points. For example, in the spring of 2002, Al Gore's vice presidential running mate Joseph Lieberman, who had long defended executive options, proposed a zero capital gains tax rate for companies that offer options to at least half of its nonexecutive ranks. Although he did so to fend off the critics that spoke out after the Enron debacle, the idea won support from some others as well. "Stock options are one way capitalism has been democratized in recent years, but too many companies still have plans that exclude all but the top echelons of management or give a disproportionate percentage of options to those top executives," Lieberman said in a speech.

Or Congress could require companies with top-heavy option plans to subtract the cost of the options from their profits, as critics such as Greenspan and Levin had proposed in mid-2002. After it became clear in 2002 that top Enron executives had enriched themselves through options by artificially pumping up the company's profits, the Federal Reserve's Greenspan and others proposed that corporations be required to count all options as a corporate expense. Doing so would make investors more aware of the true cost of options, the reformers argued, and prompt them to curb excessive executive options. The idea triggered a storm of protest from corporate America, particularly high-tech and Internet firms that make liberal use of options. They argued that their profit statements would be devastated if they had to take this approach.

However, requiring companies to expense options unless most grants go to a broad group of employees could help to achieve two purposes. It could put a damper on runaway executive options, and simultaneously spur the spread of broad-based option plans. If executives were willing to share the corporate bounty with employees, as so many high-tech firms do, they could keep getting options without damaging their profit records, although they might get fewer options than they do when most are given only to the company's top tier. The mere suggestion of this strategy raised anxiety even among high-tech firms, who feared that any proposal to expense options might steamroll through Congress or other oversight bodies without the exception being made for broad-based option plans. This would be a big mistake.

Still, the strategy of excluding broad-based options firms from any expensing requirements squares with the nature of employee options as we've elucidated it. The reform advocates argued that companies get a tax deduction for the options they issue even though they don't have to count them as a cost of doing business when it comes to reporting profits to shareholders. Many made the argument that executive options are compensation and thus should be treated just like salaries, bonuses, and other forms of pay, which also are counted as a corporate expense.

But as we've said, options, at least for nonexecutives, in fact aren't compensation at all. Instead, they represent risk-sharing profits that workers receive on top of their normal market wages and benefits. As such, it makes little sense to deduct the value of those options from profits. Unlike wages, which companies must pay out in cash, options require no expenditure by the corporation. Instead, they come out of the pockets of the company's shareholders, in the form of dilution.

Some experts contend that companies incur an opportunity cost when they grant options. They argue that if an employee gets an option at say $50, and the stock has climbed to $75 when they vest, the company loses $25. After all, it could have sold that share in the public market for $75, but instead it receives only the $50 the employee must pay to cash in the option. Others point out that this logic doesn't account for the economic benefit that options can bring to the company. When options work right, employees create extra value, which companies and their shareholders share in along with workers.

The only cash expense that a company incurs from options comes when they're actually exercised. This happens if the firm buys back shares to offset the dilution involved. Some experts have suggested that companies should deduct this expense from their profits, which makes more sense than trying to predict what the cost will be when the options are actually issued. If they did, the company should only expense the true cost, that is, the amount required to buy back an option minus the strike price it receives from the employee who exercises it.

A public policy favoring options for all employees would also be a more equitable use of taxpayer subsidies. In the late 1990s, options provided U.S. corporations with a break from federal taxes that added up to a stunning 27 percent of all corporate net income, according to a study by Mihir A. Desai, a Harvard Business School economist. In 2000, the largest 150 corporations alone used options, the bulk of which go to top executives and managers, to take $78 billion worth of tax deductions. Desai concluded that stock options emerged in the past decade as one of corporate America's main tax shelters. They are a key reason why corporations only paid about 10 percent of all the tax money collected by the U.S. government in 2001, down from 20 percent in 1977.

The United States. might consider other policies if many more employers and workers pursue a partnership approach. Congress, for example, could endorse the idea as a national policy, just as it did with ESOPs in the 1970s. To give companies more choices, it might reinstate some of the ESOP tax incentives and expand those for profit sharing. The SEC also might consider requiring companies to disclose more details about employee option ownership.

Stock options have been thoroughly abused by most major companies, whose executives have used them to transfer ownership of 10 percent of the nation's corporate wealth from public shareholders to a small coterie of top officials. But companies that have offered options to their entire workforce offer a much different example. They illustrate the potential to unleash an explosion of entrepreneurial activity, which undeniably has occurred in the United States, the dot-com crash notwithstanding. They also have changed the entire idea of a wage from a fixed salary to a share in capitalism itself. Together with the alternative work culture embraced by partnership companies, the new model illustrates how a different kind of corporation can be organized. "You're seeing a transformation of capitalism as a whole here, in that no longer are workers seen as tools for companies to expend as they see fit," said Vivek Ragavan, the CEO of Redback Networks. "I don't think the fundamental rules of valuation will be changed significantly. But the relationship of the corporate organization to its employees, and of management to its employees, has to be transformed to a different type of relationship. This is the type of corporate model that is more sustainable in the long term."

# Appendix A: The High Tech 100

| Corporation | Services and Products | Web Site (www.+) |
|---|---|---|
| 3Com | Networks and connectivity for business | 3com.com |
| Adtran | Network access products for digital telecom | adtran.com |
| Aether Systems | Extend business applications to any wireless device | aethersystems.com |
| Agile Software | Software for product chain management | agilesoftware.com |
| Akamai Technologies | Outsourced e-business infrastructure | akamai.com |
| Alteon Websystems (1) | Web performance acceleration appliances | alteonwebsystems.com |
| Amazon.com | Online shopping site | amazon.com |
| America Online (2) | Interactive services, Web brands and technologies | corp.aol.com |
| Ameritrade Holding (3) | Online brokerage products and services | ameritrade.com |
| Ariba | Web services for the CFO and procurement office | ariba.com |
| Art Technology Group | Online customer relations management applications | atg.com |
| Bea Systems | Applications infrastructure software | bea.com |
| Broadcom | Silicon solutions for broadband communications | broadcom.com |
| Broadvision | Enterprise business portal applications | broadvision.com |
| Cacheflow | Secure content networking appliances | cacheflow.com |
| Checkfree Holdings | Financial electronic software and services | checkfree.com |
| Cisco Systems | Networking for the Internet | cisco.com |
| Citrix Systems | Virtual workplace software and services | citrix.com |
| CMGI | Diversified Internet operating company | cmgi.com |
| CNET Networks | Services for buyers and sellers of technology | cnet.com |
| Commerce One | Global supplier network, software, and services | commerceone.com |
| Concentric Network (4) | Provider of broadband communications | xo.com |
| Copper Mountain | Intelligent broadband access solutions | coppermountain.com |
| Covad (5) | High-speed Internet and network access | covad.com |

*(continues)*

243

*(continued)*

| Corporation | Services and Products | Web Site (www.+) |
| --- | --- | --- |
| Critical Path | Software to maximize the value of the Internet | cp.net |
| Digex | Web and applications hosting | digex.com |
| Digital Lightwave | Technology for management of optical networks | lightwave.com |
| Doubleclick | Online advertising, email, and database marketing | doubleclick.com |
| E.piphany | Customer relationship management software | epiphany.com |
| Ebay | Online marketplace | ebay.com |
| Efficient Networks (6) | Designer and manufacturer of DSL solutions | efficientnetworks.com |
| E*Trade Group | Online investing, banking, lending, and advice | etrade.com |
| Entrust | Enhanced Internet security services | entrust.com |
| Espeed | Business-to-business electronic marketplace trading | espeed.com |
| Excite@Home (7) | Online portal | excite.com |
| Exodus (8) | Web hosting | exodus.com |
| Extreme Networks | Ethernet network infrastructure equipment | extremenetworks.com |
| Foundry Networks | Enterprise and service provider switching and routing | foundrynetworks.com |
| Freemarkets | Sourcing software and service solutions | freemarkets.com |
| Globespan (9) | High-speed broadband equipment and solutions | globespanvirata.com |
| Go2Net (10) | Online portal | go2net.com |
| Healtheon/WebMD | Internet services for physicians and consumers | webmd.com |
| Homestore.Com | Online information for real estate industry | homestore.com |
| i2 Technologies | Value chain management software solutions | i2.com |
| Informatica | Business analytics software | informatica.com |
| Infospace.com | Wireless and Internet software and services | infospace.com |
| Inktomi | Network infrastructure software solutions | inktomi.com |
| Internap | Centrally managed Internet connectivity services | internap.com |
| Internet Capital (11) | Business-to-business e-commerce network | internetcapital.com |
| Interwoven | Enterprise content management software | interwoven.com |

| Company | Description | Domain |
|---|---|---|
| ISS Group | Protect information from online threats | iss.net |
| Juniper Networks | Core, edge, mobile, and cable Internet services | juniper.net |
| Kana Communications | Software for managing customer relations | kana.com |
| Liberate Technologies | Digital video solutions for telephone networks | liberate.com |
| Lycos (12) | Web portal, search engine, and related sites | lycos.com |
| Macromedia | Multimedia Internet applications | macromedia.com |
| MarchFIRST (13) | Was an Internet professional services firm | No longer on the web |
| Mercury Interactive | Testing for IT infrastructure | mercuryinteractive.com |
| Metromedia Fibre (14) | Digital communications fibre infrastructure | mfn.com |
| Micromuse | Service and business assurance software | micromuse.com |
| Microstrategy | Business software for web, wireless, and voice | microstrategy.com |
| MMC Networks (15) | Network processors for feature-rich products | mmcnet.com |
| MRV Communications | High-bandwidth low-cost Ethernet access solutions | mrv.com |
| Netegrity | Solutions for securely managing e-business | netegrity.com |
| Network Associates | Network security and availability technology | nai.com |
| Network Solutions (16) | Internet domain names and related services | networksolutions.com |
| Next Level | Integrated multimedia access systems | nlc.dom |
| Niku | Services relationship management software | niku.com |
| Novell | Net business solutions | novell.com |
| Pairgain (17) | DSL broadbase access systems | adc.com |
| Phone.com (18) | Software for multinetwork communication services | openwave.com |
| Portal Software | Strategic billing for convergent network services | portal.com |
| Priceline.com | "Name Your Own Price" e-commerce | priceline.com |
| PSI Net (19) | Commercial Internet service company | cogentco.com |
| PurchasePro.com | Procurement and strategic sourcing applications | purchasepro.com |
| Quest Software | Application management solutions | quest.com |

*(continues)*

*(continued)*

| Corporation | Services and Products | Web Site (www.+) |
|---|---|---|
| Rational Software | Business software development platforms | rational.com |
| RCN Corporation | Phone, cable TV, and high-speed Internet services | rcn.com |
| RealNetworks | Internet media delivery | realnetworks.com |
| Redback Networks | Solutions for broadband networks | redback.com |
| Retek | Software services for the retail industry | retek.com |
| RSA Security | Builds secure e-business processes | rsasecurity.com |
| Sapient | Business and technology consultancy | sapient.com |
| Scient [20] | Internet technology consulting | scient.com |
| Siebel Systems | E-business applications software | siebel.com |
| Software.com [21] | Software for multinetwork communication services | openwave.com |
| Sonicwall | Internet security solutions | sonicwall.com |
| Symantec | Internet security solutions | symantec.com |
| Terayon Communications | Broadband networking equipment | terayon.com |
| Tibco Software | Business solutions for infrastructure software | tibco.com |
| Ticketmaster Online [22] | Online local network for information on cities | citysearch.com |
| Verio [23] | Internet business solutions | verio.com |
| VeriSign | Digital trust services for businesses and consumers | verisign.com |
| Verticalnet [24] | Collaborative supply chain solutions software | verticalnet.com |
| Vignette | Online content management applications | vignette.com |
| Virata [25] | High-speed broadband equipment and solutions | globespanvirata.com |
| Vitria Technology | Integration solutions on collaborative platforms | vitria.com |
| WebMethods | Integration software within and across enterprises | webmethods.com |
| Winstar [26] | Broadband network | idt.com |
| Yahoo | Global consumer and business Internet services | yahoo.com |

The numbers refer to notes about acquisitions, mergers, and bankruptcies that can be found on the web version of this appendix at www.inthecompanyofowners.com.

Source: Authors' analysis of NASDAQ.com, plus SEC filings and company web sites.

# Appendix B:
# The High Tech 100's Mixed Track Record

*Shareholder Returns from*
*Each Firm's IPO to July 26, 2002*

A majority, or 57 percent, lost money over this period:
- On average, these fifty-seven companies posted losses of 73 percent.
- Twenty-one of them traded below $1 as of July, putting them in danger of being delisted by NASDAQ.
- Another eight had gone bankrupt by then.

The other 43 percent still traded above their IPO price:
- 8 percent were more than 1,000 percent ahead.
- 19 percent were more than 500 percent ahead.
- 27 percent were more than 100 percent ahead.
- Cisco was 18,812 percent higher.
- AOL was 12,038 percent higher.
- Network Solutions was 4,587 percent higher.

How much money would a High Tech 100 mutual fund have made?
- Cost of one share of each company at the IPO    $725
- Value of the fund on 7/2002                                   $430
- Investor return over the period of the fund           –41 percent

Returns from IPO through July 2002:
- 32 percent had a return of at least 10 percent a year.
- 68 percent had less than 10 percent a year.

The total shareholder return used for bankrupt companies is zero. For firms that were merged or acquired, the return is calculated to the last price at which they traded or the price at which they were sold. Companies that trade on the NASDAQ for under $1 for thirty consecutive days are in danger of being delisted, although they can return if their stock price improves.

For more detail on the High Tech 100's share performance, see the web version of this appendix at www.inthecompanyofowners.com.

Source: Authors' analysis of publicly available stock prices.

# Appendix C: How Workers Took a Beating on Employee Ownership

| Type of Ownership | No. of Companies | No. of Employees Owning Stock | Stock Value in March, 2000 | Stock Value in August, 2002 | Loss |
|---|---|---|---|---|---|
| KSOPs* | 1,397 | 4.8 million | $229 billion | $174 billion | $107 billion |
| 401(k)s** | 2,813 | 13.6 million | $191 billion | $147 billion | $ 94 billion |
| ESOPs | 6,431 | 3.4 million | $ 96 billion | $ 58 billion | $ 49 billion |
| Profit sharing | 174 | 0.9 million | $ 18 billion | $ 12 billion | $ 8 billion |
| Employee Stock Purchase Plans | 746 | 1.4 million | $ 6 billion | $ 4 billion | $ 3 billion |
| Total | 11,561 | 24.1 million | $540 billion | $395 billion | $261 billion |

*A KSOP is a hybrid between an ESOP and a 401(k).

**Includes only 401(k)s that hold employer stock.

Total as a percent of all publicly traded U.S. stock in August 2002: 4.8%.

Source: Authors' analysis of corporate filings to the U.S. Department of Labor and of SEC filings.

The losses are larger than the drop in value from March 2000 to August 2002 because employees were buying more stock even as share prices fell. So they also lost money on most of what they purchased after March, 2000. For more detail, see the notes as well as the web version of this appendix on www.inthecompanyofowners.com.

# Appendix D:
# The Corporate America 100

| Corporation | Web Site (www.+) |
|---|---|
| 99 Cents Stores | 99only.com |
| Abercrombie & Fitch | abercrombie.com |
| Aetna | aetna.com |
| Alberto Culver | alberto-culver.com |
| Alliant Energy | alliantenergy.com |
| Alltel | alltel.com |
| American Express | americanexpress.com |
| American Standard | americanstandard.com |
| Anheuser Busch | anheuser-busch.com |
| Appalachian Power | aep.com |
| Atlas Air | atlasair.com |
| Automatic Data Processing | adp.com |
| Baker Hughes | bakerhughes.com |
| Barr Laboratories | barrlabs.com |
| Bergen Brunswig (1) | amerisourcebergen.net |
| BJ Services | bjservices.com |
| C.R. Bard | crbard.com |
| Berkshire Hathaway | berkshirehathaway.com |
| Boston Properties | bostonproperties.com |
| Brinker International | brinker.com |
| Brunswick | brunswick.com |
| Campbell Soup | campbellsoup.com |
| Capital One Financial | capitalone.com |
| Cendant | cendant.com |
| Charles Schwab | schwab.com |
| Cigna | cigna.com |
| Cinergy | cinergy.com |
| City National | cityntl.com |
| Colgate Palmolive | colgate.com |
| Compaq Computer (2) | hp.com |
| Conoco | conoco.com |
| Cooper Industries | cooperindustries.com |
| Cox Radio | coxradio.com |
| Darden Restaurants | darden.com |
| Diamond Offshore Drilling | diamondoffshore.com |
| Dollar General | dollargeneral.com |
| DQE | dqe.com |

(continues)

| | |
|---|---|
| Dun & Bradstreet | dnb.com |
| Eastman Chemical | eastman.com |
| El Paso Energy (3) | cmenergy.com |
| EMC | emc.com |
| Entergy | entergy.com |
| Equifax | equifax.com |
| Fairchild Semiconductor | fairchildsemi.com |
| FedEx | fedex.com |
| Florida Progress (4) | progress-energy.com |
| Ford Motor | ford.com |
| Gannett | gannett.com |
| GATX | gatx.com |
| Georgia Pacific | gp.com |
| Global Marine (5) | gsfdrill.com |
| Guidant | guidant.com |
| Halliburton | halliburton.com |
| HealthSouth | healthsouth.com |
| H.J. Heinz | hjheinz.com |
| Hollinger International | hollinger.com |
| Hon Industries | honi.com |
| IMC Global | imcglobal.com |
| IMS Health | imshealth.com |
| International Rectifier | internationalrectifier.com |
| Ipalco Enterprises (6) | aesc.com |
| Johnson & Johnson | jnj.com |
| Kemet | kemet.com |
| King Pharmaceuticals | kingpharm.com |
| Kroger | kroger.com |
| La Branche & Company | labranche.com |
| Lexmark | lexmark.com |
| Lockheed Martin | lockheedmartin.com |
| Mandalay Resort Group | mandalayresortgroup.com |
| Martin Marietta Materials | martinmarietta.com |
| Medicis Pharmaceutical | medicis.com |
| McDonalds | mcdonalds.com |
| Metro-Goldwyn-Mayer | mgm.com |
| Mitchell Energy (7) | devonenergy.com |
| M & T Bank | mandtbank.com |
| Murphy Oil | murphyoilcorp.com |
| Neiman Marcus Group | neimanmarcus.com |
| Nordstrom | nordstrom.com |
| OGE Energy | oge.com |
| Pactiv | pactiv.com |
| PepsiCo | pepsico.com |
| Pitney Bowes | pb.com |
| Pride International | prde.com |
| Questar | questar.com |
| Reynolds Tobacco | rjrt.com |

| | |
|---|---|
| SPX | spx.com |
| Scientific Atlanta | scientificatlanta.com |
| Smith International | smith-intl.com |
| St. Joe | joe.com |
| Sunoco | sunoco.com |
| Target | target.com |
| Temple Inland | templeinland.com |
| Time Warner (8) | aoltimewarner.com |
| Tribune | tribune.com |
| Ultramar DiamondShamrock (9) | valero.com |
| Unocal | unocal.com |
| Venator (10) | footlocker-inc.com |
| Vulcan Materials | vulcanmat.com |
| Wells Fargo | wellsfargo.com |
| Wilmington Trust | wilmingtontrust.com |

The numbers refer to notes about acquisitions, mergers, and bankruptcies, which can be found on the web version of this appendix at www.inthecompanyofowners.com.

Source: Authors' analysis of NYSE.com and corporate web sites.

# Notes

For an expanded version of the notes, see the web site for our book: www.inthecompanyofowners.com.

## Preface

xii    "As Federal Reserve Board chairman Alan Greenspan noted in mid-2002 . . .": Schaffler and Marchini (2002).

xvi    "Just as important is the corporate governance . . ." See Millstein ( 1998).

## Chapter 1

3    The genealogy of the concept of risk sharing has not been addressed as the principal theme in the many histories and studies of the high-tech industry, although it has been mentioned in passing in some of the studies of specific companies. The research for this chapter was based on four primary sources: original archival material, such as oral histories available at the Stanford University Library's Silicon Genesis Oral Histories Project; original interviews done for this book; newspaper and magazine articles; and filings made to the SEC. We also used secondary sources, including books, doctoral theses, and articles that often mention these issues briefly as a corollary to their main subject. For overview studies of the industry, see Chandler (1977), Riordan and Hoddeson (1998), and Campbell-Kelly and Aspray (1996).

3    "Eight cocky young semiconductor whizzes . . .": The story is told in an oral history by Gordon Moore, one of the eight and a cofounder of Intel. See Moore (1995). The names of the "Traitorous Eight" are: Julius Blank, Jean Hoerni, Victor Grinich, Eugene Kleiner, Jay Last, Gordon Moore, Robert Noyce, and Sheldon Roberts.

3    William B. Shockley: Shockley was named one of the most influential scientists and thinkers of the twentieth century by *Time* magazine. There's no extensive biography of Shockley, although Riordan and Hoddeson (1998) give him extensive coverage and were an invaluable source for this chapter. See also two brief biographies by

Moll (1996) of the National Academy of Sciences and the Nobel Foundation (1973) and Hiltzik (2001).

4    Shockley's discontentment with a lack of royalties and equity: This has been discussed by Moore (1999), Seitz and Einspruch (1998), Riordan and Hoddeson (1998), and Lewis (2000). Manners and Makimoto (1995) provide the context, discussing how engineers watched Texas Instruments' stock go up from $5 in 1952 to $191 in 1959.

5    "Your objective in this undertaking . . . ": Riordan and Hoddeson (1998), p. 234. They found the letter from A. Beckman to W. Shockley dated September 3, 1955, in the Shockley Papers, Stanford University Archives, Stanford California, Accession Listing 95–153.

5    Shockley Semiconductor Laboratory: For first-person accounts by members of the lab see the Stanford University Archives interviews with Moore (1995), Sello (1995). See also Moore (1999). For a complete account, see Riordan and Hoddeson (1998).

5    "For example, Moore described . . . ": Moore (1995).

6    "A commercially viable silicon transistor . . . ": Moore (1999).

6    Arthur Rock: Authors' interview with Arthur Rock on January 10, 2002. See also Anthony Perkins (1994), Rock (2000).

6    "Each of the eight . . . ": Perkins (1994).

7    "Being their own boss . . . ": Lecuyer (2000).

7    "Treat workers well . . . ": Authors' interview with Arthur Rock (2002).

7    Corporate culture at Fairchild: See Moore (1995) on the egalitarian philosophy that he and Noyce shared; Wolfe (1983) on Noyce's mindset; Manners and Makimoto (1995) and Berlin (2001).

7    Fairchild Semiconductor: For the story from the key actors, see interviews with Moore (1995), Hodgson (1995), Sello (1995), and Sporck (2000). The story of the breakup of the Shockley group and Fairchild is told in more detail by Wolfe (1983), Rostky (1995, 1997), Riordan and Hoddeson (1998), the Public Broadcasting System's program "Transistorized" (1999), Berlin (2001), and Lecuyer (2000).

7    "$250,000" and "Suddenly it became apparent . . . ": Manners and Makimoto (1995) and Fox (1997).

8    Noyce wanted to extend options . . . : From our interview with Arthur Rock (2002). For the Arthur Rock quote see Perkins (1994). See also Fox (1997), Rostky (1997), Berlin (2001), and Sporck (2000).

9    John Carter visit: Wolfe (1983).

11    "By 1970 . . . ": Seitz and Einspruch (1998) provide the most comprehensive map with company names showing 42 companies by 1970 and about 120 companies that they trace to Fairchild Semiconductor through Shockley, and their offspring's offspring (and so forth) by 1986. Several emerged directly from Bell Labs and were not included in this count.

11    "Exploded like a seed pod . . . ": Malone (1985).

11 "Many of the region's . . . ": Saxenian (1994a).

12 National Semiconductor: According to Berlin (2001), Charles Sporck quit Fairchild in March 1967 after articulating views similar to those of Noyce. He took over National Semiconductor. See Sporck (2000).

12 Advanced Micro Devices: Bruener (2000), Levering, Moskowitz, and Katz (1984).

13 "Since Intel . . . ": Authors' interview with Arthur Rock (2002).

14 ". . . around the Stanford area . . . ": On the seminal role that Stanford University played in nurturing a focus on intellectual capital before it became a common theme, see Tajnai (1985). On the role of Stanford's legendary dean, Frederick Terman, see Saxenian (1994a), Norr (1999), and the evidence of a recent dean in Gibbons (2000).

14 Regis McKenna: McKenna (2000), pp. 373–374.

15 ". . . they were never all of one opinion . . . ": Saxenian (1994a), Ward (2000), Rostky (1997).

15 Intel: Jackson (1997), Faggin (1995), Zielenziger (1988), Kehoe (1997), Grove (1999), and Intel's web site at www.intel.com/jobs/workplace/benefits.htm.

16 J. Robert Beyster: Authors' interview with Beyster (2001). See also Beyster (2002) for additional interviews on employee ownership. SAIC's employment and sales are from its 4/17/2001 10-K on file with the SEC.

16 Cray: Cray's company went public in 1976 at $1.10 a share adjusted for subsequent stock splits. An investment of $15,500 would have appreciated to $1 million by 1986, the year that Microsoft went public (see Flanagan 1986). Our description is based mostly on Clifford and Cavanagh (1985) of McKinsey & Co. See also Neimark (1986). Cray was named one of the one hundred best companies to work for in America in the early 1990s, Levering, Moskowitz, and Katz (1993). Later it was acquired by Silicon Graphics in a failed merger and became an independent company again in March of 2000.

17 Apple: Davidson and Bailey (1985), Musil (1997), Associated Press (1997), and the company's December 5, 1997, 10-K report to the SEC.

18 "Wozplan" and "Woz couldn't say no . . . ": Moritz (1984).

18 "A lot of people took advantage of him . . . ": Butcher (1988), Malone (1985).

19 "Of course you want . . . ": Schlender (1998).

19 Oracle: Posner (1985), Stone (2002), Kaplan (1999), and company's proxy filed September 11, 2000, with the SEC. Other key companies that used and later expanded stock options include Advanced Micro Devices, Computer Associates, Intuit, Silicon Graphics, and Sun Microsystems (Southwick 1999).

19 Seagate and Tandem: Mamis (1983), Seagate (1999), Kang and Quinlan (2000), Levering, Moskowitz, and Katz (1984), *Business Week* (1980), and Ristelheuber (1995).

19    Leland Stanford: Clark (1931), Tutorow (1971), and Norr (1999).

20    "A casual dress code . . . ": Adapted from Kehoe (2002).

20    "If a company has the attitude . . . ": See Verespej (1990) and Packard (1995).

20    "If people have some part . . . ": Packard (1995). The company introduced an employee share purchase plan in 1957 just before it went public. Professor Frederick Terman of Stanford played a key role in the launch of Hewlett-Packard. Also Said (2001) and Saxenian (1994a).

21    Varian Associates: Gullixson (1998), Ginzton (1996).

21    "What I learned . . . ": Allen (2001).

22    Adobe: Verespej (1996), and company web site at www.adobe.com.

22    3Com: Mamis (1983). Sales and employment are from 10-K filed with the SEC on August 8, 2001.

23    "They all run together in a more or less indistinguishable mass . . . ": Malone (1985).

23    ". . . many techies knew each other . . . ": These ideas are a summary of the analysis of Saxenian (1994a, 1994b).

23    . . . "unusually high levels of job-hopping . . . ": Saxenian (1994a).

23    Venture capitalists: For the Valentine and Hambrecht quotes, see Mamis (1983). Also see Perkins (1994) and Gupta (2000).

24    Microsoft history: Ichbiah and Knepper (1991), Microsoft Corporation (2000), Manes and Andrews (1993), Ballmer (2000), Stross (1997), Buckman (2000), *Financial Times* (2001), Egan (1992), Matthews (1998), Cusumano and Selby (1995). The other two software companies with large market share in 1986 were Lotus and Ashton-Tate. They held 30 percent of an estimated $5 billion market in 1985, Ichbiah and Knepper (1991). Ashton-Tate gave options only to employees above the position of director. Clancy (1989).

24    Microsoft founding: Microsoft Corporation (2000).

24    ". . . Gates balked . . . ": Manes and Andrews (1993).

24    ". . . creating stock initially held . . . ": Manes and Andrews (1993).

25    "Expanded the option program to cover all . . . ": Microsoft public relations.

25    "We never thought . . . ": Microsoft Corporation (2000).

25    "We're using ownership . . . ": Stross (1997).

25    "Early on Bill and I . . . ": Authors' interview (by email) with Ballmer (2001).

25    "Once Microsoft workers are hired . . . ": Authors' interview (by email) with Malloy (2001).

25    ". . . at the end of April 2000 . . . ": Stock prices are from SiliconInvestor.com, operated by Infospace. See Ballmer (2000) for the text of Ballmer's memo discussing this. See also Buckman (2000), *Financial Times* (2001).

26    "Not even the height of the Wall Street . . . ": Egan (1992). The stock went up 1,200 percent from the IPO to the time of this newspaper article.

26     "Gates and Ballmer take no options . . ." and their ownership stakes: Based on Microsoft's proxy filing of September 27, 2001, with the SEC and market value of $326.59 billion on March 29, 2002, according to SiliconInvestor.com.

26     "Still, all the other employees owned 20 percent . . . ": Based on a 1993 statement in a Microsoft internal publication called *Micronews,* quoted in Stross (1997). This is the only credible estimate in the public record.

26     ". . . average workers reaped the rewards of the bull market . . . ": For a look at how much employees made from options at leading high-tech firms over the decade, see web Appendix 1 at: www.inthecompanyofowners.com

26     ESOPs: ESOPs that have tended to foster a participatory culture are the smaller closely held companies. For publications and case studies of such companies, see the National Center for Employee Ownership, www.nceo.org, and the Beyster Institute for Entrepreneurial Employee Ownership, www.beysterinstitute.org. For smaller high-tech firms, the ESOP Association, www.the-esop-emplowner.org/, the Ohio Employee Ownership Center, www. dept.kent.edu/oeoc/, and the Profit Sharing Council of America, /www.psca.org/sig/sigaward.html.

27     "Smaller less noticeable firms . . . ": The reference is mainly to high-tech firms that are not well-known and often remained private or were later acquired.

27     John Cullinane: Mamis (1983).

27     Compaq: Davis (1987) and Dell (1999).

27     Rolm: Based entirely on Dolan (1984) and Richards (1988). Rolm had been named one of the hundred best companies to work for in America before its merger with IBM. Levering, Moskowitz, and Katz (1984).

28     IBM CEO Thomas J. Watson Jr.: Watson (1987). The article was written by Mr. Watson at *Fortune* magazine's invitation.

29     "IBM extended stock options broadly at the end of the 1990s": Lohr (2002). After he became chairman and CEO of IBM, Louis V. Gerstner Jr. extended options from 300 to 60,000 employees.

29     VentureOne: MacGregor (1994). Other studies shed light on this, too. A nonrandom survey of engineers by *Electronic Engineering Times* in 1993 showed that about 25 percent got stock options, while that figure had increased to 44 percent by 1995. Bellinger (1993, 1995). Another survey by iQuantic showed that stock options had still not completely penetrated high-tech companies in the 1996–2000 period. For options granted to new hires, these companies increased participation rates from 50 percent to 75 percent between 1996 and 2000 for individual contributors and from 0 percent to 60 percent for nonexempt employees. Ongoing option grants went to 100 percent of executives, 80 percent of managers, 51 percent of individual contributors, and 20 percent of nonexempt employees and increased by one-third to one-half over the period. The authors say penetration was highest in the smallest firms. Buyniski and Silver (2000).

# Chapter 2

31    Advanced Research Projects Agency, SAGE and ARPANET: Hafner and Lyon (1996), Abbate (1999), Segaller (1999), the Public Broadcasting System at www.pbs.org/internet/timeline/timeline-txt.html; Robert H Zakon at www.isoc.org/zakon/Internet/History/HIT.html; and the San Antonio Public Library at www.sat.lib.tx.us/Displays/itintro.htm.

32    @: Hafner and Lyon (1996).

32    First international connection: The connection used NORSCAR, one of the world's largest seismological observatories, which is based in Norway. For details, see www.norsar.no/NORSAR/.

32    Email: Hafner and Lyon (1996), Abbate (1999), and Segaller (1999).

32    Discussion groups: See timeline at www.pbs.org/internet/timeline/timeline-txt.html for 1979.

32    Gradual linking up of the Internet: Hafner and Lyon (1996), Segaller (1999), Abbate (1999).

32    ". . . inter-networking of networks": On the origins of the term, see Segaller (1999).

32    "broke the 10,000 mark": Segaller (1999).

32    World Wide Web: Berners-Lee (2000).

32    727,000 and 175 million: Hafner (2002).

32    40 billion and 1.4 trillion: Weinstein (2002).

32    115 million and 19 hours: Nielsen/Net Ratings (2001).

34    ". . . then flamed out . . . ": On dot-com flameouts, see Kaplan (2002) and Kuo (2001).

34    Rachel: Authors' interviews of Portal Software Employees (2001).

35    Byland: 03/16/2000 Congressional Testimony by Federal Document Clearing House Inc.

35    "We would be crucified . . . ": Authors' interview with Chris Wheeler of Internap (2001).

36    "High technology isn't about . . . ": Clark (1999).

37    "Not long ago . . . ": Speech of John T. Chambers available at www.cisco.com. For similar views, see Bostrom (2002).

38    Bezos story: Authors' interviews of Amazon employees (2001).

39    "First and foremost": Authors' interview with Frank Marshall of Covad.

39    "AOL's merger with Time Warner had been a big mistake": For a detailed study, see Munk (2002).

40    ". . . cyber-cockroach . . . ": Brophy (1999). Stiegman (2000) ascribes the quote to former AOL CEO James Kimsey. Also Stauffer (2000) and Brophy (1999). Call center: Adapted from Pressman (2000). The average wage is from an industry benchmark study in Rouzer (2000).

41    "I learned a long time ago . . . ": Heymann, Caron, and McLean (1996).

42    Portal employees: Authors' interview with Portal Software Employees (2001).

43    "I had no problem . . . ": Authors' interview with Rasipuram "Russ" V. Arun of Infospace Inc (2001).

43    Tibco employee: Authors' interview of Tibco Software Employees (2001).

44    "When the company's profits . . . ": Authors' interview with Vivek Ragavan of Redback Networks (2001).

44    "We have a saying . . . ": Authors' interview with Marcel Gani of Juniper Networks (2001).

45    "We tell workers . . . ": Authors' interview with Sandy Gould of RealNetworks (2001).

45    Jack: Authors' interview at Portal Software Employees (2001).

46    ". . . tend to feel that it's their right . . . ": Authors' interview with Jay Wood of Kana Communications (2001).

46    Meg Whittman of eBay: Tempest (1999). On eBay's culture, see also Bunnell and Luecke (2000) and Cohen (2002).

46    ". . . they feel as accountable to employees as the employees do to them": Michael Lewis (2000) says Thorsten Veblen (1921) predicted this. Jim Clark told Lewis, "The power is shifting to the engineers who create the companies."

47    "The challenges for executive . . . ": "When the company's profits . . . ": Authors' interview with Vivek Ragavan of Redback Networks (2001).

47    Silicon Graphics: Lewis (2000) and Clark (1999).

48    ". . . disenfranchised entrepreneur . . . ": Clark (1999).

48    Netscape: Clark (1999).

49    "Netscape's dress code is . . . ": Web site accessed on 11/01 at home.netscape.com/jobs/hr/culture/index.html.

49    Barksdale and teams: Cusumano and Yoffie (1998).

49    "Each of the teams working . . . ": Andreessen talk at MIT on November 14, 1996, quoted and cited in Cusumano and Yoffie (1998).

50    Groupware example: Quittner and Slatalla (1998), and Radosevich (1996).

52    ". . . motivates people . . . ": and "This is a great reward . . . ": Kadlec (1995).

52    Browser market share: Pitta (1996), *Wall Street Journal* (1997), and Fordahl (2002).

52    Netscape-Microsoft legal battles: Shiver and Hiltzik (2000), Hiltzik and Shiver (2001), and Hopper (2002).

52    Cisco history and culture: Bunnell (2000), Greenfeld (2000), and Young (2001).

53    ". . . more than 90 percent . . . ": Based on the table Option Grants in Last Fiscal Year from Cisco's corporate proxies of 9/28/01, 9/28/00, 9/24/99, 9/23/98, 10/1/97, 10/4/96 on file with the SEC and available at www.sec    v.

54    ". . . sixty-nine acquisitions . . . ": See list on the company's web site under "About Cisco" www.cisco.com/warp/public/750/acquisition/summarylist.html.

54    "When you combine companies . . . ": O'Reilly and Pfeffer (2000).

54    Cisco's acquisition process: O'Reilly and Pfeffer (2000). See also Thurm (2000), Bunnell (2000), and Paulson (2001).

55    "This is an empowerment . . . ": Hall (2000).

55    "The buddy system": O'Reilly and Pfeffer (2000).

55    ". . . 8 percent . . . 6 percent . . . ": Byrne (1998), and O'Reilly and Pfeffer (2000).

55    "Most people forget . . . ": Barner (2000).

55    Sales and employment: These data are from Cisco's web site, the Factsheet, under About Cisco: newsroom.cisco.com/dlls/corpfact.html. Cisco's inventory problems and building halts: Piller (2001); Cerent and Monterey: Hall (2000).

57    $300,000. per person: See Chapter 4, How High Tech Firms Share the Wealth.

58    James at Tibco: Authors' interview of Tibco employees (2001).

59    Francine at Portal: Authors' interview of Portal employees (2001).

59    Robert at Tibco: Authors' interview of Tibco employees (2001).

59    "A company that is owned . . . ": Authors' interview with Rick Tavan of Tibco Software Inc. (2001).

60    "The Internet Age": Authors' interview with Vivek Ranadive of Tibco Software (2001).

# Chapter 3

63    Thales: Aristotle (1996), McCarty (2000), Also Malkiel and Quandt (1969) and Bernstein (1996).

64    "Options granted to employees to purchase their company stock . . . ": For an overview of employee stock options, see Bernstein, Binns, Hyman, Staubus, and Sherman (2002), and National Center for Employee Ownership (2001a, 2001b).

64    "Most companies choose three to five years": In high tech, 65 percent of vesting schedules are four years, Buyinski and Silver (2000). For vesting variations in broad-based plans in many industries, see Weeden, Carberry, and Rodrick (2001).

66    ". . . most employees simply sell the stock when they exercise their option . . . ": We are referring to nonexecutive employees in this statement. Indeed, the research by Huddart cited below suggests that two-thirds of the stock option exercises of lower level employees happen six months after options vest if they're "in the money." This suggests they may be too eager to take quick profit from options.

66    ". . . research on the stock option behavior . . . ": Huddart and Lang (1996, 2002), and Heath, Huddart, and Lang (1999).

66   U.S. futures and option markets: On the history, see Bernstein (1996). For commodities options, see the web site of the Chicago Board of Trade on the board's history at www.cbot.com. For stock options, see the web site of the Chicago Board Options Exchange at www.cboe.com/AboutCBOE/History.asp.

67   Tulip craze: Malkiel (1996). Bernstein (1996) says new research on this tulip market suggests that "options gave more people an opportunity to participate in a market that had been previously closed to them." He concludes that the bad name for options was cultivated by vested interests who resented the interlopers. Also see Garber (1989).

67   Barnard's Act: Morgan and Thomas (1962). However, efforts to curtail option-like instruments were not effective and subsequent legislation to make them more effective failed to pass Congress.

67   History of options in the United States: New York Stock Exchange (1917), Kairys and Valerio (1997), and Baskin and Miranti (1997). A form of option trading on foxes developed in New England in the early part of the twentieth century (Balcom 1916).

67   Norton: Cheape (1985) and Tymeson (1953). Originally, Norton gave low-interest bank loans to these employees to buy stock at book value, with the remaining cost—up to 90 percent—paid by dividends.

68   "Ownership widened. . ." : Stock purchase plans in these days had elements of both today's stock purchase plans and stock option plans. All the way up until the 1950s, it was common to refer to both as "stock purchase options." The key aspect was that workers didn't have to take inordinate risks with their savings to gain equity. They primarily benefited in the potential upside of the stock's movement.

What we know as stock options today typically required no upfront money from the employee, whereas stock purchase plans offered executives stock at a discount. Often, the plans used low-interest loans and dividends to pay for the stock and reduce the risk to executives. Both approaches tried to offer them the opportunity to take an equity position without tying up as much of their own capital as would be required if they paid for it with cash from a savings account. However, if the discount on a stock purchase plan was large enough, it would look more like a stock option plan. See also an earlier use of stock by the English East India Company in Baskin and Miranti (1997).

68   "The separation of ownership and control . . . ": Chandler (1977). See also Berle and Means (1997).

68   ". . . exposes of insider dealing and stock speculation by executives": For a famous early case, see the Erie Railroad story in Gordon (1988). For a study of the important railroad corporations in these days and a review of railroad corruption, see Perrow (2002). On dilution of shareholders through issuing shares at a discount and as bonuses to railroad executives, see Baskin and Miranti (1997). Fabozzi and Zarb (1986) say Congressional and private investigations exposed widespread trading of

options and the underlying securities. See also Pecora (1939). Executives who owned large amounts of company shares gave themselves and employees discounts to buy the stock using privileged subscriptions. Mitchell (1905) and Dewing (1941) say the discounts on these purchases often amounted to 15 to 25 percent.

68    "Stock options . . . spread steadily throughout the 1920s and 1930s": Taussig and Barker (1925) studied 400 corporations between 1904 and 1915 and found that virtually none of them paid any form of incentive compensation. Earlier, options were used by bankers, utility holding companies, and investment trusts, Baker (1940) and Dewing (1920).

68    McKinsey and Chrysler: Guthmann and Dougall (1955). Wage substitution for executives in troubled companies was a common motive for the early use of stock options. For a copy of Eastern Air Lines CEO E. V. Rickenbacker's option contract see Washington (1942).

69    John Calhoun Baker quotes: Baker (1940) is the best study of options and the controversy they raised in this early period. See also Baker (1937, 1938).

69    "Shareholders filed lawsuit after lawsuit . . . ": A young Harvard graduate student, Jay Eliasberg, filed a lawsuit against Standard Oil of New Jersey, U.S. Steel, May's Department Store, and CIT charging that companies were committing fraud by having stock options and asserting that the options were unnecessary because their executives had no intention of leaving the companies: *Business Week* (1952a). For a review of other cases challenging stock options, see Washington (1942) and Washington (1951). See also Johnson (2000) on options as corporate waste.

69    IRS and Supreme Court: Commissioner v. Smith, 324 U.S. 177, 65 Sup. Ct. 591 (1945), rehearing denied, 324 U.S. 695, 65 Sup. Ct. 891 (1945). On court battles, see Washington (1951). On the Supreme Court decision, see *Business Week* (1945).

69    New York Supreme Court: Baker (1938).

70    "In 1950 Congress overruled . . . ": Congress called them "restricted stock options" because they made rules that restricted them. See *Business Week* (1953b). On the battles over taxes, see Washington (1951).

70    ". . . the capital gains rate was just . . . ": Tax rates from Fox (1997).

70    "By 1952, a third of the 1,084 companies. . . ": *Business Week* (1953a), Garcia (1942) notes how the postwar bull market expanded option profits. Some companies included rank-and-file employees, but these were mainly bargain share purchase programs called stock options, *Business Week* (1951a).

70    1953–1959 bull market: Garcia (1942).

70    ". . . the business press ran articles . . . ": *Business Week* (1951a, 1952b, 1963), *U.S. News* (1961). See also Henry Ford's (1961) defense, and Ewing and Fenn (1962). On the significant option-related wealth for executives from 1929 to 1958, see Burgess's study (1963). Husband and Dockeray (1972). De Figueiredo (1994) examines the use of options in the 1960s to transform newspapers from control by founding families to control by professional managers.

70    Senator Albert Gore Sr.: *Commonweal* (1961).

71    "Then in 1976 . . . ": Fox (1997). Whenever stock options were in disfavor, corporations simply found other ways to transfer value to executives, as the Conference Board's detailed published surveys of executive comp over this period indicate (1970–1983, 1985–2000). When options did not qualify for tax breaks, companies set up "nonqualified plans." For example, after 1982, most corporations had both qualified and nonqualified plans, although the number with nonqualified plans fluctuated. Fox (1997) additionally reports that the combination of restrictions on options and high capital gains taxes after 1976 led to option grants that "tended to be, by previous standards, huge." From 1946 to 1958, Union Carbide had a famous plan where executives were given loans to buy stock, the stock was collateral on the loan, and dividends were used to repay the loan, Burgess (1963).

71    Black-Scholes: For a very readable explanation, see Bernstein (1996). See also Bodie, Kaplan, and Merton (2002).

72    On options after 1981: A July 1979 U.S. Department of Labor ruling gave managers of pension plans more flexibility to use options and expanded their use by institutional investors, *Forbes* (1980). On the 1981 law, see *Business Week* (1981). Congress called them "incentive stock options" since emphasizing the incentive side was a large part of policy discussions at the time (Jassy 1982). Because inventive stock options put certain restrictions on companies, many also continued to maintain "nonqualified" (for tax incentives) option plans. This allowed them to have a freer hand in structuring options as they pleased. The next Conference Board survey (1982) shows that corporations began the switch to government "qualified" stock options after the 1981 law. By 1990, Conference Board (1990), 75 percent of top corporations had both plans, 5 percent qualified plans only, and 20 percent nonqualified plans only.

72    Toys "R" Us: Fox (1997). Before 1981, Firestone Tire chief John J. Nevins pushed stock options to many levels of the company (Sull 1999). Lee Iacocca's option profits at Chrysler received a lot of press attention at the time, Reuters (1984), Dworkin (1985), and Helyar and Lublin (1998).

73    "In 1992 . . . $2.4 billion": Based on an analysis of Standard and Poor's Execucomp data by the authors for the first year national data is available. These are profits on the exercises of stock options, net of the exercise price.

74    Goldstein: Fox (1997).

74    "Relatively few major companies . . . .": The extremely slow broadening of who was included in option plans can be traced by examining the Conference Board's regular surveys (1970 to 2000), especially Buenaventura and Peck (1993).

74    "The best opinion seems to be . . . ": Casey and Lasser (1952). They also report stock option overhang (potential shareholder dilution) for the 1950s from a McKinsey & Company study. Mr. Casey argues that options may not even be appropriate to junior executives who would prefer cash.

74    Thomas Ware: Ewing and Fenn (1962). The median overhang in 100 NYSE plans was 4.7 percent at the time.

75    Conference Board: Buenaventura and Peck (1993).

# Chapter 4

79    "... a host of ways to extend ownership ... ": Many companies allow employees to purchase discounted stock through employee stock purchase plans. In the past, some employers have used company stock to pay for deferred profit-sharing plans. Before 401(k)s came along in 1978, many old thrift/savings plans were partly invested in company stock.

80    High Tech 100: They are the hundred publicly traded corporations with the largest market value as of October 2000 that had more than half of their revenues related to the Internet.

80    "... all those ephemeral dot-coms ... ": The *Wall Street Journal* reported 500 recent dot-com failures (Kelly 2002), and 690 companies delisted from the NASDAQ since the end of 2000 (Edmondston 2002). Many are described in the book *F'd Companies* (Kaplan 2002) and on the web site www.F**kedcompany.com. On the bursting of the Internet bubble, see Mandel (2000) and Perkins and Perkins (2001).

80    High Tech 100 index: The index is the sum of the stock prices of all companies on the list whose stocks were trading on that date. The peak of the recent technology market boom was March 10, 2000, when the NASDAQ Composite was at 5,048. The lowest point as of this writing was July 26, 2002, when the NASDAQ was at 1,262. Stock prices are from public market sources and exclude companies that went bankrupt, were acquired, or merged with another company. Daily market statistics on the NASDAQ are from www.nasdaq.com.

80    $1.3 trillion: This market value of the High Tech 100 on March 10, 2000, is rounded and is based on Standard and Poor's Compustat database. It includes all companies that weren't acquired or bankrupt over the period, so AOL is excluded.

80    $162 billion: This market value number is rounded and is based on prices from July 26, 2002.

80    Market values for the NASDAQ: According to the NASDAQ's market data research (www.marketdata.nasdaq.com/mr4b.html), the total market value of the entire NASDAQ was $6.71 trillion on March 10, 2000. It declined to $1.95 trillion on July 26, 2002. Values for the NASDAQ National Market are somewhat lower. See also Adiga (2002), Vickers and others (2002).

81    "... eight ... had declared bankruptcy ... ": They are: Excite@Home Corporation, Covad Communications Group (which later reorganized and continues to trade on the NASDAQ as a public company), Exodus Communications, marchFIRST Inc., Metromedia Fibre Network Inc., PSI Net Inc., Scient, and Winstar Communications. By January 2002, the following companies had merged with other

companies or been acquired: Alteon Web Systems Inc., America Online Inc., Concentric Network Corp., Efficient Networks Inc., Go2Net Inc., Lycos, MMC Networks Inc., Network Solutions Inc., Pairgain Technologies Inc., Phone.com Inc., Software.com Inc., Ticketmaster Online Citysearch Inc., Verio Inc., and Virata.

81    Total employment of the High Tech 100: Based on end of the year SEC filings for 1999 through 2001. In order to arrive at a strict comparison, the figures exclude companies that were bankrupt, merged, or acquired, unless both companies were originally part of the High Tech 100.

81    "These companies have real customers and real sales . . . ": Sales are net revenues from SEC filings at the end of the 1999 fiscal year and the end of the 2001 fiscal year. These figures exclude companies that went out of business or were acquired so that the comparison between both points in time includes the same group of companies. They also don't show some declines in sales between these two points. We show 1999 and 2001 sales for the High Tech 100 on the web version of Appendix A.

81    "As Federal Reserve Board chairman Alan Greenspan . . . ": Schaffler and Marchini (2002).

81    Employee equity: Employee equity is the total claim on the equity of a corporation that all its employees have. It is the sum of all direct stock ownership by employees as reported in SEC filings (which provide direct ownership for the top five managers and typically the stock owned and reserved for the employee share purchase plan), plus all stock options currently held by employees and available for future issue. We compute the potential ownership as if all options were exercised. All ownership stakes are then diluted by the ownership represented by the stock options.

82    ". . . stupendous amount of paper wealth . . . ": We estimated paper wealth using the stock price on the day for which the wealth was determined, the total number of stock options outstanding, and their weighted average exercise price as of the most recent SEC filings. We included both vested and unvested options. This table usually appears in the stock option plan section of a company's annual report (Form 10-K) to the SEC and is labeled "Other information regarding options outstanding and options exercisable as of (date)." The figure of $1 million per employee was computed by dividing by 177,000 employees as of December 31, 1999, for the High Tech 100. All wealth figures in this chapter are averages. They assume that all employees shared equally in paper wealth. This is obviously not the case, but no better figure can be provided based on publicly available records of the SEC.

82    ". . . 83 percent of employee options were below their company's stock prices . . . ": We computed this based on an examination of actual exercise prices for all one hundred companies from their most recent SEC filings for 2001, including all vested and unvested options.

83    ". . . a total of some $78 billion . . . ": This figure may sound somewhat unbelievable in light of all the negative press high-tech stock options received following the market slump. But if anything, our method gives a conservative estimate. For ex-

ample, in 2001, the California State Department of Finance (Morain 2001) estimated that some $84 billion worth of stock options were exercised in that state alone in 2000, accounting for a remarkable 10 percent of its total wages and salaries that year. This includes options issued by all companies, not just high-tech ones, as well as those held by top executives. But the agency believed that the majority were at high-tech companies, mostly Internet ones in Silicon Valley where most of the High Tech 100 are headquartered. Since our number includes high-tech companies nationwide, the department's findings gave us some comfort that we hadn't overestimated.

83    ". . . actual cash profits employees and executives made . . . ": We computed the profit on stock options by taking all those that High Tech 100 companies reported as exercised in their SEC filings for 1994 to 2001. We imputed an exercise price using the conservative assumption that each employee sold at a price midway between the high and low price of the company's stock for the period in which the options could have been exercised. This assumes that the average employee neither beat the market by always selling at the highest point nor missed the market by selling at the lowest point.

If the company had previously gone public, all employees were presumed to have exercised during a year beginning after the exit date for the IPO. The exit date is the date before which a specific group of insiders are prohibited from selling their stock or exercising options when there has been an IPO. We assumed that all employees who exercised options abided by the exit date and then immediately sold the stock and pocketed the cash profits. For nonexecutive employees, the notion that they exercised and sold is one reasonable assumption based on the research of Huddart and Lang (1996, 2002) and Heath, Huddart, and Lang (1999). However, to the degree that employees held onto their stock, our estimates of their profits are excessive.

The figure of $53 billion is for all employees who are not the top five executives of the companies. The total profit was divided between this group of employees and top five executives using the recent share of options actually held by both groups for each company based on its SEC filings. It includes profits on sales immediately after the company's IPO and thereafter. The smaller group of employees who worked for the companies immediately after the IPO made amounts larger than the average per worker overall.

83    ". . . dot-conned investors . . . ": Cassidy (2002).

84    $70,000 a year: This is an estimate by the authors based on those firms that made compensation information available to Compustat.

85    ". . . data we gathered came mostly . . . from the SEC . . . ": All numerical data used in this chapter were calculated based entirely on SEC filings. The determination of whether a company actually granted stock options to most of its employees was gathered mainly from SEC filings. When this was not discernable from SEC filings, we used publicly available sources such as Dow Jones Interactive and Lexis/Nexis to find

the answer. When that did not work, we requested an answer from the public relations departments of the company by email or telephone.

86    "This is called dilution": Several perspectives and measures of potential dilution are provided in this book. The type discussed here involves taking all currently issued and outstanding options as a percent of total shares outstanding. "Employee equity" is figured using what's called overhang. It's calculated by summing all currently issued and outstanding options, plus all options available for future grants. These are then considered as a percent of total shares outstanding. A final perspective is the run rate, which measures how many options a company issues every year. We compute it by taking the annual option grants from SEC filings (subtracting cancelled options) as a percent of total shares outstanding. For comparable dilution and employee equity figures for the 1,500 largest U.S. corporations, see Siegl, Loayza, and Davis (2002).

87    Table 4.2: Who Owns the High Tech 100?: Direct ownership for the board and top executives is available in each company's proxy statement (Form DEF–14A). So is the share of all employee options outstanding that are currently in the hands of the top five executives. The figure for options held by board members is an estimate based on those companies that report this information, which all companies don't do.

Total stock options outstanding, and the total number of options available for future issue (the sum of which equals the overhang, or total employee equity), is available in a company's Annual Report (Form 10-K) in the stock option section and in the table on stock option activity. Shares reserved or held in the employee share purchase plan (ESPP) are also available in this document. The figure for direct ownership through ESPPs is based on the shares reserved for these plans from the companies for which information is available. Not all companies disclose this. Because the SEC requires executives to report their beneficial ownership by adding their actual direct stock ownership and the ownership potentially resulting from options exercisable within sixty days, there may be some double-counting in the columns expressing top five executive ownership from stock and options. This is not avoidable using publicly available information.

88    Employee share purchase plans: On the operation of these plans, see Carberry and Rodrick (2000).

89    401(k) Plans: Data on company stock in High Tech 100 401(k) plans was based on an analysis of the Form 5500 report on file with the U.S. Department of Labor. These data are accessible at the web site www.FreeErisa.com. While most High Tech 100 did not stuff their 401(k)s with company stock, they also didn't offer traditional pension plans (defined benefit plans), so the 401(k) was, in general, the only potentially diversified retirement plan available.

90    ". . . employee equity didn't shrink as companies grew . . .": Based on an analysis we did of option overhangs and employee equity of the High Tech 100.

Another survey finds that the largest companies actually provide employees the greatest potential value from stock options (Buyniski and Silver 2000).

90    Microsoft not in the High Tech 100: It wasn't included because more than half its sales don't come from the Internet.

90    "Microsoft's employee option program . . . ": Based an analysis of the company's recent SEC filings.

91    Table 4.3: How Founders Share the Wealth: The founders' diluted equity was computed by taking his or her beneficial ownership in these filings (which also includes options exercisable within sixty days according to SEC rules), adding potential ownership represented by options, and arriving at their total potential equity stake. This was then diluted by assuming that all stock options outstanding or available for future issue to nonexecutive employees were exercised. The information on total nonexecutive employee equity was computed as follows: We took all options outstanding or available for future issue from the accompanying 10-K for each company and computed the percent of potential ownership it might represent, adding all shares reserved for employee share purchase plans that principally cover nonexecutive employees, and diluting this total amount by assuming that all stock options outstanding or available for future issue to nonexecutive employees were exercised.

92    ". . . ninety-eight of the High Tech 100": The best available survey of participation rates, by iQuantic (Buyniski and Silver 2000), found that software and e-commerce companies that have fewer nonexempt employees than equipment makers actually grant options to 33 percent and 48 percent of their nonexempt employees, respectively. One-third of the High Tech 100 were identified as being in this survey. Most of them are in the counties surrounding San Jose, California. A 2000 Gallup poll, (*Financial Times* 2000), showed that one in three households in the surrounding Santa Clara County owned options, with 23 percent in San Mateo, 21 percent in San Francisco, and 15 percent in Contra Costa counties.

93    $21 billion: We used the method described above for computing profits on stock options, but focused entirely on exercises in the year immediately after the IPO. The figure assumes that the profits on these option exercises were equally divided among all employees working for the company at the time of exercise. Using public information, it's not possible to determine precisely how many employees shared in these option exercises.

93    39,000 employees: Based on SEC filings for the IPO year or Dow Jones Interactive or Lexis/Nexis.

93    "Higher-paid employees also often received a larger number of options than lower-paid ones . . . ": For a comparison of CEOs' annual option grants to those of other employee groups in companies with broad-based option plans, see web Appendix 2 at: www.inthecompanyofowners.com.

93    $1.27 a share: Based on an averaging of the exercise prices by the authors.

93   $8.61 a share: Based on an averaging of the IPO offering prices by the authors.

93   "A rapid, and we now know irrational, runup . . . ": The percentages were computed by the authors from stock exchange data and IPO offering prices. *Note the percentages cited express not the stock price increases relative to the offering price of the stock in the IPO, but relative to the price of the cheapest stock option granted.*

94   Portal Software: Based on a case study by the National Center for Employee Ownership (2000) and analysis of recent SEC filings.

95   Francine and Jack: Authors' interviews.

95   Jennifer: Authors' interviews.

96   Owen: Authors' interviews.

96   Tibco Software option exercises: Based on our analysis of the company's SEC filings using the estimation methods for option profits described above.

96   VeriSign Inc. option exercises: Based on our analysis of the company's SEC filings using the estimation methods for option profits described above.

97   Excite@Home option exercises: Based on our analysis of the company's SEC filings using the estimation methods for option profits described above.

97   Mitch and Rachel: Authors' interviews.

98   Peter: Authors' interviews.

98   Jay Wood: Authors' interviews.

98   Wendy: Authors' interviews.

100   Jerry and John: Authors' interviews.

100   Taxes and Alternative Minimum Tax: See Bernstein and others (2002), Fenton, Stern, and Gray (2000), NCEO (2001a, 2001b), Curtis (2001), and Ungar and Sakanashi (2001). The authors do not extend a personal endorsement regarding any stock option advice to any source or approach mentioned in this book. Any review of approaches is for general discussion purposes only.

101   "That's not fair": Schwanhausser (2001b) and (2002), report that the bill never passed. The tax bills for this problem initially became due for thousands of employees on April 15, 2001. These citizens created a lobbying organization called Reform AMT (www.reformamt.org/).

102   Oppenheimer Funds survey: Schwanhausser (2001b). On this question see also Buyniski and Silver (2000).

102   "This happened to dozens of Microsoft employees . . . ": Morgenson (2001a).

103   Rosen: Authors' interviews. The authors do not extend a personal endorsement regarding stock option advice to any source mentioned in this book. The concept of "critical capital" is trademarked by MyCriticalCapital(TM).com (Business Wire 2000) and was developed by veteran certified financial planners, Alan B. Ungar and Mark Sakanashi (2001).

# Chapter 5

105    ". . . what experts call the run rate": In the context of stock options, the run rate is the number of stock options granted in any particular year (minus those options cancelled), as a percent of total shares outstanding at the end of that year. For run rates of the 1,500 largest companies in the United States and by industry group, see Siegl, Loayza, and Davis (2002). The 2001 national average is 2.1 percent. For run rates of a large diversified sample of firms offering broad-based options, see Weeden, Carberry, and Rodrick (2001). The average is 5.4 percent, including technology and some Internet firms. The authors used the Standard and Poor's Execucomp database on the top 1,500 companies to compute that the average national burn rate (similar to the run rate without excluding cancelled options) went up by 48 percent from 1992 to 2000, climbing from 2.23 percent to 3.29 percent per year. For the 500 largest firms it more than doubled, from 1.3 percent to 2.88 percent per year.

Stock options that are cancelled and forfeited: When employees leave the company, their options are often forfeited and thus canceled. Options whose term expires also disappear. Also, if the stock price falls dramatically, companies may cancel existing options and issue new repriced ones, or cancel existing options and exchange them for other options

106    "the run rate": The run rate for any particular company can be computed by going to the Form 10-K (Annual Report) of that company at the SEC web site, www.sec.gov. Every public corporation is required to report its annual option grants and option cancellations in a table, and its total shares outstanding.

106    "High Tech 100 firms gave employees about 90 percent of all outstanding stock options . . . ": We determined the percent of *annual* option grants that were given to average employees, i.e., not the top five officers, based on grants over previous years in the following way. The SEC requires that all public companies specify in their proxies the percent of option grants in the last fiscal year given to the top five executives as a percent of those given to all employees. In order to arrive at the percent of option grants for a broad group of non-top five officers, you subtract this percent from 100 percent.

107    Chambers: Duffy (2000).

107    Lawler: Heath (1999).

109    The Annual Option Spigot Chart: The average (median) run rates for the High Tech 100 *before dilution* are: 2001: 5 percent (3 percent); 2000: 7.2 percent (8.2 percent); 1999: 8.4 percent (7.5 percent); 1998: 10.4 percent (7.7 percent); 1997: 10.8 percent (8.8 percent). The distribution between Employees' Share and Top Officer's Share was figured using the actual percent of options given to these groups (as described above) for 1999 (namely 83.5 percent) and 2000 (namely 89.1 percent) and the average of these two years for previous years (namely 86.3 percent). We assume that cancellations and forfeitures were randomly distributed between the top five officers and other employees for the purpose of these figures. Note that the drop in run

rates from 1997 to 2000—especially the drop from 1999 to 2001—can be best explained not by a decrease in the number of options granted by the High Tech 100 but rather by an increase in cancellations and forfeitures. For other studies on run rates, see iQuantic's on the broad high-tech industry showing a doubling of the burn rate (their comparable measure that excludes cancelled options) from 3.3 percent to 6.9 percent from 1996 to 1999. Buyinski and Silver (2000).

109   1.5 billion options: This is an estimate based on the total options granted by the High Tech 100 in 2000. Companies that had been acquired as of January 2002 or are out of business have not been included. The estimate does not include cancellations and forfeitures.

110   80 percent of outstanding options in the hands of employees by 2000: This percent is based on determining the *aggregate* percent of ALL option grants that are in the hands of average employees (not the top five officers). To do this, you take all the stock options available for employees other than the top five executives as a percent of total stock options outstanding. This was computed by going to the company's Proxy, called DEF 14-A.

110   Estimate of all options given over the High Tech 100 history: This rough estimate assumes that companies gave the same number of options granted in their last fiscal year (adjusted backward for stock splits) for all years they were public and for two years before their IPO. It also assumes that all bankruptcies and mergers took place in 2000 for those companies that underwent such transactions from 1999–2000. These estimates do not include cancellations and forfeitures.

110   Yahoo: On Yahoo's corporate culture, see Angel (2002) and Vlamis and Smith (2001). All Yahoo equity stakes are not the actual stakes reported in the proxies. Rather, as is the practice of this book, they have been diluted with the assumption that all outstanding stock options and those available for future issue were exercised.

111   Ragavan: Authors' interview.

112   Gani: Authors' interview.

112   Siebel: Haines, Farber, and Froehlich (2001).

113   Callisch: Steen (2000).

113   Wood: Authors' interview.

113   Sclavos: Authors' interview.

114   ". . . psychological impact of the crash . . . ": Many business stories suggested the stock option culture was dead. See *San Jose Mercury News* (2001), *Denver Post* (2001), *Houston Chronicle* (2001), *Financial Times* (2000). The issue was raised in countless major newspapers and business magazines, some of which bordered on wrongly claiming that all options were worthless and that the concept of stock options had no real future in tech companies.

114   Steve Ballmer's memo: Available from ZD Wire (2000) through Dow Jones Interactive at Rutgers University Library. Also cited by Buckman (2000). The number of employee levels at Microsoft was provided by the company's public relations firm in

response to our query on February 27, 2002. Microsoft has 32 levels including the following numbered levels: 50–70 and 80–92. Thus, all levels below level 67 would be the 18 lower levels. See also *Newsweek* (2000).

115    Microsoft temporary workers: Kelley (1999).

115    Microsoft special stock option grant: See Pender (2001), who writes: "Last April, Microsoft said it would give all its employees an extra one-time stock grant. It didn't cancel the old options, so there was no charge to earnings." Mulligan and Piller (2000) write: "In an action sure to reverberate through the high-technology world, software giant Microsoft on Tuesday granted new stock options to all 34,000 full-time employees, aiming to compensate them for the stock's 40 percent dive this year."

115    "Overall 47 percent . . . . While the other 53 percent . . . ": Here is how High Tech 100 companies compensated their workers for underwater options:

| | |
|---|---|
| An Announced Repricing | 3 percent |
| An Announced Special Additional Share Grant | 6 percent |
| An Announced Option Exchange | 35 percent |
| An Announced Restricted Stock Grant | 5 percent |
| An Unannounced Additional Share Increase in the Run Rate | 47 percent |
| An Announced or Unannounced Additional Share Grant | 53 percent |

This covers the period January 1, 2000, to March 1, 2002. All the percentages in the table add up to more than 66 percent because a handful of companies took multiple actions. In some cases it is possible that a large increase in the run rate was the result of additional stock option programs of acquired companies. This table is based on our study of the SEC filings for 2000 and 2001 of all High Tech 100 companies.

115    "We will go and look at the entire base . . . ": Authors' interview.

116    Repricing: Formal repricing was made difficult by the Financial Accounting Standards Board, so companies found several ways around it. The Board said that when companies reprice stock options, they must record any increase in the value of the repriced options as a compensation cost. See Harbert (2000) who reports an iQuantic.com study that 61 percent of tech companies repriced in a ten-year period before the board's new ruling. Ittner, Lambert, and Larcker (2001) found that 59.6 percent of 217 high-tech firms had repriced their stock options at least once since their IPO and more than 31 percent did it twice. For the board's home page see, www.fasb.org. The SEC's material on "Repricing," is available at www.sec.gov/divisions/corpfin/repricing.htm. The Division of Corporation Finance has other materials available at www.sec.gov/divisions/corpfin.shtml. To avoid lots of underwater options, many consultants recommended giving staggered option grants throughout the year instead of one big package, so that employees in falling markets would get options at varying exercise prices, a kind of "dollar price averag-

ing for stock options." See Herhold (2000) and Gomes (2001). On past executive repricing, see Brenner, Sundaram, and Yermack (2000) and Chance, Kumar, and Todd (2000).

116   ". . . exchanged old options for new options after six months . . . ": While we say this approach essentially repriced options, it did not officially count as repricing. The method was called "Six month and a day," "slow-motion swaps," or "voluntary option exchanges." Employees surrender their underwater options, cancel the old options, and wait six months for new options at an unknown exercise price. The accounting penalties can be avoided by setting the new strike price more than six months after employees cancel the old options. If it does this the company can avoid taking charges against earnings as required by Financial Accounting Standards Board rules. It was widely used by High Tech 100 companies. We collected and analyzed the press releases of all companies that used this method.

116   "Well, no one is repricing . . . ": Authors' interview.

116   Owen of Amazon: Authors' interview.

117   Janes of Amazon: Authors' interview.

117   Amazon: On the option grant see Pulliam (2000), which points out this new grant was already underwater by the time of her November 2000 article. This is probably why Amazon took further action with repricing and later an option exchange. On the Bezos email, see *Electronic Commerce* (2000). See also Schroeder and Simon (2001), Norris (2001), Simon (2001), Weiss (2001), *Investors Daily* (2000), and Edwards (2001). We have attempted to adjust all references to Amazon's stock prices in employee interviews for splits to March 2, 2002, so that they are consistent. For this purpose, we consulted SiliconInvestor.com of Infospace. On Amazon's corporate culture, see Saunders (2002), Daisey (2002), Spector (2000), Alpert and Pollock (1999).

118   "The FASB rules . . . ": Authors' interview.

118   Sprint: Sprint (2000).

119   "Companies must ask shareholders permission . . . ": 40 percent of the High Tech 100 went to their shareholders for approvals for new stock option and stock ownership programs in 2000. In these shareholder meetings, 32 percent of the companies asked and got shareholder approval for new stock option programs or to increase the shares available in such programs. About 5 percent of the companies asked and got shareholder approval for new stock option plans, 27 percent asked and got shareholder approval for increasing the shares reserved for stock option plans, 13 percent asked and got shareholder approval to increase the shares reserved for employee share purchase plans, and 9 percent asked and got shareholder approval for automatic evergreen plans that replenish options outstanding each year.

119   "Some of us have tried other creative ways . . . ": Authors' interview.

119   Bill Coleman: Authors' interview.

120    "When you throw in those who jacked up their run rates . . . ": Companies need to have enough extra authorized but unused options to do this. To compare 1999 and 2000 run rates, using SEC filings, we computed them for the High Tech 100 for December 31, 2000, (including some special fiscal years when available) and compared them to the fiscal year ending December 31, 1999, (or special fiscal years when available) for 86 of the 100. All companies for which data was available in both years were included, even Excite@Home, Covad, and Exodus, which later declared bankruptcies.

120    Curry of Amazon: Simon (2001).

121    Jain: Authors' interview.

121    ". . . Amazon did surveys of labor markets to determine how much it should pay employees . . . ": Based on interviews by Aaron Bernstein.

122    Sclavos: Authors' interview.

122    Owen: Authors' interview.

122    Zach Works at Amazon: Bernstein and Hof (2000).

123    Bezos at Amazon's 2001 Annual Meeting: These are direct quotes from questions and answers addressed to Jeff Bezos at the 2001 Annual Meeting before 200 shareholders as reported by Edwards (2001).

123    Unions at Amazon: Bernstein and Hof (2000) and *Newsday* (2001).

125    "You bet the wage substitution . . . ": Authors' interview.

125    Wheeler: Authors' interview.

125    "Our executive salaries . . . ": Authors' interview.

125    "Two surveys back up this notion . . . ": The iQuantic survey was mentioned to us in a confidential interview with a human resource management executive. The pre-IPO dot-com survey is by WetFeet.com, an Internet job recruitment site, and Hewitt Associates LLC, a corporate consulting firm (Wetfeet 2000).

126    Francine, Tom, Jack, and Goeff at Portal: Authors' interview.

126    Jerry and Sue at Excite: Authors' interview.

127    Tibco story: Authors' interview. For his view on business and corporate culture, see Ranadive (1999).

128    "It can be risky for management to hype potential option winnings . . . ": Authors' interview.

128    Bell: Authors' interview.

128    Bill of Tibco: Authors' interview.

129    ". . . they needed options to make sure they didn't lose the talent they had worked so hard to get . . . ": Experts such as Matt Ward of Westwardpay.com (Handel 2000), and Corey Rosen of the NCEO recommend more frequent option grants and longer option terms to deal with market ups and downs and its impact on employee morale and commitment. But before the bust, Buyinski and Silver (2000) report a trend toward shorter even monthly vesting and this raises troubling issues about the holding power of options, which was their original goal.

# Chapter 6

132     Dilution: There are several aspects to the dilution public shareholders face when an employee option is cashed in for a share of stock. First, any increase in the company's market capitalization will be shared with option holders, leaving less for prior stockholders. Also, any profits the company pays out in dividends will be spread out over more shares, which means less per share for each stockholder. The added shares also dilute existing shareholders' percentage control of the company, which could, for example, make some investors ineligible for board seat if they are based on such percentages. Shareholders' voting rights are diluted as well. In addition, all these dilution effects can make the company's shares look less attractive to new investors, which means that the stock price may rise more slowly than it otherwise would.

133     ". . . stock option overhang . . . ": For a benchmark on overhangs in the 1,500 largest corporations in the country and by economic sector, see Siegl, Loayza, and Davis (2002), which shows average overhang in these companies as 14 percent at the beginning of 2002.

133     "Of course, employees have to pay money to buy the stock that an option entitled them to purchase.": When employees exercise options, they must pay the company the exercise price in order to receive the stock to which the option entitles them. They're then free to sell the share at the higher market price, reaping an immediate profit that the company forgoes. Still, from this perspective, options aren't a pure giveaway, but rather are at least in part a way for a company to raise capital by selling shares. For example, in 1999, Amazon employees exercised 16 million shares, paying the company $320 million in the process (Henig and Sperling 2000).

133     "Companies that offer options typically publish the information needed to compute this figure in their annual SEC": To learn how to use public SEC filings to find the overhang for a company, see www.inthecompanyofowners.com, the web site for our book.

133     "Total equity": Total equity is the same concept as "employee equity" used in Chapter 4, except in this case we're referring to the total equity of all the insiders at a company, including the top five executives, all other employees, and board members. In Chapter 4 and throughout the book, "employee equity" refers only to employees other than the top five executives.

137     ". . . a break on Federal taxes": For a detailed study of options and taxes see Desai (2002).

137     "This can be a whopping number": Tax benefit estimates from Henry and Conlin (2002).

138     ". . . they don't have to treat that very same option as an expense . . . ": Desai (2002) reports option exercises as a percent of operating cash flow for 1996 through 2000 in general and for 150 corporations.

138     Microsoft's earning and options and Maffei quote: Norris (1997). Also see Jereski (1997), which says: "But a telltale footnote to its income statement revealed

that pretax earnings would have been $2.8 billion—$570 million less—if Microsoft had compensated its employees entirely with cash." At "its $83.75 closing stock price on the Nasdaq Stock Market yesterday would reflect an earnings multiple of nearly 30 times last year's earnings instead of about 24 times."

139    ". . . Enron had received a large tax break for options . . . ": Leonhardt (2002b). Enron also gave options to a broad group of employees.

139    Greenspan: Hitt and Schlesinger (2002).

140    "Silicon Value is now . . . ": Authors' interview.

140    "Today, 80 percent of the workforce is involved in nonmanufacturing activities . . . ": OCED (2000). We are indebted to James Sesil of Rutgers University for this reference. The growing role of intellectual property in capital was the subject of a Federal Reserve Bank of Kansas City conference in Jackson Hole, Wyoming (Murray 2001).

141    "Knowledge is not like a stock of ore . . . ": Griliches (1994).

142    "There is a trade-off . . . ": Authors' interview.

142    "We're creating a company in which human resources . . . ": Authors' interview.

143    "When you start a company, you own 100 percent of this pie . . . ": Authors' interview.

143    Warren Buffett: For "royalty on the passage of time," see Tully (1998). For his letters to shareholders, see www.berkshirehathaway.com/.

148    "The crazy thing . . . ": From Joseph Blasi's interview with Beyster in 1988. Also see www.saic.com.

148    "Here in Seattle it all centers around Microsoft . . . ": Authors' interview.

# Chapter 7

153    High performance work system: The most careful definition of a high-performance work system is by Huselid in Becker, Huselid, and Ulrich (2001). It's based on the characteristics that reduce a company's turnover and improve its market value, including return on assets and sales per employee. This approach emphasizes the importance of all parts of a company culture supporting each other.

154    ". . . various forms in the United States . . . ": For an overview of the different types of employee ownership, see Bernstein, Binns, Hyman, Staubus, and Sherman (2002). For more detailed descriptions, see the web sites of the primary nonprofit organizations that address employee ownership: The Beyster Institute for Entrepreneurial Employee Ownership (www.beysterinstitute.org); the ESOP Association (www.the-esop-emplowner.org); the National Center for Employee Ownership (www.neco.org); the Profit Sharing/401k Council of America (www.psca.org); the Kelso Institute (www.kelsoinstitute.org/); the Center for Economic and Social Justice (www.cesj.org/index.html); and the Capital Ownership

Group (www.capitalownership.org/). Various states also have special centers, including the Ohio Employee Ownership Center (dept.kent.edu/oeoc/); the Virginia ESOP Education Services (www.vlsc.bus.vcu.edu/va_esop.htm); The Global Equity Organization (www.global equity.org); and Ownership Associates (www.ownership associates.com).

See also the International Association of Financial Participation (perso.wanadoo.fr/iafp/); Employee Benefits Research Institute (www.ebri.com); WorldatWork, the professional association for compensation, benefits, and total rewards (www.worldatwork.org); the National Association of Stock Plan Professionals (www.naspp.com); and the ICA Group (www.ica-group.org).

154   ". . . 9,000 private companies, mostly smaller ones . . . ": For a list and the web sites of the 100 largest mostly private employee ownership companies, see: www.business-ethics.com/employee.htm#EO Chart.

154   Appendix C: Many companies have more than one type of employee ownership plan. So we lumped the employees and the assets of all secondary plans in with the primary one at each firm. This approach allows us to measure the number of companies and employees in the United States involved in employee ownership without double counting, as all previous estimates have done—including our own.

Also, Labor Department data on new contributions of company stock to KSOPS, 401(k)s, and profit-sharing plans weren't available after 1999. So we assumed that they continued at 9.4 percent a year, the average between 1994 and 1999. We used the same 9.4 percent assumption for employee stock purchase plans, for which no specific data were available even before 1999. We assumed that contributions to ESOPs didn't grow at all after 1999, based on the flat growth of ESOPs reported by the Labor Department. To the extent that these assumptions understate the degree to which employees pulled back from employer stock purchases during the market drop, both the stock values and the losses as of August 2002 would be smaller.

154   ". . . researchers have done more than seventy . . . ": Kruse (2002).

155   Books: See Blasi (1987, 1988), Kruse (1984, 1993b), Blasi and Kruse (1991), and Quarrey, Blasi, and Rosen (1986). We warned about the risk of employee ownership and corporate governance problems in *The New Owners* (1991). We specifically warned about the risk of employee ownership investments in company stock (such as those in 401(k) plans) and the need for a corporate governance response to this risk. For the reviews, see Kruse and Blasi (1995) (updated in Kruse and Blasi [1997, 2000a, 2000b] and Blasi and Kruse [2001a]), and Sesil, Kruse, and Blasi (2001).

155   ". . . synthesize all the findings gathered over the years . . . ": As we were writing this book, the NCEO published a partial synthesis (2002c).

155   Definition of "major" study: A major study is a comprehensive study using careful statistical techniques that relies on a large sample of the population or all of the companies for which data is available in the population being researched.

157   ". . . the companies in all these studies granted roughly 8 percent of their shares to employees": This is our estimate of the average total employee ownership found in studies involving ESOPs, defined-contribution plans, employee stock purchase plans, and stock options. The ownership at companies in which employees own more than 5 percent is about 12 percent (Blasi and Kruse 1991, and Blasi, Conte, and Kruse 1992). It's about 2 percent to 3 percent in ESOP companies. The total overhang from stock options among companies with broad-based option plans is about 11 percent on a post-dilution basis.

158   Iroquois: Johansen and Mann (2000), Johansen (1999, 1998).

158   Indentured servitude: Galenson (1981, 1984), Morgan (1995), Hofstadter (1973), Phillips (1987), Taylor (2001), Carr, Menard, and Walsh (1991), Perkins (1988), Weiss and Schaefer (1994), Paulson (1981), Bogart and Kemmerer (1942), Williamson (1944), and Hawke (1988). Indentured servitude could benefit both landowner and servant when the owners followed the terms of the indenture. But because there was such unequal power, some owners took advantage of their servants by prolonging their terms. In addition, those who finished their indenture in areas such as Pennsylvania were much more likely to get land than those in areas like the Chesapeake, where rising land prices shut them out of the market.

158   Whaling: Hohman (1926). We are indebted to Paul Cyr, librarian at the New Bedford, Massachusetts Free Public Library Whaling Collection Archives, who helped us do research on how compensation schemes worked on whaling vessals. See also Melville (1998), Bemis (1886), Clark (1886).

159   Homestead Act: United States (1862), Gates (1936, 1962), Poulson (1981), Bogart and Kemmerer (1942), Republican Association of Washington (1859), Union Republican Congressional Committee (1868), Hibbard (1924), Cowan (1936–1940), Shannon (1936), and Davis, Hughes, and McDougall (1969).

160   ". . . promises and plans to extend land ownership to free blacks . . ." : Cimbala (1989), Cox (1958), Bentley (1955), and *The Sea Islands: An Experiment in Land Redistribution* available at chnm.gmu.edu/courses/122/carr/seaframe.html.

Sharecropping: See Ransom and Sutch (2001), Royce (1993), Reid (1973), Nieman (1994), Mitchell (1979), U.S. Special Committee on Farm Tenancy (1937), Davis (1982). On the theory, see Stiglitz (1974), Braverman and Stiglitz (1982), and Cheung (1968). Cohn (1948).

161   ". . . sharing profits with employees . . . ": French companies largely pioneered profit sharing at the French National Fire Insurance Company in 1820 and in 1842 at the Paris painting and decorating firm E.J. The practice spread to other French firms such as Godin of Guise and Bon Marche store, and then to England. Plans of the day typically involved sharing profits with a substantial proportion of ordinary employees and didn't vary year to year at the discretion of the employer, according to an 1889 report by the International Congress on Profit Sharing. There were about 240 plans set up in England between 1880 and 1910. Some took a form called "copartner-

ship," in which employees were given their profit shares in company stock and had representatives on the board of directors. In the United States, 50 plans were known to exist as of 1896, and 67 plans were identified in 1937.

161   Albert Gallatin: U.S. Congress (1939), Encyclopedia Brittanica (2001), Derber (1970).

162   ". . . small groups of skilled craft workers . . . ": Commons (1918–1935). Carpenters in Philadelphia set up an employee-owned company in 1791, as did cordwainers in 1806, Boston tailors in 1849, and German tailors in New York in 1850.

162   ". . . late 1800s . . . ": See Bemis (1886) and Shaw (1886) for regional reviews of profit sharing and employee ownership plans in the Midwest and New England done for the American Economic Association. The Minneapolis barrel-making industry had significant employee ownership, while fishing in New England had extensive profit sharing. On WalthamWatch in Massachusetts, see Gitelman (1965). At this time, Andrew Carnegie gave ownership to his top managers to create "golden handcuffs," but he felt wider employee ownership and profit sharing ran counter to human nature (Derber 1970). He said that if workers wanted to become owners of wealth, they should purchase the stock with their savings (Carnegie 1933).

162   Clark: See Clark (1886), who made the basic argument of our book: "Cooperation aims to increase the margin from which the increment of gain is drawn. It makes industry more productive. It goes to the employer somewhat more and to the laborer much more than they now receive." The British political economists John Stuart Mill and Alfred Marshall also supported employee ownership (Jensen 2001). We are indebted to Christopher Mackin of Ownership Associates and David Ellerman of the World Bank for this reference.

162   Pillsbury: Shaw (1886). Pillsbury's theory connected the incentive effect and the corporate culture, as Shaw makes clear: "The habitual attention to one's work and the work of one's fellows that is developed by a personal interest in the business is a great advantage in the modern manufacture of flour. By infinite pains and great enterprise 'Pillsbury's Best' has been made the standard flour of the world and the maintenance of its enviable reputation depends much on the workmen in the mills."

162   Rand McNally: Gilman (1889).

162   Brookings: Brookings (1925, 1929, 1932). Abram Hewitt, the manufacturer, former mayor of New York City, and congressman, espoused a combination of employee ownership and profit sharing.

162   Procter & Gamble: Howert (1986) and Lief (1958). For studies on a number of well-known cases at the time, see Zahavi (1983) on the Endicott Johnson shoe company; Taylor (1928) on the Leighton retail chain; Atkins (1922) on the A. Nash clothing company; Meine (1923) on the Dennison Company (which is Avery Dennison Inc. today); and Hultgran (1924) on the Dix manufacturing facilities. On Endicott Johnson and General Electric, see the SUNY/Albany historical web site at www.albany.edu/history/histmedia/.

162    Filene: La Dame (1930), Filene (1924, 1930). Kodak's 1912 profit-sharing plan was tied to stock dividends to remind employees that they had a stake in the company similar to the shareholders. Sears considered its profit-sharing plan "the unifying symbol around which the entire organization revolved," and posted its current stock price in all buildings.

162    Illinois Central Railroad: National Industrial Conference Board (1928), Foerster and Dietel (1927), and Tead (1926).

162    King Camp Gillette: Sobel and Sicilia (1986), Gillette (1924), and Severy (1907).

163    "In 1900 . . . ": National Industrial Conference Board (1928).

163    DuPont: National Industrial Conference Board (1928), and Wall (1990) where Alfred DuPont writes: ". . . the solution to the problem of industrial discontentment . . . lies in the proper distribution of wealth between capital and labor in years to come based on some economic principle which will be satisfactory and which can be defended on the grounds of science and fairness."

163    George Eastman: National Industrial Conference Board (1928).

163    Gallatin quote: U.S. Senate (1939).

164    National Civic Federation: See McQuaid (1986). For a later study on welfare capitalism after the New Deal, see Jacoby (1997).

164    ". . . Harvard University's President . . ." See Eliot (1917), who said the level of profit sharing was not meaningful enough in most plans to create a significant incentive effect. On profit sharing before World War II: See Gilman (1889), Emmet (1917a, 1917b), National Civic Federation (1920, 1921), Groton, Dennison, Gay, Kendall, and Burritt (1926), and Derber (1970).

164    Special Conference Committee: For the Rockefeller quote, see Brookings (1932). He told the Industrial Relations Commission in their 1914–1915 hearings that he believed capital and labor were partners and that in any industry in which he was connected he would gladly welcome the workers as stockholders. On the committee, see Hirao and others (1998) and an Internet library summarizing original historical materials on the subject by a Japanese professor on the web site of his university at: comp-irh.tamacc.chuo-u.ac.jp/comp-irh/SCC/SCC.html    and    comp-irh.tamacc. chuou.ac.jp/comp-irh/SCC/scc-tbl.html. An English-language abstract of the Hirao (1998) book, *Big Business and Workers in the U.S.: The Formation of the Nonunion Industrial Relations System in the 1920s*, by Professor Takelusa Hirao, is available at: comp-irh.tamacc.chuo-u.ac.jp/comp-irh/SCCProject/Labor-Policy.html. On Clarence Hicks and employee ownership, see Hicks (1924).

164    Employee ownership figures for various companies: See National Industrial Conference Board (1928). On Standard Oil, see also, Rukeyser (1927). The U.S. Department of Labor did a thorough review of employee ownership publications (1927). On Philadelphia Rapid Transit, see Mitten (1926). On the Columbia Conserve Company, see Douglas (1926), Vance (1956), and Bussel (1997). Another unique em-

ployee ownership program founded at this time was the American Cast Iron Pipe Company, see www.acipco.com. Gardiner C. Means at the Columbia Law School took a cynical view of this big push to get workers to buy stock with their savings in the twenties: ". . . the great popularity of customer and employee stock-selling plans was to a considerable extent due to a drying up of the market for corporate stock among the rich and the necessity of seeking new capital among individuals of moderate means" and not "a permanent trend." For evidence, see Advertising Council (1957).

165   GE and Owen Young of GE: See National Industrial Conference Board (1928), pp. 26–29, McQuaid (1986), and Jensen (1956). On Swope, see Strother (1927).

165   ". . . 800,000 employees owned . . . ": See National Industrial Conference Board (1928). For a second source on this estimate, see United States Federal Trade Commission (1923).

165   ". . . underscoring the excessive risk workers bore when employee ownership was based almost entirely on the use of their savings to buy company stock": Two corporate executives who emerged as spokespeople for employee ownership warned against excessive risk to workers. Henry S. Dennison (n.d.) of the Dennison Company wanted to use stock to pay bonuses but not to encourage the use of worker savings to buy stock. To reduce risk, Gerard Swope of GE wanted workers to have stock in only established companies (Strother 1927).

165   Profit sharing after World War II: The profit-sharing spurt began with a new tax ruling, Section 162, subsection h of the Internal Revenue Code. On the War Labor Board's boost to profit sharing, see Jacoby (1997). Vandenberg comments: See U.S. Senate (1939); General developments: Knowlton (1954), Simons (1948), Encyclopedia Britannica (1961), which is the most thorough discussion of profit sharing during this period. For the best summary of research immediately after the war, see Latta 1979. On the use of stock plans before the salary stabilization board, see U.S. Salary Stabilization Board (1952).

166   "Profit sharing reached its peak . . . ": For a summary of survey data on the prevalence of profit-sharing plans, the percent of employees involved, and the profit share as a percent of payroll, see Kruse (1993a).

167   ". . . 401(k)s have been squeezing out most serious attempts at profit sharing . . . ": The best statistical evidence is in Kruse (2002), which shows that only 355 deferred profit-sharing plans that were not part of 401(k) plans existed among all public and private companies at the end of 1998 in all corporations with more than 100 employees.

167   Kelso: See Kelso and Adler (1958, 1961). Kelso's articles, books, and lectures are available at the web site of the Kelso Institute: www.kelsoinstitute.org/. Two other institutes have developed around these broad themes: The Center for Economic and Social Justice, at (www.cesj.org/index.html); and the Shared Capitalism Institute at (www.sharedcapitalism.org/). See also Gates (1999, 2000).

167   "While ESOPs can be structured in several ways . . . ": ESOPs and other forms of employee ownership dilute current shareholders, except those in which workers use their own money to buy the stock at the full market price. However, this happens in less than 5 percent of ESOPs, studies show.

169   ". . . now often have a majority of their stock in the hands of employees": The ability to use tax-subsidized credit to buy large blocks of stock—an idea pioneered by Louis Kelso—has resulted in ESOPs being the driving force behind most majority employee ownership corporations. While the general growth of ESOPs has stalled in recent years, the number of majority employee ownership firms is on the rise as a result of smaller ESOPs buying more of their company and newer tax incentives for larger employee stakes as a result of S corporation law. For example, a decade ago, the membership of the ESOP Association, the major Washington-based lobbying organization for ESOPs, consisted mainly of companies with less than 50 percent ESOPs. Today, 70 percent of its membership are in firms with more than 50 percent ESOPs.

170   Census Bureau data on self-directed work teams: See Blasi and Kruse (2000). This also provides a complete review of the high involvement workplace literature. See also Kruse and Blasi (2000a, 2000b) and Bailey, Berg, and Sandy (2001).

170   ". . . only 1 percent to 2 percent make widespread use of innovative work methods": This is based on Blasi and Kruse's (2000) measurement of high-performance work cultures. These are workplaces that have more than half of their employees in self-directed work teams, work-related meetings to solve problems, job rotation, and where the average training hours, the total recruitment costs, and the flatness of their organization, and pay and benefits are significantly different than that of their industry group.

170   Stock Options: Study of 490 corporations: See Sesil, Kroumova, Kruse, and Blasi (2000). For a full version of the report see Blasi, Kruse, Sesil, Kroumova, and Carberry (2000). For "knowledge industry" companies, see Sesil, Kroumova, Blasi, and Kruse (2002). For the Wharton study, see Ittner, Lambert, and Larcker (2001).

172   ESOPs: See Kruse and Blasi (1995, 1997, 2000a, 2000b), Kruse (1999), Blasi and Kruse (2001a), and Sesil, Kruse, and Blasi (2001). For a comparison of 1,200 ESOP and non-ESOP firms, see Kruse and Blasi (2001).

173   Stock gains of 562 companies: See Blasi, Conte, and Kruse (1992). On equity gains, see also Blasi, Conte, and Kruse (1996). On 382 companies, see Mehran (1999). See also Blair, Kruse, and Blasi (2000).

174   ". . . ESOPs effect on sales and employment growth": Kruse and Blasi (2001).

175   Profit sharing: Kruse (1993a, 1993b). See also: Weitzman and Kruse (1990), Kruse (1999), and Azfar and Danninger (2001).

176   ". . . 760 randomly selected": Black and Lynch (2000).

176   Employee participation: For an excellent review of the literature on participation, see Ichniowski, Kochan, Levine, Olson, and Strauss (1996). For examples of
individual workplaces or industries that have at times combined various forms of partnership capitalism with participation, see Rubenstein (2001) in autos; Ichniowski,
Shaw, and Prennushi (1995) in steel; Dunlop and Weil (1996) in textiles; and Kelley
(1994) in machine tools. Also see Blasi and Kruse (2000), Appelbaum and Batt
(1994), and Appelbaum (2000).

176   Robert of Tibco: Authors' interview.

176   *Reinventing the Workplace*: Levine (1995).

177   ". . . randomly choose 193 manufacturing worksites . . . ": Black and Lynch
(2000). They also found that employee voice had a larger effect on productivity when
it was done in unionized workplaces and that the proportion of nonmanagers using
computers also positively influenced productivity.

177   ". . . 433 worksites over a sixteen-year period and 660 more over nineteen
years.": Cappelli and Neumark (1999).

177   *The HR Scorecard*: Becker, Huselid, and Ulrich (2001). The most successful
companies were extremely serious about performance management. They gave 95 percent of employees performance appraisals, tied incentive or merit pay to performance
for 82 percent of employees, made 86 percent of employees eligible for incentive pay,
targeted total compensation at the 59th percentile, and made sure a low-performing
employee had a more than 6 percent difference in incentive pay compared to a high
performing employee. One strength of Huselid's approach is a very specific system to
measure companies' move toward a high-performance work system that the company
itself can manage. But a very small number of companies say they actually track these
items.

A key focus of this work is how the compensation system, among others, can be
out of alignment with the rest of the company's work system. The authors measured
the percentage of employees owning stock in each company and the percentage of
stock employees owned in each company. As expected, employee ownership alone did
not predict improved performance. One limitation is that the study did not measure
the use of stock options or stock as incentive pay, but focused on incentive pay in the
form of cash bonuses. One lesson from high-tech companies and broad-based stock
option companies, Weeden, Carberry, and Rodrick (2000, 2001), is that most integrate performance appraisal, incentive pay, AND stock options together in a seamless
system of performance management.

178   ". . . Harvard Business Review . . . ": Rosen and Quarrey (1987) and Quarrey
and Rosen (1986). Rosen, Klein, and Young (1986) explained how this worked and
were the first to determine that the initial annual stock grant had to equal 15 to 25
percent of pay at a minimum.

178   General Accounting Office: U.S. GAO (1987). The National Center for
Employee Ownership wrote on its web site in April 2002: "The measures the GAO

used were controversial because they assumed that employee ownership firms did not increase overall compensation when they set up an ESOP. In fact, it appears that about half of all ESOP companies do increase compensation, and few decrease it. The GAO results are probably too conservative because of this assumption."

179    National Opinion Research Center: Kalleberg, Knoke, Marsden, and Spaeth (1996). See also Lawler, Mohrman, and Ledford (1992).

179    Harvard University study: Freeman and Dube (2000).

180    ". . . a strong tie between higher pay and the more widespread use of various participation methods": Blasi and Kruse (2001b) show that nonunion companies tend to pay workers significantly higher fixed wages if self-directed work teams and other high-performance work practices are used comprehensively in the company. However, only companies that systematically use many high-performance work practices with most of their workers provide a meaningfully large compensation premium.

# Chapter 8

185    ". . . less than 2 percent . . . in joint decisionmaking": Blasi and Kruse (2000).

186    ". . . employees paid for about 64 percent of all this stock ownership themselves . . .": This 64 percent consists of $72 billion worth of shares workers bought through employee share purchase plans and $5 billion they purchased through company profit-sharing plans. Workers also used savings they diverted from other investments to buy $178 billion worth of employer shares through 401(k)s. Only the remaining 36 percent of the $400 billion represents true property sharing. Included here is $10 billion in company contributions to profit-sharing plans, $46 billion in ESOPs, and another $87 billion in the matching stock that many companies contribute to their employees' 401(k) plans, Kruse (2002), U.S. Department of Labor, Bureau of Labor Statistics (1997). ESPP assets are based on the Corporate America 100, supplemented by unpublished data on all retirement plans with less than 100 participants by Douglas Kruse. Market values have been updated to December 31, 2001. On excessive use of company stock, see also Meulbroek (2002), Benartzi (2001), and Benartzi and Thaler (2001).

186    "As of 2000 . . . 12 billion options . . .": Based on authors' computations from Standard and Poor's Execucomp data for the 1,500 largest U.S. corporations. This is an estimate of the total outstanding options available for all employees. See also Hitt and Schlesinger (2002), based on Ciesielski (2001).

186    "$1.2 trillion . . .": The value of all the stock on the major exchanges on 12/31/2000 was $12.2 trillion, according to Wilshire Associates. The $1.2 trillion is 10 percent of that figure. Of course, executives and employees must pay the exercise price to buy this stock, so their options wouldn't have netted them this amount. However, they control shares worth $1.2 trillion.

186   "... 10 percent ...": Based on authors' computations from Standard and Poor's Compustat. This is a conservative number because it does not include options available for future issue but not yet granted. Siegl, Loayza, and Davis (2002) show the average total overhang in these companies as 14.1 percent, including those options available for future issue.

186   "Roughly, 30 percent of them ...": Based on the Corporate America 100. This is the aggregate percent of all options outstanding at these companies that are held by the top five executives. It includes options that are both exercisable and unexercisable. On the slow trend toward wider distribution, see Mehran and Tracy (2002).

187   "... comprise less than 5 percent of traditional companies": U.S. Department of Labor, Bureau of Labor Statistics (2000).

187   "We estimate that only about 6 percent of the country's 10,000 public companies ...": This figure comes from an extrapolation of the 6 percent of the Corporate America 100 that have broad-based option plans. The 2 percent figure comes from the U.S. Department of Labor, Bureau of Labor Statistics (2000), which showed that 1.7 percent of all private industry employees received stock options in 1999, including after-hire and signing-bonus stock options. Both estimates exclude private companies, many of which also offer options to their workers.

187   "... up from 5 percent in 1992": Authors' computations from Standard and Poor's Compustat show average dilution was 5.2 percent in 1992. The median dilution was 2.2 percent that year, almost quadrupling by 2000 to 8.2 percent.

189   Construction of the Corporate America 100: The index excludes members of the High Tech 100, of which there was only one, America Online, as of October 2000. There is one significant difference between the High Tech 100 and the Corporate America 100. The first describes the hundred largest companies in the Internet industry, as measured by their market value. The Corporate America 100, however, is a random sample of all companies on the New York Stock Exchange that had market values similar to those of the High Tech 100 (i.e., only in the sense that they were above the threshhold $1.6 billion as of October 2000). We thought this was the best way to compare a single industry to the rest of Corporate America. Another option would have been to use the hundred largest firms on the NYSE, but that comparison would not have provided a picture of the average ownership of traditional corporations. We choose a random sample to make the Corporate America 100 as representative as possible of the mainline public stock market, excluding technology companies, which are mainly traded on the NASDAQ. Four of the Corporate America 100 do not offer a stock option plan to any of their employees, including executives. They are Warren Buffett's Berkshire Hathaway, Florida Progress Corporation and Appalachian Power, both utilities, and Diamond Offshore Drilling.

190   Table 8.1 Corporate America's Top-heavy Wealth Sharing: For a detailed description of our calculations see the book's web site. Figures for direct stock ownership by nonexecutive employees are based on Form 5500 records filed by each company

with the U.S. Department of Labor. While the High Tech 100 information is from 2000, the data for the Corporate America 100 covers 1999.

191    "However, this group typically constitutes less than 5 percent of the workforce . . . ": U.S. Department of Labor, Bureau of Labor Statistics (2000).

192    Run rate: Actual average run rates for the Corporate America 100 before dilution are: 1997: 1.86 percent; 1998: 1.63 percent; 1999: 1.87 percent; 2000: 2.27 percent; indicating a gradual rise over the period. The average is 1.9 percent, or 1.86 percent on a post-dilution basis, hence, almost 2 percent. The most recent numbers closely match the average run rate for the 1,500 largest U.S. companies (Siegl, Loayza, and Davis 2002).

192    ". . . 27 percent went to the top five executives alone": Based on our analysis of SEC filings for 2001.

192    Mercer study: William M. Mercer (2001b).

193    ". . . worth an average of about $6,727 . . . ": This is based on our calculations using the public records the companies have on file with the U.S. Department of Labor (Form 5500) regarding their retirement benefit plans.

193    "$40,000 in 1999": Authors' computation based on Standard and Poor's Compustat.

193    "In 1980 . . . ": See *Business Week* (1991) for 1980 and *Business Week* (2002) for the current figure. See also Reingold and Grover (1999). According to Hall and Liebman (1998), only 19 percent of total executive pay in 1980 came from stock options. They contributed 80 percent by 2001, Lavelle, Jespersen, and Arndt (2002). This reflects the value of exercised options, but excludes unexercised ones. For the trend from 1992 to 1999 for the top five executives, see Mehran and Tracy (2002).

194    Arthur Rock: Authors' interview.

194    "We calculated how much the top five executives . . . ": As of our press date, information for 2001 was only available for a third of executives. They had option profits of $6 billion at that stage, so it's possible that their total for the year could exceed that of 2000, despite the sharp downdraft in the stock market. The computations for all years are based on our analysis of the Execucomp database of Standard and Poor's, covering the largest 1,500 companies. For an explanation of how we computed these numbers, see more detailed footnotes on the book web site, www.inthecompanyofowners.com. To see how much the top five made every year, go to web Appendix 3 (also on www.inthecompanyofowners.com.)

194    "In sum, executives granted themselves higher annual increases . . . ": For a comparison of annual percentage executives and employees each received in the 1990s, see web Appendix 4 on www.inthecompanyofowners.com.

194    ". . . a total net profit of nearly $80 billion at the end of 2000 . . . ": This figure for 2001 had come close to $25 billion by our press time, with data in for only a third of executives. So the total paper wealth for 2001 might surpass the prior year, as occurred with annual option profits.

195    "... a 1999 article by Kevin J. Murphy ...": Murphy (1999). However, Murphy cites research evidence on both sides of this question and writes: "Based on my own observations and extensive discussion with executives, board members, and compensation consultants, I tend to dismiss the cynical scenario of entrenched compensation committees rubber-stamping increasingly lucrative pay programs with a wink and a nod." He also says: "Although there are undoubtedly exceptions outside board members approach their jobs with diligence, intelligence, and integrity regardless of whether they have social or business ties with the CEO. Faced with a range of market data on competitive pay levels, committees tend to err on the high side. Faced with a choice of a sensible compensation plan and a slightly inferior plan favored by the CEO, the committee will defer to management. Similarly, faced with a discretionary choice on bonus-pool funding, the committee will tend to over- rather than under-fund. The amounts at stake in any particular case are typically trivial from a shareholder's perspective, but the overall impact of the bias has likely contributed to a ratcheting of pay levels."

Murphy's comprehensive review is on his web site at: www-rcf.usc.edu/~kjmurphy/jmjpe.pdf. For the empirical evidence on CEO influence over these committees, see also Newman and Mozes (1997).

195    "A 2001 study by a Harvard University Law School professor": Bebchuk, Fried, and Walker (2002).

195    Federal Reserve chairman: See Greenspan (2002). The speech was given March 26, 2002, at Stern School of Business, NYU, and is available at www.federalreserve.gov.

196    *Fortune*: Loomis (2001).

197    Harvard study: Hall and Liebman (1998). Results are for the median CEO. They conclude: "We do however believe that our results contradict the claim that there is little or no link between performance and CEO pay." Hall and Liebman carefully look at the changes in the value of stock and stock options as the firm's market value changes. They conclude that: "both the level of CEO compensation and the sensitivity of CEO compensation to performance has increased sharply over the past fifteen years." They also write: "We do not claim that the current relationship between CEO pay and firm performance is sufficiently strong or that current contracts are efficient."

The Hall and Liebman article is available for PDF download on Prof. Liebman's web site at: www.ksg.harvard.edu/jeffreyliebman/papers.htm, or from the working papers section of the National Bureau of Economic Research at www.nber.com or www.nber.org. The working paper is # W6213, October 1997. An earlier study of the 1969–1983 period did not find a strong link between CEO compensation and company performance, but it was before the huge expansion in stock options, see Jensen and Murphy (1990). Murphy and Conyon (2000) found similar findings to these in comparing U.S. and British firms, with a stronger association between executive wealth and firm performance in the United States than in Britain.

198    "On this score, Murphy is clear . . . ": Murphy (1999). He also says that options give executives an incentive to avoid dividends and favor share repurchases, because they're tied to stock price appreciation and not total shareholder return. Options also give executives an incentive to pursue riskier investments, since option value will increase with more stock price volatility. Also see Stabile (1999).

199    ". . . CEOs should be paid . . . ": Hall and Liebman (1998). For a review, see Murphy (1999).

199    ". . . E*Trade Group Incorporated CEO Christos M. Cotsakos managed to earn a total of $80 million . . ." Craig (2002), Leonhardt (2002a), and Kirby (2002).

199    "Across corporate America, even a rough calculation . . . ": Authors' estimates based on comparing the increase in market value of the 1,500 corporations in Execucomp to the increase in actual profits from stock option exercises for the top five executives.

200    U.S.-English comparisons: Murphy and Conyon (2000), available at www.rcf.usc.edu/~kjmurphy/Pauper.pdf. The 1.48 percent refers to the combination of stock ownership, option ownership from options, and Long Term Incentive Plan grants.

200    "share of the option pie . . . ": The study was performed by the authors in 2001 using Execucomp. The average share of options granted annually to the top five, out of all options granted by the company, was 31 percent. Using standard, median, and robust regressions, this share doesn't predict total shareholder return in the year the option grant is given over all years tested. The previous year's percent of option grants doesn't predict total shareholder return in the following year.

201    ". . . they've surrendered tremendous ownership to executives with no clear evidence . . . ": The *Wall Street Journal*'s Holman W. Jenkins Jr. (2002) raised a similar point recently in his regular *Business World* column: ". . . if options have a genuine incentive effect but management is capturing too much of the gains, the mystery is easily solved: options grants are too big. Now if academic economists want to do something useful, they would explore whether CEOs have gained outsized bargaining power in relation to shareholders and boards. Our guess is yes because so much of a company's stock-market value these days depends on the image and reputation of the CEO."

202    General Motors: Proxy filed with the SEC on April 18, 2002, for the quote. On the Stock Incentive Plan, see Proxy filed with the SEC on April 16, 1997.

202    General Electric: Proxy filed with the SEC on March 23, 2001.

203    Ayn Rand: Rand (1943, 1957).

203    Michael Eisner: Lambert (2001). *Business Week* did a recent rating of how Eisner stacks up against his industry peers in terms of his pay relative to shareholder return. He received the lowest grade the magazine gets. See Lavelle, Jespersen, and Arndt (2002).

204    Pepsi: See Solomon (1989), Anfuso (1995),

# Chapter 9

205   "thousands of mostly closely held companies that have used ESOPs . . ." Employees in these companies often use them to buy the company from a small business owner who wants to cash out or retire, Bernstein, Binns, Hyman, Staubus, and Sherman (2002), and NCEO (2002g). Case studies of many of these companies can be found on the web sites of the nonprofit groups working with employee ownership. For the hundred largest majority employee-owned companies, see NCEO (2002h) available at: www.nceo.org/library/eo100.html.

205   ". . . a more attractive and versatile approach than ESOPs . . . ": ESOPs undoubtedly would have a greater role to play if the U.S. government hadn't significantly cut back the tax incentives for them in public companies in recent years.

206   ". . . hourly paycheck, which has risen by a grand total of only about 3 percent since 1973, after adjusting for inflation . . . ": See Mishel, Bernstein, and Boushey (2002).

206   ". . . capital has provided a far greater source of increased income in America in the past three decades . . . ": Capital income is from rent, dividends, interest income, and realized capital gains. In 1999, the bottom four-fifths of households got 46 percent of the wage income in the economy and 20 percent of the capital income. Overall, labor income has fallen as a share of national income since 1950 while the capital share has grown. Mishel, Bernstein, and Boushey (2002).

207   ". . . the single largest form of worker ownership today . . . 401(k)s . . . ": Appendix C. This is true when KSOPs, which are a hybrid of 401(k)s and ESOPs, are included with 401(k)s.

208   "If you are not able to allow people to criticize you . . . ": Authors' interview.

209   ". . . $65,000 worth of equipment, while the Corporate America 100 . . . with $250,000 worth . . . ": Based on an average property, plant, and equipment per worker using 2000 SEC filings.

210   Run rates: We computed run rates as options granted minus options cancelled as a percent of total shares outstanding. We estimated the run rates for the 490 companies for a sample using their 2000 SEC filings. The run rates for 150 traditional companies are from an average of non-Internet/e-commerce/software industry groups, Weeden, Carberry, and Rodrick (2001). The run rates of the 1,500 companies are from Seigl, Loayza, and Davis (2002). The doubling of run rates is based on our analysis of Standard and Poor's Execucomp from 1992 to 2000 using the burn rate. (The burn rate is the same as the run rate, except that it doesn't include cancelled options, which are not given in Execucomp). For all 1,500 companies, average burn rates went from 2.2 percent in 1992 to 3.1 percent in 2000, an increase of 143 percent. For the 500 largest corporations, they went from 0.77 percent in 1992 to 2.5 percent in 2000, a 324 percent increase.

211   "it could make sense to use at least part . . . ": While there may be a case to be made for reducing the stock options going to top executives and managers and us-

ing them for other levels in some companies, in fact, this isn't what companies with broad-based options have done. Instead, most increase their run rates. On average, these firms provide 39 percent of their options to top executives, compared to 29 percent in the Corporate America 100, Weeden, Carberry, and Rodrick (2001).

212    ". . . the U.S. stock market has risen by 10 percent a year . . . ": The exact numbers from 1925 to 2001 are 10.7 percent for large company stocks and 12.5 percent for small company stocks. This is the annual compound growth rate with dividends reinvested, based on the geometric mean. Adjusted for inflation, which was 3.1 percent annually over the period, the return was 7.4 percent for large-company stocks and 9.2 percent for small-company ones. In the 1990s, large-company returns averaged 18.2 percent a year before inflation, while small-company ones came in at 15.1 percent, Ibbotson Associates (2002).

213    "mixing option grants with ESOPs, employee share purchase plans, or profit-sharing plans": When companies can't or don't want to provide enough stock options to give workers a meaningful annual return—a minimum of 15 percent—they could use these other forms of employee ownership to achieve the same purpose. For example, the stock parceled out each year through an ESOP will deliver employees much the same wealth as they would receive from options. If a company aimed to give its hourly workers $1,600 a year in ownership profits, it could set up an ESOP that gives them $1,000 a year initially. After five years, this would grow to $1,600 if the company's stock grew by 10 percent a year.

Similarly, employee stock purchase plans are an underused vehicle for promoting employee ownership, because they can be designed to function like short-term stock options. One way is to allow workers to accumulate money through payroll deductions, then give them a long offering period in which to buy the stock. That way, they can wait to buy until they know they have a profit that's even greater than the standard 15 percent discount such plans typically provide.

Cash bonuses and profit sharing, too, can be use to promote partnership capitalism, by helping to firm up the connection between employees' extra effort and rewards for better performance.

215    ". . . study of the 490 non-Internet firms . . . ": Blasi, Kruse, Sesil, Kroumova, and Carberry (2000).

215    ". . . compared 1,200 ESOP firms to 1,200 similar non-ESOP ones . . . ": Kruse and Blasi (2001).

215    "Two smaller studies . . . ": Kardas, Scharf, and Keogh (1998), Mackin, Rodgers, and Scharf (2000), and Buchele and Scharf (2001).

215    ". . . wealth of literature on profit sharing . . . ": Kruse (1998).

216    "workers should get a minimum of 15 percent of their annual paycheck annually . . . ": Various studies indicate that incentives below the range of about 5 percent annually do not even get the attention of employees: Honeywell-Johnson and Dickinson (1999), Bucklin and Dickenson (2002), Kruse (1993a), Rosen, Klein, and

Young (1986). They also indicate that group incentives are at least as good as individual ones in affecting performance, and that social interactions among employees are generally better under group incentives. There appears to be a tradeoff between effort and reward for employees; when significant effort is required to improve company performance, larger incentives are required.

217    Table 9.1: What Employees Could Expect to Earn from Partnership Capitalism: The source is National Center for Employee Ownership. Weeden, Carberry, and Rodrick (2001). This workbook is invaluable in setting up a broadbased stock option plan because it includes benchmarks for every major industry.

217    ". . . the bull market of the late 1990s, when stocks climbed by 20 percent to 30 percent a year . . . ": Ibbotson Associates (2002).

219    "Average wages": Mishel, Bernstein, and Boushey (2002).

219    "Workers would come out ahead if they could sell their ESOP shares and diversify . . . ": Federal regulations allow workers nearing retirement to diversify their ESOP shares. Workers leaving companies with ESOPs before their retirement can take the value and roll it over into an IRA without waiting until retirement.

219    "At Enron, for example, 60 percent of the company's 401(k) . . . ": Oppel (2002).

220    "The more senior people get more stock options . . . ": Authors' interview.

221    "If you look at a seventy-five-year-old smoke-stack industry company . . . ": Authors' interview.

# Chapter 10

223    "Awarding stock options to all . . . ": Authors' interview.

224    "Many also skimped on the amounts . . . ": On the importance of using financial incentives to get employees to share private knowledge and discretionary effort for the benefit of the firm, see Laffont and Martimort (2002), and Nalbantian (1987).

224    "We don't have any manufacturing . . ." Authors' interview.

225    "As late as the early 1980s, tangible assets . . ." Ip (2002).

225    "In emerging industries that depend as heavily as the Internet . . ." For the amount of options granted in the biotechnology industry, see web Appendix 5 on www.inthecompanyofowners.com.

225    "As far back as 1979 . . . ": Jensen and Meckling (1979). Also Blair (1995, 1996).

226    "They also must extend the changes across the entire organization . . . ": Becker, Huselid, and Ulrich (2001) actually have designed a system companies can use to evaluate the degree to which they have achieved this goal. It can be used to evaluate whether a company has created an entrepreneurial culture. See also Huselid, Jackson, and Schuler (1997), and Heckscher and Donnellon (1994) on the postbureaucratic kind of corporation high-performance work practices imply. On measuring ownership

culture, see Mackin (1998, 2002) and NCEO (2002f). In addition, the two professors among us have developed a national survey of employees to assess the extent of partnership capitalism in large U.S. companies. This is a three-year project separately funded by the Rockefeller Foundation and the Russell Sage Foundation at the National Bureau of Economic Research. We developed the survey with Richard Freeman of Harvard University, Christopher Mackin of Ownership Associates, and several other scholars.

226    Frank Marshall: Authors' interview.

226    "Skeptical economists have long argued . . . ": Alchian and Demsetz (1972), Kandel and Lazear (1992), Weitzman and Kruse (1990), and Laffont and Martimort (2002).

227    "Even in the New Economy . . . ": Authors' interview.

227    "Equity in a bigger company . . . ": Authors' interview.

227    "In recent years, experts on employee ownership have come to believe that the free rider problem can be overcome by encouraging cooperation . . . ": Laffont and Martimort (2002), Axelrod (1984), Bonin and Putterman (1988), Fudenberg and Maskin (1986), Jensen and Meckling (1979), Kandel and Lazear (1992), Leibenstein (1966), Nalbantian (1987), and Putterman and Skillman (1988).

228    "Many high-tech companies back up this approach by awarding larger option grants to team players . . . ": Becker, Huselid, and Ulrich (2001). This is done by creating stark differences between the incentive pay of high-performing employees and low-performing ones.

228    "You can be a real star . . . ": Authors' interview.

228    "The culture of employee ownership": Authors' interview.

228    "The biggest thing I notice . . . ": Authors' interview.

229    "There is a psychological buy-in . . . ": Authors' interview.

229    "The partnership culture is transferable . . . ": Authors' interview.

229    Beyster: Authors' interview.

230    "We don't have nearly as much of the politics . . . ": Authors' interview.

230    "They handed out options like they were going out of style . . . ": Authors' interview.

231    "I think there is a legitimate question . . . ": U. S. Senate Committee on Banking, Housing, and Urban Affairs (2002).

231    ". . . a strong, independent board of directors . . . ": Monks and Minow (1996, 2001). Also see Millstein (1998).

232    "We looked more closely . . . ": Based on our analysis of board structures using recent SEC filings.

232    "High-tech boards tend to have fewer . . . ": See IRRC (2000b).

232    "Partnership capitalism also would seem to call for an employee representative . . . ": Olson (1994).

232 "Workers on boards . . . European countries": See Rogers and Streeck (1995).

233 "I think the ownership culture . . . ": Authors' interview.

235 Vivek Rawadive: Authors' interview.

235 $11 million a year: Lavelle, Jespersen, and Arndt (2002).

236 "You need to be more persuasive . . . ": Authors' interview.

236 "We try to set up an environment . . . ": Authors' interview.

237 "Most shareholders have more information . . . ": Authors' interview (2001).

237 "I know as a manager . . . ": Authors' interview.

239 "Stock options are one way capitalism has been democratized . . . ": Schlesinger (2002)

241 "In the late 1990s, options provided U.S. corporations with a break from federal taxes . . . ": Desai (2002). On the devastating effect on state budgets from the ups and downs of taxes on option profits, see Sterngold (2002).

# Bibliography

Abbate, Janet. 1999. *Inventing the Internet.* Cambridge: MIT Press.

Acosta, Jack. 2001. Interview. Conducted by Joseph Blasi. New Brunswick, N.J.: School of Management and Labor Relations. (Mr. Acosta was the chief financial officer of Portal Software.)

Adiga, Aravind. 2002. "Nasdaq Redux?" *Money* Magazine, June 1.

Advertising Council. 1957. The American Round Table Discussions on People's Capitalism at Yale University, New Haven, Connecticut, November 16 and 17, 1956. Digest report by David M. Potter. New York: Advertising Council.

Alchian, Armen A., and Harold Demsetz. 1972. "Production, Information Costs, and Economic Organization." *American Economic Review* 62(5), December, pp. 777–795.

Allen, Frederick. 2001. "Present at the Creation: William Hewlett and the Birth of Silicon Valley." New York: American Heritage.

Alpert, Gary, and Steve Pollock. 1999. *Amazon.com: The WetFeet.com Insider Guide.* San Francisco, Calif.: Wet Feet Press.

Amazon.com Employees. 2001. Interviews. Conducted by Joseph Blasi. New Brunswick, N.J.: School of Management and Labor Relations. (Pseudonyms of employees are Owen, James, Alisha, George, and Thomas.)

Anfuso, Dawn. 1995. "PepsiCo Shares Power and Wealth With Workers." *Personnel Journal*, June 1, p. 42.

Angel, Karen. 2002. *Inside Yahoo: Reinvention and the Road Ahead.* New York: John Wiley & Sons.

Angwin, Julia, and Martin Peers. 2000. "Workers to Get Stock Options: AOL, Time Warner Merger Offers Perks." *Wall Street Journal*, December 8.

Anthes, Gary H., and Kim S. Nash. 1992. "High-Tech Benefits Herlad Brave New Office." *Computerworld*, April 27.

Aoki, Naomi. 2002. "NYSE Seeks Changes to Directors' Ties to Companies." *Boston Globe*, June 7.

AP Online. 1998. "Thursday's Standard & Poor's." Associated Press Online, December 31.

Appelbaum, Eileen, Thomas Bailey, Peter Berg, and Arne L. Kalleberg. 2000. *Manufacturing Advantage: Why High-performance Work Systems Pay Off.* Ithaca, N.Y.: Cornell University Press, ILR Press.

Appelbaum, Eileen, and Rosemary Batt. 1994. *The New American Workplace: Transforming Work Systems in the United States.* Ithaca, N.Y.: Cornell University Press.

Aristotle. 1996. *Politics,* Books I and II. Oxford: Oxford University Press.

Arnold, Chris. 1998. "Employee Ownership: NPR's Chris Arnold Reports that While Employee Ownership has Become Commonplace in Silicon Valley, the Practice has Yet to Catch on Outside." "Morning Edition," July 27, with Bob Edwards in Washington, D.C. Washington, D.C.: Federal Document Clearing House.

Arun, Rasipuram "Russ" V. 2001. Interview. Conducted by Joseph Blasi. New Brunswick, N.J.: School of Management and Labor Relations. (Chief technology officer of Infospace Inc.)

Associated Press. 1997. "Apple Going Back To 'Egalitarian' Core." *Ottawa Citizen,* August 16.

Atherton, Angela Lipscomb. 1993–1997. "ACS Employee Ownership Index Update." *Journal of Employee Ownership Law and Finance* 5(3) (Summer 1993), pp. 117–118, through 9(3) (Summer 1997).

Atkins, Willard E. 1922. "The Personnel Policies of the A. Nash Company." *Journal of Political Economy* 30(2), April, pp. 212–228.

Atlanta Constitution. 2002. "Online Sessions Show Increase." *Atlanta Constitution,* June 16.

Auvil, Paul. 2001. Interview. Conducted by Joseph Blasi. New Brunswick, N.J.: School of Management and Labor Relations. (Mr. Auvil is the chief financial officer of Vitria Technology.)

Axelrod, Robert M. 1984. *The Evolution of Cooperation.* New York: Basic Books.

Azfar, Omar, and Stephan Danninger. 2001. "Profit Sharing, Employment Stability, and Wage Growth." *Industrial and Labor Relations Review* 54(5), April.

Bailey, Thomas, Peter Berg, and Carola Sandy. 2001. "The Effect of High Performance Work Practices on Employee Earnings in the Steel, Apparel, and Medical Electronics and Imaging Industries." *Industrial and Labor Relations Review* 44(2), March.

Baker, John Calhoun. 1937. *The Compensation of Executive Officers of Retail Companies, 1928–1935.* Boston, Mass.: Harvard University, Graduate School of Business Administration, Bureau of Business Research.

———. 1938. *Executive Salaries and Bonus Plans.* New York, McGraw-Hill.

———. 1940. "Stock Options for Executives." *Harvard Business Review,* pp. 106–122.

Balcom, A. B. 1916. "Fox Farming in Prince Edward Island: A Chapter in the History of Speculation." *Quarterly Journal of Economics* 30(4), August, pp. 665–681.

Ballmer, Steve. 2001. Interview. Conducted via email by Joseph Blasi. New Brunswick, N.J.: School of Management and Labor Relations. (Mr. Ballmer is CEO of Microsoft Inc.)

———. 2000. "The Text of Ballmer's Employee Memo." December 19. Special to ZDNet from ZDWire by ZD Inc. Available on Dow Jones Interactive at Rutgers University Library.

Barner, Robert. 2000. "Talent Wars in the Executive Suite: Six Trends Shaping Recruitment." *The Futurist,* May 1.

Barnes, Jane E. 2002. *Human Resource Metrics.* New Brunswick, N.J.: School of Management and Labor Relations, Rutgers University, June 27. Overheads presented at the Center for Human Resource Strategy Board of Advisors meeting.

Baskin, Jonathan Barron, and Paul J. Miranti Jr. 1997. *A History of Corporate Finance.* Cambridge, UK; New York: Cambridge University Press.

BCI Group. 2000. North American Employee Ownership Survey Results. Appleton, Wis.: Benefit Consultants Inc. (Joint survey with Western Compensation and Benefits Consultants, Schaumberg, Ill. Contact: BCI Group, tregnitz@bcigroup.com.)

Bebchuk, Lucian Arye, Jesse M. Fried, and David I. Walker. 2002. "Managerial Power and Rent Extraction in the Design of Executive Compensation." National Bureau of Economic Research, Working Paper 9068.

Becker, Brian E., and Mark A. Huselid. 1998. "High Performance Work Systems and Firm Performance: A Synthesis of Research and Managerial Implications." In G. Ferris, ed. *Research in Personnel and Human Resources.* Vol. 16, Greenwich, Conn.: JAI Press.

Becker, Brian E., Mark A. Huselid, and Dave Ulrich. 2001. *The HR Scorecard: Linking People, Strategy, and Performance.* Cambridge, Mass.: Harvard Business School Press.

Bell, George. 2001. Interview. Conducted by Joseph Blasi. New Brunswick, N.J.: School of Management and Labor Relations. (Mr. Bell is the former president, CEO, and chairman of Excite@Home.)

Bellinger, Robert. 1993. "Profession: 1993 IEE Salary Survey." *Electronic Engineering Times,* May 17.

———. 1995. "Worldwide Salary And Opinion Survey." *Electronic Engineering Times,* July 31.

Bemis, Edward W. 1886. "Cooperation in the Northeast." *Publications of the American Economic Association* 1(5) (November 1886), pp. 7–136.

Benartzi, S. 2001. "Excessive Extrapolation and the Allocation of 401(k) Accounts to Company Stock." *Journal of Finance* 56(5), pp. 1747–1764.

Benartzi, S., and R. Thaler. 2001. "Naïve Diversification Strategies in Defined Contribution Savings Plans." *American Economic Review* 91(1), pp. 79–98.

Bentley, George R. 1955. *A History of the Freedmen's Bureau*. Philadelphia: University of Pennsylvania.

Berle, Adolph A., and Gardiner C. Means. 1997. *The Modern Corporation and Private Property*. New Brunswick, N.J.: Transaction Publishers.

Berlin, Leslie R. 2001. "Robert Noyce and Fairchild Semiconductor." *Business History Review* 75(1), pp. 63–101.

Berners-Lee, Tim. 2000. *Weaving the Web: The Original Design and Ultimate Destiny of the World Wide Web*. New York: HarperBusiness.

Bernstein, Aaron, and Rob Hof. 2000. "A Union for Amazon: Organizing Efforts Couldn't Come At a Worse Time." *Business Week,* December 4.

Bernstein, Peter L. 1996. *Against the Gods: The Remarkable Story of Risk*. New York: John Wiley & Sons.

Bernstein, Ronald. 2001, 2002. Interviews. Conducted by Joseph Blasi. New Brunswick, N.J.: School of Management and Labor Relations. (Associate director, Beyster Institute for Entrepreneurial Employee Ownership).

Bernstein, Ronald, David Binns, Marshal Hyman, Martin Staubus, and Debra Sherman (eds.). 2001. *Designing an Employee Stock Option Plan: A Practical Approach for the Entrepreneurial Company*. La Jolla, Calif.: Beyster Institute for Entrepreneurial Employee Ownership.

———. 2002. *The Entrepreneur's Guide to Equity Compensation*. La Jolla, Calif.: Beyster Institute for Entrepreneurial Employee Ownership.

Beyster, J. Robert. 1988. Interview. Conducted by Joseph Blasi. New Brunswick, N.J.: School of Management and Labor Relations. Seminar with California Polytechnic School of Business Undergraduates, San Luis Obispo, California. (Dr. Beyster is the founder, chairman, and CEO of Science Application International Corporation, or SAIC).

———. 2001. Interview. Conducted by Joseph Blasi. New Brunswick, N.J.: School of Management and Labor Relations.

———. 2002. Interviews and Remarks. La Jolla, Calif.: Science Application International Corporation. Available at: www.saic.com/about/profile.html.

Bialek, Paul. 2001. Interview. Conducted by Joseph Blasi. New Brunswick, N.J.: School of Management and Labor Relations. (Mr. Bialek was chief financial officer of RealNetwortks Inc.)

Binns, David. 2001, 2002. Interviews. Conducted by Joseph Blasi. New Brunswick, N.J.: School of Management and Labor Relations. (Associate director, Beyster Institute for Entrepreneurial Employee Ownership.)

Black, Sandra E., and Lisa N. Lynch. 2000. *What's Driving the New Economy: The Benefits of Workplace Innovation*. Cambridge, Mass.: National Bureau of Economic Research, Working Paper No. W7479, January.

Blair, Margaret. 1995. *Ownership and Control: Rethinking Corporate Governance in the Twenty-first Century*. Washington, D.C.: The Brookings Institution.

_____. 1996. *Wealth Creation and Wealth Sharing: A Colloquium on Corporate Governance and Investments in Human Capital.* Washington, D.C.: The Brookings Institution.

Blair, Margaret, Douglas Kruse, and Joseph Blasi. 2000. "Employee Ownership: An Unstable Form or a Stabilizing Force?" In *The New Relationship: Human Capital in the American Corporation,* edited by Margaret Blair and Thomas Kochan. Washington, D.C.: Brookings Institution, pp. 241–298.

Blasi, Joseph. 1987. *Employee Ownership Through ESOPs: Implications for the Public Corporation.* Work in America Institute Studies in Productivity. New York: Pergamon Books, 1987. (Now available from Elsevier Science Ltd.)

_____. 1988. *Employee Ownership: Revolution or Ripoff?* New York: HarperCollins.

Blasi, Joseph, Michael Conte, and Douglas Kruse. 1992. "The New Owners: Stock Price Performance for Public Companies with Significant Employee Ownership." *Journal of Employee Ownership Law and Finance* 4(3) (Summer 1992), pp. 95–130.

_____. 1996. "Employee Stock Ownership and Corporate Performance Among Public Companies," *Industrial & Labor Relations Review,* Volume 50, October, pp. 60–79.

Blasi, Joseph, and Douglas Kruse. 1991. *The New Owners: The Mass Emergence of Employee Ownership in Public Companies and What It Means For American Business.* New York: HarperCollins.

_____. 2000. *High Performance Work Practices at Century's End: Incidence, Diffusion, Industry Group Differences and the Economic Environment.* New Brunswick, N.J.: School of Management and Labor Relations Working Paper. (Presented at the American Sociological Association August 2000 Conference, Economic Sociology Session.) Available from the authors.

_____. 2001a. "Employee Equity: Employee versus Owners Issues in Organizational Behavior." In *Trends in Organizational Behavior: Employee versus Owner Issues in Organizations,* edited by Cary L. Cooper and Denise M. Rousseau. New York: John Wiley and Sons, pp. 1–18.

_____. 2001b. *The Implication of Pay Patterns in High Performance Work Systems.* New Brunswick, N.J.: School of Management and Labor Relations Working Paper. (Presented at the American Sociological Association August 2001 Conference.)

Blasi, Joseph, Douglas Kruse, James Sesil, Maya Kroumova, and Ed Carberry. 2000. *Stock Options, Corporate Performance and Organizational Change.* Oakland, Calif.: National Center for Employee Ownership. (The full research report is available at www.nceo.org/library/optionreport.html.)

Bodie, Zvi, Robert S. Kaplan, and Robert C. Merton. 2002. "Options Should Be Reflected in the Bottom Line." *Wall Street Journal,* August 1.

Bradley, Keith, and Alan Gelb. 1983. *Worker Capitalism: The New Industrial Relations.* Cambridge, Mass.: MIT Press.

Bloom, Steven Marc. 1986. "Employee Ownership and Firm Performance." Ph.D. dissertation, Harvard University Department of Economics.

Blumenthal, Adam. 2001, 2002. Interview. Conducted by Joseph Blasi. New Brunswick, N.J.: School of Management and Labor Relations. (Blumenthal is the first deputy comptroller of New York City.)

Bogart, Ernest L., and Donald L. Kemmerer. 1942. *Economic History of the American People.* New York: Longmans, Green and Co.

Bonin, John P., and Louis Putterman. 1988. *Economics of Cooperation and Labor-Managed Economy.* Chur, Switzerland: Harwood.

Bostrom, Sue. 2002. "Leading in the Internet Economy." Available at www.cisco.com at: newsroom.cisco.com/dlls/tln/exec_team/bostrom/vision.html.

Branch, Shelly, Mark Borden, and Tyler Maroney. 1999. "The 100 Best Companies To Work For In America." *Fortune* Magazine, January 11.

Braverman, Avishay, and Joseph E. Stiglitz. 1982. "Sharecropping and the Interlinking of Agrarian Markets." *American Economic Review* 72(4), September, pp. 695–715.

Brenner, M., R. Sundaram, and D. Yermack. 2000. "Altering The Terms of Executive Stock Options." *Journal of Financial Economics* 57, pp. 103–128.

Brohawn, Dawn, and ESOP Association. 1997. *Journey to an Ownership Culture.* Lanham, Md.: Scarecrow Press.

Brookings, Robert S. 1925. *Industrial Ownership, Its Economic and Social Significance.* New York: The Macmillan Company.

_____. 1929. *Economic Democracy; America's Answer to Socialism and Communism. A Collection of Articles.* New York: The Macmillan Company.

_____. 1932. *The Way Forward.* New York: The Macmillan Company.

Brophy, Beth. 1999. "You've Got Money." *Washingtonian* Magazine, October.

Bruener, Richard. 2000. "Keeping Employees the Financial Way." *Electronic News,* October 9.

Buchele, Robert, and Adria Scharf. 2001. *The Wealth and Income Effects of Employee Ownership.* New Orleans, La.: Industrial Relations Research Association Study Group of Pay Systems, January 4–7 Annual Meeting.

Bucklin, Barbara R., and Alyce M. Dickinson. 2002. "Individual Monetary Incentives: A Review of Different Types of Arrangements between Performance and Pay." *Journal of Organizational Behavior Management* 21(3), forthcoming.

Buckman, Rebecca. 2000. "Microsoft Plans to Cut Costs, Not Salaries." *Wall Street Journal,* December 19.

Buenaventura, Maria Ruth M., and Charles Peck. 1993. *Stock Options: Motivating Through Ownership.* New York: Conference Board.

Bunnell, David. 2000. *Making the Cisco Connection: The Story Behind the Real Internet Superpower.* New York: John Wiley & Sons.

Bunnell, David, and Richard Luecke. 2000. *The eBay Phenomenon.* New York: John Wiley & Sons.

Burgess, George H., and Miles C. Kennedy. 1949. *Centennial History of the Pennsylvania Railroad Company, 1846–1946.* Philadelphia: Pennsylvania Railroad Co.

Burgess, Leonard. 1963. *Top Executive Pay Packages.* New York: Free Press.

*Business Week.* 1945. "A Blow to Options." August 2.

———. 1951a. "Stock Options for the Rank-and-File." December 8.

———. 1951b. "Are Options Legal?" December 8.

———. 1952a. "Are Options Legal?" August 2.

———. 1952b. "Bobby Trap in Stock Options." September 6.

———. 1953a. "Making Options Stand Up." August 8.

———. 1953b. "The Idea and Its Dangers." October 24.

———. 1963. "Tightening Tax Laws on Stock Options." March 2.

———. 1980. "What Makes Tandem Run." July 14.

———. 1981. "A New Life for Stock Options." October 12.

———. 1991. "The Flap Over Executive Pay." May 6.

———. 2002. "Executive Pay." April 15.

Business Wire. 2000. "MyCriticalCapital.com Gives Individual Stock Option Owners a Game Plan for Financial Independence: Companies Can Become Partners Too, Offering New Employee Benefit." October 9.

Bussel, Robert. 1997. "Business Without a Boss: The Columbia Conserve Company and Workers' Control, 1917–1943." *Business History Review,* September 22.

Butcher, Lee. 1988. *Accidental Millionaire: The Rise and Fall of Steve Jobs at Apple Computer.* New York: Paragon House.

Buyniski, Ted, and Daniel Silver. 2000. *Trends in Equity Compensation: An Executive Summary of iQuantic's High-Tech Equity Practices Survey.* San Francisco, Calif.: iQuantic. Available in PDF format at www.iQuantic.com.

Byland, Timothy. 2000. Treatment of Stock Options. Transcript of Congressional Testimony. Washington, D.C.: Federal Document Clearing House, March 16. (Available on Dow Jones Interactive.)

Byrne, John A. 1991. "The Flap Over Executive Pay." *Business Week,* May 6.

———. 1998. "The Corporation of the Future." *Business Week,* August 31.

Campbell-Kelly, Martin, and William Aspray. 1996. *Computer: A History of the Information Machine.* Sloan Technology Series. New York: Basic Books.

Cappelli, Peter, and David Neumark. 1999. "Do 'High Performance' Work Practices Improve Establishment-Level Outcomes?" Cambridge, Mass.: National Bureau of Economic Research, Working Paper 7374.

———. 2001. "Do 'High-Performance' Work Practices Improve Establishment-Level Outcomes?" *Industrial and Labor Relations Review* 54(4), July.

Carberry, Ed, and Scott Rodrick. 2000. *Employee Stock Purchase Plans.* Oakland, Calif.: National Center for Employee Ownership.

Carnegie, Andrew. 1933. *The Gospel of Wealth, and Other Timely Essays.* New York: The Century Co.

Carr, Louis Green, Russell R. Menard, and Lorena S. Walsh. 1991. *Robert Cole's World: Agriculture and Society in Early Maryland.* Chapel Hill: University of North Carolina Press.

Casey, William J., and J. K. Lasser. 1952. *Executive Pay Plans: 1952–1953.* Roslyn, N.Y.: Business Reports.

Cassidy, John. 2002. *Dot.con: The Greatest Story Ever Sold.* New York: HarperCollins.

Cha, Ariana Eunjung. 2000. "Deal Partners Taking New Look at Stock Perks; Options Common For AOL Employees." *The Washington Post,* January 14.

Chance, D., R. Kumar, and R. Todd. 2000. "The Repricing of Executive Stock Options." *Journal of Financial Economics* 7(1) July, pp. 129–153.

Chandler, Alfred Dupont. 1977. *The Visible Hand: the Managerial Revolution in American Business.* Cambridge, Mass.: Harvard University Press, Belknap Press.

———. 2001. *Inventing the Electronic Century: The Epic Story of the Consumer Electronics and Computer Industries.* New York: Free Press.

Cheape, Charles W. 1985. *Family Firm to Modern Multinational: Norton Company, a New England Enterprise.* Cambridge, Mass.: Harvard University Press.

Cheung, Steven N. S. 1968. "Private Property Rights and Sharecropping." *Journal of Political Economy* 76(6), November-December, pp. 1107–1122.

Ciesielski, Jack T. 2001. "2000 Stock Compensation: Sizing Up The Beast." *The Analyst's Accounting Observer* 10(8 and 9), July 31.

Cimbala, Paul. 1989. "The Freedman's Bureau, The Freedmen, and Sherman's Grant in Reconstruction Georgia, 1865–1867." *Journal of Southern History* 55(4), November, pp. 597–632.

Cisco Systems Employees. 2001. Interviews. Conducted by Joseph Blasi. New Brunswick, N.J.: School of Management and Labor Relations. (Pseudonyms of employees are Tom, Henry, Quentin, and Lewis.)

Citrix Systems. 2001. Citrix Systems Press Release. Business Wire, November 6.

Clancy, Heather. 1989. "A Look at Long-term Stock Option Plans." *Computer Re-seller News,* December 18.

Clark, George T. 1931. *Leland Stanford: War Governor of California, Railroad Builder, and Founder of Stanford University.* Stanford, Calif.: Stanford University Press.

Clark, Jim. 1999. *Netscape Time: The Making of the Billion-Dollar Start-up that Took on Microsoft.* New York: St. Martin's Press.

Clark, John Bates. 1886. *The Philosophy of Wealth.* Boston, Mass.: Ginn & Company.

Clifford, Donald K., and Richard E. Cavanagh. 1985. "Cray Research Draws Best from All Worlds—And It Works." *Chicago Sun-Times,* December 27.

Cohen, Adam. 2002. *The Perfect Store: Inside eBay.* New York: Little Brown.

Cohen, Don, and Laurence Prusak. 2001. *In Good Company: How Social Capital Makes Organizations Work.* Boston, Mass.: Harvard Business School Press.

Cohn, David. 1948. *Where I Was Born and Raised.* Notre Dame: University of Notre Dame Press.

Coleman, William T. III. 2001. Interview. Conducted by Joseph Blasi. New Brunswick, N.J.: School of Management and Labor Relations. (Mr. Coleman is a founder, chairman and former CEO of BEA Systems.)

Commons, John R. 1918–1935. *History of Labour in the United States.* 4 volumes. New York: The Macmillan Company.

*Commonweal.* 1961. "Inducement for Executives: Proposed Gore Bill." April 28, p. 117.

Conference Board. 1970–1983, 1985–2000. *Top Executive Compensation.* New York: Conference Board. Series: Conference Board Report.

Conlon, Jerome. 2001. Interview. Conducted by Joseph Blasi. New Brunswick, N.J.: School of Management and Labor Relations. (Mr. Conlon was chief marketing officer for Internap Network Services Inc.)

Conte, Michael, Joseph Blasi, Douglas Kruse, and Rama Jampani.1996. "Financial Returns of Public ESOP Companies: Investor Effects vs. Manager Effects." *Financial Analysts Journal,* July/August, pp. 51–61.

Core, John E., and Wayne R. Guay. 2001. "Stock Option Plans for Non-executive Employees." *Journal of Financial Economics* 1, pp. 253–287.

Cowan, Miss Effie. (Interviewer) 1936–1940. "Interview with Mrs. Belle Little, Pioneer, Mart, Texas." *American Life Histories: Manuscripts from the Federal Writers' Project, 1936–1940.* File No. 240, McLennan County, Texas, District 8. Available at Library of Congress Website: rs6.loc.gov/ammem/wpaquery.html.

Cox, La Wanda. 1958. "The Promise of Land for the Freedmen." *Mississippi Valley Historical Review* 45(3), December, pp. 413–440.

Craig, B., and J. Pencavel. 1992. "The Behavior of Worker Cooperatives: The Plywood Companies of the Pacific Northwest." *American Economic Review* 82, pp. 1083–1105.

_____. 1993. "The Objectives of Worker Cooperatives." *Journal of Comparative Economics* 17(2), June, pp. 288–308.

_____. 1995. "Participation and Productivity: A Comparison of Worker Cooperatives and Conventional Firms in the Plywood Industry." *Brookings Papers on Economic Activity,* pp. 121–160.

Craig, Susanne. 2002. "No Discount: E*Trade CEO Gets Pay Deal of $80 Million." *Wall Street Journal,* May 1.

Curtis, C. E. 2001. *Pay Me in Stock Options.* New York: John Wiley & Sons.

Cusumano, Michael A., and Richard W. Selby. 1995. *Microsoft Secrets.* New York: Simon & Schuster.

Cusumano, Michael A., and David B. Yoffie. 1998. *Competing on Internet Time.* New York: Simon & Schuster.

Dahl, Robert. 1985. *Preface to Economic Democracy.* Berkeley, Calif.: University of California Press.

Daisey, Mike. 2002. *21 Dog Years: Doing Time @ Amazon.com.* New York: The Free Press.

Davis, E. 1933. *Employee Stock Ownership and the Depression.* Princeton: Princeton University Press.

Davis, Jo Ellen. 1987. "Who's Afraid of IBM?—Not Compaq, The Feisty No. 2 in Office PCs Is Picking a Fight." *Business Week,* June 29.

Davis, Lance E., Jonathan R. T. Hughes, and Duncan M. McDougall. 1969. *American Economic History: The Development of a National Economy.* Homewood, Ill.: Richard D. Irwin, Inc.

Davis, Ronald L. 1982. *Good and Faithful Labor: From Slavery to Sharecropping in the Natchez District, 1860–1890.* Westport, Conn.: Greenwood Press.

Davidson, J. Lang, and Douglas M. Bailey. 1985. "It Cleared in Massachusetts." *New England Business,* May 28.

Dean, A. H. 1953. "Employee Stock Options." *Harvard Law Review,* June, pp. 1403–1449.

de Figueiredo, Elizabeth MacIver Nieva. 1994. "Pressing Change: The Consolidation of the American Newspaper Industry, 1955–1985." Ph.D. dissertation, Harvard University.

Dell, Michael. 1999. *Direct from Dell: Strategies That Revolutionized an Industry.* New York: HarperCollins.

Dennison, Henry S. (N.D.) "The Employee Investor." *Academy of Political Science Proceedings* 11(3), pp. 29–31.

*Denver Post.* 2001. "Economic Downturn Casts New Light on Stock Options." June 24.

Derber, Milton. 1970. *The American Idea of Industrial Democracy, 1865–1965.* Urbana: University of Illinois Press.

Desai, Mihir. 2002. *The Corporate Profit Base, Tax Sheltering Activity, and the Changing Nature of Employee Compensation,* Working Paper 8866. Cambridge, Mass.: National Bureau of Economic Research.

Dewing, Arthur Stone. 1920, 1941. *The Financial Policy of Corporations.* New York: Ronald Press Company.

Dolan, Carrie. 1984. "Rolm's Merger Could Fulfill Dream of Fighting AT&T on Equal Footing." *Wall Street Journal,* September 27.

Douglas, Paul H. 1926. *The Columbia Conserve Company.* Chicago, Ill.: University of Chicago Press.

Dreazen, Yochi J. 2002. "U.S. Says Web Use Has Risen to 54% of the Population." *The Wall Street Journal,* February 4.

Duffy, Jim. 2000. "One on One with Cisco's Honcho." *Network World Fusion,* May 29.

Dunlop, John T., and David Weil. 1996. "Diffusion and Performance of Modular Production in the U.S. Apparel Industry." *Industrial Relations* 35(3), July, pp. 334–355.

Dworkin, Peter. 1985. "Purse Strings Tight at Many Firms." *San Francisco Chronicle,* April 22.

Edmondston, Peter. 2002. "Deals & Deal Makers: Numbers Didn't Lie in '01, and a Few Bear Repeating." The Wall Street Journal Online, *Wall Street Journal,* January 3.

Edwards, Marcelene. 2001. "Amazon.com CEO Says Future Looks Strong Despite Poor Stock Performance." Knight Ridder/Tribune Business News, *News Tribune,* May 24.

Egan, Timothy. 1992. "Microsoft's Unlikely Millionaires." *New York Times,* June 28.

Eisenmann, Thomas R. 2000. "The U.S. Cable Television Industry, 1948–1995: Managerial Capitalism in Eclipse." *Business History Review,* March 22.

Ellerman, David. 1990. *The Democratic Worker-Owned Firm.* Malden, Mass.: Routledge. Also published by Brodart.

––––––. 1991. *Property and Contract in Economics: The Case for Economic Democracy.* Williston, Vt.: Blackwell. (Also published by Brodart.) Available online at: www.capitalownership.org/Author/Author.htm.

*Electronic Commerce.* 2000. "Amazon Reprices Options As Stock Lags." August 3, 2000.

Eliot, Charles W. 1917. "The Road to Industrial Peace." *Nation's Business,* August, p. 17.

Emling, Shelley. 2002. "AOL's Growing Gap; Membership Is Growing And Usage Is Up . . . ." *Austin American-Statesman,* March 26.

Emmet, Boris. 1917a. "Extent of Profit-sharing in the United States: Its Bearing on Industrial Unrest." *Journal of Political Economy* 25(10), December, pp. 1019–1033.

––––––. 1917b. "Profit Sharing in the United States." Bureau of Labor Statistics, Bulletin No. 208. Washington, D.C.: U.S. Department of Labor.

Engelbart, Douglas. 1986. Interview. Stanford University Library Archives, Stanford and Valley Archives Project Interview 1, December 19, 1986. Available at: www. sul.stanford.edu/depts/hasrg/histsci/ssvoral/engelbart/main1-ntb.html.

*Encyclopedia Britannica.* 1961. Entry for "Profit Sharing." Vol. 18, New York: William Benton, pp. 558–563.

––––––. 2001. Entry for "Albert Gallatin." Brittanica.com, July.

Ewing, David, and Dan Fenn. 1962. *Incentives for Executives.* New York: Macmillan.

Excite@Home Employees. 2001. Interviews. Conducted by Joseph Blasi. New Brunswick, N.J.: School of Management and Labor Relations. (Pseudonyms of employees are Jerry, John, Jeff, Randall.)

Fabozzi, Frank J., and Frank G. Zarb, eds. 1986. *Handbook of Financial Markets.* Homewood, Ill.: Dow Jones-Irwin.

Faggin, Federico. 1995. Interview. Conducted by Rob Walker. Stanford, Calif.: Stanford University Library Archives, Silicon Genesis Oral Histories Project. Transcript available at: www-sul.stanford.edu/depts/hasrg/histsci/silicon%20genesis/fredbody-ntb.html#anchor941041. Video available at: www.sul.stanford.edu/depts/hasrg/histsci/silicon%20genesis/intro-ntb.html.

Fenton, Gabriel, Joseph S. Stern III, and Michael Gray. 2000. *Employee Stock Options: A Strategic Planning Guide for the 21st Century Optionaire.* San Francisco, Calif.: Stillman Publishing.

Filene, Edward. 1930. *The Model Stock Plan.* New York: McGraw-Hill.

Filene, Lincoln. 1924. *A Merchant's Horizon, Lincoln Filene.* New York: Houghlin & Mifflin.

*Financial Times.* 2000. "Survey: Pockets of Optimism As the Mood Changes to Gloom." London, December 6.

———. 2001. "News: Microsoft To Issue Share Options Six Months Early." January 21, Global News Wire.

Fitz Simon, Jane. 1990. "Cullinet: Drawn and Quartered By Wall Street." *Boston Globe,* May 15.

Flanagan, James. 1986. "Success of New Stock Offerings Stuff of Dreams." *Los Angeles Times,* April 1.

Foerster, Robert F., and Else Dietel. 1927. *Employee Stock Ownership in the United States.* Princeton, N.J.: Princeton University, Industrial Relations Section, Department of Economics.

Foner, Eric. 1988. *Reconstruction: America's Unfinished Revolution, 1863–1877.* New York: HarperCollins.

*Forbes* Magazine. 1980. "Stock Options Come of Age." November 24.

Ford, Henry. 1961. "Stock Options Are In the Public Interest." *Harvard Business Review,* July, p. 45–51

Fordahl, Matthew. 2002. "Netscape Long Ago Lost Browser Battle With Microsoft." Associated Press Newswires, January 22.

Fox, Harland. 1983. *Executive Incentives: Long-term Performance Share/unit Plans.* New York: Conference Board. Research Bulletin Number 132.

Fox, Justin. 1997. "The Next Best Thing to Free Money: Silicon Valley's Stock-option Culture Is Doing a Whole Lot More than Making Techies Rich. It's Taking Over the Country. Is That Good or Bad?" *Fortune* Magazine, July 7.

Freeman, Richard B., and Joel Rogers. 1999. *What Workers Want.* New York and Ithaca: Cornell University Press and Russell Sage Foundation.

Freeman, Richard, and Arindrajit Dube. 2000. *Shared Compensation and Decision-making in the U.S. Job Market.* Cambridge, Mass.: Harvard University Department of Economics and National Bureau of Economic Research.

French, Kristin. 2001. *Personal Finance: Below the Radar, Roaring '90s Didn't Leave Middle Class with Much Cushion.* Thestreet.com, November 5.

Frisch, Robert A. 2001. *ESOP: The Ultimate Instrument in Succession Planning.* New York: John Wiley & Sons.

Fudenberg, Drew, and Eric Maskin. 1986. "The Folk Theorem in Repeated Games with Discounting or with Incomplete Information." *Econometrica* 54(3), May, pp. 533–554.

Galenson, David. 1981. *White Servitude in Colonial America: An Economic Analysis.* New York: Cambridge University Press.

_____. 1984. "The Rise and Fall of Indentured Servitude in America: An Economic Analysis." *Journal of Economic History* 44(1), March, pp. 1–26.

Gani, Marcel. 2001. Interview. Conducted by Joseph Blasi. New Brunswick, N.J.: School of Management and Labor Relations. (Chief financial officer and head of Information Systems and Human Resources of Juniper Networks Inc.)

Garber, Peter M. 1989. "Who Put the Mania in Tulipmania?" *Journal of Portfolio Management* 16(1), Fall, pp. 53–60.

Garcia, F. L. 1991. "Option." In the *Encyclopedia of Banking and Finance,* edited by Glenn G. Munn, F. L. Garcia, Charles J. Woelfel. 9th edn. Rolling Meadows, Ill.: Bankers Publishing Company, pp. 558–559.

Gates, Jeff. 1999. *The Ownership Solution: Toward a Shared Capitalism for the Twenty-first Century.* New York: Perseus Books.

_____. 2000. *Democracy at Risk: Rescuing Main Street from Wall Street—A Populist Vision for the 21st Century.* New York: Perseus Books.

Gates, Paul Wallace. 1936. "The Homestead Law in an Incongruous Land System." *American Historical Review* 41(4), July, pp. 632–681.

_____. 1962. "Land Policy and Its Relation to Agricultural Production and Distribution." *Journal of Economic History* 22(4), December, pp. 473–466.

Gibbons, James F. 2000. "The Role of Stanford University." In *The Silicon Valley Edge,* edited by Chong-Moon Lee, William F. Miller, Marguerite Gong Hancock, and Harry R. Rowen. Stanford, Calif.: Stanford University Press, pp. 200–217.

Gillette, King C. 1924. *The People's Corporation.* New York: Boni and Liveright.

Gilman, Nicholas Paine. 1889. *Profit Sharing Between Employee and Employer.* New York: Houghton-Mifflin.

Ginzton, Edward L. 1996. *Times to Remember: The Life of Edward L. Ginzton.* Edited by Anne Ginzton Cottrell and Leonard Cottrell. Berkeley, Calif.: Blackberry Creek Press.

Gitelman, H. M. 1965. "The Labor Force at Waltham Watch During the Civil War Era." *Journal of Economic History* 25(2), June 1965, pp. 214–243.

Gogoi, Pallavi, and Louis Lavelle. 2000. "When Good Options Go Bad." *Business Week* E.Biz, Number 3711, December 11.

Gomes, Lee. 2001. "Cisco Issues Grim Profit, Sales Warning." *Wall Street Journal,* April 17.

Gordon, John Steele. 1988. *The Scarlet Woman of Wall Street: Jay Gould, Jim Fisk, Cornelius Vanderbilt, the Erie Railway Wars, and the Birth of Wall Street.* New York: Weidenfeld & Nicolson.

Gordon, Robert J. 2002. "Technology and Economic Performance in the American Economy." Cambridge, Mass.: National Bureau of Economic Research, Working Paper 8771.

Gould, Sandy. 2001. Interview. Conducted by Joseph Blasi. New Brunswick, N.J.: School of Management and Labor Relations. (Director of Recruiting of RealNetworks Inc.)

Greenfeld, Karl Taro. 2000. "The Network Effect: Cisco." *Time* Magazine, April 10.

Greenspan, Alan. 2002. Text of Alan Greenspan's Speech on Corporate Governance. March 26, New York University's Stern School of Business. Available from Rutgers English News Service on Dow Jones Interactive.

Griliches, Zvi. 1994. "Productivity, R&D, and the Data Constraint." *American Economic Review* 84(1), March, pp. 1–23.

Grimes, Christopher. 2002. "AOL Slashes Executive Bonuses." *Financial Times,* March 27.

Groton, James, Henry S. Dennison, Edwin F. Gay, Henry P. Kendall, and Arthur W. Burritt. 1926. *Profit Sharing and Stock Ownership for Employees.* New York: Harper & Row.

Grove, Andrew S. 1999. *Only the Paranoid Survive: How to Exploit the Crisis Points that Challenge Every Company.* New York: Currency Doubleday.

Gullixson, Paul. 1998. "Silicon Valley Pioneers: How Varian and Its Klystron Tube Illuminated the Future." *San Francisco Chronicle,* June 5.

Gupta, Udayan. 2000. *Done Deals: Venture Capitalists Tell Their Stories.* Boston, Mass.: Harvard Business School Press.

Guthmann, Harry G., and Herbert E. Dougall. 1955. *Corporate Financial Policy.* New York: Prentice-Hall Inc.

Hafner, Katie. 2002. "The Internet's Invisible Hand; At a Public Utility Serving the World, No One's Really in Charge. Does It Matter?" *New York Times,* January 10.

Hafner, Katie, and Matthew Lyon. 1996. *Where Wizards Stay Up Late: the Origins of the Internet.* New York: Simon & Schuster.

Haines, Mark, David Farber, and Robert Froehlich. 2001. *Siebel Systems CEO— Interview.* CNBC/Dow Jones Business Video. April 19.

Hall, Amanda. 2000. "Cisco's E-vangelist Silicon Giants John Chambers Believes Passionately That the Internet Is Changing The World." *Sunday Telegraph* (London), August 27.

Hall, J. Brian, and Jeffrey B. Liebman. 1998. "Are CEOs Really Paid Like Bureaucrats?" *Quarterly Journal of Economics* 113, August, pp. 653–691. Available in PDF format at Prof. Liebman's website at www.ksg.harvard.edu/jeffreyliebman/papers.htm or from the working papers section of the National Bureau of Economic Research at www.nber.com or www.nber.org. Working paper # W6213, October 1997.

Halstead, Tammy. 2001. Interview. Conducted by Joseph Blasi. New Brunswick, N.J.: School of Management and Labor Relations. (Ms. Halstead is chief financial officer of Infospace.com.)

Handel, Jeremy. 2000. "Take a Deep Breath: Dealing with Underwater Options." *Workspan,* January 1.

Harbert, Tam. 2000. "Repricing No Longer a Viable Option." *Electronic Business,* October 1.

Hawke, David Freeman. 1988. *Everyday Life in Early America.* New York: Harper & Row.

Heath, Chip, Steven Huddart, and Mark Lang. 1999. "Psychological Factors and Stock Option Exercise." *Quarterly Journal of Economics* 114(2), May, pp. 601–627.

Heath, David. 1999. "Software Payrolls Surpass Aerospace: Stock Options Cause Momentous Shift in Puget Sound Area." *Seattle Times,* August 22.

Heckscher, Charles, and Anne Donnellon. 1994. *The Post-Bureaucratic Organization: New Perspectives on Organizational Change.* Thousand Oaks, Calif.: Sage Publications.

Helyar, John, and Joann S. Lublin. 1998. "America 1998: High on Stock Options: Corporate Coffers Gush with Currency of an Opulent Age." *Wall Street Journal,* August 10.

Henig, Pete, and Nicole Sperling. 2000. "The Fantasy World of Jeff Bezos." *Red Herring* Magazine, October 2000.

Henry, David, and Michelle Conlin. 2002. "Too Much of a Good Incentive?" *Business Week,* March 4.

Herhold, Scott. 2000. "Stocks.comment Column." *San Jose Mercury News,* June 19.

Heymann, Leonard, Jeremiah Caron, and Michelle Rae McLean. 1996. "Q&A: The Star Chambers." *LAN Times,* July.

Hibbard, B. H. 1924. *A History of the Public Land Policies.* New York: The Macmillan Company.

Hicks, Clarence, J. 1924. "What Can the Employer Do to Encourage Saving and Wise Investment By Industrial Employees?" *Harvard Business Review* 2, January, pp. 194–200.

Hiltzik, Michael A. 2001. "The Twisted Legacy of William Shockley: Perhaps No Other Nobel Laureate Had a Greater Impact on California's Industrial Stature Than the Man Who Brought the Silicon to Silicon Valley. So How Did He End Up an Object of Worldwide Scorn?" *Los Angeles Times Magazine,* December 2.

Hiltzik, Michael A., and Jube Shiver Jr. 2001. "The Microsoft Ruling: Breakup of Microsoft Is Overturned on Appeal; Law: Federal Court Vacates Order to Split Computer Giant and Rebukes Trial Judge for 'Egregious' Ethical Violations. But It Rules that the Company Did Violate Antitrust Laws." *Los Angeles Times,* June 29.

Hirao, Takehisa, Akira Morikawa, Kenichi Ito, and Teiichi Sekiguchi, eds. 1998. *How Nonunion Industrial Relations Systems Work: Corporate Labor Policies and the Workers in the U.S., the 1920s.* Hokkaido, Japan: Hokudai Tosho Kankou-kai (Hokkaido University Press).

Hitt, Greg, and Jacob M. Schlesinger. 2002. "Perk Police: Stock Options Come Under Fire in Wake of Enron's Collapse." *Wall Street Journal,* March 26.

Hoch, Detlev J., Cyriac R. Roeding, Gert Purkert, and Sandro K. Lindner. 2000. *Secrets of Software Success: Management Insights from 100 Software Firms Around the World.* Boston, Mass.: Harvard Business School Press.

Hodgson, Richard. 1995. Interview. Conducted by Rob Walker. Stanford, Calif.: Stanford University Library Archives, Silicon Genesis Oral Histories Project, 1995. Video available at: www-sul.stanford.edu/depts/hasrg/histsci/silicon%20genesis/intro-ntb.html.

Hofstadter, Richard. 1973. *America at 1750: A Social Portrait.* New York: Random House.

Hohman, Elmo P. 1926. "Wages, Risk, and Profits in the Whaling Industry." *Quarterly Journal of Economics* 40(4), August, pp. 644–671.

Hollod, Lisa. 1998–1999. "ACS Employee Ownership Index Update." *Journal of Employee Ownership Law and Finance.* Selected volumes and numbered issues from 10(3) through 11(4) in 1998–1999.

Honeywell-Johnson, Judith A., and Alyce M. Dickinson. 1999. "Small Group Incentives: A Review of the Literature." *Journal of Organizational Behavior Management* 19(2), pp. 89–120.

Hopper, D. Ian. 2002. "AOL Time Warner Files Antitrust Lawsuit Seeking Damages from Microsoft Over Browser." Associated Press Newswires, January 22.

Howert, I. W. 1986. "Profit-sharing at Ivorydale." *American Journal of Sociology* 2(1), July, pp. 43–57.

*Houston Chronicle.* 2001. "Bust Takes Fun Out of .coms The Theme Now: Get Back to Work." April 1.

Huddart, Steven, and Mark Lang. 2002. "Information Distribution Within Firms: Evidence from Stock Option Exercises." *Journal of Accounting and Economics,* Forthcoming.

———. 1996. "Employee Stock Option Exercises: An Empirical Analysis." *Journal of Accounting and Economics* 21(1) February, pp. 5–43.

Hultgran, Thor. 1924. "The Dix Transfer." *University Journal of Business* 2(4), September, pp. 406–413.

Husband, William, and James C. Dockeray. 1972. *Modern Corporate Finance.* Homewood, Ill.: Irwin.

Huselid, Mark, Susan Jackson, and Randall Schuler. 1997. "Technical and Strategic Human Resource Management Effectiveness as Determinants of Firm Performance." *Academy of Management Journal* 40(1), pp. 171–188.

Ibbotson Associates. 2002. *Stocks, Bonds, Bills, and Inflation: 2002 Yearbook, Market Results for 1926–2001.* Chicago, Ill.: Ibbotson Associates.

Ichbiah, Daniel, and Susan L. Knepper. 1991. *The Making of Microsoft: How Bill Gates and His Team Created the World's Most Successful Software Company.* Rocklin, Calif.: Prima Publications.

Ichniowski, Casey, Kathryn Shaw, and Giovanni Prennushi. 1995. *The Impact of Human Resource Management Practices on Productivity.* Cambridge, Mass.: National Bureau of Economic Research, Working Paper Number 5333.

Ichniowski, Casey, Thomas A. Kochan, David Levine, Carig Olson, and George Strauss. 1996. "What Works at Work: Overview and Assessment." *Industrial Relations* 35(3), July. (The entire issue of this journal is devoted to industry and national studies of high-performance workplaces and company performance.)

Infospace.com Employees. 2001. Interview. Conducted by Joseph Blasi. New Brunswick, N.J.: School of Management and Labor Relations. (Pseudonyms of employees are Agatha and Franklin.)

Internap Network Services Employees. 2001. Interview. Conducted by Joseph Blasi. New Brunswick, N.J.: School of Management and Labor Relations. (Pseudonyms of employees are Frederick and Marcia.)

Investor Responsibility Research Center (IRRC). 2000a. *Potential Dilution—2000: The Potential Dilution from Stock Plans at the S&P Super 1,500 Companies.* Washington, D.C. Investor Responsibility Research Center.

_____. 2000b. "Study Finds Dot-Com Boards Are Less Independent, In Conflict with Governance Principles." *Business Wire* press release from Investor Responsibility Research Center, Jan 10.

*Investor's Daily.* 2000. "Amazon Reprices Options As Stock Lags." August 3.

Ip, Greg. 2002. "Mind Over Matter, Why Many Highfliers Built on Big Ideas Are Such Fast Fallers." *The Wall Street Journal,* April 4.

Iquantic. 2000. Trends in Equity Compensation: An Executive Summary of Iquantic's High Tech Equity Practices Survey, 1996–2000. San Francisco, Calif.: iQuantic.com. Available on Adobe PDF at www.iQuantic.com under articles, at www.iquantic.com/flash/ArticlesPress/ArticlesiQArticles.html.

Ittner, Christopher, Richard Lambert, and David Larcker. 2001. *The Structure and Performance Consequences Of Equity Grants to Employees of New Economy Companies.* Philadelphia, Pa.: University of Pennsylvania, Wharton School of Business, January.

Jackson, Tim. 1997. *Inside Intel: Andy Grove and the Rise of the World's Most Powerful Chip Company.* New York: Dutton.

Jacoby, Sanford M. 1997. *Modern Manors: Welfare Capitalism Since the New Deal.* Princeton, N.J.: Princeton University Press.

Jarman, Max. 1998. "Stock Plans For Workers: Companies Vesting Employees in Deals." *Arizona Republic,* June 14.

Jain, Naveen. 2001. Interview. Conducted by Joseph Blasi. New Brunswick, N.J.: School of Management and Labor Relations. (Mr. Jain is the chairman and CEO of Infospace.)

Jassy, Everett L. 1982. "Incentive Stock Options: The Reincarnation of Statutory Stock Options Under the Economic Recovery Tax Act of 1981." *Tax Law Review,* Summer, 1982.

Jenkins, Holman W. Jr., 2002. "Business World: Is the Problem Stock Options—or Stock Prices?" *Wall Street Journal,* April 24.

Jensen, Gordon Maurice. 1956. "The National Civic Federation: American Business in an Age of Social Change and Social Reform, 1900–1910." Ph.D. dissertation, Princeton University.

Jensen, Hans E. 2001. *John Stuart Mill and Alfred Marshall on Worker Ownership.* Knoxville, Tenn.: University of Tennessee at Knoxville, Department of Economics.

Jensen, Michael C., and William H. Meckling. 1979. "Rights and Production Functions: An Application to Labor-Managed Firms." *Journal of Business* 52(4), October, pp. 469–506.

Jensen, Michael, and Kevin Murphy. 1990. "Performance Pay and Top-Management Incentives." *Journal of Political Economy* 98(2), pp. 225–265. (Available on Prof. Murphy's web site at: www-rcf.usc.edu/~kjmurphy/jmjpe.pdf.

Jereski, Laura. 1997. "Share the Wealth: As Options Proliferate, Investors Question Effect on Bottom Line—FASB Rules Would Outline What Worker Incentives Really Cost Companies—Microsoft Invents a Security." *Wall Street Journal,* January 14.

Johansen, Bruce E. 1998. *Encyclopedia of Native American Legal Tradition.* Westport, Conn. : Greenwood Press.

———. 1999. *The Encyclopedia of Native American Economic History.* Westport, Conn.: Greenwood Press.

Johansen, Bruce E., and Barbara Alice Mann. 2000. *Encyclopedia of the Haudenosaunee (Iroquois Confederacy).* Westport, Conn.: Greenwood Press.

Johnson, Eric L. 2000. "Waste Not, Want Not: An Analysis of Stock Option Plans, Executive Compensation, and the Proper Standard of Waste." *Iowa Journal of Corporation Law* 126, 26 Iowa J. Corp. L. 145.

Jones, Derek. 1982. *Participatory and Self-Managed Firms: Evaluating Economic Performance.* Lexington, Mass.: Lexington Books.

Jones, Derek, and Jan Svejnar. 1985–2003. *Advances in the Economic Analysis of Participatory and Labor-Managed Firms.* Vol. 7. New York: Elsevier/JAI Press.

Kadlec, Daniel. 1995. "Netscape Insiders: Thanks A Million!" *USA Today,* November.

Kairys, Joseph P. Jr., and Nicholas Valerio III. 1997. "The Market for Equity Options in the 1870s." *Journal of Finance* 52(4), September, pp. 1707–1723.

Kalleberg, Arne L., David Knoke, Peter V. Marsden, and Joe L. Spaeth. 1996. *Organizations in America: Analyzing Their Structures and Human Resource Practices.* Thousand Oaks, Calif.: Sage Publications.

Kandel, Eugene, and Edward P. Lazear. 1992. "Peer Pressure and Partnerships." *Journal of Political Economy* 100(4), August, pp. 801–817.

Kang, Cecilia, and Tom Quinlan. 2000. "Disk-Drive Maker Seagate Technology Going Private." *San Jose Mercury News,* March 30.

Kaplan, David. 1999. *The Silicon Boys and their Valley of Dreams.* New York: HarperCollins.

Kaplan, Philip J. 2002. *F'd Companies: Spectacular Dot-Com Flameouts.* New York: Simon & Schuster.

Kardas, Peter, Adria L. Scharf, and Jim Keogh. 1998. "Wealth and Income Consequences of ESOPs and Employee Ownership: A Comparative Study from Washington State." *Journal of Employee Ownership Law and Finance* 10(4), Fall.

Keeling, Michael. 2001, 2002. Interviews. Conducted by Joseph Blasi. New Brunswick, N.J.: School of Management and Labor Relations. (President, The ESOP Association.)

Kehoe, Louise. 1997. "Intel Pays $820m in Employee Bonuses." *Financial Times,* February 12.

_____. 2002. "Keeping the HP Way Is No Picnic: Hewlett-Packard Management Led Astray By 'Warm and Fuzzy' Myths." *Financial Times,* January 17.

Kelly, Kevin. 2002. "The Web Runs on Love, Not Greed." *Wall Street Journal,* January 3.

Kelley, Maryellen. 1994. "Participative Bureaucracy and Productivity in the Machined Products Sector." *Industrial Relations* 35, pp. 374–399.

Kelley, Tina. 1999. "Temporary Microsoft Workers Win Stock Ruling." *New York Times,* May 14.

Kelso, Louis O., and Mortimer Adler. 1958. *The Capitalist Manifesto.* New York: Random House.

_____. 1961. *The New Capitalists: A Proposal to Free Economic Growth From the Slavery of Savings.* New York: Random House.

Kelso, Louis O., and Patricia Hetter Kelso. 1986. *Democracy and Economic Power: Extending the ESOP Revolution.* Cambridge, Mass.: Ballinger Pub. Co., HarperCollins.

_____. 1968. *How To Turn Eighty Million Workers Into Capitalists On Borrowed Money.* New York: Random House.

Kenney, Martin. 2000. *Understanding Silicon Valley: The Anatomy of an Entrepreneurial Region.* Palo Alto, Calif.: Stanford University Press.

Kirby, Carrie. 2002. "E-Trade Executive Takes Heat For Pay." *San Francisco Chronicle,* May 25.

Knowlton, Phillip A. 1954. *Profit Sharing Patterns.* Evanston, Ill.: Profit Sharing Research Foundation.

Koretz, Gene. 1999. "Economic Trends: An Overlooked Labor Cost. Options Way More Than Just a Perk." *Business Week,* September 13.

Krimmerman, Len, and Frank Lindenfeld. 1992. *When Workers Decide: Workplace Democracy Takes Root in North America.* St. Paul, Minn.: New Society Publishers, Consortium Books.

Kroumova, Maya. 1999. "Employer Stock As A Vehicle For Retirement Savings: Is There a Reason For Concern?" New Brunswick, N.J.: Rutgers University School of Management and Labor Relations, Ph.D. dissertation. (Available full-text from Dissertation Abstracts.)

Kruse, Douglas. 1984. *Employee Ownership and Employee Attitudes: Two Case Studies.* Norwood, Penn.: Norwood Editions.

_____. 1992. "Profit Sharing and Productivity: Microeconomic Evidence from the United States." *Economic Journal* 102(410), pp. 24–36.

_____. 1993a. *Profit Sharing: Does It Make A Difference?* Kalamazoo, Mich.: W. E. Upjohn Institute for Employment Research.

_____. 1993b. *Does Profit Sharing Affect Productivity?* Cambridge, Mass.: National Bureau of Economic Research, Working Paper No. 4542, November.

_____. 1998. "Profit Sharing and the Demand for Low-skilled Workers." In *Generating Jobs: Increasing the Demand for Low-skilled Workers,* edited by Richard Freeman and Peter Gottschalk. New York: Russell Sage Foundation, pp. 105–153.

_____. 1999. *Economic Democracy or Just Another Risk for Workers: Reviewing The Evidence on Employee Ownership and Profit Sharing.* New York: Columbia University Department of Economics and School of International and Public Affairs, Democracy, Participation and Development Conference, April 23–24.

Kruse, Douglas. 2002. Research Evidence on Prevalence and Effects of Employee Ownership: Testimony Before the Subcommittee on Employer-Employee Relations, Committee on Education and the Workforce, U.S. House of Representatives, February 13.

Kruse, Douglas, and Joseph Blasi. 1995. *Employee Ownership, Employee Attitudes, and Firm Performance.* Cambridge, Mass.: National Bureau of Economic Research, NBER Working Paper No. W5277, September.

_____. 1997. "Employee Ownership, Employee Attitudes, and Firm Performance: A Review of the Evidence." In *The Human Resource Management Handbook, Part I,* edited by David Lewin, Daniel J. B. Mitchell, and Mahmood A. Zaidi. Greenwich, Conn., and London: JAI Press, p. 113–152.

_____. 1998. "Profit Sharing and the Demand for Low-Skill Workers." In *Generating Jobs: Increasing the Demand for Low-Skill Workers,* edited by Richard Freeman and Peter Gottschalk. New York: Russell Sage Foundation, pp. 105–153.

_____. 2000a. "The New Employee-Employer Relationship." In *A Working Nation: Workers, Work and Government in the New Economy,* edited by David T. Ellwood, Rebecca M. Blank, Joseph Blasi, Douglas Kruse, William A. Niskanen, and Karen Lynn-Dyson. New York: Russell Sage Foundation, pp. 42–91.

_____. 2000b. "The New Employee-Employer Relationship." In *Global Competition and the American Employment Landscape: As We Enter The 21st Century.* Proceedings of the New York University 52nd Annual Conference on Labor. Edited by Samuel Estreicher. Boston, The Hague, London: Kluwer Law International, pp. 305–376.

_____. 2001. *A Population Study of the Performance of ESOP and Non-ESOP Privately-held Companies.* New Brunswick, N.J.: School of Management and Labor Relations, Rutgers University, May. For a summary and the tables, see www.nceo.org/library/esop_perf_tables.html.

Kuo, J. David. 2001. *Dot.bomb: My Days and Nights at an Internet Goliath.* New York: Little Brown & Company.

La Dame, Mary. 1930. *The Filene Store; a Study of Employees' Relation to Management in a Retail Store.* New York: Russell Sage Foundation.

Laffont, Jean-Jacques, and David Martimort. 2002. *The Theory of Incentives: The Principal-Agent Model.* Princeton, N.J.: Princeton University Press.

Lambert, Emily. 2001. "The Big Executive Rip-off: While CEOs Get Big Bucks Shareholders' Returns Sink." *New York Post,* April 29.

Latta, Geoffrey. 1979. *Profit Sharing, Employee Stock Ownership, Savings, and Asset Formation Plans in the Western World.* Philadelphia: The Wharton School, University of Pennsylvania, Industrial Research Unit.

Lavelle, Louis, Frederick F. Jespersen, and Michael Arndt. 2002. "Executive Pay: Special Report." *Business Week,* April 15.

Lawler, Edward III, Susan Albers Mohrman, and Gerald E. Ledford Jr. 1992. *Employee Involvement and Total Quality Management: Practices and Results in Fortune 1000 Companies.* San Francisco, Calif.: Jossey-Bass.

Lecuyer, Christopher. 2000. "Fairchild Semiconductor and Its Influence." In *Silicon Valley Edge,* edited by Chong-Moon Lee, William F. Miller, Marguerite Gong Hancock, and Henry S. Rowen. Stanford, Calif.: Stanford University Press.

Leonhardt, David. 2002a. "Battle Lines Drawn on Stock Options." *New York Times,* March 17.

_____. 2002b. "E*Trade Chief Accepts A Cut in Compensation." *New York Times,* May 10.

Lev, Baruch. 2000. "Knowledge Management: Fad or Need?" *Research Technology Management,* September.

_____. 2001. *Intangibles: Management, Measurement, and Reporting.* Washington, D.C.: Brookings Institution.

Levering, Robert, Milton Moskowitz, and Michael Katz. 1984. *The 100 Best Companies to Work for in America.* 1st edition. New York: Doubleday.

_____. 1993. *The 100 Best Companies to Work for in America.* 2nd edition. New York: Doubleday.

Levine, David I. 1995. *Re-inventing the Workplace: How Business and Employees Can Both Win.* Washington, D.C.: The Brookings Institution.

Lewis, Michael. 2000. *The New New Thing.* New York: Penguin.

Leibenstein, Harvey. 1966. "Allocative Efficiency versus 'X-Efficiency.'" *American Economic Review* 56, pp. 392–415.

Lewellen, Wilbur G. 1968. *Executive Compensation in Large Industrial Corporations.* New York: National Bureau of Economic Research; distributed by Columbia University Press.

Lieber, James B. 1995. *Friendly Takeover: How an Employee Buyout Saved a Steel Town.* New York: Viking.

Lief, Alfred. 1958. *It Floats.* New York: Rinehart & Winston.

Lipman, Frederick D., and David Richardson. 2001. *The Complete Guide to Employee Stock Options: Everything the Executive and Employee Need to Know About Equity Compensation Plans.* Roseville, Calif.: Prima Publishing.

Little, Kenneth E. 2000. *Ten Minute Guide: Employee Stock Option Purchase Plans* (10 Minute Guides). Indianapolis, Ind.: Alpha/Pearson Education.

Logue, John, Richard Glass, Wendy Patton, Alex Teodosio, and Chris Cooper. 1998. *Participatory Employee Ownership: How It Works: Best Practices In Employee Ownership.* Kent, Ohio: Ohio Employee Ownership Center, Kent State University.

Logue, John, and Jacquelyn Yates. 2001. *The Real World of Employee Ownership.* Ithaca, N.Y.: Cornell University Press.

Lohr, Steve. 2002. "He Loves to Win. At I.B.M., He Did." *New York Times,* March 10.

Long, Senator Russell. 1981. "S. 1162—Expanded Ownership Act of 1981." *Congressional Record* (May 12), vol. 127, no. 72, pp. S 4779–4796.

Loomis, Carol J. 2001. "'This Stuff Is Wrong'; That's the Conclusion of Most of the Insiders Who Talked to FORTUNE—Candidly—About CEO Pay. And You Know What's Even Worse? They Don't See How the Overreaching Can Be Stopped." *Fortune* Magazine, June 25.

MacGregor, Bruce. 1994. "Enticements Aid New Ventures." *Portland Oregonian,* June 10.

Mackin, Christopher. 1998. "Surveys and Employee Ownership." Cambridge, Mass.: Ownership Associates. Available at: www.ownershipassociates.com/survey.html.

———. 2002. "The Ownership Culture Survey™: An Example of How The Survey Results For Your Company Would Look." Cambridge, Mass.: Ownership Associates. Available at: www.ownershipassociates.com/ocssample.html.

Mackin, Christopher, Loren Rodgers, and Adria Scharf. 2000. Census of Massachusetts Companies with Employee Stock Ownership Plans (ESOPs). Boston: Commonwealth Corporation.

Maich, Steve. 2002. "Tech Sector Gloom Deeper Than Appeared: New Merrill Lynch Report: Biggest U.S. Firms Inflated Earnings An Average Of 67%." *Financial Post, National Post,* March 16.

Malkiel, Burton G. 1996. *A Random Walk Down Wall Street.* New York: Norton.

Malkiel, Burton G., and Richard E. Quandt. 1969. *Strategies and Rational Decisions in the Securities Options Market.* Cambridge, Mass.: MIT Press.

Malloy, John. 2001. Interview. Conducted by Joseph Blasi. New Brunswick, N.J.: School of Management and Labor Relations. (Senior director, Microsoft.)

Malone, Michael S. 1985. *The Big Score : The Billion-dollar Story of Silicon Valley.* Garden City, N.Y. : Doubleday.

Mamis, Roger. 1983. "Golden Handcuffs." *Inc.* Magazine, August.

Mandel, Michael. 2000. *The Coming Internet Depression.* New York: Basic Books.

Manes, Stephen, and Paul Andrews. 1993. *Gates: How Microsoft's Mogul Invented an Industry and Made Himself the Richest Man in America.* New York: Doubleday.

Manners, David, and Tsugio Makimoto. 1995. *Living With the Chip.* London and New York: Chapman & Hall.

Marshall, Frank. 2001. Interview. Conducted by Joseph Blasi. New Brunswick, N.J.: School of Management and Labor Relations. (Mr. Marshall is the vice chairman of Covad Communications and was the interim chief executive officer at the time of this interview.)

Matthews, Jay. 1994. "FINANCIAL: Stock Options Rule Fight Escalates; Study Shows Few Workers Get Them, but Defenders Challenge Figures." *Washington Post,* September 1.

Matthews, Joe. 1998. "Baby Bills Follow Leader To Success: Microsoft Bill Gates' Ex-employees Are Using His stock and Even His Strategies to Start Up their Own High-tech Firms." *Baltimore Sun,* August 14.

McCarty, Mariu Hurt. 2000. *The Nobel Laureates: How The World's Greatest Economic Minds Shaped Modern Thought.* New York: McGraw Hill.

McGough, Robert. 2000. "Heard on the Street: Firms Face Options Pickle as Stocks Fall." *Wall Street Journal,* October 16.

McKenna, Regis. 1995. Interview. Conducted by Rob Walker. Stanford, Calif.: Stanford University Library Archives, Silicon Genesis Oral Histories Project. Transcript available at: www-sul.stanford.edu/depts/hasrg/histsci/silicon%20genesis/regis-ntb.html. Video available at: www-sul.stanford.edu/depts/hasrg/histsci/silicon%20genesis/intro-ntb.html.

_____. 2000. "Free Advice: Consulting the Silicon Valley Way." In the *Silicon Valley Edge,* edited by Chong-Moon Lee, William F. Miller, Marguerite Gong Hancock, and Harry R. Rowen. Stanford, Calif.: Stanford University Press, pp. 370–379.

McMinn, Charles. 2001. Interview. Conducted by Joseph Blasi. New Brunswick, N.J.: School of Management and Labor Relations. (Mr. McMinn is the founder and chairman of Covad Communications.)

McQuaid, Kim. 1986. *A Response to Industrialism: Liberal Businessmen and the Evolving Spectrum of Capitalist Reform, 1886–1960.* New York: Garland Publishing Company.

Mead, Edward Sherwood. 1912. *Corporation Finance.* New York: D. Appleton.

Means, Gardiner C. 1930. "The Diffusion of Stock Ownership in the United States." *Quarterly Journal of Economics* 44(4), August, pp. 561–600.

Mehran, Hamid. 1999. *Unleashing the Ownership Dynamic—Creating Connections Through Engaged Ownership—A Research Summary.* Lincolnshire, Ill.: Hewitt Associates, 1999. (Dr. Mehran is now at the Federal Reserve Bank of New York.)

Mehran, Hamid, and Joseph Tracy. 2001. "The Effect of Employee Stock Options on the Evolution of Compensation in the 1990s." *Economic Policy Review,* December 1. (See also, Federal Reserve Bank of New York Economic Policy Review, December 1.)

————. 2002. "The Impact of Employee Stock Options on the Evolution of Compensation in the 1990s." July, Working Paper Number 8353. (Available at www.nber.org.)

Meine, Franklyn. 1923. "Dennison Company's Works Committee Part II. Growth of the Works Committee from January 1, 1920 to January 1, 1921: Its Problem and Procedure." *University Journal of Business* 2(1), December, pp. 81–111.

Melville, Herman. 1998. *Moby Dick.* New York: Oxford University Press.

Meulbroek, Lisa. 2002. "Company Stock in Pension Plans: How Costly Is It?" Cambridge, Mass.: Harvard Business School, Division of Research. Working Paper 02–058.

Microsoft Corporation. 2000. *Inside Out: Microsoft—In Our Own Words.* New York: Warner Books.

Microsoft Employees. 2001. Interviews. Conducted by Joseph Blasi. New Brunswick, N.J.: School of Management and Labor Relations. (Pseudonyms of employees are Carrie, Victor, Elaine, Christina, Paul, and Evan.)

Millstein, Ira, Michel Albert, Sir Adrian Cadbury, Robert E. Denham, Dieter Feddersen, and Nabuo Tateisi. 1998. *Corporate Governance: A Report to the OECD.* Paris: Organization for Economic Development and Cooperation (OECD).

Mishel, Lawrence, Jared Bernstein, and Heather Boushey. 2002. *The State of Working America: 2002/2003.* Ithaca, N.Y.: Cornell University Press.

Mitchell, H. L. 1979. *Mean Things Happening in This Land: The Life and Times of H. K. Mitchell, Co-founder of the Southern Tenant Farmers Union.* Montclair, N.J.: Allenheld, Osmun.

Mitchell, Thomas Warner. 1905. "Stockholder Profits on Privileged Subscriptions." *Quarterly Journal of Economics* 19(2), February, pp. 231–269.

Mitten, Thomas E. 1926. "Humanizing the Capitalistic System." *Service Talks* (Publication of the Philadelphia Rapid Transit Company) 7(21), September 27.

Moll, John L. 1996. "William Bradford Shockley." in National Academy of Sciences. Biographical Memoirs, Volume 68, Office of the Home Secretary. Washington, D.C.: National Academy Press, pp. 305–324. Available at books.nap.edu/books/0309052394/html/305.html#pagetop or www.nap.edu/readingroom/books/biomems/wshockley.html.

Monks, Robert A. G., and Nell Minow. 1996. *Watching the Watchers: Corporate Governance for the 21st Century.* Oxford, UK: Blackwell.

————. 2001. *Corporate Governance.* Oxford, UK: Blackwell.

Moore, Gordon M. 1995. Interview. Conducted by Rob Walker. Stanford, Calif.: Stanford University Library Archives, Silicon Genesis Oral Histories Project.

Transcript available at: www-sul.stanford.edu/depts/hasrg/histsci/silicon%20genesis/ moorebody-ntb.html#anchor491986. Video available at: www.sul.stanford.edu/ depts/hasrg/histsci/silicon%20genesis/intro-ntb.html.

_____. 1999. "Solid-State Physicist: William Shockley." *Time 100: Builders and Titans, Scientists and Thinkers*. Editors of Time Magazine. New York: Time Incorporated. Available at: www.time.com/time/time100/scientist/profile/shockley.html.

Morgan, E. Victor, and W. A. Thomas. 1962. *The Stock Exchange: Its History and Functions*. London: Elek Books.

Morgan, Edmund S. 1995. *American Slavery American Freedom: The Ordeal of Colonial Virginia*. New York: W. W. Norton.

Morgenson, Gretchen. 2001a. "Some Suffer Tax Hangovers from Microsoft Option Spree." *New York Times*, April 18.

_____. 2001b. "Holding Executives Answerable To Owners." *New York Times*, April 29.

_____. 2002. "Business Lobby Seeks to Limit Investor Votes on Options." *New York Times*, June 6.

Morain, Dan. 2001. "State's Economy More Robust Than in Rest of U.S., Chief Analyst Says." *Los Angeles Times*, January 6.

Moritz, Michael. 1984. *The Little Kingdom: The Private Story of Apple Computer*. New York: William Morrow and Company.

Mulligan, Thomas S., and Charles Piller. 2000. "Microsoft's Option Grants May Signal Trend For Tech Firms: Firm Hopes To Make Up Shares 40% Plunge By Doubling What Employees Can Exercise." *Los Angeles Times*, April 26.

Munk, Nina. 2002. "AOL Time Warner's Civil War." *Vanity Fair*, July.

Murphy, Kevin J. 1997. "Executive Compensation and the Modern Industrial Revolution." *International Journal of Industrial Organization* 15, July. Available at: www-rcf.usc.edu/~kjmurphy/kjmijio.pdf.

_____. 1999. "Executive Compensation." In *Handbook of Labor Economics*, edited by Orley Ashenfelter and David Card. Amsterdam: North Holland. Available online at: www-rcf.usc.edu/~kjmurphy/ceopay.pdf.

Murphy, Kevin, and Martin Conyon. 2000. "The Prince and the Pauper? CEO Pay in the US and UK." *Economic Journal*, November.

Murray, Alan. 2001. "Capital: Intellectual Property: Old Rules Don't Apply." *Wall Street Journal*, August 23.

Musil, Steve. 1997. "Jobs Takes on Exec Perks in 'Egalitarian' Gesture." *MacWeek*, August 18, p. 1.

Nalbantian, Haig R. 1987. *Incentives, Cooperation, and Risk Sharing: Economic and Psychological Perspectives*. Totowa, N.J.: Rowman and Littlefield.

New York Stock Exchange. 1953. *Stock Ownership Plans For Employees*. New York: New York Stock Exchange.

National Center for Employee Ownership (NCEO). 2000. "Case Study: Portal Software." Employee Ownership Newsletter. Oakland, Calif.: National Center for Employee Ownership, May-June, p. 8.

_____. 2001a. *The Stock Options Book.* Oakland, Calif.: National Center for Employee Ownership.

_____. 2001b. *Leveraged ESOPs and Employee Buyouts.* 4th edn. Oakland, Calif.: National Center for Employee Ownership.

_____. 2001c. *The Employee's Guide to Stock Options.* 4th edn. Oakland, Calif.: National Center for Employee Ownership.

_____. 2001d. *Communicating Stock Options.* 4th edn. Oakland, Calif.: National Center for Employee Ownership.

_____. 2002a. *The Employee's Guide to Stock Options.* Oakland, Calif.: National Center for Employee Ownership.

_____. 2002b. *A Statistical Profile of Employee Ownership.* Oakland, Calif.: National Center for Employee Ownership. Available at: www.nceo.org/library/eo_stat.html.

_____. 2002c. "Special Issue: Employee Ownership and Corporate Performance: A Comprehensive Review of the Evidence." *Journal of Employee Ownership Law and Finance* 14(1), Winter.

_____. 2002d. *Stock Options: Beyond the Basics.* Oakland, Calif.: National Center for Employee Ownership.

_____. 2002e. *Model Equity Compensation Plans.* Oakland, Calif.: National Center for Employee Ownership.

_____. 2002f. *Ownership Management: Building a Culture of Lasting Innovation.* Oakland, Calif.: National Center for Employee Ownership.

_____. 2002g. *Selling to an ESOP.* Oakland, Calif.: National Center for Employee Ownership.

_____. 2002h. "The Largest 100 Majority Employee Owned Companies." *Employee Ownership Report* 22(4), July/August. Oakland, Calif.: National Center for Employee Ownership. Available at: www.nceo.org/library/eo100.html.

National Civic Federation. 1920. *Profit Sharing by American Employers.* New York: National Civic Federation.

_____. 1921. *A Report of the Profit Sharing Department of the National Civic Federation.* New York: E. P. Dutton.

National Industrial Conference Board. 1928. *Employee Stock Purchase Plans in the United States.* New York: National Industrial Conference Board.

_____. 1930. *Employee Stock Purchase Plans and the Market Crises of 1929.* Supplement to *Employee Stock Purchase Plans in the United States,* published in January 1928. New York: National Industrial Conference Board.

_____. 1943. *Employee Savings and Investment Plans.* New York: National Industrial Conference Board, Studies in Personnel Policy, Number 133.

_____. 1953. *Stock Ownership Plans for Workers*. New York: National Industrial Conference Board, Studies in Personnel Policy, Number 132.

Neimark, Jill. 1986. "The Mystical Corporation: New-age Management and the Bottom Line." *Success* Magazine, *San Francisco Chronicle*, November 2.

New York Stock Exchange. 1917. *Essays in the History of the American Corporation*. Cambridge, Mass.: Harvard University Press.

Newman, H., and H. Mozes. 1997. *Compensation Committee Composition and Its Influence on CEO Compensation Practices*. New York: Fordham University.

*Newsday*. 2001. "Laid-Off Amazon Workers Cite Union Drive, Call For Investigation of Cutbacks." *Newsday* from Reuters, February 1.

*Newsweek*. 2000. "The Geeks Microsoft Cares About: When It Comes to Reported Profits, Even the Sharp-elbow Types in Redmond Have to Occasionally Give In." *Newsweek*, May 15.

Nielsen/Net Ratings. 2001. "Internet Usage Climbs to Record High in October, with 115 Million Americans Online, According to Nielsen//NetRatings." *Business Wire*, November 13.

Nieman, Donald G. 1994. *From Slavery to Sharecropping: White Land and Black Labor in the Rural South, 1865–1900*. New York: Garland Publishing.

Nobel Foundation. 1973. *Nobel Lectures, Physics 1901–1970*. 4 vols. Amsterdam: Elsevier Publishing Company. Biography available at: www.nobel.se/physics/laureates/1956/shockley-bio.html. Nobel Lecture available at: www.nobel.se/physics/laureates/1956/shockley-lecture.html.

Norr, Henry. 1999. "Growth of a Silicon Empire: Bay Area's Fertile Intellectual Ground Helped Sprout High Technology Industry." *San Francisco Chronicle*, December 27.

Norris, Floyd. 1997. "Microsoft, A Pioneer In Quality Accounting." *New York Times*, November 16.

_____. 2001. "Funny Math No Joke for Investors." *New York Times*, February 4.

Olson, Deborah Groban. 1994. "Giving Employee Owners a Real Voice as Stockholders." *Journal of Employee Ownership Law and Finance* 6(4), Fall.

Oppel, Richard A., Jr. 2002. "Enron's Many Strands: Retirement Money." *New York Times*, April 12.

Organization for Economic Cooperation and Development (OECD). 2000. *Is There A New Economy?* First Report of the OECD Growth Project. Paris: OECD.

O'Reilly, Charles A., III, and Jeffrey Pfeffer. 2000. "Cisco Systems: Acquiring and Retaining Talent in Hypercompetitive Markets." *Human Resource Planning*, January 1.

Packard, David. 1995. *The HP Way: How Bill Hewlett and I Built Our Company*. New York: HarperBusiness.

Paulson, Barry. 1981. *Economic History of the United States*. New York: Macmillan Publishing Co.

Paulson, Ed. 2001. *Inside Cisco: The Real Story of Sustained M & A Growth.* New York: John Wiley & Sons.

Pearl Meyer & Partners. 2002. *Executive Pay Trends.* New York: Pearl Meyer & Partners. Available at www.execpay.com/Pearl%20PDF/Trends%202002.pdf.

Peers, Martin, and Julia Angwin. 2000. "AOL, Time Warner Plan Stock Options for All Employees." *Wall Street Journal,* December 8.

Pecora, Ferdinand. 1939. *Wall Street Under Oath.* New York: Simon and Schuster.

Pender, Kathleen. 2001. "Cisco's Option Plan Opens Door For Others to Make Adjustments: Repricing, Grants, Slow-motion Swaps All Have Costs." *San Francisco Chronicle,* April 18.

Perkins, Anthony B. 1994. *Venture Pioneers.* Interview with Arthur Rock and Thomas Perkins. *The Red Herring.* February 1. pp. 54–59.

Perkins, Anthony B., and Michael C. Perkins. 2001. *The Internet Bubble.* New York: HarperBusiness.

Perkins, Edwin J. 1988. *The Economy of Colonial America.* New York: Columbia University Press.

Perrow, Charles. 2002. *Organizing America: Wealth, Power, and the Origins of Corporate Capitalism.* Princeton, N.J.: Princeton University Press.

Perry, Stewart E., and Raymond Russell. 1998. *Collecting Garbage: Dirty Work, Clean Jobs, Proud People.* New Brunswick, N.J.: Transaction Publishers.

Phillips, W. Louis. 1987. *Warren County, Ohio Records of Apprenticeship and Indenture 1824–1832 and 1864–1867.* Bowie, Md.: Heritage Books.

Piller, Charles. 2001. "Cisco's Slump Kills Off Some High-tech Myths." *Los Angeles Times,* May 6.

Pitta, Julie. 1996. "Showdown on the Web Microsoft, Netscape Battle for Net Dominance." *Los Angeles Times,* July 8.

Poletti, Therese. 2001. "Intel Issues Special Stock Option Grant." *San Jose Mercury News,* April 5.

Portal Software Employees. 2001. Interviews. Conducted by Joseph Blasi. New Brunswick, N.J.: School of Management and Labor Relations. (Pseudonyms of employees are Rachel, Francine, Jack, Goeff, Mitch, Tom.)

Posner, Bruce G., Nelson W. Aldrich Jr., Nell Margolis, and Robert A. Mamis. 1985. "In Search of Equity." *Inc.* Magazine, April 1.

Poulson, Barry W. 1981. *Economic History of The United States.* New York: Macmillan.

Pressman, Aaron. 2000. "Call Forward." *The Industry Standard,* November 6.

Public Broadcasting System. 1997. 2001–2002. *Big Dream, Small Screen. The American Experience Series.* Boston, Mass.: WGBH Educational Foundation. Available at: www.pbs.org/wgbh/amex/technology/bigdream/bigdreamts.htm.

———. 1999. "Transistorized!" Alexandria, Va.: PBS. Available at: www.pbs.org/transistor/index.html.

Pulliam, Susan. 2000. "Heard on the Street New Dot-Com Mantra: 'Just Pay Me in Cash, Please'." *Wall Street Journal,* November 28.

Putterman, Louis, and Gil Skillman. 1988. "The Incentive Effects of Monitoring Under Alternative Compensation Schemes." *International Journal of Industrial Organization* 6(1), pp. 109–119.

Quarrey, Michael, and Corey Rosen. 1986. *Employee Ownership and Corporate Performance.* Oakland, Calif.: National Center for Employee Ownership.

Quarrey, Michael, Joseph Blasi, and Corey Rosen. 1986. *Taking Stock: Employee Ownership at Work.* New York and Cambridge, UK: Harper and Row/Ballinger Books.

Quittner, Joshua, and Michelle Slatalla. 1998. *Speeding the Net: The Inside Story of Netscape and How It Challenged Microsoft.* New York: Atlantic Monthly Press.

Radosevich, Lynda. 1996. "Internet Plumbing Comes to Groupware. (Internet-enabled groupware coming to market)." *Datamation,* May 15.

Ragavan, Vivek. 2001. Interview. Conducted by Joseph Blasi. New Brunswick, N.J.: School of Management and Labor Relations. (Former chief executive officer of Redback.)

Ranadive, Vivek. 1999. *The Power of Now.* New York: McGraw-Hill.

_____. 2001. Interview. Conducted by Joseph Blasi. New Brunswick, N.J.: School of Management and Labor Relations. (Mr. Ranadive is the chairman and CEO of Tibco Software Inc.)

Rand, Ayn. 1943. *The Fountainhead.* Indianapolis, New York: The Bobbs-Merrill Company.

_____. 1957. *Atlas Shrugged.* New York: Random House.

Ransom, Roger L., and Richard Sutch. 2001. *One Kind of Freedom: The Economic Consequences of Emancipation.* New York: Cambridge University Press.

RCN Employees. 2002. Interviews. Conducted by Joseph Blasi. New Brunswick, N.J.: School of Management and Labor Relations.

Rega, John. 2002. "CEOs Propose More Oversight on Boards." *Bergen County Record,* May 15.

Reid, Joseph D. 1973. "Sharecropping As An Understandable Market Response: The Post-Bellum South." *Journal of Economic History* 33(1), The Tasks of Economic History, March, pp. 106–130.

Reingold, Jennifer. 1999. "Dot.com Boards Are Flouting the Rules: They're Small and Packed With Insiders. Does It Matter?" *Business Week,* December 20.

Reingold, Jennifer, and Ronald Grover. 1999. "Executive Pay." *Business Week,* April 19.

Republican Association of Washington. 1859. *Lands for the Landless.* Washington, D.C.: The Republican Association of Washington, under the direction of the Congressional Republican Executive Committee. Available in the Princeton University Firestone Library.

Reuters News Agency. 1984. "Chrysler." *Globe and Mail,* April 26.

Richards, Evelyn. 1988. "IBM Shedding Key Parts of Rolm Corp; Deal Said to Show Strategy Foundered." *Washington Post,* December 14.

Riordan, Michael, and Lillian Hoddeson. 1998. *Crystal Fire: The Invention of the Transistor and the Birth of the Information Age.* Sloan Technology Series. New York: W.W. Norton and Company.

Ristelhueber, Robert. 1995. "What's Behind Management Pay?" *Electronic Business,* December 1.

Rock, Arthur. 2000. "Arthur Rock: Arthur Rock & Co." In *Done Deals: Venture Capitalists Tell Their Stories,* edited by Udayan Gupta. Boston: Harvard Business School Press, pp. 139–128.

———. 2002. Interview. Conducted by Joseph Blasi. New Brunswick, N.J.: School of Management and Labor Relations.

Rock, Edward B., and Michael L. Wachter. 1999. "Tailored Claims and Governance: The Fit Between Employees and Shareholders." In *Employees and Corporate Governance,* edited by Margaret M. Blair and Mark J. Roe. Washington, D.C.: Brookings Institution Press.

Rodrick, Scott. 2001. *Section 401(k) Plans and Employee Ownership.* Oakland, Calif.: National Center for Employee Ownership.

Rogers, Joel, and Wolfgang Streeck. 1995. *Works Councils.* Chicago: University of Chicago Press.

Ros, Agustin J. 2001. *Profits for All?: The Cost and Benefits of Employee Ownership.* Hauppauge, N.Y.: Nova Science Publishers.

Rosen, Corey. 2001, 2002. Interviews. Conducted by Joseph Blasi. New Brunswick, N.J.: School of Management and Labor Relations. (Executive director and co-founder of the National Center for Employee Ownership in Oakland, California.)

Rosen, Corey, Katherine Klein, and Karen M. Young. 1986. *Employee Ownership in America: The Equity Solution.* Lexington, Mass.: D. C. Heath, Lexington Books.

Rosen, Corey, and Michael Quarrey. 1987. "How Well Is Employee Ownership Working." *Harvard Business Review* 65, September-October, pp. 126–130.

Rostky, George. 1995. Interview. Conducted by Rob Walker. Stanford, Calif.: Stanford University Library Archives, Silicon Genesis Oral Histories Project, 1995. Video available at: www-sul.stanford.edu/depts/hasrg/histsci/silicon%20genesis/intro-ntb.html.

———. 1997. "25th Anniversary-Electronics at the Threshold of the New Millennium. The Transistor: A Biography." *Electronic Engineering Times,* October 30.

Rowe, R. L. 1949. "Profit Sharing Plans in Industry." *Harvard Business Review* 27(5), September, pp. 559–584.

Royce, Edward. 1993. *The Origins of Southern Sharecropping.* Philadelphia, Pa.: Temple University Press.

Rubinstein, Saul A., and Thomas A. Kochan. 2001. *Learning from Saturn: Possibilities for Corporate Governance and Employee.* Ithaca, N.Y.: Cornell University Press, ILR Press.

Rukeyser, M. S. 1927. "Labor Shares in the Prosperity of Standard Oil." *Forbes Magazine*, April 1.

Runge, Carlisle Ford. 1984. "Institutions and the Free Rider: The Assurance Problem in Collective Action." *Journal of Politics* 46(1), February, pp. 154–181.

Russell, Raymond. 1985. *Sharing Ownership in the Workplace*. Albany: State University of New York Press.

Said, Carolyn. 2001. "High-tech Pioneer Hewlett Dies: With Packard He Founded Electronics Giant and Left A Legacy." *San Francisco Chronicle*, January 13.

*San Jose Mercury News*. 2001. "Economic Downturn Casts New Light on Stock Options." October 7.

Saunders, Rebecca. 2002. *Big Shots, Business the Amazon.com Way: Secrets of the World's Most Astonishing Web Business*. New York: John Wiley & Sons.

Saxenian, AnnaLee. 1994a. *Regional Advantage: Culture and Competition in Silicon Valley and Route 128*. Cambridge, Mass.: Harvard University Press.

————. 1994b. "Lessons From Silicon Valley." *Technology Review*, July 1.

Schaffler, Rhonda, and Deborah Marchini. 2002. CNNFn Special Events, Testimony on July 17, 2002, before the House Financial Services Committee.

Schlender, Brent. 1998. "The Three Faces of Steve." *Fortune Magazine*, November 9.

Schlesinger, Jacob. 2002. "Lieberman Would Expand Option Grants to Include Less Highly Paid Employees." *Wall Street Journal*, April 2.

Schroeder, Michael, and Ruth Simon. 2001. "Tech Firms Object, as SEC Gets Tougher On Their Practice of Repricing Options." *Wall Street Journal*, February 2.

Schwartz, Evan I. 2002. *The Last Lone Inventor: A Tale of Genius, Deceit, and the Birth of Television*. New York: HarperCollins.

Sclavos, Stratton. 2001. Interview. Conducted by Joseph Blasi. New Brunswick, N.J.: School of Management and Labor Relations. (Mr. Sclavos is the chairman, president, and CEO of VeriSign Inc.)

Seagate Technology. 1999. "Seagate Announces Reorganization Of Seagate Software Subsidiary." PR Newswire, September 3.

Segaller, Stephen. 1999. *Nerds 2.0.1: A Brief History of the Internet*. New York: TV Books.

Sello, Harry. 1995. Interview. Conducted by Rob Walker. Stanford, Calif.: Stanford University Library Archives, Silicon Genesis Oral Histories Project, 1995. Video available at: www-sul.stanford.edu/depts/hasrg/histsci/silicon%20genesis/intro-ntb.html.

Seitz, Frederick, and Norman G. Einspruch. 1998. *Electronic Genie: The Tangled History of Silicon*. Urbana and Chicago: University of Illinois Press.

Sesil, James, Maya Kroumova, Joseph Blasi, and Douglas Kruse. 2002. "Broad-based Employee Stock Options in U.S. New Economy Firms." *British Journal of Industrial Relations* 4(2), June, pp. 273–294.

Sesil, James, Maya Kroumova, Douglas Kruse, and Joseph Blasi. 2000. *Broad-based Employee Stock Options in the U.S.: Company Performance and Characteristics.* Academy of Management National Conference, Toronto, Canada, 2000.

Sesil, James, Douglas Kruse, and Joseph Blasi. 2001. *Sharing Ownership via Employee Stock Ownership.* Helsinki, Finland: United Nations University, World Institute for Development Economics Research (WIDER), Discussion Paper No. 2001/25.

Severy, Melvin L. 1907. *Gillette's Social Redemption.* Boston: H. B. Turner & Co.

Schwanhausser, Mark. 2001a. "Profits Were on Paper, but the Tax Bite is Real: Last Year's Nouveau Riche This Year Face Financial Ruin." *Seattle Times,* April 2.

———. 2001b. "Democrats Push for Tax Relief on Stock Options." *San Jose Mercury News,* April 6.

———. 2002. "Workers Seeking Help with Alternative Minimum Taxes Face Defeat in Washington." *San Jose Mercury News,* April 15.

Shannon, Fred A. 1936. "The Homestead Act and the Labor Surplus." *American Historical Review* 41(4), July, pp. 637–651.

Shaw, Albert. 1886. "Cooperation in a Western City." *Publications of the American Economic Association* 1(4), September, pp. 7–106.

Shiver, Jube, Jr., and Michael A. Hiltzik. 2000. "The Microsoft Ruling: Microsoft Violated Federal Antitrust Laws, Judge Rules." *Los Angeles Times,* April 4.

Siegl, Annick, Chris Loayza, and Glenn Davis. 2002. *IRRC: Stock Plan Dilution 2002.* Washington, D.C.: Investor Responsibility Research Center.

Simmons, John, and William Mares. 1983. *Working Together.* New York: Knopf.

Simon, Ruth. 2001. "Techs Retool Option Plans Amid Plunge." *Wall Street Journal,* March 14.

Simon, Ruth, and Ianthe Jeanne Dugan. 2001. "Companies Overdose On Stock-Option Plans—Now, a Backlash Brews as Downside Emerges." *Wall Street Journal Europe,* June 6.

Simons, Gustave. 1948. "Economic and Legal Aspects of Profit Sharing Plans." *Industrial and Labor Relations Review,* October.

Sobel, Robert, and David Sicilia. 1986. *The Entrepreneurs: An American Adventure.* New York: Houghton Mifflin.

Solomon, Jolie. 1989. "Workplace: Pepsi Offers Stock Options To All, Not Just Honchos." *Wall Street Journal,* June 28.

Southwick, Karen. 1999. *High Noon: The Inside Story of Scott McNealy and the Rise of Sun Microsystems.* New York: John Wiley & Sons.

———. 2001. *The King-makers: Venture Capital and the Money Behind the Net.* New York: John Wiley & Sons.

Spector, Robert. 2000. *Amazon.com, Get Big Fast: Inside the Revolutionary Business Model That Changed the World.* New York: Harper Business.

Sporck, Charlie. 2000. Interview. Conducted by Rob Walker. Stanford, Calif.: Stanford University Library Archives, Silicon Genesis Oral Histories Project, 1995. Video available at: www-sul.stanford.edu/depts/hasrg/histsci/silicon%20genesis/intro-ntb.html.

Sprint Inc. 2000. "Sprint Board Approves Motivation and Retention Initiative Providing Employees a Choice to Cancel and Replace 2000 Stock Options." PR Newswire, October 17.

Stabile, Susan. 1999. "Motivating Executives: Does Performance-based Compensation Positively Affect Managerial Performance?" *Journal of Labor & Employment Law* 2, Fall.

Stashower, Daniel. 2002. *The Boy Genius and the Mogul: The Untold Story of Television.* New York: Broadway Books.

Staubus, Martin, Ron Bernstein, David Binns, Marshal Hyman, and Debra Sherman, eds. 2002. *Transitioning Ownership in the Private Company.* La Jolla, Calif.: Beyster Institute.

Stauffer, David. 2000. *It's A Wired World: Business the AOL Way.* Milford, Conn.: Capstone.

Steen, Margaret. 2000. "Market Volatility Makes Company Stock Options Suddenly Less Attractive." *San Jose Mercury News,* April 22.

Sterngold, James. 2002. "California Stunned to Find $20 Billion Hole in Budget." *New York Times,* May 11.

Stewart, Bryce M., and W. J. Crouper. 1945. *Profit Sharing and Stock Ownership for Wage Earners.* New York: Industrial Relations Counselors.

Stewart, Thomas A. 2001. *The Wealth of Knowledge: Intellectual Capital and the Twenty-first Century Organization.* New York: Currency.

_____. 1998. *Intellectual Capital: The New Wealth of Organizations.* New York: Bantam.

Stiegman, Patrick. 2000. "America Online-Time Warner Merger: The Internet Grows Up; Left For Dead, AOL Creates a New Media Landscape." *Milwaukee Journal Sentinel,* January 16.

Stiglitz, Joseph E. 1974. "Incentives and Risk Sharing in Sharecropping." *Review of Economic Studies* 4(2), April, pp. 219–255.

Stone, Florence M. 2002. *The Oracle of Oracle.* New York: AMACOM, the American Management Association.

Stross, Randall E. 1997. *The Microsoft Way.* Reading, Mass.: Addison-Wesley, Inc.

Strother, French. 1927. "What Big Business Owes the Public: A Notable Interview Given to French Strother (by Gerard Swope of GE), in World's Work, March.

Sull, Donald L. 1999. "The Dynamics of Standing Still: Firestone Tire & Rubber and the Radial Revolution." *Business History Review* 73, September 22.

Tajnai, Carolyn E. 1985. *Fred Terman, The Father of Silicon Valley.* Stanford, Calif.: Stanford University, Stanford Computer Forum, Technical Report # STAN-CS-85-1052, May, pp. 85–276. Available at the Stanford University Library and online at: www.internetvalley.com/archives/mirrors/terman.html.

Taussig, F. W., and W. S. Barker. 1925. "American Corporations and Their Executives: A Statistical Inquiry." *Quarterly Journal of Economics* 40(1), November, pp. 1–51.

Tavan, Rick. 2001. Interview. Conducted by Joseph Blasi. New Brunswick, N.J.: School of Management and Labor Relations. (Senior vice president of Tibco Software Inc.)

Taylor, Alan. 2001. *American Colonies.* New York: Viking.

Taylor, Paul S. 1928. "The Leighton Co-operative Industries." *Journal of Political Economy* 36(2), April, pp. 212–228.

Tead, Ordway. 1926. "The Rise of Employee Stock-Ownership: The Possibilities and the Dangers of This Trend in Business and Industry." *Industrial Management* 712, March, pp. 157–160.

Tempest, Nicole. 1999. *Meg Whitman at eBay, Inc.* Boston, Mass.: Harvard Business School Publishing, October 1.

Thurm, Scott. 2000. "Joining the Fold: Under Cisco's System, Mergers Usually Work; That Defies the Odds—Ms. Gigoux's SWAT Teams Oversee the Integration Of Newly Acquired Units—'The Borg' of Silicon Valley?" *Wall Street Journal*, March 1.

Tibco Software Employees. 2001. Interviews. Conducted by Joseph Blasi. New Brunswick, N.J.: School of Management and Labor Relations. (Pseudonyms of employees are Joe, Jennifer, Peter, Wendy, Bill, Robert, James, Paul.)

Tully, Shawn. 1998. "Smart Managing/Special Report: CEO Pay. Raising the Bar Stock Options Have Become Even the Subpar CEO's Way to Wealth." *Fortune* Magazine, June 8.

Tutorow, Norman E. 1971. *Leland Stanford: Man of Many Careers.* Menlo Park, Calif.: Pacific Coast Publishers.

Tymeson McClary, Mildred. 1953. *The Norton Story.* 1st edn. Worcester, Mass.: Norton Company.

Uchitelle, Louis. 2002. "Economic View: Do 401(k)'s Give Workers An Illusion of Wealth?" *New York Times*, May 26.

Ungar, Alan B., and Mark T. Sakanashi. 2001. *Your Employee Stock Options.* New York: HarperCollins, HarperBusiness.

Union Republican Congressional Committee. 1868(?). *Homes for the Homeless: What the Republican Party has Done for the Poor Man.* Washington, D.C.: The Union Republican Congressional Committee. Available in the Princeton University Firestone Library.

*U.S. News.* 1961. "Under Fire: Stock Options." May 8, pp. 111–112.

United States Congress (Senate). 1939. Committee on Finance. Survey of Experiences in Profit Sharing and Possibilities of Incentive Taxation: Hearings Before a Subcommittee of the Committee on Finance, United States Senate, 75th Congress, 3d session, Pursuant to S. Res. 215, Providing for an Investigation of Existing Profit-sharing Systems Between Employers and Employees in the United States.

November 21 to December 16. Washington, D.C.: U.S. Government Printing Office.

United States Congress. 1973. Joint Economic Committee. Subcommittee on Priorities and Economy in Government. Executive Compensation Rules. Hearing, 93d Congress, 1st Session. June 5, 1973. Washington, D.C.: U.S. Government Printing Office.

United States Department of Labor, Bureau of Labor Statistics (US DOL BLS). 1927. Employee Stock Ownership in the United States: A Selected Bibliography. Washington, D.C.: U.S. Government Printing Office.

_____. 1997. *Employee Benefits in Medium and Large Establishments.* Washington, D.C.: U.S. Department of Labor, Bureau of Labor Statistics.

_____. 2000. Press Release. *Pilot Survey on the Incidence of Stock Options in Private Industry in 1999.* Washington, D.C.: U.S. Department of Labor, Bureau of Labor Statistics, USDL 00-290.

United States Department of Labor (US DOL PWBA). 1997. Pension and Welfare Benefits Administration. "Abstract of 1993 Form 5500 Annual Reports." *Private Pension Plan Bulletin* 6, Winter.

_____. 2001–2002. "Abstract of 1998 Form 5500 Annual Reports." *Private Pension Plan Bulletin* 11, Winter.

United States Department of Labor (US DOL). 2001. *2001 Report on the American Workforce.* Washington, D.C.: U.S. Department of Labor.

United States Federal Trade Commission (US FTC). 1923. National Wealth and Income: A Report . . . in Final Response to Senate Resolution No. 451. Washington, D.C.: 69th Congress, 1st Session, Senate Document 126, February 23.

United States General Accounting Office (US GAO). 1986. *Employee Stock Ownership Plans.* Washington, D.C.: U.S. General Accounting Office, December.

_____. 1987. *Employee Stock Ownership Plans.* Washington, D.C.: U.S. General Accounting Office, October, GAO/PEMD-88-1.

United States, Government of the. 1862. The Homestead Act, May 20. U.S. Statutes at Large, Vol. XII, p. 392 ff.

United States Salary Stabilization Board. 1952. *Stock Option and Stock Purchase Plans.* The Report of a Special Panel to the Salary Stabilization Board, October 23, 1951. Washington, D.C.: U.S. Salary Stabilization Board. (Available at the Princeton University Library).

United States Securities and Exchange Commission (US SEC). 2002. *Final Rule: Disclosure of Equity Compensation Plan Information.* (17 CFR Parts 228, 229, 240 and 249. [Release Nos. 33–8048, 34–45189; File No. S7–04–01] RIN: 3235-AI01. Washington, D.C.: U.S. Securities and Exchange Commission. Available at: www.sec.gov/rules/final/33–8048.htm.

United States Senate Committee on Banking, Housing, and Urban Affairs. 2002. "U.S. Senate Committee on Banking, Housing, and Urban Affairs Holds Hearings on the Collapse of Enron." February 14. Washington, D.C.: Federal Document Clearing House Inc., Political Transcripts.

United States Special Committee on Farm Tenancy. 1937. *Farm Tenancy.* Report of the President's Committee. Washington, D.C.: U.S. Government Printing Office. Prepared under the auspices of the National Resources Committee. February.

Vance, Russell E., Jr. 1956. "An Unsuccessful Experiment in Industrial Democracy: The Columbia Conserve Company." Ph.D. dissertation, Indiana University.

Veblen, Thorstein. 1921. *The Engineers and the Price System.* New York: B. W. Huebsch Inc.

Verespej, Michael A. 1990. "Where People Come First, Part 7." *Industry Week,* July 16.
———. 1996. "Empire Without Emperors." *Industry Week,* February 5.

Vickers, Marcia, Mike France, Emily Thornton, David Henry, Heather Timmons, Mike McNamee. 2002. "How Corrupt Is Wall Street? New Revelations Have Investors Baying for Blood, and the Scandal Is Widening." *Business Week,* May 13.

Vlamis, Anthony, and Bob Smith. 2001. *Do You?: Business the Yahoo Way.* Milford, Conn.: Capstone Publishing.

Wall Frazier, Joseph. 1990. *Alfred I. DuPont: The Man & His Family.* New York: Oxford University Press.

*Wall Street Journal.* 1997. "Netscape to Unveil Technology in Race With Rival Microsoft." September 29.
———. 2002. "Almost $40 Billion was Spent Last Year to Scoop Up Dot-Coms at Bargain Prices." January 11.

Ward, Leah Beth. 2000. "TI Execs Announce 2000 Goals: CEO Promises Greater Shareholder Returns." *Dallas Morning News,* March 3.

Washington, George Thomas. 1942. *Corporate Executives' Compensation: Legal and Business Aspects of Salary and Bonus Plans, Stock Options, Pensions, Indemnity Agreements, and Related Matters.* New York : The Ronald Press Co.
———. 1951. *Corporate Executives' Compensation: Legal and Business Aspects of Salary and Bonus Plans, Stock Options, Pensions, Indemnity Agreements, and Related Matters.* Rev. edn. New York: The Ronald Press Co.

Watson, Thomas J., Jr. 1987. "The Greatest Capitalist in History (Thomas J. Watson, Jr.)." *Fortune* Magazine, August 31.

Weeden, Ryan, Ed Carberry, and Scott Rodrick. 2000. *Current Practices in Stock Option Plan Design.* Oakland, Calif.: National Center for Employee Ownership.
———. 2001. *Current Practices in Stock Option Plan Design.* Oakland, Calif.: National Center for Employee Ownership.

Weinstein, Elizabeth. 2002. "Help! I'm Drowning in E-Mail!—Many Users Give Up Hope, But Some Devise Tricks That Keep Them Afloat." *Wall Street Journal,* January 10.

Weiss, Miles. 2001. "Amazon Option Offer Could Affect Finances." *San Francisco Chronicle*, February 1.

Weiss, Thomas, and Donald Schaefer. 1994. *American Economic Development in Historical Perspective*. Stanford, Calif.: Stanford University Press.

Weitzman, Martin. 1986. *Share Economy: Conquering Stagflation*. Cambridge, Mass.: Harvard University Press.

Weitzman, Martin, and Douglas Kruse. 1990. "Profit Sharing and Productivity." In *Paying for Productivity: A Look at the Evidence*, edited by Alan Blinder, pp. 95–140. Washington, D.C.: Brookings Institution.

WestwardPay.com. 1998. *Biotechnology Stock Compensation Practices*. San Francisco, Calif.: Westward Pay Strategies, March.

WetFeet.com. 2000. "Dot Coms Doling Out Mega-Salaries and Perks in Race to Attract And Retain Top Talent: Silicon Valley Dot Coms Increase Compensation as Well as Non-Monetary Benefits As Talent Shortage Becomes More Acute." PR Newswire, August 1.

Wheeler, Chris. 2001. Interview. Conducted by Joseph Blasi. New Brunswick, N.J.: School of Management and Labor Relations. (Senior vice president and chief technology officer of Internap Network Services Corporation.)

William M. Mercer Company. 2001a. "CEO Compensation Study Reveals Subtle Shifts in Emphasis." *Executive Compensation Perspective* (12), June.

———. 2001b. "Broad-based Stock Options—2002 Update: Increasing Prevalence Among Major Companies," November 16. Available at www.mercerhr.com:80/attachment.dyn?idContent=1009105&idFile=101370.

Williamson, Harold F. 1944. *The Growth of The American Economy: An Introduction to the Economic History of the United States*. New York: Prentice Hall.

Williamson, Oliver. 1975. *Markets and Hierarchies*. New York: The Free Press.

Winther, Gorm. 1995. *Employee Ownership: A Comparative Analysis of Growth Performance*. Aalborg, Denmark: Aalborg University Press.

Wolfe, Tom. 1983. "The Tinkerings of Bob Noyce." *Esquire*, December, pp. 346–374.

Wood, Jay. 2001. Interview. Conducted by Joseph Blasi. New Brunswick, N.J.: School of Management and Labor Relations. (Chairman and former CEO of Kana Communications Inc. and founder of Silknet, acquired by Kana.)

Wray, David. 2001, 2002. Interviews. Conducted by Joseph Blasi. New Brunswick, N.J.: School of Management and Labor Relations, March. (Executive director, Profit Sharing/401(k) Council of America and Profit Sharing Research Foundation.)

Young, Jeffrey S. 2001. *Cisco Unauthorized*. Roseville, Calif.: Forum, Prima Publishing.

Zahavi, Gerald. 1983. "Negotiated Loyalty: Welfare Capitalism and the Shoeworkers of Endicott Johnson, 1920–1940." *Journal of American History* 70(3), December, pp. 602–620.

Zalusky, John. 1986. "Labor's Collective Bargaining Experience with Gain-sharing and Profit-sharing." Madison, Wis.: Industrial Relations Research Association, 39th Annual Proceedings.

———. 1990. "Labor-Management Relations: Unions view Profit Sharing." In *Profit Sharing and Gain Sharing,* edited by Myron J. Roomkin. Metuchen, N.J.: Scarecrow Press, pp. 65–78.

ZD Wire. 2000. "The Text of Ballmer's Employee Memo." December 19.

Zielenziger, David. 1988. "The Recovery Lives On At AMD, Intel." *Electronic Engineering Times,* July 18.

# Index

# About the Authors

**Joseph R. Blasi** is a professor at Rutgers University's School of Management and Labor Relations. A sociologist, Professor Blasi is a former Mellon Foundation Fellow of the Institute of Advanced Study in Princeton, New Jersey.

**Douglas L. Kruse** is a professor at Rutgers University's School of Management and Labor Relations. An economist, Professor Kruse is a Research Fellow at the National Bureau of Economic Research in Cambridge, Massachusetts.

**Aaron Bernstein** is a senior writer at *Business Week* magazine, where he has won numerous awards. Bernstein studied political philosophy at Oxford University.